REFLECTING ON THINGS PAST

REFLECTING ON THINGS PAST

The Memoirs of
Peter Lord Carrington

A Cornelia & Michael Bessie Book

HARPER & ROW, PUBLISHERS, New York
Cambridge, Philadelphia, San Francisco
London, Mexico City, São Paulo, Singapore, Sydney

LIBRARY OF CONGRESS CATALOG CARD NUMBER 88-45542
ISBN 0-06-039090-5

89 90 91 92 93 HC 10 9 8 7 6 5 4 3 2 1

'Reflect on things past, as wars, negotiations, factions, and the like; we enter so little into those interests, that we wonder how men could possibly be so busy, and concerned for things so transitory: Look on the present times, we find the same humour, yet wonder not at all.'

JONATHAN SWIFT, 'Thoughts on Various Subjects'
(1711)

ACKNOWLEDGEMENTS

I owe a great deal to many people in the preparation of this book – the personal record of a fairly public life – and I have owed even more to many more in the career it describes. On the first count I am indebted to those friends who have read and advised on all or parts of the typescript; particularly to David Fraser who has devoted much time and care to the task, to Anthony Duff, Brian Fall, Ian Gilmour, Roderic Lyne, Pat Nairne, Dick Nugent and George Walden. Some of them appear, whether by name or anonymously, in the narrative itself; and have given their time and wisdom generously to help me. I also wish to thank Joyce Smith who has, for years, struggled to bring some sort of order to my life and papers; and Carol Aldridge who has patiently typed, re-typed and re-typed again the book itself.

Those whose support throughout my political life has enabled me to do anything I have managed to do are legion. I must particularly, however, mention the ministerial colleagues who made my work both possible and enjoyable in a number of Cabinet posts; Ian Gilmour and Robin Balniel at the Ministry of Defence; at the Foreign Office Ian once more (as Lord Privy Seal), Humphrey Atkins, Peter Blaker, Douglas Hurd, Richard Luce and Nick Ridley. But no Minister would achieve anything without the dedicated and selfless assistance and advice of his Private Secretary and secretaries, and here I was invariably served in a way for which I am most deeply grateful. Pat Nairne appears in several guises in these pages; Robert Andrew, Brian Fall (in several incarnations), Marc Grossman and Bill McCahill (brilliant State Department men), Roderic Lyne, Michael Matthiessen and Kai Eide (from Denmark and Norway) whose work was invaluable, Jane Pearey, Kevin Tebbitt, George Walden – all were beyond praise and all, I am proud to feel, became personal friends.

Last, and first, nothing I have attempted or achieved would have been possible without the untiring support of my wife – invariably selfless, patient, loyal and wise.

CONTENTS

*Sixteen pages of illustrations appear following
page 214.*

PREFACE

I have met many of the world's leaders in the course of the past twenty-five years. None has impressed me more than Lord Carrington.

My admiration for Peter Carrington did not start as personal friendship—although we are now good friends—but was due to his extraordinary performance over the decades. He is a statesman who has performed with a grace and style that have nearly vanished from our pedestrian age.

I suppose each generation believes that its era is plagued by unprecedented problems; in our case this may be closer to correct than is usual. The role of the policymaker is, as it has always been, in part to take those he represents from the familiar to the new and as yet unknown. Until the end of the Second World War this process, although difficult, was eased by reason of its gradual character. But in the past few decades circumstances have altered with increasing speed. Experience is often irrelevant and sometimes dangerous. Changes in technology transform the face of the world around us with agonizing rapidity, while politics have become global at one extreme, and increasingly provincial at the other. Nations that until recently lived in isolation and ignorance now interact and, due to modern communications, instantaneously. But, at least in the democracies, the qualities required to reach office and the promises that must be made to achieve it are not necessarily—to put it mildly—the qualities necessary for government.

Fortunate are the societies whose leaders still emerge from a tradition of public service acquired through the centuries so matter-of-factly that it requires no special affirmation.

One of the glories of the British political system has been the existence of such public servants. Unlike most modern politicians, they do not require polls to tell them what they must do; their commitment to the common good is anchored in their style of life and in their dedication to the service of their nation. Though not free of human vanity, they do not require office to confirm their values, and therefore they do not cling to public office at the cost of a compromise of their principles.

Peter Carrington represents that tradition; indeed, he *is* that tradition. He would never make such a claim for himself, yet his amusing, readable account of his family nearly makes one forget the central point, that for centuries these sometimes eccentric, always madly individualistic personalities were linked by one common thread: to serve the common weal, their people, and their sovereign. A sense of duty emerges so powerfully that it can be put forward as a series of anecdotes underlining the personalities and foibles of a way of life that requires no affirmation to underline its principles.

It was this matter-of-fact commitment to service that enabled Peter Carrington to participate in such an astonishing range of his period's history: as First Lord of the Admiralty, British High Commissioner of Australia, Minister of Energy, Secretary of Defence, Secretary of State for Foreign Affairs, and finally as Secretary-General of NATO. In these jobs Carrington made seminal contributions—in helping to establish an International Energy Agency, in negotiating the independence of Rhodesia, in managing the transition of British defense policy from an imperial to a regional role, and lastly in shepherding the Western Alliance through a period of changing strategic and political concepts. In describing these events he draws vivid portraits while characteristically claiming much less credit for himself than I know to be his due.

The special relationship with America was to Carrington's generation the core of British foreign policy. In all the time that I dealt with him, I never thought of him as a foreign statesman from a friendly country, but as a colleague on the ramparts defending the common values of the West. He would, of course, shrink from so portentous a formulation, not because it would not be true, but because it would seem to him that one demeans duty by personalizing it.

To me, the quintessential Carrington appeared in the aftermath of the Falkland crisis. He resigned as Foreign Secretary, the office he treasured above all others, because it was the honorable thing to do. Though one finds no reference to his personal feelings on that subject in the book, I know that it was a difficult —and indeed a traumatic—parting. Weeks later the Franks Report not only exonerated him but pointed out that his repeated warnings of the danger had been ignored. (There is, characteristically, no reference to the Franks Report in his book.) I called Peter to say that I had expected the exoneration but was moved that he had never mentioned the warnings even to good friends in small circles. "There is no sense assuming responsibility," he replied, "if you then whisper that you are not really responsible."

Peter Carrington is a Western treasure and a wholly remarkable man. But I must guard against being too fulsome. For I cannot forget his opening remarks when I introduced him somewhere in a particularly pretentious manner: "After these remarks I can hardly wait to hear what I am going to say."

—HENRY KISSINGER

CHAPTER 1

Early Years

As it happens, I never belonged to the Conservative Club, a most respectable institution founded in the nineteenth century, which used to stand at the lower end of St James's Street, on the right as one faced the clock tower of St James's Palace itself. I might have had difficulty in getting support for election since memories are long in that quarter of London and it was on the steps of the Conservative Club, one June evening in 1869, that Lord Carrington (my great-uncle) ambushed a journalist by name Grenville Murray. Grenville Murray owned a gossipy paper, the *Queen's Messenger,* and the current edition had contained an abusive article about my great-uncle which included what Carrington described as a scurrilous attack on his father, who had died the preceding year and whom his son had much loved. Carrington had armed himself. In his own words:

> I bought a small rhinoceros-hide whip at Briggs in St James's Street and waited for Mr Murray outside the Albany till midnight, but he never appeared. I also watched for him all next day without success, but hearing he generally went to the Conservative Club about eleven in the evening, I fortunately ran across him in St James's St, and after asking him his name I told him who I was, and that he had written infamous things about my father, and then I hit him with the whip across the face as hard as I could. The whip cracked like a pistol shot under his nose. He ran into the Conservative Club and I got another blow in. I followed him into the Club, gave him my name and address and said, 'If you write any more filth about any of my family I will give you the same again.' I think I must have hurt him, as the point came off the whip – it lapped round his face just under the nose and he jumped two foot off the ground.

1

My great-uncle then went to Pratt's Club nearby, where he saw a number of friends, told them the story, and asked them to testify if need be that he was neither excited nor drunk. His own account of the incident ends, 'I then went to bed happy.' I know how he felt. He received a large number of letters of support, telling him that he had done admirably. That always helps, although the ultimate comfort, if one has behaved with difficult or controversial individualism, lies within oneself. In my great-uncle's case few doubts about the rightness of his actions seem to have disturbed him. He went to bed happy! Ultimately he was bound over for the assault: Grenville Murray, charged with perjury, fled the country never to return.

This great-uncle, Charles, 3rd Lord Carrington, was born in 1843. I don't remember him, although he died only in 1928. His life straddled the ages. When he died Britain was about to have her second Labour Government, warfare had entered the age of the tank and the aeroplane, the map of Europe had been torn up and remade. While a boy he had seen the Chartist riots of 1848, with the family's gamekeepers sitting in the hall of Carrington House in London (where the War Office building now stands, opposite Horse Guards), loaded guns across their knees.

An intimate friend of King Edward VII, my great-uncle sat in the House of Commons as Liberal Member for Wycombe for three years from the age of twenty-two (while simultaneously holding a commission in the Royal Horse Guards); and in the House of Lords from 1868, when he inherited the peerage from his father. Thereafter Great-Uncle Charles, 'Uncle Charlie' to us, and 'Champagne Charlie' to a wide circle, was a popular, dutiful and not, I think, particularly controversial public servant. He was a large landowner in both Buckinghamshire and Lincolnshire – the family's home was at Wycombe Abbey, a house built by Wyatt just outside the town of High Wycombe. He was made Privy Councillor in 1881, in which year he became Captain of the Gentlemen-at-Arms and Chief Government Whip in the House of Lords until Gladstone's Liberal Government resigned in 1885. Later, Uncle Charlie was Queen

Victoria's Lord Chamberlain (1892–5) and for fifteen years was Member of the London County Council for West Pancras. He had, I think, a certain light-heartedness of character, in spite of this creditable record. The appointment of Lord Chamberlain was, in those days, political. I have seen the letter in which Queen Victoria thanked him for his services after he gave up that office and it is extremely chilly, even expressing words of warning about his language!

Nevertheless Uncle Charlie persevered with a career in public life. The *Dictionary of National Biography* describes him, in terms I find curious, as 'a sturdy Liberal of an extreme type'. By today's or even yesterday's standards I doubt if Uncle Charlie's politics were extreme. In 1905 he was made President of the Board of Agriculture, and during the long Liberal ascendancy of Campbell-Bannerman followed by Asquith he took a large number of agricultural Bills through the House of Lords, including a smallholdings Bill (a cause in which he greatly believed) and a so-called 'Farmers' Charter' – successfully piloted through Parliament, according to the magazine *Vanity Fair*, by Uncle Charlie's 'sheer good humour and brains'. Neither Bill was very popular with the landowning fraternity. In fact Uncle Charlie applied his smallholdings philosophy to his own estate, and created a number of such which caused me no little difficulty in later times. In 1912 he was made Marquess of Lincolnshire. Having inherited through his mother what is technically called a moiety in the office of Hereditary Lord Great Chamberlain, one of the great Offices of State and carrying responsibility for the Palace of Westminster among other things, he officiated as Lord Great Chamberlain at the Coronation of King George V.

It was in 1885, however, after the Liberals were beaten and Disraeli took office, that Uncle Charlie received an appointment which came to have a more direct bearing on my own life. He was sent out to Australia as Governor of New South Wales. And at this point I should introduce Uncle Charlie's brothers.

*

3

Champagne Charlie had two brothers, and was a generous and popular elder, supporting them in whatever they attempted and backing them in what were – at least in the case of the youngest of the family – some pretty difficult times. Both brothers held commissions in the Grenadier Guards.

The second brother, William – 'Bill' within the family – was close to Uncle Charlie in age and followed him as Liberal Member of Parliament for Wycombe, our local constituency. In spite of the first Reform Bill of 1832 with its abolition of 'rotten' boroughs, this sort of succession was regarded as a natural development in 1868, when Uncle Bill took his seat in the Commons, a seat he held for fifteen years. He combined this, in the manner of the times, with military service of an undemanding kind, comfortably compatible with his parliamentary duties – although he went to Egypt in 1882 in the 2nd Battalion Grenadiers, with Wolseley's expedition which culminated in the victory of Tel-El-Kebir in September, followed by the occupation of Cairo. Uncle Bill also held a number of positions at Court. Like his elder brother he was an intimate friend of King Edward VII who, as the young Prince of Wales, had been attached to the Grenadiers, in a determined effort by Prince Albert to bring order and purpose into the Prince's life. The experiment was only partially successful – in fact it was always said to be Uncle Charlie who had manoeuvred an actress into the Prince's bed, when he was with the Regiment in Ireland. I daresay word of this reached the Queen and contributed to what I suspect was lifelong disapproval of Uncle Charlie, who had been visiting his younger brother at the time. Uncle Bill seemed untarred by this. He was, successively, Equerry to Queen Victoria, Comptroller to the Prince of Wales and, from 1910, Keeper of the Privy Purse. Leader, by all accounts, of a blameless life, he married but died childless in 1914.

The youngest brother, Rupert, was my grandfather. Also (somewhat improbably) a Member of Parliament from 1880 until 1885, he originally joined the Grenadiers like his brother William, his elder by seven years. Troubles soon came. My grandfather at once displayed an extravagance which was to remain throughout life his most, perhaps his only, constant characteristic. The army was, from one viewpoint, a suitable profession for him. He enjoyed soldiering. He took part in the Zulu War in 1879, arriving only just before the close of hostilities but writing home with interest and enthusiasm, keen to see action, observant and perceptive, uncomplaining of hardship or discomfort, thoroughly proud of the men he commanded (like many Guardsmen he had volunteered, and was serving with another regiment in Zululand). But, from another angle, service with the Grenadiers meant long periods spent in London, and London, in every epoch, meant expense. Volunteering to join the Zululand expedition probably brought temporary relief from financial pressure ('I can't thank you enough about the bills,' one letter from Africa to his mother ran, 'so like you!'): but debt was my grandfather's besetting problem, and the problem, it is clear, was also a running sore for his eldest brother, Uncle Charlie. Some years ago I found a bill made out to my grandfather. From Beale and Inman, famous shirtmakers, it was for £900 and covered the early 1870s, when he was a young Grenadier. £900 is about £22,000 in today's money. I expect that the price of shirts and underwear has inflated at the same sort of rate as everything else, but that, by any standards, is a good deal of linen.

I remember my grandfather late in his life, when occasionally coming to stay with us. He was a tall, white-moustached old gentleman with piercing, blue eyes, somewhat alarming although undoubtedly a person of great gaiety and charm. Contemporaries all swore to his geniality, his good looks and his universal popularity. Without any doubt, however, he spent and spent – I daresay often with much generosity: but he had not the wherewithal.

Grandfather's four-year stint in the House of Commons would also have involved a good deal of money. There was no remuneration for Members in those days and the expense of elections was proverbial. Thus, in 1885, the appointment of his long-suffering and moderately distinguished eldest brother Charlie to the governorship of New South Wales appeared to offer hope of relief from creditors and, at least temporarily, certain economies. Australia is a long way from London and in 1885 seemed further still. His brother Charlie had always been kind and would, Rupert was confident, support him out there while he found his feet. And there were reported to be considerable heiresses in Australia, potential inheritors of the wealth the great Australian farmers were amassing from sheep and cattle. Rupert was unmarried and completely broke. He too sailed to Australia. In 1891 he married Edith, eldest daughter of John Horsfall, one of the greatest sheep farmers in New South Wales.

In 1957, when I was British High Commissioner to Australia, I found myself sitting in the Union Club in Sydney next to a venerable-looking old gentleman.

He peered at me.

'Your name Carrington?'

I admitted it.

'I remember old John Horsfall', the old gentleman said, 'coming into this club sixty-six years ago and saying to me, "My daughter's going to marry Rupert Carington." I looked at him and I said, "John, that's the most expensive ram you've ever bought!"'

The old gentleman chuckled. So did I, but wryly. It had been a prescient remark. My grandfather ran through his wife's fortune with the same ease he had shown at similar exercise in England. He made his home in Australia, where his brother's position and his wife's money established him at first most comfortably. He never lost his taste for military life – he went to the South African War as a major in the New South Wales Mounted Rifles in 1901 at the age of forty-nine, and when in South Africa formed and commanded a regiment, 'The Imperial Bushmen'. He enjoyed campaigning, just as he had enjoyed Zululand over twenty years earlier, and his letters were vigorous and vivid. But he did not lose his early and ingrained habit of spending more than he possessed. He and his wife had only one child, born and brought up in Australia. A son. My father.

*

My father's circumstances and those of his family were d
cally transformed by tragedy. When war broke out in
my Uncle Charlie's son (he had one son and five daugl
was serving in the Royal Horse Guards, the Blues, lik
father before him. In May 1915 he died of wounds receiv
France. Thereafter Uncle Charlie's heir was his only surv
brother, Rupert, my grandfather. Rupert thus once mor
certain prospects.

He did not live long to enjoy their fruition. Uncle C
died in 1928, his Marquessate and other titles exce|
barony of Carrington dying with him. My grandfathe:
ceeding as Lord Carrington, died seventeen months later
1915, however, my father had known that if he surviv
war he was likely to inherit one day.

The Carrington inheritance was founded on ba
Thomas Smith, of Nottingham, born in 1631 and descr
'a respectable draper', kept accounts for and looked af
cash of a number of neighbouring farmers. This activit
him an early 'Country Banker' and his descendants ke|
founding in London as well as Nottingham a family
Smith, Payne and Co. Thomas Smith thus began it al
magnificent stained glass window in the south transe|
Church of St Mary the Virgin in Nottingham comme
his achievements. He died in 1699. I am thoroughly |
him. He came of good yeoman stock, raised himsel
own efforts and founded a pretty successful family
was a Puritan tradition, directed towards sobriety, w
success. Daughters tended to bear names like Fortun

Thomas had three sons. The eldest produced only da
The second, Samuel, became the progenitor of the
Smiths of Tresco Abbey in the Scillies. The third s
Smith, was my ancestor.

This Abel, by now described as a banker, also h
sons. The eldest, George, was made a baronet and ch.
name to Bromley. The second, John, was the fore
large number of Smith families. The youngest, anot
had several children of whom the eldest surviving so
Smith, became in 1796 the first Lord Carrington. 1

7

been an earlier, seventeenth-century, peerage of Carrington granted to another (fiercely Royalist) family of Smiths. Our family also, in 1839, adopted the surname of 'Carington' – why differently spelled I have no idea. On Robert Smith's reasons for taking the title of Carrington the editor of *The Complete Peerage*, Vicary Gibbs, was cutting: 'The title "Carrington" was doubtless selected because the ancient family of Smith, *alias* Carrington (though in *no* way connected with the family of the grantee) had, under the latter name, been ennobled in 1643.'

In another place the same publication quotes one of our relations, Augustus Smith, as describing our family of Smiths as 'altogether plebeian in its source'! And Vicary Gibbs finally observes (1913) with what reads like a sigh of relief, 'Although retaining Carington as its surname the family has now abandoned any claim to a Carrington descent.'

Plebeian in origins or not, Robert, 1st Lord Carrington, was a very successful banker and, I suspect, an extremely agreeable man. Born in 1752, he was described by Maria Edgeworth, the Irish novelist and writer of children's books, as 'most amiable and benevolent, without any species of pretension, thinking the best that can be thought of everything and everybody'. This endearing pen-picture of a man trustful and genial might be thought at slight variance with a sound banking career, but in fact Robert combined charm with acumen. His face in the portraits at my home, whether young or middle-aged, shows engaging friendliness and good nature, and he was as famous for unobtrusive benevolence as for worldly success. Cowper wrote about him:

> I mean the man who, when the distant poor
> Need help, denies them nothing but his name.

But there is shrewdness in the face and the worldly success was there too. He began life as a Whig, first elected to the House of Commons in 1779: but he became a devoted friend of the younger Pitt, and remained thereafter a most loyal political supporter. A partner in the family bank from the age of twenty-one (the bank now operated both in Nottingham

and London, the original Payne of Smith, Payne and Co. having provided the London connection), Robert did much to advise Pitt on Government loans. When the long war with France started in 1792 Government loans were increasingly necessary, and more and more funds were attracted to London by the rates there obtaining. Robert gave up his partnership in the Nottingham bank and concentrated on London. He prospered greatly.

It was, of course, Pitt who obtained for him his peerage in 1796. People said that he lent Pitt money personally, but I don't believe it. Robert firmly denied it – denied, indeed, that Pitt and he had ever discussed money at all, in a private sense; and Robert was a man of utter integrity, by every report. He is said to have given Pitt some advice, early in the latter's political life, about how to manage his affairs, but it went no further than that. King George III, nevertheless, strongly opposed the peerage grant, on the grounds that banking was an unsuitable occupation for a nobleman. Pitt had his way, however, and Robert had his peerage. When he took his seat in the Lords his fellow peers, or some of them, walked out in protest because he was 'in trade'.

The family were by now firmly established in Buckinghamshire. Robert's son, my great-grandfather, another Robert, represented Wendover, Buckinghamshire and High Wycombe, successively, in the House of Commons, as a Whig, being first elected in 1818; and at Wycombe keeping out the young Disraeli* in both the 1832 and 1834 Elections. I do not know what his reactions were when, in 1832, Robert's father in the Lords voted against the final reading of Lord Grey's Reform Bill. This limited extension of the electoral franchise had become a great popular cause. There had been riots and talk of revolution. Ultimately, Wellington had advised the Tory peers to abstain rather than oppose the measure, and most of them took that advice. Lord Carrington, however, was

---

* Disraeli, nevertheless, remained a great personal friend of the family. In his later years, when Dizzy was old and almost blind at Hughenden, my Uncle Charlie used to ride over to read to him. Civilities of that kind between political opponents are all too rare today.

9

one of the twenty-two 'Stalwarts' as they were called (in a more recent, twentieth-century, confrontation the same sort of resolute minority were to be known as 'Ditchers') who voted against Reform to the bitter end.

His son, in the Commons (for High Wycombe), supported it. He succeeded to the peerage on the first Robert's death in 1838 and continued to support Liberal administrations and measures from his place in the House of Lords until his own death in 1869, when he was succeeded by Uncle Charlie. One matter deserves record, however. Unlike his party colleagues my great-grandfather opposed Peel's repeal of the Corn Laws. Where he thought the agricultural interest threatened he was as Tory as his political enemies; and certainly more Tory than Peel. I suspect that, like his youngest son, my great-grandfather was extravagant. He had, beside Wycombe and Carrington House, a castle in Wales and another house, Gayhurst, in north Buckinghamshire. Uncle Charlie inherited, with a peerage and large possessions, equally substantial debts. This did not in the least diminish his love and loyalty for his father, as the incident of the horsewhip and his language at the time make clear.

My father thus came to an inheritance whose roots were in banking, in Whig and Liberal politics mixed with a dash of support for Pitt, and in land – for since Thomas Smith's heirs had first started to make their banking fortunes they had invested in land. In addition, the generation immediately preceding my father had all served in the army.

His own immediate background was very different. Growing up in Australia, and educated at Melbourne Grammar School (with some distinguished contemporaries such as Lord Bruce of Melbourne, at one time Prime Minister, and Dick Casey, later Governor-General), he only came to England shortly before the First World War. In the closed society of those days he probably felt and was regarded as something of an outsider, and I suspect it took him time to adjust. 1914 found him an officer in the 5th Dragoon Guards. 1915 made him an heir – I suspect a somewhat resented heir. There were other areas of sensitivity. I remember once feeling mild surprise that he did not become a Grenadier when he joined the army at the beginning of the war. It was the regiment of his father, and of Uncle Bill; and he in fact transferred to the Grenadiers in 1916 and remained with them until he retired. An aunt enlightened me.

'It would not have been thought proper. Not in 1914.'

'Why not?'

'Your grandfather, it was well known, had two illegitimate children by a certain lady. She lived in Hampstead. The son was in the Grenadiers. People would have thought it in bad taste if your father had joined the regiment in which his bastard brother was serving!'

Grandfather Rupert certainly cast a long shadow. Sadly, that son was killed early in the war. Thereafter, I imagine, it was thought decent for my father to exchange.

My father never returned to Australia. In 1916 he married. My sister Elizabeth was born in 1917 and I in 1919. My mother was Sibyl Colville, daughter of Lord Colville of Culross. The Colvilles were Scottish and more often than not sailors or soldiers. Their lives had been different from those of the Smiths – until the Victorian era when, like the Carringtons, several Colvilles served at Court and became close friends of the Sovereign's family. The Colville family had befriended my father when he first came to England, asking him often to stay. He and my mother became engaged when she was still very young.

My father, twice wounded in the First World War, retired from the army in 1924 and made his home in Devon. He might, I suppose, have moved to Buckinghamshire, where the family were well based, where he might ultimately inherit responsibilities, where Uncle Charlie Lincolnshire reigned. He did not do so. His position as a nephew who had, so to speak, supplanted a first cousin dying for his country, was invidious – or so I think he felt, and so his cousins, Uncle Charlie's daughters, undoubtedly and perhaps naturally felt. So, probably, felt Uncle Charlie, who had adored his son and with whom my father had little in common. He had sold Wycombe

Abbey to the distinguished girls' school which now inhabits it. He had then built a huge and hideous bungalow within the park, tacking it on to an older farmhouse on high ground, and looking down from this eminence on the school and its formidable headmistress, Miss Dove, with undisguised loathing which was certainly reciprocated. The new house was called Dawes Hill, ultimately to be sold to the school by my father, who said it was the ugliest house he had ever seen – built on a slope, every room seemed to have a sort of dais, better suited to scholastic than domestic use. Meanwhile my parents reckoned they had their own lives to live. They stayed in Devon where they had bought Millaton House, an agreeable Georgian house of medium size, after my father left the army. In lovely country on the north-western edge of Dartmoor, that was my childhood home.

My boyhood was uneventful, happy and dull. It didn't feel dull at the time but when I later learned of the dramas or exotic backgrounds which some contemporaries enjoyed or suffered, my own comfortable and ordinary family home seemed unexciting. I am grateful for it. I grew up living a placid country life and learning country pursuits and sports, shooting, riding, hunting. My sister and I didn't see many other children – neighbours were few and there was little social activity. Outings were rare. We did, however, go to France several times, because after we left the nursery and before going to boarding school we were taught by my mother's French governess; and she used to take us to Le Havre, her home, where we stayed in a boarding house with box hedges and a garden overlooking the harbour. Box has a particular smell. It always now brings back to me Le Havre, and the sight of the great liners, the *Paris*, the *Île de France*, steaming out into the Channel for the Atlantic passage.

On one memorable occasion we were taken not to Le Havre but to Guernsey. We crossed from Weymouth by sea to St Peter Port and the inevitable boarding house. I got chickenpox on the day of arrival and for thirteen days of the holiday was confined to bed, itching and miserable. The boarding house was opposite an Ebenezer Chapel whence the sound of hymns thundered – in my recollection every day and all day – as I lay wretchedly scratching. My sister contracted the disease the day I got up.

Very occasionally we went to London, where we stayed in some grimy and uncomfortable hotel, peopled with cats and depressing old ladies and needing shillings put in a gas fire to produce warmth in the bedroom. This was characteristic of the age. I find that a younger generation supposes our lives to have been gilded by privilege in those days, and certainly families like ours regarded it as usual – indeed necessary – to employ a good many servants in house and garden (no great expense at that time) and to live according to the sort of formality and routine which that imposes. In that way life had changed little from Victorian times, and – which would have been true for most of my school-fellows – I hardly remember an evening at home after I was old enough to dine downstairs when I did not put on dinner jacket, stiff shirt and collar, all laid out by a footman, as a matter of course. Comfort, still less luxury, however, was a different matter. My mother, a gentle, sweet-natured person whose character tended to soften the sternness of my father's outlook as far as we children were concerned, would have regarded a more agreeable hotel in London as entirely inappropriate – extravagant certainly, and with a strong undertone of sin. One should not, by her principles, 'spend much money on oneself'. I think that this was a pretty widespread attitude, and by no means contemptible. Maintenance of a proper routine at home was a different matter. We live today in less dignified but on the whole more comfortable ways.

A domestic staff and the sort of regimen under which I grew up necessitate punctuality. If those who prepare and serve a meal are to do so exactly at the time ordered, they have a right to expect that their employers who sit at table will be equally punctual – punctual and properly dressed, as they are properly dressed. That was the system. Both employers and employed lived under discipline. My father was a stickler for the rules. Strict in most ways, he demanded that we should never be late. The habit has stuck, and it is a good one: I have wasted more time waiting for other people than anybody else in the world.

My father did not accompany us to the depressing London hotels. If he went up to the House of Lords he would stay at his club. He never seemed greatly to exert himself physically. It was only later that I realized he was ill for a long time, that he had a bad heart and knew it. At the time I was happy in Devon and always longed to get back there if away at school – I spent some years at Sandroyd, a preparatory school at Cobham, in Surrey. I loved our home, and was enormously sad when, in later years, circumstances led me to sell it.

At the age of thirteen I was sent to Eton.

Eton has changed a good deal since my day, mostly, I suspect, for the better. I was perfectly happy there but neither in academic nor in sporting ways did I shine. Games inevitably bulk large in any boys' school, and they bulked larger at Eton then than they do now. To be good at games was, on the whole, the route to social eminence. I was short-sighted and an indifferent performer. I was not, therefore, an enormous success.

Eton, however, was a large and diverse place, and I doubt if many people failed to find friends and congenial pursuits there sooner or later, even if, like I, they failed to reach any of the summits of schoolboy achievement and adulation. It depended a good deal on which house one was in – the school was divided into College (for the seventy King's Scholars) and about twenty-five boarding houses, each with some forty boys. One's housemaster was the king of one's immediate surroundings and his character greatly affected the life of every boy in the house and produced its tone.

My own housemaster, J. C. Butterwick, was a person of considerable quality – a very cultivated, civilized man who much later joined Sotheby's after giving up schoolmastering. He had what was generally regarded as a pretty good house. Certainly it was a most successful house, since Cyril Butterwick had a sharp appetite for success. That kind of thing feeds itself:

'Butterwick's' was known as a place to which stars of the schoolboy firmament were drawn and preparatory school-masters as well as parents noted the fact. One summer we had, I think, five members of the Eton Cricket Eleven, including a future Captain of England, George Mann.

I was not in that sort of category, and might have felt a failure and suffered thereby in so competitive a milieu. That I did not, says much for Eton, and much, too, for Cyril Butterwick. He taught me a great deal. A man of wide interests, he discovered and stimulated interests in his boys, however various. I was extremely fond of him and remain grateful to him. Many years afterwards I was elected a Fellow of Eton – a member of the governing body – and I felt proud and touched that an Etonian with so mediocre a record should be thus recognized. It somehow made the record itself feel a little less dim. My son was a boy there at the time. The Fellows on some occasion walked in procession to Chapel and he watched. Afterwards he simply observed,

'You were the only one not wearing a Master of Arts gown!'

He was right.

Eton was, therefore, agreeable even for an undistinguished boy. It was not, however, comfortable. Throughout the winter one tended to freeze. There were very few baths – enjoyed by roster and for extremely short periods. Getting clean after football mud and in the cold of winter was difficult: a tiny little old lady, Annie North, the 'Boys' Maid', lugged a hipbath and a can of tepid water into one's bedroom in the morning but it was not very effective. I am sure boys should not be pampered, and we weren't. In summer the hazards were different. Bathing – there was no swimming pool at Eton until quite recently – took place in the Thames. There were three bathing places, each with a raised stone structure called the Acropolis off which diving could take place. One of the bathing places – 'Athens' – was in the Thames itself: a human corpse was fished out of Athens during my time. The other two – 'Cuckoo Weir' and 'Ward's Mead' – were on a concrete-edged channel running out of the main river. The water in all cases was indescribably filthy. The river itself was very dirty in those

15

days and debris of every description – and defying description
– flowed through Cuckoo Weir and Ward's Mead. Orange peel
and garbage mixed with fragments of the carcasses of drowned
animals. We swam around with great enjoyment, and I remember no boy suffering from any sort of infection in consequence. In fact I do not recall the possibility even being
mentioned. I suppose Etonians were immune.

As schools go Eton was, I think, a tolerant place. There were
none of the daunting rituals for new boys, the institutionalized
bullying, about which one has heard or read of other places.
One had one's own room – a small bedroom/study with bed
folding by day against the wall – from the first day one arrived.
One thus had a certain possibility of privacy – and I think even
very young boys appreciate that. Order in each house was
kept by a small, self-elected team of senior boys called the
'Library', who saw that the rules were observed and who
punished miscreants by caning. This sort of discipline of the
young by the young can be abused, naturally; and has been
largely abolished. But in a good house – and this was the large
majority – it was carefully monitored by the good sense of the
housemaster: and by the boys themselves it was entirely
accepted.

Nevertheless children and adolescents can be cruel, and
are quick to mock and mob deviations from the norm, as I
witnessed on my first day. The supreme, self-elected boys'
governing body at Eton, the 'Eton Society', known as 'Pop',
had great privileges. Members of Pop could stop any Lower
Boy in the street and send him on an errand. They had the
use of a special clubroom. They were tremendous swells, about
twenty-five in number I think, who were allowed to carry
furled umbrellas, walk arm-in-arm, and – rather obscurely –
had blobs of sealing-wax, imprinted 'Pop', at various points
on their top hats.

They also wore different clothes from the rest of us, of great
splendour – braided tailcoats, coloured waistcoats, and grey
spongebag trousers instead of the regulation black. On my first
morning at Eton I went down to breakfast, wearing for the
first time my Eton jacket – an alarming experience as I walked

16

into the house dining room packed with boys, noisy, knowing, intimidating. With me was another new boy, Hugh Rock-savage – later to become Lord Great Chamberlain as Cholmondeley, one of the families dividing that office in turn with ourselves. Hugh and I knew nothing of such things in those days. What we did know, with terrible suddenness, was that Hugh was wearing 'Pop' grey trousers with his Eton jacket. His parents had been insufficiently briefed, and the gale of laughter and jeers hit us like a water cannon. Hugh told me many years later that it had remained one of the most appalling experiences of his life. I remember, young and raw as I was, my own indignation at the sheer unkindness of it. Physical violence is almost easier to forgive than the united derision of a mob. I also remember, with contempt, that my Dame – at Eton houses there is a matron/housekeeper known as the Dame – joined in the mockery of the new boy. Fortunately feminine influence on our lives could also be exerted by Mrs Butterwick, who was as gentle and kind a person as one could wish to meet and was loved by us all.

Eton was less demanding academically then than now, and probably – no doubt unfortunately – England was a less competitive place. Examinations did not play a large part in the lives of any but the most gifted scholars. If one aspired to go to Oxford or Cambridge it was taken for granted one would get there. Great idleness was penalized by lines to be copied out or by the forfeiture of some privilege: or, in extreme and rare cases, by flogging with a birch at the hands of the Lower Master (for the younger boys) or Headmaster (for the older). Great brilliance was rewarded by prizes, advertised on notice-boards and in the *Eton Chronicle*, the school newspaper, edited by boys. Most of us spent our days well clear of either of these extremes. Our education was, I believe, both good and enlightened despite a certain lack of pressure. Few boys worried greatly about future employment or the gaining, one day, of qualifications. They supposed they would find some sort of work to do. They knew they would have to earn their livings – great wealth was certainly rare, and anyway most boys were sufficiently intelligent to know that idleness is

17

deadly boring. Meanwhile, Eton was a small, self-sufficient, and – of great albeit generally unacknowledged benefit, I think – visually beautiful world of its own.

The system, too, was closer to that of a university than in most schools of those days. A good deal of work was done in what was called 'Private' – a small collection of boys discussing a particular theme with a tutor, generally in the evening. Much had to be performed in one's own room and one's own time. One learned about arranging that time. One learned the pleasures and the penalties of putting work off until the last possible minute. One learned the rudiments of organization.

One had to speak, too – to orate. There was, in many divisions of the school, a weekly 'Saying Lesson', which meant the memorizing and then the delivery of some piece of poetry or prose, sometimes selected by the form master, sometimes by oneself. The masters included a good number of eccentrics. Some of them were men of independent means, and they certainly had independent minds: I doubt if all their habits would go down well with Her Majesty's Inspectors of Schools today. One mathematics master (also a housemaster, and a terrifying one) used to hit boys over the head with the heavy key of the classroom if their calculations were inadequate. One charming man, an ex-regular army officer who later inherited an estate in Yorkshire, was so long-sighted that if one moved to the front benches in his classroom he could see one not at all: he taught French, a language of which he had only limited knowledge (so low was the teaching of French rated at Eton then that in one whole block of the school it was taught by the classics masters, totally unqualified in another modern tongue). It is the eccentrics, the oddities, the absurdities that remain in the mind: but most Eton masters were civilized, gifted and genial men and more of us owe more to more of them than we always confess.

Eton was, and remains, a very good school, and if its pride in being a centre of excellence is offset by criticism of such places as divisive and 'élitist' I think the pride justified and the criticism misplaced. A country needs excellent institutions, and a wisely governed country, with a sense of history, nurtures them. Eton has, with remarkable success, moved with the often perplexing times while retaining its essence and its ideals; it is no small achievement to stand for sound learning, for sensible discipline and for a decent moral code when many boys get little of the kind at home. Eton has had the advantage of intelligent guidance in our testing era: I think of the provostships of Harold Caccia and Martin Charteris, while I am confident Michael McCrum and Eric Anderson will be judged great headmasters by any standard.

When I was sixteen my father asked me what I wanted to do after Eton. I had few ideas. The subject was seldom discussed with schoolfriends until shortly before leaving. I was somewhat in awe of my father and looked at him with indecision.

He said, rather sharply, 'I think you'd better go into the army.'

I had no better plan. I rather enjoyed the Officers Training Corps at Eton – 'the Corps' to all of us. We wore heather-coloured uniforms with facings and rank badges of Eton blue. There were many stories current about why our dress was different from every other School Corps, who of course wore khaki – one version had it that we had murdered a boy at Corps camp and the monarch had decreed we be distinguished by a different uniform, a sort of mark of Cain, until Judgement Day. I don't know who invented this tale – a Harrovian, probably. Another, more credible, explanation was that when the Volunteer movements got going in the last century the Quartermaster General's department found huge quantities of cloth nobody wanted since some uniform had changed; and managed to sell it to the Buckinghamshire Volunteer Association, Eton's parent. Whatever the reason, we wore heather-colour, from our peaked caps to our ill-wound puttees; and formed a battalion, six hundred strong.

Sometimes we took part in great events. As a member of the Corps I lined the route within Windsor Castle down which passed the funeral procession of King George V. 'Resting on arms reversed', head bowed over up-ended rifle, one is meant to keep eyes on ground, but most of us squinted upwards, against orders, to see something of the great assembly of crowned heads, and notables, gorgeously uniformed, marching slowly past us on that moving occasion. King after king was there. Marshal Mannerheim was there from Finland, magnificent in his furred cap and pelisse: the Prince of Piedmont* from Italy, in gold helmet and white cloak; and many more.

I doubted whether the army would be much like the Corps: I told my father, however, that I agreed. He explained that it was possible to get a commission by way of going to Oxford and getting a degree.

'Or you could go to Sandhurst. Which do you choose?'

The Sandhurst course was eighteen months, divided into three terms. I felt under pressure and a little sulky. I said – I think mistakenly – that if I was going into the army I might as well do it properly and go to Sandhurst. When I returned to Eton I told Mr Butterwick. Speaking rather elliptically, in his nasal and much-imitated voice, he explained that for the really stupid boy, in his experience, three professions could be pursued with some hope of success: farming, soldiering and stockbroking. I have never been a stockbroker.

---

* Later King Umberto.

CHAPTER 2

The Army

Like Eton, Sandhurst has changed greatly and yet retains certain aspects recognizable to one of my generation. The most recognizable are sounds: principally the sounds of the voices of warrant officers and NCOs, raised to incredible volume in exhortation or rebuke. Also reminiscent is the sound of the stamping of boots on the parade ground.

In most ways, however, Sandhurst was a very different institution in 1937 when I arrived there. Arrival itself was alarming: perhaps it still is. When I walked up the steps of the Old Building and reported to the Sergeant Cadet (a senior, in his third and final term) he ordered me out of the room and to march into it again, smartly this time: and repeated the procedure fifteen times before he was grudgingly satisfied and I was accepted as a Gentleman Cadet. A 'Gentleman Cadet' – the difference from today is not a matter of courtesy but of status. We were not enlisted, we were not paid, we were only a part of the British Army in the sense that Sandhurst was a military institution, run and financed by the War Office. In most cases we paid to be there: or our parents did.

The curriculum was peculiar and seemed to have little coherence and not much relevance to our future duties except in the most basic, physical sense. There was a great deal of drill, several hours a day. Every movement was a drill movement. Mounting and moving by bicycle was done as a drill. Drill dominated life. Experience in the Corps at Eton had done little to prepare me for this. The other pursuit which filled our waking hours in the first term was cleaning our uniforms. Boots, leatherwork, bayonet scabbard, all had to

21

shine like reflective mirrors, and the slightest mist or dullness led to punishment and extra drill.

There were also kit inspections, with every article displayed, gleaming and clean. One's rifle had to be stripped down to its component parts: and anyone who thinks a Lee-Enfield rifle consists simply of magazine, bolt and body doesn't know much about a Lee-Enfield rifle. There were more than a hundred (so I recall) tiny screws, springs and parts which had to be laid out, spotless, on a sheet on one's bed for inspection. At my first such inspection the Senior Under Officer found a speck of dust on one part, picked up the sheet and threw the lot out of the window. It took me ages to find all the components of my rifle on the grass below.

Oddly enough, after loathing those first weeks, I came to derive a certain satisfaction from much of this. Drill well-performed – and at Sandhurst there is no doubt it was extremely well-performed – can be thoroughly satisfying. Rather to my surprise, too, I found that I was quite good at it, and at most of the other Sandhurst activities. There was a lot of riding – before breakfast there would be 'blanket rides', jogging without saddles on Barossa Common, behind the college: the 'Saddle' was awarded at the end of one's time to the best equestrian cadet, and although I never won it I was in the top four, competing to ride off for first place. There were cadet promotions – in one's second term one could be a corporal which, to my surprise, I was made. In one's last term one had the chance of being an Under Officer, and, again to my surprise, I was made Senior Under Officer, the senior cadet in my company (there were four companies). The best of the four Senior Under Officers was awarded the Sword of Honour. I didn't attain this – it was deservedly won by Chan Blair; later, as Lieutenant-General Sir Chandos Blair, he used to address me as 'Sir' (if anybody else was present) when I was Secretary of State for Defence – a source of mild satisfaction.

I therefore, and for the first time, won certain modest successes at Sandhurst, and I think it did me good and helped my confidence. Our more academic hours were unmemorable.

There was a good deal of military history; book-keeping – I am unsure why; and French, at which my instructor was Bernard Fergusson, a charming man, and later a distinguished soldier, author, Governor-General of New Zealand – who I don't remember as knowing more French than me, although someone has since told me he had the reputation of being almost bilingual. But Sandhurst had enjoyable moments. The quality of our instructors – both officers and NCOs – was high. 'Mr So-and-so, Sir', the latter used to bawl – one was always 'Mr', and 'Sir' – and then the address would be followed by a terrible stream of vituperation. There were a number of cadets from foreign countries, and generally a Prince of the Thai Royal House, it seemed. 'Prince, Sir,' the roar used to come, *'Stand up straight!'* At the passing out parade – which culminated, then as now, in the senior term marching up the steps of the grand entrance in slow time to the strains of 'Auld Lang Syne', followed by the Adjutant on his charger – we once heard, and every spectator heard, an agonized roar from the Regimental Sergeant Major, a Grenadier, as he surveyed the line, 'Stand up, Prince, Sir! Stand up! You're standing like a ruptured rook!'

There was little to do outside the college, off duty. London was out of bounds. One was allowed a car in one's last term if one could arrange and finance its garaging in Camberley, but recreation, apart from visits to a local pub, didn't play much part in our lives in term time: and on returning to the college one had to march the length of the gymnasium to report to the officer on duty – with ferocious penalties for signs of unsteadiness.

Sandhurst was not, perhaps, the most progressive or enlightened officer-training establishment in the world in those days, and I doubt if in usefulness we much surpassed our brother officers who came from universities when finally we gained our commissions. We drilled better, of course. We were tidier – on the whole, much tidier. We were more disciplined, more punctual, more instinctively acceptant of rank and order. I suppose we were less educated. One thing we certainly knew, which has never left me – we knew how to change our clothes quickly: we were forever having to switch from drill uniform, to riding kit, to physical training order (white flannels, red and white striped blazer, pillbox hat) and back again in no time at all, with no excuses admitted for lateness. The curriculum exacted it. It was at least one lesson.

During my final term, in November 1938, my father died and I succeeded him. Apart from natural grief I cannot say I felt any sense that unusual responsibilities had come to me early. The responsibilities and privileges which loomed largest were those of Senior Under Officer of my Sandhurst company. In that respect I had arrived. In the world of Sandhurst I was a person of some importance and felt it. This sensation was abruptly overturned in January 1939 when, the Sandhurst course completed, the last procession up the steps of the Old Building faultlessly accomplished, I joined the 2nd Battalion Grenadier Guards at Wellington Barracks, in Birdcage Walk, London.

Osbert Sitwell, also a Grenadier in his time, has described the respective headquarters of the five regiments of Foot Guards as being housed – in his day as in mine – in small edifices similar to miniature Doric temples near the railings of Wellington Barracks, each serving a particular cult. I reported to the officer commanding Grenadier Guards, the High Priest of my own particular cult. He looked at me with great seriousness.

'I only want you to remember two things. On no account are you to marry until you are twenty-five: and you are to hunt in Leicestershire at least two days a week.'

I naturally did not then and do not particularly now dispute that the virtues developed in the hunting field – nerve, speed of reaction, an eye for country – have military advantage. But this was 1939 and I wondered if there might, perhaps, be something more. As a matter of fact a contemporary tells me there was a third injunction – never to wear a grey top hat before the June race meeting at Epsom – but if so I have forgotten it. I was disobedient to the two orders I do recall. Love and Hitler intervened.

24

It was the custom in the Grenadiers to make newly joined Ensigns – a second lieutenant in the Foot Guards of the British Army is known as an Ensign – sharply aware of their insignificance. This was intended to induce humility, to knock out of the newcomer any false feeling of grandeur or achievement in having joined so distinguished a regiment. The salient method was not to talk to him, so when I joined nobody talked to me. My brother officers behaved as if I wasn't there. This was the system and it generally went on for some months, about three in my case. One went into the Officers' Mess – no word spoken, no glance of awareness that one existed. To break the silence oneself, to say, 'Good morning', would have been regarded as insufferable impertinence. One moved like a ghost, without substance, carrying out under instruction one's appointed duties. This, at least in barracks, led to a certain loneliness. I sat, when off parade, in a corner of the Mess ante-room and wrote letters. I have never written more letters in my life.

Wellington Barracks had been condemned as unfit for human habitation in 1871, the year my grandfather there joined the Regiment. The barracks have now, albeit fairly recently, been splendidly rebuilt behind the familiar and elegant façade that fronts St James's Park. In 1939 the façade was gunmetal grey and I doubt if much had been done inside the barrack blocks since Grandfather's time. Living conditions for the Guardsmen were primitive. Food, however, was plentiful and healthy, there were plenty of athletics and games for the soldiers of the battalion – whose Commanding Officer, Lieutenant-Colonel 'Boy' Browning, had been an Olympic hurdler – and there was excellent discipline, order, an impeccable appearance on parade and scrupulous domestic administration so that everything was done promptly, exactly, smartly and fairly – as was the tradition of the British Army at its best. This administration was largely executed by the Warrant Officers and Sergeants, a breed I had, of course, experienced already at Sandhurst; and very formidable they were. A good deal of a newly joined Ensign's time was spent, in the manner of Sandhurst, marching up and down the parade ground under

25

the orders of a Drill Sergeant, being periodically reproved for inadequacy by the Adjutant – clanking over menacingly to the officers' and corporals' drill squad with a jingle of spurs and sword scabbard. 'Had a good breakfast?' the Drill Sergeant used to roar at the troops. 'Sir!' they would roar back in assent. 'You lucky so-and-so's,' used to be his sally. 'Look at those poor sods licking the paint off the railings for theirs!' and, indeed, knots of onlookers used to peer curiously in at us from Birdcage Walk whenever the battalion was at drill. We young officers were almost invariably put into a squad and chased round the square with the rest. During the infrequent 'stand easy's' we were subjected to questions on Regimental and Brigade of Guards custom, lore and history. The first, put with enjoyment by the Drill Sergeant, tended to be, 'When did Julius Caesar command the Brigade of Guards?' – which, improbably, a distinguished officer of that name had done in the eighteenth century.

One was, therefore, treated from the start as a very unimportant person, more likely to do wrong than right, an object for eagle-eyed scrutiny at every moment of life, certainly incompetent as yet for the important task of commanding Guardsmen. Curiously, however, our instruction in order to fit us for more professional duty seemed hardly to exist. It was fairly clear as 1939 passed that Europe was heading for catastrophe. In March Hitler sent the German Army into Czechoslovakia, in defiance of the Munich agreement which had joined the Sudetenland to the Reich and had been declared by the Führer to satisfy his territorial ambitions in that area. This was generally thought to be the last straw. Conscription, for the first time ever, was voted in peacetime by the British Parliament. Everyone knew that German eyes were now on Poland, where the Danzig corridor separating East Prussia from the Reich was resented by every German. There was foreboding, tension and a sense of inevitable doom in the air. But in Wellington Barracks we marched up and down, and were rebuked for the smallest irregularities of dress (dress played a huge part in our lives) as if little else in the military sense mattered at all. My own company commander had taken a house in the south of France and between January and April I never saw him.

Nor, it must be said, would there have been much, if anything, for him to do had he been in Birdcage Walk rather than Provence. The system made serious training, when in London, impossible. There was, of course, minor training – individual weapon training and drill, drill, drill – but the battalion had not even its correct complement of light machine guns, and the infantry battalion anti-tank rifle (a heavy and almost entirely ineffective weapon as it happens) was represented, during our one period of field training in the summer, by a broom handle. Field training involved a fortnight at Pirbright; but in London our duties were ceremonial – the mounting of the various public duties, King's Guard, the Bank of England Picquet and so forth. There was always a shortage of men for these duties and the shortage meant that rosters for guard had to be controlled on a strictly centralized basis by Adjutant and Regimental Sergeant-Major. In these circumstances a company commander, had he been present, would have found absolutely no opportunity to train his company: indeed, he would have seldom found it possible to see it, since the men would have been dispersed over London or barracks on public duties or fatigues. Inevitably, therefore, officers were given a good deal of leave, and the more senior the officer the longer the leave. Battalions of Foot Guards, furthermore, spent very long periods in the London District with little hope of change or relief. It was a poor way to fit any part of an army for war, at least in modern times; and particularly in 1939.

We junior officers had, like the Guardsmen, a certain amount of ceremonial and routine duty to perform: and, like the Guardsmen, we were treated without much mercy if it was performed imperfectly. In my case this was not infrequent. My first duty as Ensign of the King's Guard – that is, carrying the Colour – was a nervous occasion, but was improved by finding that the Ensign of the Old Guard (from another Grenadier battalion, also in London) was a great friend and exact Sandhurst contemporary, Dickie Rasch. Equally nervous, he knew as little as I about it, although we had both been put through our paces intensively and were determined not to go wrong. There is a long period during the ceremony of Changing the Guard in the forecourt of Buckingham Palace when the two Ensigns walk slowly up and down together, the men standing easy, and the sentries at the various posts being relieved from the New Guard. I don't know where the Captains of the Guards, Old and New, were or are at that moment, but for a while the Ensigns seem to have the forecourt to themselves, without any obvious way of doing something wrong. We strolled contentedly, Colours sloped with their silks draped in the approved way over our shoulders. The crowds beyond the railings gawped at us. We felt confident, dignified.

The Sergeant of the Guard approached and saluted.

'Their Royal Highnesses the Princesses just going out, Sir.'

Princess Elizabeth and Princess Margaret were on their way out by car to their swimming lesson. There was, there assuredly is, an order as to what to do when a member of the Royal Family passes through the forecourt during Guard Mounting (and I have no doubt the action differed depending on which member of the Royal Family was involved): the trouble was that neither of us knew what it was. All we both knew, for certain, was that there would be an almighty rumpus if we got it wrong. The back of the Sergeant of the Guard was visible marching off, having conveyed to us his warning. There was something smug about it. We had a hurried consultation.

My friend Rasch said that he thought we ought to face the Princesses, take our respective Colours from our shoulders, bring them to the ground in that gracious, sweeping movement which accompanies a formal Royal Salute by troops, when given (rarely) to a personage entitled to the Colours of the Foot Guards being lowered. Something told me this was wrong. I doubted, correctly, whether an Ensign strolling up and down with a Colour should act as if he were standing in front of a body of troops, as far as ceremonial was concerned! I didn't know what to do, but I was sure it wasn't that. I suggested, instead, that we should pretend we hadn't noticed, and keep strolling, preferably as far from the Royal car as possible. This solution anyway came naturally to me since I was short-sighted: was forbidden to wear spectacles in full dress (and they do undoubtedly detract from the *empressement* of scarlet tunic and bearskin); and always found it difficult to identify who was who on the parade ground, in front of Buckingham Palace or anywhere else. We each did our own thing.

We were, of course, both wrong. My own punishment (and I think Dickie's was similar) was one month's extra duty as Picquet Officer – that is, confined to barracks and performing all the regular daily duties and chores that need an officer's presence during the twenty-four hours.

'Extra picquets' were the ordinary way of punishing us subaltern officers, and the punishment was undoubtedly tedious because it necessitated cancelling one's social arrangements, forgoing parties and festivities and fun. It followed that one man's extra picquets constituted other men's freedom: and my own sentence of a month was probably my most popular achievement in the Grenadiers so far. Any officer congenitally liable to get things wrong and do punishment was a godsend to the others, and fortunately we had one such colleague, to whom we all owed much. Not long after completing my own month's punishment he attended divine service in the Guards Chapel on a Sunday, dressed, as was the Picquet Officer's duty, in tunic and bearskin. He had such an appalling hangover from some Saturday night debauch that he went to sleep (in the front row where, by order, he sat) and fell off his seat into the aisle with an unbelievable clatter, sword emerging from scabbard, bearskin and gloves and Picquet Officer sprawling in the middle of the (rather smart and customarily morning-coated) congregation. He was given so many extra picquets – I cannot remember exactly how many – that the rest of us had a clear run for months. He may be doing them still.

My own other memorable contretemps with a Colour – when, raising it for the Royal Salute in the Mall as the King and President Lebrun of France were driving past on the latter's state visit, the tassels got caught in a tree – passed without awful consequences: the Drill Sergeant managed to disentangle the gold cords with his pace stick and I got away with it.

Less trouble-free was my first command of the Bank of England Picquet which in those days (and ever since the eighteenth-century Gordon Riots) used to march to Threadneedle Street from barracks, a drummer bearing a lantern at its head: and, of course, me. Nobody had made clear to me that if it rained we were allowed to take the Picquet to the Bank by Underground, and when we were marching down Queen Victoria Street and a storm broke I halted the troops and ordered: 'Capes on'. The Guardsman's cape was at that time worn folded in a very smart square at the small of the back. It was, as I could soon tell by the consternation on the sergeant's face, not meant to be used in this unrehearsed fashion and soon Queen Victoria Street was profusely littered with bits of cardboard, old newspapers and various other unsightly devices used by the Grenadiers to shape up their folded capes to the requisite standard. Leaving our litter, we marched on.

This was ceremonial, this was participation in the great and colourful state occasions of the London scene, this, at first, was almost the sum of military duty. I will not pretend I did not enjoy it. Of course it was all agreeable. Going on Guard, once one got through the ceremony without mishap, was agreeable. Dining on Guard, in the Officers' Guardroom at St James's Palace, was agreeable: one was allowed to entertain girls there to lunch and to drinks before dinner, and that was agreeable. And there were, in addition, all the pleasant distractions of the London season, invitations to balls, often several on one night, dinner parties, theatres, freedom and fun. I was nearly twenty and life was good; and the rigorous conventions of those days were accepted, as part of an unchanging order. Exactly the right clothes had to be worn on every occasion, whether on duty or off – and fearful retribution followed any backsliding. For theatres, dances, dinners in restaurants one wore white tie and tails, always. In London, out of barracks, it was a dark suit, bowler hat, rolled umbrella and gloves. No parcel could be carried by an officer in any circumstances, nor could he get on a bus. On parade, of course, precision of dress and the fitting of each garment was rated of immense importance, and the same attitude was applied to every aspect of life. To be 'improperly dressed', whatever the occasion, was to sin indeed.

I don't think this sort of attention to detail, this insistence on correctitude in small observances, is contemptible, but it should be kept in proportion, and by some the proportions were in those days unhealthily exaggerated. The theory in the Brigade of Guards – probably seldom articulated because they were not great theorists – was that officers and men who had been trained and disciplined to get every small personal detail right, whether in drill, dress, cleanliness or whatever, would similarly expect and observe the highest possible standards in every duty they were called on to perform. 'If it's worth doing, it's worth doing properly' was often heard, and so far as it goes it is a valid maxim. The trouble was that a lot of things were also worth doing which we didn't do at all. I must not exaggerate the inadequacy of our instruction: some principles were inculcated which were absolutely sound. In particular we were left in no doubt that the interests and care of our men (when we had the chance to see them) came first, always: and our own concerns and comfort came last, always. We were very proud – indeed I suspect we often appeared arrogant in our pride – of how our battalion looked, drilled, responded to orders, did its duty. It was a fine battalion and there was not only first-class discipline but a splendid spirit within all ranks. We laughed at our deficiencies of equipment, mocked 'The Army', which we thought of as a vague, remote, enormously incompetent authority quite outside ourselves. We reckoned we were very good. We knew our Regiment's history and traditions. Many of us had fathers who were Grenadiers. We were supremely confident. If war came – and it was obvious throughout 1939 that sooner or later it *would* come – I don't think anybody doubted we would do as well as our parents had, in the war which had culminated in total victory only twenty-one years before.

Yet this confidence was misplaced. We were, in fact, not well trained. The system I have described made it virtually impossible. Boy Browning, our Commanding Officer, impeccably turned out and impressive, was a first-class and inspiring soldier but neither he nor any other man could have trained a battalion in those conditions. Our short annual period at Pirbright was painfully inadequate – although he used it to test and break a number of non-commissioned officers and I suspect might with advantage have included some commissioned officers as well. Our older officers had spent too long in the deadening routine of a peacetime army which – as happened between 1919 and 1939 – is told that it has won the War to end all Wars and won't take part in another conflict on any significant scale. In such an atmosphere the small minutiae of regimental life dominate and replace all else. They have their place but they should not dominate.

The priorities, the code, which governed us were defective. I think it now – with a certain anger – and I believe I sometimes thought it then. There was, despite all the fun, the loyalty, the pride of Regiment, a certain complacent lethargy, a view that life must continue according to some manifestly outdated guidelines, coming war or no coming war. To take a broader interest in any aspect of the military profession (I am not suggesting that I did) was regarded as insufferably bad form. It was, I think, not exactly thus in the Wehrmacht! Our equipment, our field training, and especially our attitudes of mind – all were inadequate. Despite the rigour with which we young ones were treated there was a certain infectious self-indulgence in the atmosphere that led to softness of fibre where the reverse was needed.

After Commanding Officer's drill parade, attended by all officers in barracks, it was usual to go at once to the Officers' Mess where most immediately had a glass of port – a wine I have never drunk since. One day we were all ordered into the dining room: it transpired that certain officers, no doubt of some seniority, had complained about the quality of the port and we were to have a tasting, to help the Mess order a better consignment. Such a concession to democracy was unusual.

32

Representatives of our wine merchants, Saccone and Speed, were present. Dry biscuits were served. Samples were poured. Eventually a vote was taken and there was unanimity that one wine was superior to all others tasted. It was, needless to say, the one we had been drinking all along, the one which was the subject of complaint. This sort of nonsense is unimportant: but concentration on it distorted men's sense of priorities. It made them sound and seem like asses, which only a few were. Asses are not good models for commanders in war.

I suppose the truth was that the shadow of our triumph in the previous war, ended in 1918, lay too heavy. In that war, because of the peculiar character the fighting assumed on the Western Front, the most important aspects had probably been discipline, minor administration, *esprit de corps*, exactly observed routine; and these attributes were undoubtedly displayed by the Brigade of Guards to the admiration of all. Harold Macmillan, a Grenadier, has referred to the twelve battalions that formed the Guards Division in that war as constituting perhaps the world's most formidable fighting body since the Macedonian phalanx. But in the war that was now coming, while those virtues remained important, other qualities and more flexible attitudes and skills would be required. To develop them, imaginative training was needed, and serious military education. We did not receive it.

On 1 September the German Army invaded Poland. Two days later we were at war. Our battalion was to be part of 7th Guards Brigade, formed from battalions in the London District on mobilization. 7th Guards Brigade was in 3rd Division, one of the first four divisions planned to be sent to France as the leading echelon of the British Expeditionary Force. The division was assembling in the West Country and we moved to Sherborne in Dorset. Our battalion commander, Boy Browning, had been taken away from us shortly before and was destined for higher things. His wife was the gifted and beautiful Daphne du Maurier, whose father was Sir Gerald, and it was said that only an intervention by a member of the

Royal Family had saved him from anathema, on the grounds that officers of the Regiment did not marry the daughters of actors. He later commanded an airborne corps. He was succeeded by one generally regarded as a nice old buffer, who was replaced in France before battle began the following spring.

Life at Sherborne – we were billeted in the town, my own company officers living in a small hotel – was properly feverish. The battalion sailed to France on 29 September, nearly four weeks after the outbreak of war; and the frenzied activity of those weeks of final preparation was further spurred and stimulated by the arrival of our divisional commander, a small, vigorous officer with a sharp-pointed nose and very penetrating blue eyes who at once gave orders that all ranks were to run up and down hills before breakfast and who seemed determined to make us and everybody else fitter than we had been; and quickly, too. His name was Major-General Bernard Montgomery. He began to instil into us what he was later to do for most of the army – a long-overdue professionalism.

Much later in life I got to know 'Monty' very well. In the House of Lords he was energetic, friendly and often entertaining – a charming parliamentary companion. He used to sit on the Conservative benches,* and if I turned would often look at me with his characteristic, impish grin when he managed to say something particularly outrageous or, as he fancied, especially provocative. Monty was lively, irreverent and often unpredictable. He had an unkind, uncharitable side, evidenced by his attitude to military colleagues in too many cases; but I never experienced it. He was conceited – bumptious, as a schoolboy can be bumptious after a run of success and until taken down a peg. The effect of this, particularly later in his ascent to grandeur, could be astonishing. I once went to the British Embassy in Rome after the war; Monty was staying there, I think when he was Deputy Supreme Commander, Europe. When we met he extended his hand and said, 'How

---

* This was unusual for an ennobled public servant, who, in most cases, would sit on the cross-benches.

do you do? Have you met me before?' I had never heard it put quite like that! He had been calling on the Pope (in retreat at the time, as it happened) to tell him how to fight communism.

I am not a military historian but I have a strong impression that Monty's generalship was on occasions described in over-generous terms by Monty. The fact remains that as the newly arrived Commander of the 3rd Division: later, as Commander of V Corps in which we were stationed; and again, as Commander of the 21st Army Group, before D-day in 1944, his arrival was invariably a strong gust of fresh air. He had a powerful will. He exuded confidence. He conveyed clarity, purpose and absolute certainty that all would be well with him in charge. It was clearly the same – and the most striking example – when he assumed command of the Eighth Army in the Western Desert in 1942. That was far away from us – we were training, training in England – but we read about it, we had experienced Monty, we could believe it and it made us feel better. Monty, as would be said now, was good news.

To my great rage I was sent away from the battalion after a few weeks, since there was an order that officers and soldiers under the age of twenty-one could not go abroad. I, therefore, did not experience Monty as divisional commander in France, but when I returned to the 2nd Grenadiers in 1941 they had been through the disastrous campaign that led to Dunkirk and by then they reckoned they knew Monty well. One and all thought him the most effective General they had encountered, the one who knew his job, the one who imposed his own will rather than danced to the tune of others, the one who made sense. It has sometimes been alleged that Monty 'didn't get on with the Brigade of Guards', that his abrasive personality and apparent disdain for convention were at odds with Guards punctilio and that he, in turn, had little time for Guardsmen. It is perfectly true that our Guardsmen were unimpressed by Monty's later gimmicks – the studied informalities, the calls to 'gather round me', the liberal scatterings of cigarettes to troops at wayside halts, were treated by our men with a certain ribald scepticism. But as a commander we recognized his quality from the very beginning, and Monty reciprocated. He paid glowing public tributes to the Brigade of Guards again and again, calling them in the House of Lords 'the best troops in the army, without question', saying, 'They're the best because you can trust them: they do what they're told.' We, in turn, thought the world of him and it pleases me to record it.

When I was rusticated from the 2nd Grenadiers I was sent to the Grenadier Training Battalion at Windsor and from there to command a demonstration platoon at the Small Arms School at Hythe in Kent. I was at Hythe when, in the summer of 1940, the 'phoney war' of those early months was succeeded by the astonishing German successes of May and June as the Wehrmacht broke through the Allied line, sent the British reeling back to Dunkirk and forced capitulation on the French in a brief, brilliant campaign that we all supposed would culminate in the invasion of England. At Hythe, we had a grandstand view of the aerial dogfights out to sea, the bombing of convoys passing through the Dover Straits. The summer of 1940 was especially beautiful, and there was a curious unreality in watching, without danger or involvement, the ships steaming slowly along the Channel with German bomb-bursts bringing up the columns of water around them, while, overhead, Spitfires fought it out with Messerschmitts and occasionally a pilot drifted down by parachute towards the cliffs of Kent or the Hythe marshes.

My demonstration platoon – composite, with men drawn from all regiments of Foot Guards – had responsibility for part of the beach defences in case of invasion. We gave demonstrations of skill at arms by day to the School students, and by night we went to the beach – our line of responsibility, I remember, extended for three and a half miles – and waited for the invasion. We were confident that if the Germans landed they would suffer appallingly. I almost pitied them. I commanded forty-eight men with three light machine guns and forty-five rifles. Personally, I had a pistol. I suppose we might have made sense of a frontage of a few hundred yards: we had three and a half miles. Nevertheless I felt for the Germans who in their rashness might come our way; and they never did. I spent my twenty-first birthday on the Hythe beaches. I came of age.

Before being returned to the 2nd Battalion, now back from Dunkirk a good deal shaken, I spent a short while at Chelsea Barracks in London, where a part of the Holding Battalion of the Grenadiers was stationed. The operation of call-up and mobilization, together with the fact that no fighting was going on and nobody was getting killed, meant that there was an enormous build-up of troops in England. Every regiment had a long queue behind its service battalions (of which three new ones were in process of being formed in the Grenadiers). This queue consisted of recruits under training – at the Guards Depot at Caterham and the Regimental Training Battalion, in our case at Windsor – but after initial training men had to go somewhere before being absorbed into the establishment of a service battalion, and the Holding Battalion, stationed at both Chelsea and Wellington Barracks, was formed to accommodate them. The Holding Battalion also, of course, did the many duties which were necessary in London itself: these ranged from providing garrisons at key points – Ministries and so forth – to furnishing the King's Guard in much the same way as before the war. The latter ceremony was unchanged from peacetime, in that the Duties marched up and back behind a band as I had done in my first year, a year that now seemed an age away. There was no Colour to confuse the Ensign now, however; while scarlet tunic and bearskin had been replaced by khaki battledress, steel helmet and gasmask.

There was also the Blitz. The great air attacks on London started in the late summer of 1940 and gave a sharp edge to the Holding Battalion's duties. Off duty, in blacked-out London, a good deal of life went on as it had done before. It was possible to dine out – not badly, for rationing had not yet started to bite with any severity. One could dance in a number of places still open – the Café de Paris, one of the most popular of these, was hit by a bomb in March 1941, and many were killed. But on many evenings we were on some sort of duty. I remember, on one occasion, sharing a guard duty in a room in the Horse Guards building with an officer in the Blues, the Royal Horse Guards. He was extremely deaf, and was reading *The Times* when I heard that peculiar whistle and screech like the approach of an express train which meant a German bomb was on its way – and coming very close. I dived under the table. The bomb fell on the Scottish Office next door with a deafening crash. There was dust, plaster and splinters everywhere. My companion looked up from *The Times* a shade thoughtfully. Had someone knocked at the door? He said, gently, 'Come in!'

It was 1941 before I rejoined the 2nd Grenadiers, by then stationed at Weymouth on the south coast, still in 7th Guards Brigade, still in the 3rd Division – although Monty had left it and was commanding V Corps in which we now were. But it was about that time, in the spring of 1941, that a decision was taken which had a considerable effect upon us all. A Guards Division was to be formed, as in the First World War – but it was to be an armoured division. Selected battalions of the Foot Guards, including ours, were to be converted into tank or motorized battalions. Long programmes of indoctrination for soldiers, officers, commanders and staffs were planned. The Guards Armoured Division was born.

The then Commander-in-Chief Home Forces, Sir Alan Brooke, had drawn up in 1940 an Order of Battle for the army he needed to defend the United Kingdom against German invasion; this included a number of armoured divisions. As the year 1940 turned and the threat of invasion receded (by the end of 1941, to vanishing point) the army in Britain became the basis less for national defence than for that counter-offensive, at first in the Mediterranean theatre but ultimately in north-west Europe, which everybody hoped would be the pattern of the war one day although the possibility seemed remote. At this stage, of course, the United States was neutral: and when it was resolved to form the Guards

Armoured Division, early in 1941, the Germans had not yet attacked the Soviet Union. Except on a small scale in the Western Desert against the Italians – and, since February, against the German Afrika Korps in addition – the British Army was training, reorganizing, but only preparing for war. It was not fighting; and it was recognized that, willy-nilly, there was likely to be plenty of time for major changes before the next round. To form new divisions and to transform, radically, the role of regiments was perfectly realistic. The need was there and time allowed.

Nevertheless, to convert the Foot Guards, or some of them, into tank battalions was, I believe, a peculiar policy. They were, at least by then and after the intensive shake-out and training of the first year of war, first-class infantry: and, as in the First World War, they proved themselves as such and set a certain standard for the whole army, a standard which was, I think, generally recognized later, both in North Africa and in Italy. This standard was achieved by a tradition of discipline and order, perhaps sometimes a touch inflexible but in infantry combat assuredly effective. The Foot Guards could be relied upon to do what they were told, and to do it conscientiously and efficiently. The tradition was less applicable to armoured warfare, or much of it. Where manoeuvre is required, so is speed and imagination and initiative. I never thought that our system was perfect for breeding those qualities. Individuals possessed them – splendidly. But the system itself was differently designed.

I have already referred to our warrant officers and non-commissioned officers, our sergeant-majors and sergeants. They were admirable men, but more in those days than today they were executants of pretty rigid orders, custodians of a fairly inflexible regime. They knew their basic infantry soldiering inside out. To find their Guardsmen separated from them by the steel walls of an armoured vehicle, apparently possessed of a will of its own, was disconcerting. Furthermore they themselves were in some cases less than rapid learners of new ways. There was also the simple fact that the tanks of the day were rather small and the Guardsmen particularly large. I remember one sergeant-major, a huge man of magnificent appearance, who seemed slow at responding on the radio – he commanded a tank – during training on Salisbury Plain. There was always a pause before he acknowledged a transmission, and one day, when his tank happened to be close to mine, I discovered why. When an officer's voice came through his earphones he stood to attention and saluted before tackling the microphone.

This sort of thing led to a certain dichotomy which I suspect was unhealthy. On the one hand was the need to embrace new ways, to learn new skills – and, inevitably, to modify and sometimes scrap time-honoured practices and attitudes of mind. On the other hand was the instinct – largely represented by the senior non-commissioned ranks and by no means unrespectable – that if certain traditional methods and standards, such as drill, appearance and minor routine, were unduly disregarded, the battalion's discipline and efficiency would ultimately suffer; because we were that sort of animal. The theory of our superiors in the Brigade of Guards was that there was no problem – our discipline was just as essential and its practice just as applicable whether we were in armour or out of it. It did not work out quite like that. At the least this dichotomy led to a partial waste of excellent non-commissioned officer material. Good soldiers in the former ways, they could not adapt: while not all those who learned about armour with most celerity were impeccable soldiers and leaders, when it came to the crunch. Of course some people were unteachable. The authorities had dreamed up what are now commonplace but then seemed revolutionary methods of testing our suitability, as individuals, for armoured warfare, and I remember the whole battalion, all ranks, taking some sort of aptitude test. When the results were published the highest score, by far, was notched up by the battalion sanitary man who performed an essential but somewhat humdrum duty in the hygiene department. The bottom score was rated by one of our squadron leaders – in fact, a brilliant commander – who was a highly successful stockbroker in civilian life. Both stayed in the armoured battalion, I'm glad to say.

I remain of the opinion that in forming the Guards Armoured Division the army had the worst of two worlds. In the words of the Division's historians: 'A large number of officers in the Brigade, holding the general view that armour rather than infantry was becoming the predominant arm, were keen to embark on the venture. The Regimental Lieutenant-Colonels all welcomed the idea, and the Major-General commanding the Brigade of Guards . . . after consultation with His Majesty the King, expressed himself as being strongly in favour of the proposal.'* So be it. I think they were wrong. There is the further point that, whatever was held in 1941, the greatest shortage as the war continued was of high-class infantry – a fact which I believe was perfectly predictable, and which, certainly in Europe, applied to mobile operations as much as to the more positional warfare which terrain such as most in Italy dictated. It is, of course, true that there was a widespread sense that the Germans were ahead of us in the matter of armoured warfare. This transformation was meant to show that we were, belatedly, taking it seriously.

All that is not to deny that it was an interesting and enjoyable experience – and we became very proud of our division. The years between Dunkirk and the British Army going to war again were difficult. Tedium threatened. The novelty of learning a different sort of soldiering helped prevent it. Furthermore, the chances of survival were higher in a tank – I have no illusions about that. Let nobody pretend that the infantryman was not and is not the most vulnerable figure on the battlefield, with the toughest, most unrewarding and in some ways most skilful job of all. We were lucky. We lost too many good and gallant friends in the armoured battalions; but I have no doubt we would have lost more had we remained on our feet.

* Rosse and Hill, *The Story of the Guards Armoured Division* (1956).

CHAPTER 3

The War

The two most important things in a war are to participate under the command of people who know their job; and to spend it with friends. The first gives a decent chance of preparedness, even survival, even success, even honour. The second ensures that amidst the most disagreeable circumstances there will still be laughter and affection.

In the Guards Armoured Division I was lucky on both counts. The division was formed with Sir Oliver Leese as its first commander. A Coldstreamer, large and energetic, he had a squeaky voice, a great command of violent language when annoyed, and a rapidly acquired mastery of every detail of an armoured division, of how its component parts ought to work, of what principles ought to guide it in battle, and of how to organize, harry and teach his mainly ignorant subordinates in order to reach his objectives. He left us in September 1942 to take command of a corps in the Eighth Army under Monty, where he made a great name as a fighting commander and later succeeded Monty in charge of Eighth Army itself. None of us was surprised. In the end Oliver Leese was appointed Commander-in-Chief of Land Forces in South-East Asia, and came to grief over a row in which he was alleged to have replaced without authority General Slim, the victorious and beloved commander of the Fourteenth Army in Burma. The ins and outs of this affair have been explored by many a writer and have no part in my own tale. I doubt if tact was Oliver Leese's longest suit, but he was a magnificent divisional commander, and in the early days of the Guards Armoured Division he worked wonders.

He was succeeded by Major General Allan Adair, a Grenadier

who, long afterwards, became Colonel of our Regiment. He was loved by everybody. He had enormous charm of personality and voice, taking great pains to make everyone feel they were valuable whatever their rank, regiment or job. He was a man of impeccable manners – in the true sense of leaving anyone he spoke to happier and better for the encounter. He was the sort of general who made his entire command feel they would do anything rather than let him down. He had joined the Grenadiers as a very young man in 1916, in the trenches of the Western Front, and had won a considerable reputation. He was brave, sensible, courteous and kind.

As to friends, I was surrounded by them. Furthermore, some of my longest-lasting friendships were formed in those years between 1939 and 1945, in my Regiment, in my battalion. Bonds are formed like no other bonds when one is young, and at war. But early in 1942, a new bond was formed. I marched into the Commanding Officer's office, known as the orderly room, immediately after he had dispensed justice for the day at a midday ceremony we called 'Memoranda'. A large, genial man, his name was Mike Dillwyn-Venables-Llewellyn. We were stationed in billets at Warminster in Wiltshire and the orderly room was in St Boniface's School. I stood rigidly to attention. It was the hour when officers' applications were received or rebukes administered. I was a (temporary) captain.

'I thank you, sir, for leave to get married.'

A few friendly enquiries and I received it, with congratulations. The injunction given to me on joining the Regiment three years before had been disregarded. In the spring of 1942 I married Iona McClean, which is far the most sensible thing I've ever done. We were married at the Guards Chapel in London with the rather restricted celebrations of wartime. I remember that the date, 25 April, coincided with one of the frequent divisional exercises on Salisbury Plain with our newly arrived tanks, or those of them which could be coaxed into movement. I had, surprisingly, been excused attendance because of an already arranged wedding, but the exercise meant that few of my friends from the battalion could be with us on the day. Our week's honeymoon in a special suite in the Lygon Arms Hotel at Broadway in the Cotswolds cost £19.10s, including all food and drink. It nearly broke me.

Our first married home, scene of Iona's first attempts at housekeeping, was in part of the battalion butcher's shop, in a semi-detached house on the outskirts of Warminster, on the road leading towards Heytesbury. We had to reach our quarters ducking under or round the hanging sides of meat and bacon. I was just under twenty-three. For the next two years we spent as much time together as we could – not always easy to arrange. We managed to find some sort of lodgings here and there on most occasions: the Guards Armoured Division moved from the West Country to East Anglia in 1943, and a few months later to Yorkshire, preparatory to the final journey to the south coast before D-day. Iona generally succeeded in turning up and we contrived to have some sort of interrupted, rather adventurous and certainly unpredictable life together. Our eldest daughter, Alexandra, was born in London in April 1943. In some areas – notably, of course, the south coast immediately before the invasion of north-west Europe – neither wives nor anyone else except residents were allowed. Random checks were made, identity cards inspected, and unauthorized persons deported – with, very properly, appropriate disciplinary action taken against those who were responsible for them. Iona and I outwitted both the regulations and the logistic problems on several occasions, although more than once she had to escape through the back door of a shop to avoid being spotted by somebody in higher authority who would have recognized her. Once, when we were quartered in Hove, our last billet in England, she was brought in by a taxi-driver, passing as his wife.

During those years before D-day the army in England was growing hugely, changing enormously and experiencing a good many difficulties. It is not easy to keep great numbers of men under arms in their own country, training for campaigns which will start at a time which none knows. Furthermore, other people were fighting – not only in Africa and, on a huge scale, in Russia: but in Burma, and, of course, at sea and in the air. We were safe. We were merely training. The consequent psychological pressure should not be exaggerated – most men, in a war, primarily wish to survive it, after all. But the pressures were there and often frustration as well. It was seldom a simple matter to create enthusiasm, preserve discipline, bring about ever-improved efficiency. The army was learning, but the learning process was protracted and sometimes tedious.

I, too, was learning. I believe I had already learned one important thing in my service, but I learned it with more force in the army as it became after war began. It was, I knew, both more agreeable and much more effective to associate one's subordinates of whatever rank with what one was trying to do, by the sharing of information, by the exercise of pleasantness and good manners, as well as by straightforward discipline. The army has to be a hierarchical institution. Obedience must be instant and absolute – anything less is inefficient and dangerous. To demand such obedience – the rendering of which doesn't come easily or naturally: most of us prefer to argue the toss, demur, delay – it seems to me essential to leaven the requirements of subordination with a good deal of humour, friendliness and commonsense. Otherwise discipline either fails, or is imposed in an atmosphere of sullenness and incomprehension. I daresay these assertions will be found by most to be blindingly obvious. I hope so.

This approach was particularly necessary in the circumstances of a major war, with the whole nation mobilized. The war was a great leveller, and the army a more variegated and egalitarian society than people who have never served in it suppose. Of course there was in the army, as in all armed services in any country, emphasis on the externals of discipline, on rank, saluting, forms of address and so forth. In a profession where performance – and, sometimes, life itself – often turns on knowing exactly who has authority, and on obeying that authority, such emphasis is essential. But within the framework of hierarchy the army contains, and particularly contained in the Second World War, a great diversity of

45

people and relationships. Most men between the ages of twenty and forty were in uniform. Very few had chosen to be soldiers. The degree to which they acquired the hallmarks of the military differed with their character, their background and the nature of the military institution they joined. Some took to army life like ducks to water, even secretly preferring it to anything previously experienced: many of these (where they survived) regarded it later with nostalgia long after resuming civilian clothes. Some took it cheerfully, dutifully, philosophically, stifling their loneliness, doing their often considerable best and on occasion bringing to the army gifts and variety which it could seldom expect from its Regulars to a like degree – but never pretending they did not eagerly await the hour of release. Some were lost, out of place, unhappy from first to last. All served together.

The circumstances of war, too, were levelling. Among the officers of a regiment, for instance, there might be considerable differences of personal wealth, differences which could be obtrusive – even divisive – in the free-spending days of peace. In the war A might have more money than B but there was remarkably little to spend it on. He might own a large house, but the chances were that it was occupied by a Government agency or some irremovable tenant; and, anyway, he couldn't live there. He might possess a smart car, but there was no petrol. His more extensive wardrobe was restrained by clothing coupons – and, in any case, we all wore uniform day in, day out, from first to last. Nobody could cut much of a dash. All lived a communal life, like school or prison but undoubtedly more fun than either.

War, too, was a leveller between ranks themselves, because one was living at very close quarters with the soldiers one commanded, and each could form a view of the other based on pretty intimate knowledge. It takes more than a badge of rank to preserve respect if an officer shows himself deficient in the qualities expected of him. Chief of these, I think, was – and no doubt is – the power of conveying that he regards others, whatever their status, as individuals and fallible human beings, like himself. And perhaps one of the principal means

46

of demonstrating this is by humour. But although the war may have been a leveller, at the best it reinforced mutual regard, made subordination human and bound a disciplined collection of men with at least some of the attributes of a loyal and devoted family. It was said, long ago and again perhaps surprisingly to those who have never served, that nobody successfully commands a battalion or a company except with the consent of every man in it. I believe that to be true; and I like it.

My abiding memory is of the quality of the men I was privileged to command, make friends with and try to look after. A large number of the soldiers in my squadron – our companies were renamed 'squadrons' in the cavalry manner when our battalion became armoured – came from pretty disadvantaged backgrounds. Two out of the four other men in my tank crew had been unemployed. Of the Regulars – and we had, in the 2nd Grenadiers, a high proportion of Regulars and Regular reservists since there were, of course, no casualties between Dunkirk when they had been evacuated and D-day when they prepared to set sail again – I think a large proportion had joined because they were hungry in civilian life; the army meant food, a roof and a job; and, once they got used to it, a job in which they could take pride as compared to the dole in which there could be no pride at all. Of course some of the Guardsmen and NCOs had been more fortunate, came from skilled trades or prosperous homes: but there were very many who didn't.

They weren't bitter. They were enormously nice, full of infectious humour, decent, honourable men who showed little rancour about a society in which they had drawn, to date, few prizes. But there was no doubt in my mind that they reckoned life after the war ought to give them at least a chance of something better. 'Current Affairs' were in vogue: an 'Army Bureau of Current Affairs' issued from the War Office pamphlets on political themes which were meant to form the basis of discussions between all ranks. 'ABCA' has been described as an agency which disseminated socialist propaganda, because it fell into the hands of enthusiastic left-wingers while other people were attending to matters purely military. There is a good deal in this, as I recollect, but it wasn't ABCA – nor the stridently anti-Establishment *Daily Mirror*, the sole newspaper read by the majority of soldiers – which ensured most of the army voted as they did in 1945. I remember, late in the war, asking the men of my squadron, 'If you would like, tell me who, were there an Election, would vote for Party A, B or C?' Not one man intended to vote other than Labour. They wanted a change. They reckoned that a change could only be for the better, and that they had had too little to cherish from life as it had been. And, as people will, they blamed the Government – the pre-war, Conservative Government. I didn't and don't regard that as entirely just, but I understand.

I understand particularly because it seemed to me that luck – merit, certainly, but a great deal of luck – plays a large part in determining who, in life, succeeds. I don't only mean the self-evident luck which decrees that A is born to a good home, decent surroundings, honourable parents, material prospects; while B has none of this. I mean also that luck which puts a person into the right place at the right time, in any calling or walk of life, so that they catch the tide and ride with it. Without luck, few who achieve great things would get started. I admire them. But there were and are a good many people whose luck never placed them near even the bottom-most rung of the ladder of success; and some of them were in my squadron. For them, in every generation, there has to be concern and understanding. And it is the duty of those who have enjoyed superior luck – and, let it not be denied, may sometimes have displayed superior qualities – to feel that concern and show that understanding. By all means let the race be to the swift, by all means let there be every effort to 'level upwards', but there should be some consolation prizes in life. And those of us who may feel that the handicapper has been generous in our case have a particular obligation to attend to them.

The Guards Armoured Division moved to France and concentrated in the vicinity of Bayeux at the end of June 1944. Our first battle was the operation christened 'Goodwood'. It was my first experience under fire.

It was not, I think, a very successful affair. Three armoured divisions, including ours, and one infantry division advanced southward over the rolling country east of the city of Caen – a narrow funnel between the suburbs of Caen itself and some wooded hills a few miles further to the east. In the clear light of a beautiful morning we halted, dismounted from our tanks, waited, and watched a vast fleet of bombers discharging their loads on the wretched inhabitants of Caen and (we hoped) the German defenders in and beyond the city whom we had been assured we were about to overrun. At last – I recall that all timings had got somewhat delayed, no doubt because of the considerable congestion at the bridges over the River Orne – we moved forward, passed a number of disconsolate-looking German prisoners wending their way northward in sad little field-grey columns, and swung southward fully deployed on to our line of advance. The first, somewhat discouraging, sight to meet the eye was a large number of British tanks blazing on the skyline. These were from the 11th Armoured Division, who had been in the lead and then directed to move south-westward, while the Guards Armoured Division were to continue south-eastward, passing into and through the German defences around Vimont and the Bourguebus ridge.

It didn't happen like that. Very soon our own tanks were being hit by German dug-in tanks and anti-tank guns, sited skilfully and in considerable depth on the edge of the villages, by the barns, and in the coppices with which the open corn-lands were studded. We saw very little of the enemy who, in spite of having been shaken to pieces by our air bombardment, had recovered enough to be picking off British tanks with enthusiasm and in large numbers. What we did see was our own blazing hulls – our battalion lost over twenty tanks from one cause or another in the first hours – and very soon we found ourselves halted while a more deliberate attack was put in on the village of Cagny. The cavalry charge – for the initial advance had resembled exactly that, and a fine sight it was – had ended. The German defensive line was dented but unbroken. Monty explained afterwards that the object of the whole thing was to draw the German Panzer reserves eastward, on to ourselves, to facilitate an American breakout from the west of the Normandy beachhead: but we thought and hoped that things would go better than that and we should find that we had broken through. So, I suspect, did he.

That night, as on so many subsequent nights until the war's end, my crew and I dug a hole sufficiently large for five bodies, drove our tank over the top of it, shovelled some of the spoil between the tank bogey wheels to give additional protection against shell blast and splinters, crawled underneath and went to sleep. Our first day of battle had been rather tiring and we had lost quite a number of friends. The Germans – allegedly now of poor quality because of their losses in Russia, bombed to distraction and outnumbered by enormous odds – had shown themselves pretty effective. Furthermore, despite what we were told of their shortages of guns, ammunition and everything else, they were proving smart hands at shelling, both with guns and mortars.

We stayed for a few more days in the Caen sector, suffering sporadic shellfire and making no further attempts to advance. The battle, we were told, was over. I remember the astonishing congestion of vehicles – the British Army had an immense array of motor transport and every sort of mechanical equipment and it was all crowded into the comparatively small space of the Normandy eastern beachhead. Finding a field for an armoured squadron to harbour was like looking for a parking space in central London at lunchtime today. On exercises in England we had been soundly rated if our vehicles were not dispersed, to impede discovery from the air and to minimize the chance of shellburst causing casualty. None of that nicety applied in Normandy. There wasn't room. Yet this great mass of vehicles had not, it seemed, led to the sort of shock effect at the sharp end of the battle which would have cracked the German defence. The truth, I suppose, was that a mass of tanks was an excellent force with which to exploit a tactical victory, but to achieve that victory needed the coordination of a limited number of tanks with a large number of skilled infantry and mortars – in order to deal with the scatter of German strongpoints which so successfully held up the armoured advance. And in the armoured brigade of our division – three armoured battalions, a force of about 180 tanks – there was only one (numerically small) infantry battalion. This was the 'Motor' battalion, 1st Battalion Grenadiers, and we needed a good deal more of it. I don't think 'Goodwood' was a very well conceived operation from the tactical viewpoint. Perhaps some of our superiors still needed stronger reminders that Western European terrain differs a good deal from the North African desert. I suspect, however, that we had such huge numbers of tanks by that stage of the war that they could be used prodigally – and were. Infantry were more scarce. Infantry needed more anxious husbanding.

The same lesson – our shortage of good infantry, our superfluity of armour and mechanized vehicles – became even clearer in the next stage of the fighting, which took place in the Normandy *bocage*. By then we had – most wisely – been reorganized. Within the Guards Armoured Division each armoured battalion was grouped with an infantry battalion, whether (as in our case) with the 1st (Motor) Battalion of the Grenadiers or with a battalion from the lorried infantry brigade of the division. It so happened that the four groups thus formed each consisted of two battalions of the same regiment – a Grenadier, a Coldstream group and so on. The result was that in every encounter a mix of tanks and infantry was available: tanks and infantry, furthermore, who came from the same regiment, who already knew each other and were quickly to know each other very well indeed – for squadrons of armour were similarly paired with companies of infantry, forming sub-groups which were so close in spirit and confidence as to be completely one. I daresay that there could be theoretical criticism of this arrangement, in that for some engagements more infantry were required or more tanks: we established our own sort of inflexibility, it could be (and by some was) said. But the compensating advantage was the truly intimate cooperation of both arms, even if not always in the most ideal proportions. And the upshot was a great improvement on what had gone before.

This was particularly necessary in the *bocage*. This country

51

consists of small meadows separated by high, steep banks topped by very thick hedges. It is a country of small hills and winding streams. Tanks could only cross the banks laboriously, and were, of course, very vulnerable when doing so to the short-range anti-tank weapons of which the Germans seemed to have plenty. Mobility – the principal characteristic of an armoured formation – was irrelevant. We pushed from hedge to hedge and farm to farm, needing at every step infantry and mortars, and using our tank guns as close-support weapons to blast the buildings, hedgerows and coppices which could contain enemy machine guns, snipers or anti-tank bazookas.

We also, of course, used them as anti-tank guns. Although intelligence officers often explained to us that the opposing Panzer divisions had been so 'written down' as to present a negligible threat, they seemed to crop up with tedious frequency, and certainly not yet to have run out of ammunition. They, too, were largely confined by the terrain to an anti-tank role: but here we made the sharp discovery that, although German industry might have been pulverized and German losses in the East might have been astronomical, their tanks were greatly superior to ours in tank-versus-tank combat. We in the Guards Armoured Division (as in most of the Allied formations) had the Sherman tank. With a robust and reliable engine, it had only moderately effective armoured protection: it burned with hideous ease if hit; and it had a 75-millimetre gun with low velocity, which was quite an effective close-support artillery piece but was remarkably ineffective against the Germans' Tigers and Panthers (the giants of the Wehrmacht) or even their Mark IVs. The German tanks could hole us in the front at anything up to two thousand yards while our 75s could do little to them except from the rear. Not until we got a proportion of our tanks (I think one in four) up-armed with a British seventeen-pounder gun did we look the German armour in the face on something like level terms. Tank design was not the Allies' proudest achievement in the Second World War.

Eventually the Normandy campaign ended. As far as we were concerned it seemed somewhat to peter out. We were ordered to a 'rest area' which was comparatively unscarred and appeared to have no Germans nearby and were told that we would be unlikely to move for several days. We could sleep, clean ourselves and our kit, write letters, visit the neighbouring squadrons. The days extended to a week or more. Then we learned that far to the west the Americans were advancing southward and eastward, moving fast. We had not, of course, realized the extent to which the German defence had been stretched, the ceaseless attrition of their line by small-scale encounters but by hugely superior forces. It was hard to believe this really was the breakout, the moment of victory for 'Overlord', the end of the battle of Normandy. While we were digesting this, largely hoping that we would nevertheless get a good period of inactivity and respite, individuals were encouraged to take a few days off, to go to the Normandy coast to swim or something of the kind, to enjoy a change. It was a generous concession. Three friends and I managed to borrow a second staff car which our Commanding Officer had acquired, I am uncertain how. We drove out of the battalion area, ostensibly to the coast. In the back were jerrycans of petrol, bedding rolls, a tank cooker and some boxed rations. We also took a jeep and two Guardsmen. When our little column was clear of the view of authority we stopped and had a quick conference. That morning the radio had reported the Americans advancing on Paris, entering Chartres. 'To hell with bathing,' we said. 'History is being made! It has to be Paris!'

The roads were packed with huge columns of Americans. We never saw another British vehicle. Somehow we passed up the columns, mingled with them, pointed to the Union Jack on our vehicles to bamboozle our way past outraged, white-helmeted American military police. We stuck to main roads — one had no idea of the situation of the Germans, and certainly a good many small German columns were moving by minor roads in the same direction as ourselves. It was anybody's guess how far we'd get. Of fighting there was no sign. At five o'clock in the afternoon we drove into Chartres. For four years

France had been beyond an impenetrable curtain of war, its enchantments recollected by those of us lucky enough to be aware of them, its people being plundered and oppressed, we supposed, by the occupying power. It was startling, on that drive, to find how normal everything and everybody appeared. Chartres, its streets filled by throngs of American soldiers, was not in the least unlike one's pictures or recollections: Normandy, with its destruction, squalor and death was miles behind us – this didn't feel like war at all. We even found a table in a Chartres café and were able to have something to eat and drink that we hadn't cooked ourselves on a tank cooker. It was an extraordinary contrast. We drove out after half an hour, on the Paris road.

At seven o'clock we drove into Versailles. Here the great, broad avenue in front of the château was filled with milling crowds of the inhabitants, all in highly festive mood and mostly waving small tricolor flags. Our Union Jack was recognized and greeted everywhere with huge enthusiasm. Military traffic had thinned out but it was hard to believe we were near any sort of front line, and we pushed on towards Paris.

Shortly before eight o'clock we drove down the Champs Élysées. The tanks of General Leclerc's Free French Armoured Division were parked under the great avenue's trees, between the Arc de Triomphe and the Rond Point. An abandoned German Panther tank was in the Place de la Concorde, near the Jeu de Paume Gallery. Otherwise, of the enemy there was little trace.

When we had left our bivouac area that morning we had slept few nights except in a slit trench or under a tank since landing in France. We had assumed that wherever we found ourselves that night something of the same would apply – shovels were in car and jeep. We were, we imagined, moving towards the front, after all. When we reached the Place de la Concorde, however – crowds large but not overwhelming, traffic minimal – it was unclear what to do next. A slit trench and bivouac cover in the Tuileries Gardens seemed inappropriate. One of us, David Fraser, knew Paris quite well – his father had been Military Attaché until after the outbreak of war.

'I know where the Ritz is,' he said. 'Let's go there.'

We did. And – contrast of all contrasts from the battlefields we had just quitted – sitting in the Ritz were a number of well-dressed people, elegant ladies perched on bar stools chatting, sipping cocktails, looking unconcerned and somewhat indifferent to the dramatic scenes of war and peace, occupation and liberation in which we supposed we were playing a part. The impression given was that the war was a distraction, an intrusion in somewhat bad taste.

In evidence at the Ritz, however, were a good many Americans already – and a good many journalists. Another of our party was Neville Berry, a son of Lord Kemsley and himself a newspaperman in peacetime. A moment's thought convinced him that Kemsley Newspapers should open a Paris office; that the office would need a Paris bank account; and that a reasonable first charge on it would be to keep a small party of Grenadier liberators for two nights at the Ritz.

'We'd better have rooms here,' he said. 'Leave it to me.'

Half an hour and several bottles of Perrier Jouet later we sat down to a perfectly tolerable dinner, interrupted by an air-raid warning which caused disproportionate alarm, we thought. I had started to order the dinner, an order being acknowledged by the suave head waiter in perfect English. Facetiously and rather foolishly I smiled at him and said, 'Did you talk English when the Germans were here?'

He was busy writing and didn't look up as he said politely, 'No. I talked German when the Germans were here.'

It put us in our place. We gathered the last Germans had left by the back door not long before our arrival at the front. A campaign is only a campaign but the Ritz is the Ritz.

Next day we went to the British Embassy, where David Fraser was keen to discover whether anything was known of his family's flat and possessions, abandoned when the Germans had conquered all in 1940. We banged on the closed gates of the huge entrance in the Rue St Honoré. After an interval a wicket gate was cautiously opened. One of the splendid tribe of expatriate porters who had been there throughout the German occupation looked at us, astonished.

On our battledress jackets was the shoulder flash 'Grenadier Guards'.

'Good heavens!' he said, 'Good heavens!'

We were the first he had seen. He told us with pride that Goering had attempted to take over the Embassy as his Paris residence.

'"You can go away," I told them,' he said. '"You can go away! This is the *British Embassy*!"'

It was a lovely reunion. David Fraser learned that his parents' furniture had been moved into the Embassy and was safe. We signed the visitors' book, the first compatriots to do so since 1940. A little later an elderly English lady, Lady Westmacott, approached me as I was returning to the Ritz.

'Young man, are you from *The Times*?'

'No, as a matter of fact I'm in the Grenadiers.'

She seemed most disappointed. No doubt she had some tales to tell. I think she had been living in the hotel throughout.

As we drove westward the next day to rejoin our battalion, in Normandy as we supposed, we saw columns of vehicles advancing towards us bearing the familiar 'Ever-Open Eye' sign of the Guards Armoured Division. In our absence 'by the sea' the division had been ordered to move. The German Army had been largely trapped and destroyed at Falaise, the Allies were in full pursuit, the hunt was on. We reached our comrades at Vernon, where the River Seine runs between pleasant, wooded hills. We had been expected back somewhat earlier but nobody seemed disposed to be very angry.

'You nearly missed a great moment,' they said. 'We're about to cross the Seine!'

'We've been crossing and recrossing it for the last forty-eight hours,' we explained softly, 'by the Pont Alexandre III and the Pont de l'Alma!'

The following days were spent in advancing through northern France, across the Somme, through Amiens and Arras, names which had been marked by years of bloody struggle in the previous war, names with depressing memories for those who had experienced 1940. Now this was 1940 in reverse and it was stimulating. We encountered a few German rearguards and lost a few tanks and men but on the whole the pursuit was more tiring than dangerous: there was much driving by night, when sleep is almost impossible to defeat. On the night of 2 September we harboured on an airfield at Douai. And next day, at six in the morning, we set out on an advance which culminated a hundred miles further with the entry into Brussels of the Guards Armoured Division that evening.

The advance to Brussels itself was only patchily opposed. One of our 'squadron-company groups' (not mine) had to fight a battle in Pont-à-Marcq against a German group of infantry and anti-tank guns while the rest of the Grenadier group found another route and pressed on. We drove into Brussels after nightfall amid scenes of extraordinary, moving, jubilation. It was difficult to get through the crowds and every tank was quickly laden with a heavy complement of flag-waving Bruxellois, bestowing kisses and wine on every head they could see. The Germans seemed to have evacuated the city. Eventually – I am unclear how we found our way or why and on whose orders – we arrived in the gardens of the Palace of Laaken in the north-east of the city, where the Queen Mother of the Belgians was standing in the darkness to shake selected hands. It was an incongruous night. A patrol was sent through well-tended rhododendrons in response to a report that a German force was in the neighbourhood. 'Are we to dig in?' NCOs asked officers, contemplating getting the men to tackle the inevitable slit trenches which had saved many a life in Normandy and without which no sensible soldier would take rest, orders or no orders. And somewhere else one heard in the darkness – 'Careful with those tanks! Keep as much as you can off the grass!' I slept on the pavement, dog-tired and very soundly.

My tank broke down – without any contriving – in Brussels, and I was some hours late in catching up with the 2nd Battalion who advanced next morning to Louvain. The division, we discovered, had overrun the principal German Armed Forces' champagne store, and hundreds of crates full of bottles marked

Reservé à la Wehrmacht fell into our hands. Twenty cases, following some pretty spirited initiative on my part, fell into my own hands. When my tank, repaired, roared down the Chaussée de Louvain to catch up with the war there were twenty cases of champagne on the engine covers. That evening I opened a case: the wine had been, more or less, boiled. It was some time before I was ready to drink champagne with pleasure again.

The next major operation in which we took part was christened 'Market Garden' – the advance to link up with the aerial assault by three airborne divisions on Arnhem and Nijmegen. They were intended to capture the two great bridges across the Waal at Nijmegen and the Nederrijn at Arnhem, the two arms of the lower Rhine. We were meant to drive up one road through Holland (a considerable German army was still in Holland, west of us, between our intended advance and the sea), link up with the airborne divisions and thus cross the Rhine barrier, so that the Allies could swing eastward and start encircling the Ruhr.

I have no idea whether this operation could, in fact, have achieved what was intended had certain things gone right which went wrong. Monty, in his memoirs, declared himself still its 'unrepentant advocate'. On the other hand we all knew that most Allied supplies were still coming across the Normandy beaches a long way behind us: the Germans had garrisoned and held the Channel ports for some time and made them unusable, and they controlled the banks of the Scheldt estuary preventing the use of Antwerp, so that our necessaries were reaching us along a remarkably extended route. This would have remained the case – and been even more so – had we at that stage got across the Rhine. Winter, too, was approaching. It was true that at the time of our advance to Brussels the Germans seemed beaten: but they had remarkable powers of recovery, and although our overall numerical superiority was massive, what counts in war is how much superiority you can muster at the point where it matters.

Ours was being mustered along one narrow road, with, for much of the way, sunken fields and soft yielding polder on either side where tanks would sink immediately. I doubt the proposition that success in 'Market Garden' would have finished the war in 1944.

We set off on the road to Holland with high hopes, nonetheless. I remember seeing the great fleets of gliders and troop-carrying aircraft moving through the afternoon sky as we sat by our tanks awaiting the hour to start. Later, when we had advanced some way but the clock had moved dangerously far, we saw the aircraft resupplying the beleaguered troops at Arnhem. Many were brought down. I thought the pilots wonderfully brave, such easy targets, such devoted men.

Our own advance went a good deal slower than the authorities had anticipated. Could it have gone faster? Was the operation feasible, so that the gallant soldiers of 1st Airborne Division at Arnhem could have been relieved? I don't know. Much has been written – and filmed. It seems to me that the rate of progress planned for the ground troops was absurdly optimistic: very minor obstacles can hold up a mechanized column if there is little chance to leave the road, and enough were created to slow the rate of advance by critical hours. It seems to me that the Americans' 82nd Division at Nijmegen were dropped in a most peculiar place, miles away in the country: the result was that the Germans were still occupying much of the town, including the approaches to the bridge, when we arrived, whereas the plan envisaged a clear run. And it seems to me that the decision not to drop troops between the Arnhem and Nijmegen bridges was most odd. It meant that even when across the Waal, somebody would have to drive along a raised road on top of a dyke between the two rivers, with no intervening support. From what I have read there seems to have been a certain failure, too, to act on intelligence about the German forces at Arnhem itself: as well as a somewhat curious choice of dropping zones for 1st Airborne Division. But at the time, of course, I knew nothing of such things.

The first major water obstacle we crossed – bridge successfully captured by the Americans – was the Maas at Grave. On
the bridge was standing the well-remembered figure of my
first Commanding Officer in the 2nd Grenadiers, Boy Browning, now commanding the Airborne Corps. As ever, he looked
immaculate, gleaming boots and belt, trim, confident and
formidable. The leading squadron commander, Alex Gregory-
Hood, had also served as a subaltern in his battalion before
the war. He dismounted and, unrecognizably covered with
dust, approached the General and saluted. This was the beginning, it seemed, of the link-up. This was a dramatic moment.

'Sir!'

'Who are you?'

'Sir, it's Alex!'

Boy Browning looked astonished. 'Good God,' he remarked,
'I always said it was cleaner to come by air!'

Later that day we drove into the outskirts of Nijmegen,
discovered it was still full of Germans, tried to rush the bridge
in the evening, lost tanks and men, and realized the unpalatable fact that the place would have to be cleared – methodi-
cally. That takes time. It also demands daylight unless it is to
go very, very slowly indeed.

Next dawn, therefore, we quartered the city and worked
through it, clearing it of the German defenders. At the same
time assault boats were brought forward – up that same
narrow, congested road – and troops of the US 82nd Airborne
Division, with enormous bravery, began crossing the Waal
west of the town. The boats were unfamiliar, the casualties
high, but a significant number of Americans got across and
began working their way eastward along the north bank. At
half past three in the afternoon our own squadrons and
companies of the Grenadier group began their attack on the
hard core of the German defence – the approaches to the
bridge, and the buildings dominating them. Some public gardens on a hill immediately above the south end of the bridge
were strongly garrisoned and were eventually taken by the
Grenadiers just after six o'clock.

At that stage my job – I was second-in-command of a

60

squadron – was to take a half-squadron of tanks across the bridge. Since everybody supposed the Germans would blow this immense contraption, we were to be accompanied by an intrepid Royal Engineer officer to cut the wires and cleanse the demolition chambers under each span. Our little force was led by an excellent Grenadier, Sergeant Robinson, who was rightly awarded the Distinguished Conduct Medal for his action. Two of our tanks were hit – not lethally – by anti-tank fire, and we found a number of Germans perched in the girders who tried to drop things on us but without great effect. Sergeant Robinson and the leading tank troop sprayed the opposite bank and we lost nobody. When I arrived at the far end my sense of relief was considerable: the bridge had not been blown, we had not been plunged into the Waal,* we seemed to have silenced the opposition in the immediate vicinity, we were across one half of the Rhine! A film representation of this incident has shown American troops as having already secured the far end of the bridge. That is mistaken – probably the error arose from the film-maker's confusion of two bridges: there was a railway bridge with planks placed between the rails and used by the Germans for road traffic, some way to the west of the main road bridge we crossed; and the gallant American Airborne men reached it. When Sergeant Robinson and his little command crossed our main road bridge, however, only Germans were there to welcome him; and they didn't stay.

The pursuit had ground to a halt, the war was clearly going on. We spent the winter of 1944 in Holland, first near Nijmegen where the Germans had flooded the land between the two great rivers, and there was little activity. There were some comic incidents: we discovered that a supply depot run by a Dutch staff from which we drew rations was also being used by the Wehrmacht! They drew and signed on different days – I don't know how long that went on! Then we moved

* In fact it seems the Germans never intended to blow the bridge. The demolition chambers were packed with German soldiers, who surrendered.

to the area north of Maastricht and manned a defensive line based on a number of farms and villages on the Dutch–German border. Meanwhile the American Army was fighting its way towards Aachen, south of us, and plans were being hatched to clear the country between Maas and Rhine. Shortly before Christmas 1944 we were withdrawn to Belgium for some sort of change, and in mid-move we learned of the German December offensive through the Ardennes. A British Corps of three divisions, including ours, was then deployed as long-stop behind the River Meuse, but the enemy never reached it.

After returning to Holland to take part in the slow, muddy series of battles to clear the Germans from the west bank of the Rhine – battles which again took us near Nijmegen and into the Reichswald Forest – we crossed the Rhine itself in mid-March and started the final advance into the heart of Germany. Everyone knew that these were the closing weeks of the war. Everybody – including myself – was loath to indulge in unnecessary adventures when the end of hostilities and personal survival at last looked very likely. Everybody, however, was astounded at the skill, tenacity and courage of the enemy.

After the Rhine crossing German defence was fragmented. Isolated detachments fought small-scale actions and withdrew if they could. There was no question, on their part, of counter-attack or manoeuvre – and, anyway, they had no petrol. They had no hope of winning, or even of much delaying defeat. The Russians, committing frightful atrocities, were hammering at the gates of Berlin. The German soldiers knew their cities were in ruins, the peoples of their eastern provinces were fleeing from the Red Army, utter disaster was engulfing their country. And yet they fought. Their discipline was remarkable. Their soldierly instincts, their tactical training and sense, were capable, right to the end, of teaching us a sharp lesson if we took liberties. They were superb fighting men, the men of the Wehrmacht against whom we fought; and my admiration and respect for them has never diminished.

They were curious weeks, those last weeks of the Second World War. We had little idea of what we would find in

Germany, and perhaps – as elsewhere – were bemused by the comparative normality of everything. Towards the end we found ourselves approaching a great raised autobahn – a novelty in those days – and along it flashed a motor column which we tried unsuccessfully to shoot. Afterwards we learned that Heinrich Himmler, the Reichsführer SS and commander of the Home Army, had been in the column. The top Nazis, creatures of Allied demonology for so long, seemed to belong to another world from these ordinary, well-behaved, not un-friendly folk who gazed at us without emotion as we drove towards Hamburg and towards the end of the war.

There were again, of course, moments of humour. I was by now commanding a squadron and together with my 'grouped' company commander from the 1st Battalion, Harry Stanley, found we had incurred the displeasure of our brigade com-mander for some inadequacy or folly. The Brigadier, Norman Gwatkin, was a very popular, fiery officer with a high colour and we stood to attention in front of him as he told us what he thought in most uncomplimentary terms. Then we both saw, as he did not, a billygoat approach him from behind. We said absolutely nothing, and as his invective reached its climax the billygoat charged. The Brigadier yelled, drew his revolver and fired six entirely ineffective shots in the direction of the complacent beast, now withdrawing. Then he relapsed into gales of laughter and our rebuke was at an end.

The ceasefire found us in the Cuxhaven peninsula, not far from Bremen. Within a few weeks we said goodbye to our tanks: the Guards Armoured Division was to revert to the infantry role. A huge parade was held on Rothenburg airfield on 9 June 1945, with Monty taking the salute as the tanks and armoured cars – all of them – started up for the last time. Some of them had come from Normandy, travelled the distance on their tracks. The massed bands of the Brigade of Guards, flown from England for the occasion, then struck up and as the tanks disappeared a column of about a thousand marching men, a detachment from each Foot Guards battalion in the division, came over a slight rise, marched to the saluting base and presented arms. Then Monty addressed us, speaking in generous terms of our divisional general, Allan Adair, whom we loved. I doubt if there was a man unmoved in that huge assembly. And then it was all over, the Guards Armoured Division, the north-west European campaign, the German war.

We moved to the Rhineland, were quartered in German houses, lived for a little while lives of peace and ease and a good deal of luxury among the increasing privations of a defeated people. I had seen the sufferings of the inhabitants of Holland, where the food situation in the winter of 1944 had been particularly severe. Now I saw the same in Germany, where physical wretchedness was increased by political confusion and despair. Germany, all-conquering a few years previously, had lost everything. And everywhere there was hunger. Was our enjoyment and abundance in the midst of misery heartless? Undoubtedly so – but it was regarded by us, then, as the not unjust outcome of a war forced on Europe by Germany. I don't defend this complacency, but it was human. It showed me, in retrospect, how easy it is to rationalize our own well-being and the deprivations of others.

The results of our bombing were a revelation. I never saw Berlin at that time, nor Dresden, nor many another crucified city, but we inspected towns of the Ruhr and the Rhineland and they showed the scale of the destruction. I believe there were about eighty undamaged buildings in the great city of Cologne. People, grey-faced, appeared from the ruins, conducting some sort of life, moving slowly with the lethargy which comes from starvation, waiting patiently for the chance of a cigarette stub thrown into the gutter by an Allied soldier. So it was throughout the industrial – and many other – towns of Germany. And everywhere people were displaced, frightened, herded into camps, posing problems to the exasperated and often bored Allies. In my own company area in the Rhineland we were responsible for a huge 'Displaced Person' camp. Largely containing Yugoslavs, the place was divided between those who had supported the Royalist Mihailovic and reckoned a return to communist Yugoslavia meant sudden death; and those who felt differently. Murder between the factions was frequent. Atrocities against the local population if, as sometimes happened, inmates of the camps went on unauthorized sprees in the countryside were equally common. All these people – Poles, Yugoslavs, Balts – were casualties of the war, million upon million of human tragedies. There were camps full of Russians, too, ex-prisoners of war and ex-slave labour in Hitler's factories. Their overwhelming terror was of being sent back to the Soviet fatherland. It is too easy, in the tranquillity of today, to condemn those in authority at that time who made harsh decisions in such matters with cruel effects. It is too easy to forget that we had just won total victory after near defeat, won it very largely through the efforts and enormous suffering of Russia; and that people were slow and understandably reluctant to admit the brutality of the Soviet system and rule. And it is too easy to forget that all over Europe were confused, unsettled multitudes who created the need for some sort of decision and administration. It was an atmosphere hard for today's generations to conceive.

When I look back and recall the twin steeples of the mighty cathedral of Cologne rising from the rubble of a city in which it appeared to be the only building standing; when I remember the desolation of Europe forty-three years ago, the populations starved, demoralized and apathetic on the one hand, filled with hatred and the desire for revenge on the other; when I remind myself of the vicious wounds inflicted by the nations of Europe upon each other in those appalling years, I marvel at what has since been achieved. It would, at the time of which I write, have been thought incredible that in a few decades we should be living in a continent at peace within itself, prosperous beyond the dreams of previous generations, and not without a certain strength, a semblance of incipient unity. New challenges confront the peoples of Europe and the Western world. Their determination and ingenuity continue to be tested, whether by the potential threat of an armed and ideologically hostile Soviet Empire, by the perplexing menace of international terrorism, or by the less violent but often intractable problems of managing their economies within a new industrial revolution. But the ferocity of actual battle between the great nations of the West is no longer conceivable; the alliances they have formed and the institutions they have adopted commit them to internal peace – peace with acrimony at times, peace amid rivalry doubtless, but peace nevertheless. A younger generation is now reminded by fiction or television – perhaps excessively reminded – of ancient animosities and past brutality but with a sense of remoteness such as that felt by myself when contemplating the Napoleonic Wars. One of my generation regards this transformation with astonishment and gratitude. Gratitude – and perhaps something additional: a resolve that if disunion, weakness and complacency contributed to the horrors we witnessed, they never shall again.

CHAPTER 4

Introduction to Public Life

I decided I wanted to leave the army.

I was a Regular soldier. Retirement was not yet permitted. Non-Regulars, of course, were being demobilized quite rapidly on a first-in first-out basis, but the Regular had no exit route. Except one: Members of either House of Parliament were – indeed had to be – permitted to return home if Regulars, or obtain their discharges if not, in order to attend to their parliamentary business.

I had long decided that after the war I wished to follow a political life. There was nothing spurious, therefore, about my application to leave my battalion and take my seat in the House of Lords. Of course personal interests played a strong part – I had inherited my family's property but knew little about it and needed to learn; our daughter, Alexandra, was two years old and I had hardly seen her; I wanted to start to build a life and a home in England. There was also a sadness: my mother was dying and I hoped to spend a little time near her if possible. All this was true, but it was also true that my eyes were on Parliament and I had no intention of pursuing further a military career. The war, including the war against Japan, was over. I reckoned peacetime soldiering, however necessary and meritorious, could manage without me. It was politics which interested me.

This went down badly with my superiors in the Regiment. They looked at me with suspicion. Successive Commanding Officers of the 2nd Battalion – to say nothing of the lieutenant colonel commanding the Regiment, now reigning in that little Doric temple* I remembered – thought I was taking an unfair

* Or near it. Wellington Barracks had been bombed and regimental headquarters was in temporary quarters nearby.

advantage as a peer, and causing a lot of unnecessary inconvenience. I understood their point of view – which was maintained with considerable warmth. I realized I was a nuisance. I appreciated that getting the right number of officers of the right seniority into the right places amid the chaos of demobilization was difficult and I was making it more so. I was aware that they thought I simply wished to get home and be idle, without serious application to politics. Nevertheless I knew what I wanted. I stuck to my rights and my (unrefusable) application. I have never regretted it. I had loved my Regiment and continued to do so but I knew it was time to turn the page.

In 1943 I had had a few days' leave and had taken Iona to Buckinghamshire to look around the estate and to build castles-in-the air about where on it we might, just might, live one day. There was no family house. Uncle Charlie's home had been sold to the school long before, and my mother had always remained in Devonshire. Iona and I had no home: she had been living in a rented house at Woolacombe in north Devon, near where my mother had spent the war.

In those few wartime days in Buckinghamshire we had seen the Manor House at Bledlow. It was fairly derelict at the time. Originally a house where the eldest son of the Carington family lived, only some eight miles from Wycombe Abbey, it had been for many years a tenanted farm and at this time half the house was the tenant's dwelling and half was occupied by evacuees. No member of my family had lived there since the mid-nineteenth century.

We had, however, decided that it was there, if possible, we should like to make our home. The evacuees had now left, so that half the house was available and in 1945 we took possession of that half, sharing the house with the tenant-farmer, Tom Wooster, a generous, independent-minded man. There were few facilities – little in the way of electricity, bathrooms or plumbing. The evacuees had by no means lived in luxury! And the state of interior decoration was, of course, most primitive.

In those days it was not possible to do any work on a house except with a permit, obtained from the local council. There was an enormous construction problem facing the building industry in the aftermath of the war, blitz and inevitable wartime neglect. It was policy – and quite right too – that priorities should be controlled and that in competition for scarce resources money should not be allowed to enable someone to jump the queue. Permits were regulated by a financial ceiling; and we were granted £400 to make the house habitable. Even in those days it wasn't a very large sum, but we managed to slap some paint on here and there, install a bathroom, and wire the house so that we could have electric fires, the only available heating. There was a fuel crisis the following winter and we weren't allowed to turn them on. I seldom remember more intense cold.

But life at Bledlow started. While work was under way we rented a London house in Campden Hill Square and travelled to Bledlow when we could, to see how things were going. The train service from Marylebone to Princes Risborough was slow, cold and uncomfortable but a new life was beginning and inconvenience was a trivial matter compared to the years of separation and war. We moved into Bledlow in April 1946. Our second daughter, Virginia, was born in June. We assembled a small domestic staff and fitted in somehow, in conditions which would now be regarded, so far as amenities went, as plumbing the depths of squalor and discomfort. We were extremely happy. We started – principally Iona started – to create the beginnings of a garden, where none had been: a garden at which she has become ever more expert and inventive and which has been a source of huge satisfaction and pride to us both.

Out of the blue I was asked to join the Buckinghamshire War Agriculture Executive Committee.

I was a landowner, one who had only just started to learn his business. As yet I was no farmer and I realized that the committee would teach me a lot. These committees, formed during the war, were designed to give advice to landowners and farmers on how to maximize production from land. I reckoned I was as yet unqualified to give very authoritative advice, but by rubbing shoulders with those who presumably were I could not fail to learn. Agricultural committees included representatives from landowners, farmers, farmworkers, land agents, veterinary surgeons and a host of others.

The country had been very short of food in wartime. Britain had for years been under siege. It is sometimes forgotten that we remained short – indeed we were for several years a good deal shorter – after the war was over. Bread, never rationed during the war, was rationed after war ended. Meat was rationed until 1954. To grow the maximum amount of food was of paramount importance. Our committee, and others like it, was meant to play its part in this.

War had in fact produced a revolution in British agriculture and attitudes towards it. Before the war agriculture had been in acute depression. Cheap food was imported, home-grown cereal crops could only be grown economically in a few counties of England, farms in Buckinghamshire seldom boasted a ploughed field. In huge areas of the country, including ours, it was a matter of what was called dog-and-stick farming. Farmers could afford no investment and received wretched returns. Wages were low, and rents were difficult to pay – and were themselves derisory, so that landowners were, as often as not, running loss-making businesses, disposed of with sadness and small profit if debts became too pressing.

The war transformed all this. It became a matter of national survival to make land as productive as possible. Every sort of grant, advisory service and guaranteed price structure was invoked to turn the British agricultural economy round; and it was turned round for ever, or at least until today. A beneficent revolution had occurred and for the first time since the repeal of the Corn Laws farmers were prosperous and well-regarded.

This prosperity, of course, owed much to national policy. It was underpinned by a mass of legislation, orders and statutory instruments. It required – or was deemed to require – direction, and the War Ag committees provided it. In my work for ours I went round the county, visited farms, agents, experts

70

of every kind. I got to know my own county pretty well and a lot of people in it. I learned, I think, a good deal about estate management and farming without benefit of a formal course.

Our committee was not purely advisory: it was armed with formidable powers. A landowner or farmer could be dispossessed if he failed to follow the so-called advice the committee gave, or if he neglected his buildings, his capital equipment, in such a way as to prejudice his or his tenant's farming enterprise. This, of course, was an interference with a man's liberty to do what he thought right with his own, and here and there would be instances of resentment – and, I daresay, of poor advice or of power abused. But I found these instances rare: and the rarity undoubtedly owed much to the general prosperity which Government policy and direction had produced for the farming community as well as to the composition of the committees. People were not being asked or advised by ignoramuses to do unprofitable things, and there was a general acceptance of the fact that to grow more food was a patriotic duty. Sometimes, of course, some independent character would get away with an act of defiance, whatever the rights and wrongs: a redoubtable lady in north Bucks had managed to disobey War Ag instructions to plough her land, and to keep her grass for her stud of horses throughout the war.

I learned much from my visits, from committee work and discussion and from my colleagues. There were three landowner representatives and the other two were friends – Ralph Verney of Claydon, a famous house of great beauty; and John Young. We had all just left the army, we were new to the work, and we helped each other and enjoyed it. The farmers on the committee were splendid men. We had a lawyer as chairman, of a very old and distinguished south Bucks family of estate agents named Rafferty. As a small boy Mr Rafferty had been caught trespassing at Hughenden by Disraeli. He described Dizzy as a terrifying figure, in a cloak; but when he beckoned the boy over he gave him no rebuke and was kind.

From time to time we were visited by ministers. The Labour Government's Minister of Agriculture was Tom Williams, a thoroughly agreeable man. It was probably not very difficult to be a successful and reasonably popular Minister of Agriculture at that time of guaranteed markets and prices, when the farming community was doing well; but Tom Williams was, undoubtedly, successful – and since he was shrewd and friendly, a cheerful, red-faced figure, everybody took to him and his popularity was genuine. His Parliamentary Secretary was George Brown. The latter had spent the previous few years as a paid official of the agricultural wing of the Transport and General Workers Union, and had no doubt formed strong views on agriculture. His manners were a good deal worse than those of his master. George Brown had admirable qualities, but he was a man of emotional prejudices and a taste for abrasive language and behaviour. Years later when he was Foreign Secretary many an Ambassador experienced this disagreeably. I think he disliked the genus ambassador. At this earlier time he probably disliked the genus landowning Conservative peer, and his and my encounters were less than polite.

I was busy with the committee, of which I became vice chairman, and chairman of the Estate Management Committee. But in 1949 our tenant Tom Wooster died, and we not only took possession of the rest of the house but also started to farm the land. At that time it was about 350 acres, to which I have been able to add by taking over other tenancies or by purchase, bringing the Bledlow farming acreage up to 1000. I also joined the Country Landowners Association, later becoming chairman of the executive committee. I began to feel more at home with the problems of practical farming and of landownership. Although farming was underpinned by guaranteed prices, we had plenty of headaches. We were still very short of materials for building and repair: and there was a general lack of capital for investment. There were plenty of challenges in life – and satisfactions. Our son, Rupert, was born in December 1948.

At about the time that I got possession of my farm I stood for the Buckinghamshire County Council and was elected – at least I have held one elected office! – and I served on the County Council until after the General Election of 1951, when

I became a junior Minister and had to give up. I enjoyed the County Council. It taught me, too, the great authority wielded under our democracy by officials. The people's representatives, whether in local government or in Parliament, come and go. They may take trouble to brief themselves on particular issues but by and large the officials who serve council or ministry know their facts better, have seen it all before and have the benefit of continuity. To challenge them needs very careful preparation; and I had the impression that too few councillors undertook that preparation, and that, in consequence, officials had things too much their own way. Certainly they never overstepped their proper role, but if mastery of a subject lies too much with a permanent servant and too little with his nominal master there is an imbalance which can create suspicion among the governed, the electors. Another lesson I learned from local government was how subjective a matter is taste. My first meeting at the Planning Committee was concerned with the architectural form to be taken by a new public lavatory in Olney. Olney is a most attractive place but tempers rose between the mock-Tudors and the neo-Georgians to a very alarming degree. Opinion was equally divided, and I realized that no arguments by one party would ever sway the other: nor could there be appeal to some impartial authority. Taste is how one feels, victory goes not to superior reason but to the most powerful or the most adroit; and victory is seldom won without acrimony.

I also became a magistrate. The county had little crime in those days and most of our business was concerned with motoring offences. We used to ballot for any of the more interesting cases likely to come before the Bench. I remember only one murder, and I didn't win the ballot. But the Court, the Council and the Agricultural Committee all helped to refresh my contacts with English society and I thoroughly enjoyed them.

I became, too, treasurer of the Wycombe Conservative Association. Wycombe – a Liberal seat for a long time, and owned by my family in the Whig interest for many years before that – had become tenuously Conservative, and then in 1945 had been captured for the first time by Labour. When

73

we first arrived at Bledlow nobody approached me from the local Conservatives – or any other party for that matter. Nobody tried to enrol either Iona or myself, or collect a subscription. After a bit I thought this was idle; and I wrote to the local chairman saying so. This, of course, was a mistake, in that it had the entirely predictable result that I was not only enrolled but given a job. Nevertheless work in the party at constituency level was another good way of meeting people and listening to them. In 1951 they made me chairman, and I remained chairman for many years. Our candidate was Bill Astor, who narrowly lost at the 1950 Election but in 1951 won the seat. He had to give it up and go to the Lords in 1952 when his father died: but then, in a celebrated by-election, John Hall won it, and it has remained Conservative. Bill Astor's wife showed me another difficulty in politics in England, particularly the post-war England of clothing coupons and shortages. If she went to a meeting in a fur coat people whispered, 'Look at her, flaunting her riches!' If she left it at home they hissed, 'She's dressing down to us! We all know she's got a mink at home!'

Life was full, and full to bursting, of course, when I started to farm. For apart from these local activities I had given up service with my Regiment on the grounds of wishing to do my duty in Parliament and pursue a political career. And at the end of 1945 I took my seat in the House of Lords.

There was at that time no possibility of disclaiming a peerage. I would have enjoyed the challenge of trying for a seat in the House of Commons in due course, and had it been possible I would have taken that road as early as I could. It was not possible. It was accepted that, rightly or wrongly, a peer, like a certified lunatic or a minor, could neither vote in an election to the House of Commons nor sit in that Chamber. I made no bones about the fact that this had been congenial in the short term, because it had enabled me to make an early start to civilian life and make a beginning in politics; but I was under no illusions – the House of Commons was the place which really mattered. Nevertheless I had long accepted that politics, for me, meant the Lords.

The House of Lords in those days was very small. The place itself was particularly small because the Commons, whose House had been damaged by bombing, had been sitting for some years in the Lords' Chamber; and the Lords sat in the King's Robing Room which was very small indeed. The House was also small in that comparatively few peers took part in most debates. The peerage itself, of course, was also smaller: until 1958, no life peers were created; and on the whole peers attended and spoke only if they felt they could contribute something to the argument, reckoned that they had something to say. Nevertheless they crowded the House on particular occasions; and they could crowd the House to vote. And here the composition of the Lords, although well-known, struck with particular force as soon as I took my seat.

For the Tory peers were in an immense majority. There was only a handful of Labour peers, and when the House was full the Conservatives filled the benches on both sides, overwhelming the Government's voting strength many times over. Labour had made one or two new creations, but they were still very thin on the ground. The situation was without parallel or precedent. Of course there had been plenty of times in history when the political balance in the Lords was somewhat different from that in the Commons, but a Government with a huge majority in the Commons and an Opposition with a huge majority in the Lords were something new.

It was a time for wisdom and restraint. If the House of Lords behaved with unreasonable obstructiveness there would clearly, and very soon, arise a constitutional crisis. This would do no sort of good to the Lords and I think most of us could see without difficulty that it would do little good to the country or its institutions. England does not prosper by revolutions. Two circumstances helped matters decisively.

The first of these was the atmosphere and traditions of the House itself. The House of Lords is, on the whole, a good-tempered and good-mannered place. The peers keep order among themselves – there is no Speaker (a very important and beneficial point in a Chamber of that kind) and the Lord Chancellor, who sits on the Woolsack, is in no sense an impartial chairman with right of intervention and control: indeed, he is a member of the Cabinet, a Minister as well as a Great Officer of State. Control is exercised by the members of the House and by them alone. Several peers may rise to speak – the others will make clear whom they wish to have the floor. A peer may go on much too long and irrelevantly – the motion may be proposed 'that the Noble Lord be no longer heard'. This is a rather laborious way of shutting up a speaker who may be out of order or, quite simply, intolerable; but it places the onus for procedure and conduct fair and square upon the House itself and it does not often need to be invoked. Add to this the obvious point that the Lords know perfectly well that theirs is not the place where great political names are made nor careers advanced, so that individual ambition and rivalry is less obtrusive than in the Commons; and you have and had a House which was, on the whole, courteous and comparatively tolerant. There could be sharp things said, but the occasional asperity of Lord Salisbury who, I remember, called Lord Nathan an oleaginous hypocrite was still more containable within civilized debate than the sort of coarse abuse occasionally hurled across the floor of the House of Commons until the Speaker intervened. It was resented by everyone in the House if a peer imputed self-interest or dis-honourable motives to another. I remember, years later, a Labour life peer (incidentally to become one of the most competent and best-liked members of the House) who implied that the same Lord Salisbury was taking a particular line about Rhodesia because he owned property there. The whole House deeply resented it and the remark – which had, I think, been made without much reflection – took a good deal of living down. There was less passion – and undoubtedly less interest and drama – in the Lords, but there was self-discipline.

In those days of the Attlee administration this was import-ant. It would have been possible to make the life of Govern-ment ministers intolerable by the sheer weight of our numbers and our noise, but it would have been bad tactics and poor behaviour, and the traditions of the House were against it. These were fortified by the second helpful circumstance: the personalities of the Leader of the House and the Leader of the Opposition peers.

The Leader of the House was Lord Addison. He had been a Liberal minister before the First World War. His experience was considerable. He seemed to someone like myself immensely old (he was, in fact, seventy-six when I took my seat) but he was obviously not only venerable but wise. He was also extremely nice. He was a sincere, albeit moderate, socialist who loved Parliament, and he understood perfectly clearly that the Government needed a certain tolerance, a certain cooperation from its opponents; and in return owed to the House a certain tact. This he displayed admirably. He could be waspish – he was no easy or compliant adversary. But he gave everyone the sense that he was an honourable man, prepared to do his parliamentary duty in a difficult situation – even when his own heart (as certainly sometimes happened) was not wholly with the Government's measures. These measures – even including those of wholesale nationalization – seldom look really revolutionary in retrospect. At the time, however, we on the Tory benches reckoned they spelled unprecedented danger, and some Government spokesmen seemed to go out of their way to exacerbate our fears, to represent the changes they were determined to foist on the country as more extreme than they were. In this atmosphere Addison kept Government going as far as the Lords were concerned: he kept his own party under control; and he kept the atmosphere acceptable.

In this he had the support of the Leader of the Opposition, Lord Cranborne. Bobbety Cranborne also had long parliamentary and ministerial experience. He had sat for a good many years in the Commons and had been a member of Baldwin's, Chamberlain's and Churchill's administrations. He had been given a peerage in 1941 in order to serve in the Lords (he continued to use his courtesy title of Cranborne until his father, the Marquess of Salisbury, died in 1947 and he succeeded). He knew the House very well and the Cecil family's long association with the government of England fortified his historical perspective.

Cranborne reckoned that it was not the duty of the House

of Lords to make our system of government inoperable. Nor, he considered, was it justified that the Opposition peers should use their voting strength to wreck any measure which the Government had made plain at a General Election that they proposed to introduce. He thus evolved guidelines, now unofficially known as the Salisbury Rules, which meant that the Lords should, if they saw fit, amend, but should not destroy or alter beyond recognition, any Bill on which the country had, by implication, given its verdict. The Lords, in other words, should not frustrate the declared will of the people.

I doubt if this amounted to a formal constitutional doctrine but as a way of behaving it seemed to be very sensible, and Cranborne's conduct of Opposition was exemplary. He had the confidence of the entire party, he dominated the House however distinguished its membership, he was wise, encouraging, clever and kind: he taught me most of whatever I've learned in politics. His parliamentary problem, of course, was that he had to give his followers a taste of blood from time to time. Many of us might feel deeply about some particular measure, which it was within our constitutional power to amend beyond repair or delay to a degree we knew could make a nonsense of Government administration. Cranborne had to allow some robust words and tactics, but still retain sufficient control to prevent the passing by the Opposition of 'wrecking' amendments – as opposed to those which could perhaps draw a good deal of the poison from a Bill without seeming to destroy it utterly. There was, of course, argument about what constituted a wrecking amendment and what did not: but, by and large, the Salisbury strategy worked and the Salisbury convention – of no wrecking amendments – was observed. To this day the convention continues that the House of Lords may amend but does not reject Bills on matters of formal and declared Government policy which have received a second reading in the Commons. Later in life I applied the same convention myself. I owed it to Cranborne. And in leading us in those days Bobbety Cranborne was brilliantly supported by his second-in-command, Philip Swinton, one of the ablest men I have ever known.

But these early experiences in the Lords also taught me the need for a revising Chamber. When there is before Parliament a heavy legislative programme – and particularly when one party has a large majority in the Commons – Bills cannot all receive the attention they need if they are to become the law of the land. It is essential they be looked at again, argued about, drafting loopholes discussed and eliminated, hypothetical difficulties exposed and answered. That is the way to make decent laws and prevent injustice – and inefficiency of administration. There is no doubt that sessions of Parliament packed with legislation are capable of turning out some pretty bad law – I regard this as equally true whichever political party is in power. Without a second Chamber Britain would be governed a good deal worse than it is. In the matter of revising Bills during the 1945 Parliament I believe our House did some excellent work, and both country and Government profited thereby.

The House of Lords, however, was and is more than a revising Chamber for legislation. It provides a forum where great issues can be discussed and opinions, even unpopular or minority opinions, can be advanced. It enables particular anomalies or injustices to be ventilated. It is a place of public debate. In my early years in the House we had formidable debates and men of great achievements and distinction. We had a number who had served in the wartime Coalition Cabinet. We had – and this has tended to be a feature of the House of Lords and one of its justifications – we had experts on every conceivable subject. There were, of course, the 'First Creations', men who had been given peerages for their records and their knowledge, presumed to have something especial to offer on their own subject. But among the hereditary peers, too, there was much depth of experience, not all of it purely agricultural, some of it recondite. The Duke of Bedford, I remember, was the world's greatest authority on parrots; and for some reason a measure affecting parrots came up! The Commons were a democratically representative body but I don't think they had a comparable authority on parrots.

The distinction of particular members, the self-discipline shown by the House collectively, and the fact that few men

79

spoke for personal gesture or effect but purely if they had something significant to say – all this made the House of Lords I joined a very worthwhile and instructive assembly. Of course one cannot make too much of the merits of objective and dispassionate debate. Who reads these debates afterwards? What is their outcome in terms of action? Perfectly fair questions, and I do not suggest and did not think that a debating society *tout simple* justifies a House of Parliament. But I believe we should be poorer if there were no place where public men can give a minority cause an airing from time to time.

There were moments, too, when a speech on an actual measure caught and turned the House. I remember the February 1947 debate on the Bill for giving independence to India. The matter had raised great passions. A lot of people thought it a betrayal – of a trust, of our history, and of a great many Indians. Some savage speeches – I recall Lord Beaverbrook's – had been made to that effect. Then Lord Halifax rose. An ex-Viceroy, an ex-Foreign Secretary, an ex-Ambassador in Washington, he was a man of great prestige. His reputation had suffered from his closeness to Chamberlain and his indefatigable search for peace before the war – as well as from the animosity of Churchill. He was not a great advocate. But he spoke with such sincerity, affecting the whole House by the obvious uprightness of his character, that I know he turned the anti-Government tide. A date had been fixed for Indian independence, a date many thought terrifyingly early in view of the state of India and the threat of violence and chaos. Halifax spoke of his own profound doubts about the timetable. But, he said, 'The truth is that for India today there is no solution that is not fraught with the gravest dangers. And the conclusion I reach is that I am not prepared to condemn what His Majesty's Government are doing unless I can honestly and confidently recommend a better solution.' It was simple, it was honourable, it was immensely effective on all who heard it. And he concluded, I remember, by saying that there could be no better way to close this chapter of history than to assist India's passage into the new order to the limits of our power. 'That', he ended, 'would be the spirit of the message that I would like to see this House send to India tonight.' Such moments raise the general level of dignity. The Government Bill passed.

Occasions of that kind were infrequent but they were precious. The House not only had a part to play but could on occasion play it with something not far from objectivity. There was a further, a constitutional function for the Lords which I came to appreciate as I took more and more part in its affairs and thought more about it. A second Chamber – provided that it was differently constituted to the Commons – represented the final constitutional barrier to an extreme majority in the House of Commons which might be determined to overthrow all our institutions, all our liberties. It was a pretty fragile barrier. We have no written constitution. We have no supreme court. Parliament has sovereign authority. The Upper House can impose an absolute veto on a vote by the House of Commons only to prolong its own life. Other measures of a revolutionary kind might be delayed, and might need to be preceded by Acts abolishing the second Chamber itself, but they would ultimately prevail if the Commons so willed. The House of Lords (in none of this have I set out any argument about its composition; I come to that issue later) was supposed to represent a mechanism against extremism. The need for this in 1945 was sometimes exaggerated, but it can never be entirely absent. Yet the mechanism was, I came to believe, inherently flawed.

At the beginning attendance at the Lords was intimidating. A large number of peers were, as I have said, men of distinction. A large number were also extremely old. A young major – until various formalities had been completed and resignations of regular officers permitted, we always wore uniform until some years after the war – was pretty small fry. But my fellow peers were exceedingly kind. There was a small clutch of us – Lloyd, Mancroft, Onslow, Fairfax, Townshend – who were all comparatively young. We kept each other company and learned the ropes together. The independent Unionist peers – the organization of backbenchers comparable to the 1922

Committee in the Commons – was chaired by Johnny Chesham. Aged fifty-one, encouraging, approachable and kindly, he took great trouble with us apprentices. He urged us to participate, to speak, saying easily that it didn't really matter if we weren't very effective so long as we had a go! The hereditary system is open to serious criticism but there is no doubt that it enables some young men interested in politics to play a useful, albeit restricted, part earlier than would otherwise be possible. We did a good deal of work and I think some of it was needed.

As I gained confidence I started to make speeches from time to time, and in view of what I was doing at home I generally chose a subject connected with agriculture. Our front bench spokesman on agriculture was Buck de la Warr, another man of outstanding charm and wide experience; in fact he had been a junior minister in Ramsay MacDonald's second Labour administration (he then became 'National Labour', sticking with MacDonald), as well as in Baldwin's and Chamberlain's Governments that followed. De la Warr was another who went out of his way to encourage the young. In 1947 I became a junior Opposition Whip.

I went often to the Peers' Gallery of the House of Commons (who were still sitting in the Lords' Chamber). I used to watch the proceedings and try to form some estimate of individuals. On the whole the famous tend to shrink in stature as one gets nearer them and in Parliament I certainly found this so. Churchill, of course, had a certain aura: I expect that imagination contributed to what seemed the magnetism of his presence, but I believe it existed all the same. Pink and white, in his short black jacket and pinstripe trousers, he stood out from all about him. In those days television had not brought statesmen into our homes – almost certainly diminishing them in the process. We had seen these renowned faces on newsfilm or in newspaper photographs. In many cases – notably Churchill's – we had heard their voices, memorably, on radio. We, or at any rate I, had not seen them in the flesh. Now I did. And Churchill did not disappoint, watched with fascination by a twenty-six or -seven-year-old from the Peers' Gallery. The other outstanding figure, I thought, was Ernest Bevin. Large, burly, rather ugly with heavy horn-rimmed spectacles and a continually moving mouth, he conveyed power and authority.

In the General Election of 1950 Labour was returned with a greatly reduced majority. Conservative tails were up. People who had, a few years before, said that they couldn't foresee another Tory Government in their lifetime, swallowed their words and were out scenting blood. The whole country seemed to be seething with discontent at what appeared to be the dreariness and loss of nerve of a bureaucracy-ridden bunch of tired ideologues with a majority of a mere six. It looked certain that the Government couldn't last long. In the autumn of 1951 Attlee asked for a dissolution, and a few weeks later Churchill, six years' disappointed unhappiness rolling away from him, was invited by the King to form a Government. We had a respectable majority in the Commons – sixteen. It wasn't impressive but it was more than that with which Labour had struggled through the last eighteen months.

The following weekend I had friends staying at Bledlow and we spent Saturday trying to shoot a few partridges. At lunchtime it transpired that there had been a telephone call from No. 10 Downing Street, and that there would be another later. Downing Street had been told I was shooting. Following instructions, I went to the telephone when we finished in the late afternoon. I thought it not impossible that I was about to be offered the job of Government Whip in the Lords, a Lord-in-Waiting, as they are called. I learned afterwards that one of the guns, a very nice farmer called Cyril Morris, addressed the others after I had gone into the house. A quiet man of few words, he had apparently said, decisively, 'Parliamentary Secretary, Ministry of Agriculture and Fisheries.'

A voice familiar from wartime broadcasts in every British home came down the telephone.

'Have you had a good shoot?'

I said, not very accurately, that we had.

'Would you like', the voice went on, 'to join *my* shoot?' Cyril Morris was right.

CHAPTER 5

In Government

To find myself sitting in the House of Lords on the Government benches was a new experience – sitting there, too, with several members of the Cabinet. Churchill brought back into Government a number of distinguished figures from the wartime years, who either were or had been created peers. It was the period of 'overlords' – the concept of grouping Departments beneath the oversight of some elevated member of the Cabinet, presumed to be sufficiently aloof from the Departmental battle to view everything, including his own Department, with sublime objectivity. In my experience this seldom works, although the experiment of a small War Cabinet (from which the idea was lineally descended) no doubt had advantages in the particular circumstance of war. We had a number of overlords in the House of Lords: Alexander, of course, was Minister of Defence, with three Service ministers under him, an arrangement I was to experience at first hand in the coming years. Woolton (Lord President of the Council) and Leathers were charged with coordinating this and that: in fact Leathers was actually 'Secretary of State for the coordination of transport, fuel and power'. I believe in the usefulness of inter-Departmental committees but I am sceptical of 'overlords'. Either they are armed with sufficient Departmental and Civil Service support, in which case bureaucracy is duplicated, wasteful and self-neutralizing: or they have no such support, in which case they are impotent. Other names from the war were among us on the front bench. Pug Ismay, for a while, was Secretary of State for Commonwealth Relations until being persuaded to go to Paris as the first Secretary-General of NATO.

Sometimes I found myself among my elders and much betters. Lady Waverley* used to have something of a political *salon* and much to my surprise invited me one day. Alexander, who shared a birthday with her, was there – it was, in fact, a birthday party. Harold Macmillan was also present. He had been Political Resident at Alex's headquarters in the Mediterranean during the war, and, full of genial party spirit, he leaned towards Alex with an expansive Macmillan gesture:

'Oh, Alex! Wouldn't it be marvellous to have our lives over again!'

'Oh no, Harold,' Alex answered, in his modest, natural way, 'that would never do! We might not do nearly as well!'

It was usual in those days for a Minister of Agriculture to have two Parliamentary Secretaries, one in the Lords and one in the Commons. A Parliamentary Secretary in the Lords tended to be used more on what might be called the external circuit – to visit, speak outside Parliament, go on tour. His colleague, the Parliamentary Secretary in the Commons, was more tied to Westminster. He had to face the House of Commons on behalf of his minister, a more taxing task than facing the Lords. He saw more of his superior, inevitably. And in my time his vote was often needed in the Commons and his presence essential, for our majority was small. So it fell to me more often than not to go round the country, to see Agricultural Committees throughout England and Wales (the Department had no such responsibility for Scotland) and talk to branches of the Country Landowners' Association, the National Farmers' Union and so forth. During the next three years I got to know a large number of the people concerned in a leading capacity with the agriculture of our country.

It was a time of change, a change whose exact nature and significance did not really come home to all of us – and certainly not to me – for some time. The Conservative administration which came in in October 1951 was determined to

* Widow of Sir John Anderson, 1st Viscount Waverley.

restore an atmosphere of freedom of choice, to stimulate consumption, to build up again liberties which wartime constraints had made impossible or irrelevant. Rationing was gradually abolished – and people, with some astonishment, found that they could buy as much as they wanted without coupons, that there were few shortages, and, furthermore, that this was accomplished without galloping inflation. Nevertheless, there was never much margin. I remember the Minister for Food, Gwilym Lloyd George, telling a Cabinet meeting that he was unhappy with food stocks if rationing disappeared, and Churchill himself saying, 'We were *elected* for this! We must do it!' There was, everywhere, a reviving sense that people's lives and properties were their own, to be lived or cared for without excessive regulation. It was very stimulating.

In January 1952 King George VI died, universally mourned. But the Queen's accession, inevitably greeted by Press and public speakers as the dawn of a New Elizabethan Age, really did coincide with a perception that the Second World War with its dreariness and privations was at last behind us.

The implications of this change for the agricultural community were by no means simple – and in some ways by no means welcome. It remained essential to grow as much food as possible, to make the industry as efficient and productive as could be managed. It was our job to encourage farmers to keep up that high input and to go for that high output which the war had, of necessity, introduced to Britain. But now, of course, the means and the language changed. We were, as a party, opposed to excessive regulation or interference. We believed in a free market – a thing inconceivable in the siege economy that had been our experience in war. There was, undeniably, a continuing national interest in maximizing production, but now farmers were to be freed from many controls, and price support would be given under a new guaranteed price system. Up to 1951 farmers had known exactly what a crop was going to fetch; and during Tom Williams's benevolent regime at the Ministry of Agriculture they had done pretty well. Now we moved to a system of deficiency payments, whereby each farmer sold in the market place and then received the national deficiency payment according to a formula negotiated periodically between the Ministry and the National Farmers' Union. A farmer, depending on the quality of his produce, could therefore receive more – or less – than the guaranteed price. It was up to him to produce what the market wanted and 'beat the average'. It sounds the same arrangement by another name, but in fact it was significantly different! And many farmers thought the difference was to their disadvantage, a thought encouraged by the official Opposition, as is the way of official Oppositions. It was the beginning of a progression wherein the farmer reckoned he was first begged to produce the maximum and to invest to do so (and be rewarded for it): and then, when the need was regarded as less pressing, was criticized for the results of his own efficiency, accused of living a feather-bedded existence off public subsidy, and blamed for destroying the countryside by clearing waste land, cleaning ditches and making larger fields – all activities to which he had been directed or exhorted in leaner times. And nowadays, of course, he is also abused for adding, at great public cost, to stacks of commodities which insufficient numbers wish to consume! Yet there has to be some guarantee, some assured support for farming, however devised. Without some certainty of return, nobody would invest and commit themselves to a process so dependent on weather and the vagaries of the international market. It was not, and is not, simple calculation of personal advantage which made me remember with dismay the agricultural depression and the poor, primitive farming of my boyhood days, with Britain utterly dependent on overseas producers for food, and with farmers and their men impoverished and resentful. There *is* a national interest. Yet assuring it, in a free society, is another matter and the nations of the European Community wrestle with it today just as we wrestled with it in those post-war years.

I felt very proud and happy on first taking possession of my office in the Ministry of Agriculture. It was a tiny room in the small block opposite the Admiralty in Whitehall, heated by a coal fire – there was, of course, no central heating in the building – and it had an iron balcony and was, to me, the last word in grandeur. I met Sir Francis Floud a little later, a most distinguished retired civil servant who had once been Uncle Charlie Lincolnshire's Private Secretary, when my uncle was President of the Board of Agriculture in Asquith's Government.

'What was it like in those days?' I asked. 'Did my Uncle Charlie work very hard?' He had, after all, made a considerable name as Agriculture Minister.

Sir Francis considered. 'No,' he said, 'I don't think he worked very hard. He used to come into the office at 11 o'clock, and he used to leave for lunch at a quarter to one, and that was that.'

Life for a minister, whether senior or junior, is somewhat different now. And it was somewhat different even in 1951.

My colleague, the Parliamentary Secretary in the Commons, was, as I have said, more tied to London than I and had a harder time. It added a great deal to my own life, however, that he happened to be one of the most charming of men and dearest of friends I have been lucky enough to know.

Dick Nugent had been a leading figure of the National Farmers' Union and was a distinguished agriculturalist. He had built up and expanded a poultry business and had then been particularly active in NFU affairs. When we took office we didn't know each other and we were at first somewhat wary. We were both farmers and we were both Tories, but I had been very involved with the CLA, the Country Land-owners and their problems, while Dick had been deeply immersed in the battles of the farmer and the tenant-farmer – and the two interests were sometimes thought to be incompatible, or worse. But gradually – and particularly a little later when the going got rough – I came to understand and hugely to value Dick's kindness, his wisdom and his sheer goodness. He saw things much more clearly than most of us, and he saw them true.

Our chief was Tom Dugdale, Minister of Agriculture and

Fisheries. Sir Thomas Dugdale, a Yorkshireman, was a delightful and kindly man, the most genial and considerate of masters. He had been Member for the Richmond Division of the North Riding since 1929 and had held a number of offices – including Parliamentary Private Secretary to the Prime Minister – before the war. He had fought in both world wars and been Chairman of the Conservative Party from 1942 to 1944. He had been Shadow Minister for Agriculture. He was the sort of Conservative, old-fashioned perhaps, who thought it was his duty to serve, that it was a tradition and an obligation. He had no major ambition. His long experience gave him a good deal of political wisdom and he was, within the party and in the House of Commons, much respected and greatly liked.

It was Tom Dugdale's fate – and, I sometimes felt, his misfortune – that he had to deal with one of the most formidable chiefs the National Farmers' Union has ever had. It was our minister's duty to negotiate the annual Price Review which determined the level of deficiency payments and thus, to a large extent, the level of farmers' prosperity. Jim Turner, later Lord Netherthorpe, President of the NFU, was an outstanding negotiator. He was also a pretty ruthless as well as persuasive advocate, and he was not easy to worst. I don't think Tom Dugdale's life was particularly easy. As a superior to us Parliamentary Secretaries, however, he was never anything but charming, and I soon began greatly to enjoy the work.

Because I was less tied to Parliament, because I was freer to travel and investigate and explore, I found myself often with the odd jobs which nobody else wanted or had time for. One of these, I remember, was a study of the myxomatosis problem. Myxomatosis was a disease fatal to rabbits and without a cure; there had been prolonged examination of it on the Continent where there were dreams of eradicating or anyway reducing the rabbit population. A French chemical scientist carried out a series of experiments in the park of his château, with a view to rabbit control. He let the virus loose, apparently unaware that it could be carried by birds and insects. Very soon myxomatosis had spread like wildfire through France.

This created uproar. The uproar was even greater in

England. To a population reared on Beatrix Potter's *Peter Rabbit*, the prospect of a hideous and incurable disease sweeping the country clean of these delightful, furry little creatures was intolerable, and the fact that the virus was likely to come from France was the last straw. The farmers, of course, hated rabbits but their voice was not the loudest in the matter. I was told to form and chair a committee to decide a policy on myxomatosis. Was its arrival in Britain inevitable (I think by then we all knew that it was) and what should be done about it?

We had first to discuss the point of principle – should myxomatosis be kept from Britain's shores, in the unlikely event that that was possible? We had a lot of expertise on my committee. Miriam Lane, née Rothschild, was the greatest living expert on fleas; and there were others. While we were deliberating, however, myxomatosis arrived. Rabbits started dying. This caused great outrage (again, muted among the farmers). The unfortunate Frenchman who had turned the virus loose was sued by a great diversity of people in his own country – by those who liked shooting rabbits and for whom *la chasse* had been spoiled: by cartridge-makers for loss of sales and takings: by hat-makers who lacked rabbit skins for hat felt. Ultimately he went bankrupt.

In 1937 the Air Ministry had compulsorily acquired as an experimental bomb site some land near Crichel in Dorset. In 1950, under the previous Government, that Ministry had decided it had no further use for the land. The Ministry of Agriculture, however, was interested in it as a site for two new farm holdings and since the land had been acquired by Government for its own purposes it was simply transferred from one Ministry to another. That was the situation we inherited. We received independent advice from the Land Commission that from the point of view of production it would be best to keep the land which had been acquired together in two units as proposed. I was sent to inspect. I agreed with the Land Commission.

Some of the land, known as Crichel Down, had been bought from Lord Alington – just under half the total. His daughter, his heiress, had married Commander Toby Marten; and the Martens protested at the transfer of what had been their family land from one Ministry to another. They pointed out that there had always been assurances given to landowners from whom land had been acquired for wartime purposes that, if it were no longer required by Government, landowners would be given the chance to repurchase. The matter turned, of course, on whether land acquired for one purpose could be retained by Government for a different purpose without breach of those assurances. The case dragged on amid a good deal of (mostly unfavourable) publicity. Eventually an Inquiry was held, Sir Andrew Clarke QC conducting it. The Inquiry's finding was that our Department had acted in an arbitrary manner. Officials were criticized by name and the minister faced a sceptical meeting of Conservative backbenchers. Eventually there was a long debate on the proceedings of the Inquiry, during which Dugdale said, stoutly, that he did not take so poor a view of the conduct of his officials as the Inquiry had: it was true, he said, that they had failed to make clear to him that the original purchase of the land had been under threat of compulsion, but he did not regard that as the dominant factor. Nevertheless he recognized, with dignity, the mood of the House and since he was an honourable man and his Department had been criticized by an Inquiry and, in effect, by Parliament, he reckoned there could only be one outcome. The Martens got their land. Tom Dugdale resigned.

Myth has collected around the Crichel Down case. Its upshot has been thought of as a triumph over bureaucracy, talked about as demonstrating the irresponsible and despotic power which civil servants can – and in wartime sometimes did – arrogate to themselves; as a failure of successive ministers to control their men; as, ultimately, a vindication of the subject against the Crown. It was not in the least like that. There was a certain amount of incompetence and administrative bungling involved in the run-up to the Crichel Down affair but at the heart of it was the point with which I began this

91

chapter – a failure to appreciate that there was, in our country, a new spirit, a new situation. The material national interest, the need to maximize farm production and to use the power of Government where desirable to promote this, was like a charted line on a graph. It had been at its highest point when we had been under siege. It had continued high in the hungry aftermath of war. Now it was following a downward curve, and was approaching the point of convergence and then the crossing of another charted line – the line of individual rights of property, the line of ordinary personal and economic freedom. This second line had been at its lowest during the war, when all personal rights and privileges had been subordinated to winning and to survival. But now this line was on a rising curve – and rightly so. The advent of the Conservative Government in 1951 had the desired effect of making it rise more steeply still. Crichel Down showed that the two lines had crossed. Personal rights mattered, and their restoration was more important than a Government Department's perception of how, one day, our land might marginally produce a little more.

  Neither our civil servants in the Department, nor Tom Dugdale, nor I realized, at the time, that those lines had crossed. Dick Nugent did. He was always perfectly clear in his mind that the Martens should be offered back the land which had been theirs before Government took it from them. He was consistent in this opinion, although the fact was not always to be guessed from the rudeness with which he was on occasion described by those who criticized our Department's conduct most virulently. Dick realized that the lines had crossed and that people now saw such matters in a different way.

  The Crichel Down case was disagreeable. It was my first job in Government and my first experience not only of being an object of public criticism but of coming to the conclusion that my judgement had been at fault and much of the criticism justified. Some people reckoned I had been let off lightly by the Inquiry, and said so: Sir Richard Acland, Labour MP for Gravesend, spread himself in the Commons debate on this particular theme.

I thought Tom Dugdale right to resign. Then Dick Nugent decided he should go too. I said, 'If you go, I go.' We wrote letters of resignation to the Prime Minister, who replied that there was no need for the step. Dick and I compared notes. We thought this private exchange inadequate and we still felt we ought to follow our chief and go. We asked to see Churchill and we saw him together. He peered at us.

'Do you both *want* to resign?'

We told him that an independent Inquiry had been critical of the Department, and I pointed out that I had played a leading role in the business. We knew that the Prime Minister himself thought our Ministry had been on the wrong side, that Government policy had been led by us in a mistaken direction; and, obviously, the whole Government had been weakened as Governments always are if an Inquiry slates a Department.

Churchill grunted. Then he said, 'I think you had better carry on,' adding, 'What do you *want?*'

We settled for a published exchange of letters, and we agreed to stay. Churchill was not an easy person for young men to gainsay. I had asked the advice of Bobbety Salisbury earlier.

'I'm the worst possible person to talk to,' he said. 'I'm a resigner by nature!'

I have often been taunted about withdrawing my resignation. These things are hard and the path often obscure. Whether I was right or wrong to stay I do not know.

Dugdale was succeeded by Derick Heathcoat-Amory, whom I much liked – perhaps the most unassuming and unambitious man I have ever known in politics, and yet one of the most able – and, when he chose, the most funny. It was summer, 1954. In October I was appointed Parliamentary Secretary to the Ministry of Defence, and began an association with defence and foreign policy which has lasted most of my ensuing years.

Harold Macmillan, the newly appointed Minister of Defence, was a senior member of the Cabinet. He had a strong reputation for getting things done, having made a great success as Minister of Housing where he had overseen the building of 300,000 houses, one of the Government's most spectacular achievements. He had been a Grenadier, and an officer with an outstanding name for bravery, in the First World War. He had known my father in the Regiment, but he knew little of me although we had casually met.

Macmillan was the kindest of men to serve. He was very punctilious in his courtesy towards so unimportant a person as the Parliamentary Secretary in the Lords. If I made a speech in the House he would send me a note the following day without fail. 'Well done!' it might say. 'You made a good speech and I am lucky to have you in the House of Lords.' I have no idea whether he read the speeches in question – I hope not! But small touches of consideration of that kind are helpful when one is young; or even not so young. Harold Macmillan, in a word, took trouble with his subordinates and was repaid by their affection.

He also provided a stimulating example as head of a Department. He had a splendid style, a sharp, witty and amusing technique. He could and did draw on an extensive experience of both Parliament and Government. He relished talking about his days as a somewhat rebellious backbencher, angry with the Government of the day about the failure to stimulate employment, angry with what he saw as indifference to the sufferings of poor people in his and similar northern constituencies. There was nothing contrived about that indignation: I knew it came from the heart, it was a mood which had marked him. He was marked, too – like most of his age – by the loss of a whole generation of his friends in the First World War. He cared very much that our Armed Forces should be decently prepared and equipped so that we could play a credible part in seeing that such things never recurred – I think most protagonists in either or both world wars incline instinctively to accept the old tag that if you want peace you had best be prepared to fight. And in those days, of course, there were also plenty of military tasks around the world with which the British armed forces had to be concerned. In attempting to see that they were ready, Harold Macmillan's heart was in the job. He liked the Services and was proud of them.

So was I. In fact of the various facets or achievements of our national life I have observed in the last forty years I am undoubtedly proudest of the Armed Services. They have adapted to a changing environment, they have responded admirably to every call, they have evolved from one sort of age to another with impressive flexibility, they have spent a lot of the time making bricks with insufficient straw. They are professionally a great deal more competent than when I first joined the army; they have preserved their traditions and their discipline and their principles; they have served us a good deal better than we have always deserved, and I have been greatly honoured by my close association with them in several posts – and have derived considerable enjoyment from it. It was clear Macmillan felt the same.

But Macmillan undoubtedly found that in trying to do something constructive for British defence management, affection was certainly not enough; and I witnessed his frustration, although he naturally enjoyed a good deal of the job as well. Macmillan as Minister of Defence was an 'overlord' in those days (I was known as the 'underlord'). There were three Service ministers, who sat on the Defence Committee of the Cabinet and who had the right to attend Cabinet when their own affairs were being discussed. They had responsibility for the running of their Services, for that Service's equipment programme, training, recruitment, discipline and general good order; and the authority of the Minister of Defence tended to appear so remote as to be invisible. Inter-Service and defence policy issues were managed by the device – capable of being pretty effective – of a large number of inter-Departmental committees. The Ministry of Defence itself (in Storey's Gate) was small, providing houseroom for the committees and manned by the few Secretariat and Joint Staffs which existed, and which had largely been inherited from the pre-war Committee of Imperial Defence. The system can be described as a run-down and reduced version of the organization with which the Second World War had been conducted: but, of course, in the Second World War each of the three fighting Services had been enormous; and the Prime Minister himself had been Minister of Defence, presiding over committees of Service ministers or Chiefs of Staff with all the authority of the head of the Government. In time of peace, and of attenuated Armed Services disputing about the distribution of resources, the writ of the Minister of Defence did not run very strongly.

Macmillan, who was Minister of Defence for only six months, found this unsatisfactory. He had responsibility but inadequate power. His three Service ministers were Jim Thomas at the Admiralty, Antony Head at the War Office and Bill De l'Isle at the Air Ministry. Macmillan would hold a meeting to try to hammer out some sort of compromise over the Services' competition for public money – competition which was entirely comprehensible, entirely justifiable, entirely predictable and will continue until there comes, in the words of *Hymns Ancient and Modern*, the promised time that war shall be no more. Each minister would return to his Department, and would, a little later, explain that he had had second thoughts. Antony Head and Bill De l'Isle had had second thoughts on reflection; Jim Thomas had had second thoughts after confrontation with bellicose admirals in the Admiralty. The recourse of a minister with second thoughts would be to ask that the matter be referred to Cabinet, himself present; and the previous meeting might just as well not have taken place. Macmillan lacked the constitutional power (he certainly possessed the intelligence) to settle these matters, and the lack exasperated him. Of course difficult matters of priority have to be settled after a good deal of informed discussion, but in those days they were difficult to settle at all except after full Cabinet: not generally the best method for detailed decisions on complex professional issues. Without doubt Macmillan was stimulated by this experience to pursue that amalgamation of the Service Ministries and that unified and stronger Ministry of Defence which came about during his premiership. A traditionalist with radical sympathies – or, perhaps, a radical with a sensitive understanding of the value of tradition – he appreciated the three Services and their individuality. But he certainly formed the view that they were instruments of, and needed to conform to, something we were increasingly calling Defence Policy.

In 1954 the British Armed Services had considerable responsibilities outside their first and, self-evidently, most important task of being ready to defend our country by participation in and contribution to a defensive alliance – NATO. Nevertheless the importance of NATO and its primacy were accepted, although the acceptance was comparatively recent and by no means ungrudging.

There were reasons for this. In the immediate aftermath of the Second World War there were several years during which attempts were made to restore something of what people told themselves had been the spirit of the wartime alliance between the Soviet Union and the Western powers. Hopes were entertained that the hostility of the Soviet Union, as well as the ruthless Soviet suppression and enforced communization of European countries 'liberated' by the Red Army and now occupied, were temporary and remediable phenomena, deriving from Russian experience of German invasion and other explicable historical factors rather than from the inherent brutality and intransigence of the system and the men who ran it. It was natural for the peaceable and somewhat exhausted populations of the West to think like this, even if not consistent with much evidence.

Optimism did not last long. Stalin soon killed it with international ruthlessness and internal atrocity. The Berlin blockade of 1948 marked the final end of the period of illusions, although a good many people had shed them soon after the war's conclusion if not before; and some had never nourished them at all. Soon after this, in 1949, the North Atlantic Treaty was signed. It was reluctantly accepted that the world in general and Europe in particular was divided by a curtain of enmity and that, yet again, we and our friends had to face the possibility of defending ourselves one day. It was clear that the situation was not going away. We were in for a long haul.

The watershed in terms of perception of the military threat, however, had been the Korean War, wherein the communist North Koreans (considered, with some accuracy at that time, to be Soviet agents or puppets) had invaded South Korea. A savage war had followed, in which a large number of non-communist nations, notably the United States and countries of the British Commonwealth but also including such stalwarts as the Turks, had fought against the North Korean invaders under the banner of the United Nations. The Korean War had broken out in 1950 and soon thereafter the Attlee Government had committed Britain to a major programme of rearmament which was to last many years. The materiel with which our Services had fought the Second World War was gradually – in some cases very gradually – to be replaced. Files from the war days were brought out and dusted; and a certain sense of urgency was communicated to the Armed Forces. The British Army of the Rhine was reorganized from being purely an occupation force into the shape of a field army, although it took many years to equip it to modern – or Soviet – standards. The Royal Navy and Royal Air Force evolved major ship and aircraft replacement programmes. Considerable expenditure was planned. The incoming Conservative administration in 1951 had inherited a certain dynamic in defence planning and, of course, took it on with a will.

But from the start I suspect that two factors had somewhat blurred the priority of NATO in British thinking; one of these was the immediacy of other problems confronting the Services, practical as opposed to speculative. The Conservatives may have inherited a rearmament programme directed towards the objects of NATO – defence of the Atlantic area – but their immediate preoccupation when they took office in the autumn of 1951 was participation in an actual war in Korea; and how to deal with a revolutionary situation in the canal zone of Egypt, where we had a large base and a small garrison and where the Egyptians had just revoked the treaty which kept us there. Through the next few years, and certainly up to the time when I went into the Ministry of Defence, we had actual operational challenges to meet in many parts of the world, and although they may have been less vital than NATO planning they involved action here and now.

The second factor which tended to mask the importance of NATO was the intractable nature of the military problem, producing a certain sense of unrealism rather than urgency.

NATO planning was predicated on the idea that, sooner or later, the Soviet Union might try in Europe what her friends had attempted in Korea – take over an easily conquered stretch of strategically desirable territory, fill a vacuum. For in terms of power Europe was, pretty well, a vacuum. The aftermath of war, economic collapse and the total destruction of Germany had made it so. Looked at from London, Washington or Paris it didn't seem, in the early days, that Stalin would have a particularly difficult military task if he decided to take it on. The Red Army was enormous, based on a lengthy period of conscription; and Russia was known to be devoting a good deal of expense to its modernization. Against this there were – I am speaking of the earliest days of NATO – a tiny handful of British and American divisions, a small, resurgent French Army already preoccupied with problems in the overseas territories, and little else. It is true that at sea, in those days, the Western powers were still dominant: Admiral Gorschev had not yet fully accomplished the remarkable process which has made the Soviet Union a major maritime power, although by the time I reached the Ministry of Defence Russia already had twelve of the new Sverdlov-type cruisers. But any edge that we possessed at sea didn't look as if it was going to do much to stop the Red Army, although it might, as so often in the past, avert defeat for ourselves and win time. For the peoples of Continental Europe it provided little comfort.

The Korean War had given the youthful NATO a certain stimulus to try to correct all this, and the Marshall Plan had started to put the European nations back on their feet. But the problem, both physical and moral, remained huge. The Europeans, very naturally, thought in terms of defence of their territory, of the threat from the vast land power lying to the east. NATO evolved a set of goals for the raising of a large number of army divisions for the defence of Europe – I think about ninety. Two things were clear from the outset. First, that it was absurd to contemplate this sort of thing – or aspire to defend Europe at all – without the reintegration of Germany into the military family of the West. Second, that to pay for ninety divisions, with air forces to match, was going to tax the European (and American) populations more steeply than they were likely to welcome. The threat argued itself: Allied manpower, given the will, was not a constraining factor: money and resources were.

The depressing nature of the military balance, however, was mitigated by one all-important circumstance: the nuclear dimension. The Soviet Union had now acquired her own nuclear weapons, but the United States at that time held a massive superiority both qualitatively and quantitatively. As it became clear that the conventional-force goals NATO had recognized as necessary were highly unlikely ever to be met, even with German participation (unless the latter were to be so preponderant as to upset everyone else, and be pretty unpopular with the Germans themselves), so more and more emphasis was placed on the instant or near-instant use of nuclear weapons as a response to any attack against the West. This was the situation when Macmillan took office as minister and I first entered the Ministry of Defence. There were goals which, anyway as far as land forces were concerned, nobody thought we would ever reach. There was thus a gap, an area of risk, which it was accepted would be filled by declared willingness to use nuclear weapons against an aggressor – both his armed forces and his homeland – if war should ever come. And there was, after much negotiation and in the face of many French reservations, acceptance of German rearmament. Germany became a full member of NATO in 1955.

It might thus be thought – and it certainly was official doctrine – that what I have called 'the intractable nature of the military problem' had been solved and the circle squared by the nuclear factor. Dependence on nuclear weapons to redress our inferiority in conventional forces was taken to its ultimate in the doctrine of so-called massive retaliation, evolved under the leadership of the United States in the aftermath of the development of the hydrogen bomb, a bomb vastly more destructive than anything conceived before. The first of these had been exploded in 1952, and another in March 1954. I started work in the Ministry of Defence late in 1954, when the ambitious force goals with which to defend Europe in traditional terms had been pretty well abandoned, and when conventional forces (in terms of East–West confrontation) had been designated a mere 'tripwire': there had to be enough of them to show that aggression had occurred and impose enough delay for someone to decide to press a button, but there was no question of them being capable of defeating that aggression. Defeat was to be inflicted by nuclear means, and hostilities were bound to be over pretty quickly. Anything else was inconceivable. Our Defence White Paper in February 1955 affirmed that deterrence of an aggressor 'must rest primarily on the strategic air power of the West, armed with its nuclear weapons'. 'The knowledge', we said, 'that aggression will be met by overwhelming nuclear retaliation is the surest guarantee that it will not take place.' And referring to the Soviet Union's conventional strength on land we said, unequivocally, 'The use of nuclear weapons is the only means by which this massive preponderance can be countered.'

But right from the start 'massive retaliation' and 'tripwire' had raised a good many questions, most of them awkward, and a few years later NATO – and thus British – strategy wobbled back towards a shift of emphasis, towards something in which people could more easily believe. Initially the Soviet Union had no delivery means with which it could hit the continental United States, so that the policy was well based in American invulnerability, and was thus credible. But this was not a situation which could be relied upon to last, and when Soviet capabilities evolved – as they did – the most obtrusive question, inevitably, became 'Won't the Soviets massively retaliate too?' or even, 'Won't they massively retaliate in anticipation?' The answer, obviously, being 'yes' there was a somewhat depressing debate on the question of who might come off worst from this exchange. Neither party to the quarrel looked like coming off at all well, and from this, naturally, it was a short step to the conclusion that action so probably suicidal might not be credible to the enemy – who might, therefore, risk aggression with his superior conventional forces on the basis that we might never dare play the one, nuclear, card that could defeat it, for fear of the consequences to ourselves. The evolution of this argument – and it is still evolving – lay well in the future, but there were plenty of people who, from the beginning, had difficulty over totally confiding in the policy of 'tripwire' and 'massive retaliation'.

I cannot pretend that I, personally, spent most of my time on these speculations about strategic philosophy. I am sure that in those early days of the hydrogen bomb and its implications we were, quite simply, awestruck at the appalling capacity for destruction which man had now acquired; and we had an instinctive feeling, I hope not unreasonably, that this horrifying power would mark the end of major war, at least between the sort of nations which possessed it. Of course we appreciated that Soviet acquisition of nuclear know-how produced a complex situation for deterrence; and I think most people felt in their bones that lesser situations than all-out nuclear war might conceivably occur, and demand a certain spectrum of possible responses – indeed the state of the world and our own responsibilities, as well as the recently ended Korean War, made that clear. Liddell Hart had written in 1950:

> If both sides possess the same weapon ... there is a fair chance that both may hesitate to unloose it from mutual fear of the common consequences.

And he continued:

> Mankind, and even its governments, can show uncommon sense and restraint when they see clearly enough that it is a matter of mutual preservation.

I think that reflected the basic feelings of most of us, and in spite of the astonishing developments in nuclear weaponry and delivery systems which the intervening decades have seen, I still believe there is a good deal in it. In presenting Defence White Paper after Defence White Paper to the House of Lords I found myself emphasizing that nuclear weapons, by making war yet more destructive, must be making it less likely. And I criticized those who would 'ban the bomb' but seemed to regard 'conventional' warfare as acceptable, or at least comparatively so. 'Perhaps there are some', I said once in the House, 'who, faced with the unknown consequences of nuclear warfare, are apt to forget that conventional warfare as we have known it in the last two world wars is utterly degrading!' It was a message I tried to express again and again, at that time and much later also. To be persuasive it demands acceptance that the possible use of nuclear weapons can, at the least, inhibit aggression itself. I was always sceptical of attempts to be too precise about what hostile actions would produce exactly what degree of destructive response. I said on another occasion to the House: 'If you announce beforehand what you will or will not do in a given set of circumstances it amounts to a direct invitation to your enemy to go as far as he dares without suffering the consequences of his actions.'

But that this frightful potential existed and *might* be used seemed, and seems, to me a crucial inhibiting factor, although I came to accept that it might not inhibit as much as we first hoped. I remain convinced, however, that those who would make war less awful could end by making it more probable. It is for that reason and on exactly the same argumentation that I have consistently opposed any declaration of resolution by NATO not to use nuclear weapons first.

For our Armed Services this explicit dependence on nuclear weapons for the waging of major war created particular problems. It might all seem somewhat theoretical, but since NATO strategy had to govern our own concepts the matter was not academic – it provided the set of assumptions to which our programmes were supposed to conform, anyway as far as preparedness for hostilities against the Soviet Union was concerned. Our White Papers and my speeches tended to refer in somewhat imprecise terms to the Forces being 'capable of dealing with outbreaks of limited war should they occur', to a 'proper system of strategical priorities' (between nuclear and conventional forces) rather than the millenarian scrapping of all tanks, all fighter aircraft. This was sincere. We all felt in our hearts that the Forces needed to be ready to do something about almost anything, expensive though that might be. Nevertheless the imprecision remained, and the difficulties.

For the navy the difficulty could be simply stated. Nobody argued that a war which included the massive use of nuclear weapons could last more than a very short time – however it went. Seapower is slow-moving and attritional in its effects. The use of the sea is vital to a nation like ours, dependent on it for the movement of essential supplies, but blockade – whether aimed at us and frustrated by our own seapower or imposed by us on somebody else – takes a considerable time to bite. In a very short war (people talked airily in terms of days or weeks at the most) what was the point of the navy? The navy, of course, could and did point to its ability to range the oceans, show the flag, influence remote situations in faraway countries (provided they had a coastline) in time of peace. In the context of major war efforts were later made to show that there might be some sort of hostile exchanges at sea before main hostilities occurred on land, thus prolonging the maritime business. Other efforts were made to show that the navy's hour would come after the nuclear exchanges were over, during the phase which came to be known as 'broken-backed war'. I never found these suggestions very convincing (I am condensing into one discussion, here, arguments which continued over ensuing years, into the time when I played a different part on the Defence scene). But in spite of being unimpressed by some of the argumentation I never doubted the need for the navy – and this was quite apart from its later role in providing our own strategic nuclear arm. I suppose that, with my instincts, I was sceptical of the premise, the easy assumption, that a war, however horrible, would be over in days. The premise was fearful: it was also convenient. Yet who knew? Who knows? Something inside me suggested that Britain, as in the past, should 'look to her moat', that assumptions about the character of future wars can err. But NATO strategy undoubtedly imposed intellectual contortions on the navy, particularly at that time.

The army, too, found 'massive retaliation' and 'tripwire' a difficult concept although more, perhaps, at the tactical level. It is not easy to explain to troops that they are a tripwire, that their function is simply to 'define aggression' and then wait for a big bang delivered by someone else. This was a time (1954) when it was being emphasized by NATO that nuclear weapons would be used by us (and presumably by the enemy, although this was less prominently advertised) from the outset, and that low-yield nuclear weapons would be used against troops on the battlefield. The army, therefore, had to organize itself on the Continent and evolve its tactics in such a way as to be as invulnerable as possible to nuclear attack; while still providing a credible tripwire – for it was conceded that even a tripwire must be of a certain thickness, or nobody will trip. The former function needed perpetual movement by highly decentralized forces. The latter tended to require concentration of rather more conventional troops and firepower. The army struggled with these obligations and experiments without, I suspect, universal belief in what they were doing; and thought of other things. Such matters were the concern of generals and their staffs rather than the Parliamentary Secretary of the Ministry of Defence, and I cannot say I envied them. Meanwhile the army's re-equipment programme lumbered along slowly, not greatly influenced as far as I could see by these theoretical concepts. During this time the soldiers were still largely subsisting on the equipment with which they, and for that matter I, had fought the Second World War – although they now had a better tank than any I had known.

Perhaps only in the Royal Air Force did 'massive retaliation' strike a chord. Trust in the historic efficacy of the Second World War strategic bomber offensive was widespread (although not universal) in that Service. It was a perfectly natural development to welcome dependence on a weapon of strategic bombardment which was now to be not only a contributory war-winner but the only one. But there were question marks for the Royal Air Force too. Assuming, as was now the fashion,

105

not only that conventional land and sea hostilities must be quickly over if they ever started, but also that conventional air attack was a thing of the past, air defence must become largely nugatory and, in any case, likely to be more and more dependent upon surface-to-air missiles – although I remember saying in 1956 that 'for some time to come' the manned fighter would have its part to play. Yet only a few years previously lecturers at Staff colleges had proclaimed as the three pillars of British strategy: the air defence of Great Britain, the maintenance of our sea communications and a firm base in the Middle East. Now it seemed that the first two pillars had little applicability. Fighter Command, Coastal Command, would be read about in history books, their functions largely gone. Massive retaliation or the threat of it would deter war; and would certainly finish it within days if it began. Except for Bomber Command the tasks of the Services in a major conflict had become somewhat perplexing.

I have said that this exaggerated (as I consider) dependence on nuclear weapons survived only a comparatively short time. Our overall policy – of believing in a strong nuclear potential – did not change but the emphasis, the strategy, did. 'Massive retaliation' and 'tripwire' did, however, last throughout the period described in this chapter and in retrospect it seems curious that some of the anomalies of their position did not strike the three Services (or parts of them) with more disturbing force at the time, and upset to a greater degree their confidence in their programmes, their *raisons d'être* and themselves than actually occurred. Without doubt one reason was the highly speculative nature of all this strategic philosophizing. Nobody really knew what might turn out to be required of people in war, and nobody really knows now; and in practice when they are serving in or commanding a ship or a regiment or a squadron of aircraft men can only do their utmost with the material at their disposal and hope for the best. I daresay many of our people, reading learned articles or attending studies on these subjects, reflected inwardly that sooner or later somebody would probably have a different idea and meanwhile one just had to keep going. But another

106

reason, as I have said, was certainly the fact that a great many actual tasks lay to be done, as well as preparing for that Third World War which all hoped, and I think most believed, would never come.

In October 1954 the Emergency in Malaya had been going on for over six years. The situation had improved dramatically after the arrival of Sir Gerald Templer with full powers at the beginning of 1952 and was to go on improving, but it still demanded a major British military presence.

Then, throughout my time, we had the fight against the Mau Mau rebellion in Kenya, which went on (albeit with diminished seriousness after 1956) until 1960. We had come into office to find a crisis in Egypt and had poured reinforcements into the Canal Zone, as pretty well our first act. By the end of 1954 – still adhering to what had been the third pillar of British strategy – we had concluded our agreement with the Egyptian Government whereby we were to remove our garrison from the Suez Canal area and resite our major Mediterranean headquarters and facilities in Cyprus: one consequence was angry rumbling from those factions who wished to see Cyprus united with Greece, and a threat of trouble which didn't take long to come. In October 1955 the Government sent out Sir John Harding as Governor of the island and Commander-in-Chief, to deal with the mounting violence, intimidation and subversion with the sort of powers which had enabled Templer to succeed in Malaya.

1953 had seen the end of the Korean War, but the ceasefire line was precarious. In addition to actual fighting or internal security in a number of places we also, of course, had garrisons in various parts of the world and responsibilities throughout the Empire – which still existed. Whether in areas of obvious economic and strategic concern like the Persian Gulf, or in regions where political obligations involved a periodic presence, like the Caribbean, our Services – all three of them – had a great deal to do, and generally suffered from a shortage of ships, aircraft and men with which to do it. These far-flung duties – by no means all unpopular – kept the minds of the people in uniform from too much introspection about their long-term roles or about nuclear Armageddon. There was too much going on here and now. British defence policy had to put NATO first, in logic; for NATO was the Alliance to which we belonged in order, ultimately, to defend our own country and continent. But in practice, and in the ordering of priorities and the spending of money, British defence policy often did no such thing.

Almost regardless of theoretical priorities there were two practical matters which particularly concerned us. The first was the question of National Service. This principally affected the army. As a more labour-intensive Service it absorbed the majority of the National Service intake. There were two – opposing – political views on National Service: and there were two, also opposing, military views.

Politically, there were those who reckoned that it was a sound principle that every able-bodied man should be required to give some part of his life to the service of his country: that this obligation – universal among our European allies – helped to involve and interest the whole nation in the defence of our land, and not simply a professional élite; and that the discipline and standards required in the Forces were, of themselves, good for the youth of Britain. On the other side were those who argued that National Service was unpopular and led to a disgruntled rather than patriotically stimulated younger generation – and that its abolition would ultimately be electorally helpful: that the removal of each generation for eighteen months or two years at a formative age interfered with education, training and the needs of industry (however the service was arranged); and that it was unnecessarily expensive, since it required an inordinately large number of servicemen to administer the system and to train others, while the resultant army strength was probably in excess of what we needed.

Militarily, some people thought that it would, without National Service, be impossible to fill the ranks; they feared that a dearth of volunteers would sooner or later lead to such reduction in the size of the Forces in general and the army in particular that they would be unable to carry out their present tasks and would contribute less than something credible to NATO deterrent strength. They also pointed to the tiny reserve which a small, all-Regular, force generated: were there ever to be major war or the threat of it, there would be too little behind the front line and too few trained men after the first battles – or even to fill the war establishments. To this others, on the other side of the argument, pointed out that there were not going to be any battles after the first ones, because of our assumptions about the use of nuclear weapons. National Service kept too many Regulars training conscripts; it led to perpetual turbulence, so that no unit or formation could train to a high standard before everybody changed places; and its abolition could lead to higher professional efficiency, albeit in a much smaller force. The latter arguments won the day. 'Massive retaliation' was accepted as compatible with a small, highly professional, long-service army, and several years later, by which time I was serving at the Admiralty, National Service was phased out. In the early days of which I write we could not have met our commitments without it. As to the political argument, I was and remain uncertain. I am dubious as to whether we could have sustained a long and periodically unpopular commitment like that in Northern Ireland with a conscript army – domestic pressures would have been much greater. On the other hand I doubt if abolition was as popular as some suggested, and although I admire the standards achieved by our professional Services I fancy we may have lost something. At the time, the military argument had swung against National Service and ministers inclined to accept that. There was no doubt that, if alternatives exist, conscription (as I said in the House of Lords several years later) 'is a most wasteful and inefficient way to raise an army'. By then we had, of course, decided to end it. Meanwhile, in 1955, we reduced the National Service intake.

The second major matter I became particularly alive to in those days was the rate at which weapon systems of all kinds – guns, ships, aircraft, ammunition, all – increased in cost. That problem has certainly persisted and accelerated, and has dominated a good deal of my life. Partly because of improved technology, partly because of the pressures of inflation, partly from causes few understand or agree about, prices have soared. A Spitfire cost £5000 in 1940. A Tornado Air Defence Fighter costs £14 million today. That is a lot of inflation! And even when all has been said about the greater effectiveness of the latter machine, so that far fewer are needed, there still remains a mighty problem. There tend to be limits to the extent to which numbers can be reduced by superior quality. A ship can only cover a certain amount of ocean, however sophisticated it may be; and the most formidable of tanks can't do much beyond the limits of its commander's sight. There is a minimum numerical requirement, and meeting it with equipment capable of taking on the enemy was already, in 1955, a source of worry.

It certainly worried Macmillan. He foresaw less and less sophisticated equipment being affordable – for the rest we would have to get by with more primitive devices. 'We are like', he used to say, using an analogy charmingly reminiscent of an Edwardian foursome at North Berwick or Sandwich in a more elegant age, 'a golfer, who finds he can afford fewer and fewer steel-shafted clubs, and when he replaces one will increasingly find he has to revert to the wooden shaft!' For my part it started me thinking about ways to get better value for money, about collaboration in arms procurement and about role specialization.

I served under three Defence Ministers. Harold Macmillan left after six months, for in April 1955 Churchill ultimately re-signed to be succeeded by Anthony Eden, and a general post of Cabinet ministers ensued. Selwyn Lloyd succeeded Macmillan at Defence, himself to last only six months before taking the Foreign Office: Defence, arguably the most complex portfolio in the Cabinet, changed regularly in those days; nobody really wanted it or could achieve much at it, for authority eluded them, whatever their vision. Attlee described it in a 1956 debate as a 'mere siding into which people are shunted before they go on somewhere else'. Selwyn Lloyd was a very *good* man – genuine, conscientious, high-principled. After him as Minister of Defence came Walter Monckton, a particularly shrewd negotiator, a finder of formulas, a squarer of circles.

Working with the Services, even as the underlord, was fun. It was also somewhat daunting at first. My debut speech as the responsible minister was about ship replacement and cruiser modernization, and speaking in the debate before me were three Admirals of the Fleet – Chatfield, Cunningham and Fraser of North Cape. They were invariably generous. The Chiefs of Staff, too, became firm friends to me. The First Sea Lord was Sir Rhoderick MacGrigor, 'Wee Mac', a fine fighting sailor better suited to the high seas than the devious ways of Whitehall. I don't think the later achievements of Dickie Mountbatten should ever be underestimated, in terms of the effectiveness with which he restored the navy to its proper place in the public consciousness – and in the priorities of politicians. Not all admirals could understand, as he could, that to persuade those who don't belong to the navy, a good deal of adroitness as well as bluff conviction is required. Mountbatten taught the navy a good deal.

Chief of the Imperial General Staff was Sir John Harding,* like MacGrigor diminutive and like him, too, a fine fighting man and a charmer. Sir Dermot Boyle was Chief of the Air Staff – a powerful and intelligent Irishman, a great believer in the nuclear arm and also a man of immense attraction. They were all three delightful people and it was a privilege to try to help here and there. From time to time I got it wrong. I remember during the visit of Bulganin and Khrushchev reading the name-card of my neighbour at dinner in the Painted Hall at Greenwich and saying,

'I imagine you are at the Russian Embassy, Mr Brimlov. How long have you been in London?'

'My name is Brimelow,' Tom Brimelow (now Lord Brimelow) replied. 'My family has lived in Worcestershire for one thousand years, and I am in the Foreign Office.'

* Succeeded as CIGS when he went to Cyprus by Sir Gerald Templer.

I know he has forgiven me.

I was, of course, sent all over the place to attend to various jobs which concerned more than one Service. As at the Ministry of Agriculture, I was most people's dogsbody. I was sent to South Uist in the Hebrides, I remember, because the Ministry of Defence was setting up a rocket range and the island people were worried. Leader of the local opposition to the range was a fierce Roman Catholic priest and I went to see him.

He was an enchanting man and after a little the difficulty became clearer. A statue of the Virgin Mary had been placed exactly at the point where the Ministry of Defence wanted to plant the rocket launch site. We talked and talked about it, and about the options. After a little he told me that Compton Mackenzie had taken the story of his book *Whisky Galore* from a real incident on the island. This was, in fact, the fictional Isle of Toddy and an immense cargo of illicit whisky had, in reality, been shipwrecked and salvaged by the islanders, and much of it had certainly escaped the excisemen. Indeed some of it was still around.

The Reverend Father and I went on talking about the rocket range. Then we found ourselves together in the pub, still talking. And I remember a good many winks and digs in the ribs as the whisky was poured and poured and the talk went on. I can't quite remember what solution we achieved to our problem, but one was found.

CHAPTER 6

Australia

I had been at the Ministry of Defence for two years when Alec Home saw me one day in the House of Lords and asked me to come to his office – 'to have a word', he said. He was Secretary of State for Commonwealth Relations, and the word was to ask whether I would be prepared to go as British High Commissioner to Australia.

I was completely unprepared for this and it astonished me. I knew that Alec was a particular friend of Robert Menzies, the formidable Prime Minister of Australia, so I assumed he not only wanted to send somebody likely to be personally acceptable, to represent the British Government, but was kind enough to think my face might fit; and I had considerable respect for Alec's competence and judgement as a minister. But I felt I had no qualifications whatsoever. I had no diplomatic training nor, as far as I could judge, aptitudes. I did not know Australia. It occurred to me that the traditional association of my family – Uncle Charlie's governorship, my grandfather's marriage, my father's birth and education – might have played some obscure part in Alec's choice, but I have never discovered that he was even aware of those connections. I asked for time for reflection and consultation with Iona.

I was thirty-seven. Politics had been for eleven years the principal part of my life and at the Ministry of Defence (which I much liked) I could reasonably feel that my foot was on the ladder. Whether it could return there – and if so on what conceivable rung – after what might be three years in Australia seemed more doubtful. Then there were domestic consider-ations. The children were all of school age and there would be educational upheavals. Bledlow was now running well

113

from a farming viewpoint but it would have to manage with the sort of very remote control which can succeed but can also lead to deterioration. And closing a house for a three-year absence is never easy.

These were all personal factors, some of them trivial, some not. Against them was the challenge and excitement of going to the other side of the world, to do something completely different which somebody seemed to think might be useful. I had travelled a good deal from the Ministry of Defence and had visited the Far East for the first time, but such visits were brief. Now we had been invited to transplant ourselves for a while. Iona and I were relatively young; and I had a feeling, which was strongly reinforced by later experience, that to get outside one's own country and look at it with something of the perspective of others is an educative venture for anyone, and particularly for a politician. As it happened my later return to politics was much facilitated by the circumstance of Harold Macmillan's assuming the premiership in 1957 and then forming a new Government after the election of 1959, the year I returned: he had been my boss at the Ministry of Defence, and he visited Australia while I was there. This was, of course, unpredictable. Meanwhile the novelty of the idea was invigorating to both of us. I told Alec Home that we would go and within a few weeks we were on our way.

He invited us to lunch at Dorney Wood, the house near Burnham Beeches used by the Foreign Secretary, particularly for entertaining. The luncheon party, we immediately realized, was very senior and very old. There was a very old High Commissioner of New Zealand. There was the very old Admiral of the Fleet, Lord Chatfield. I could see that Alec's wife Elizabeth, a particularly charming and skilful hostess, was finding the going sticky, and Iona and I were conscious of doing too little to help her lighten the atmosphere. With a touch of desperation Elizabeth said, when we'd left the lunch table and the silences began to hang heavy, 'Let's play a game!'

She then introduced us to a game whereby one had to pass a pair of scissors round and deduce something or other from whether they were passed closed or open. Chatfield participated with a bemused expression, which was nothing to that of the New Zealand High Commissioner at the next game.

'We will now', Elizabeth said, 'play Bing Bong.'

This involved the guests counting in sequence as they sat – '1, 2'. For '3' one said 'Bing'; and for '7' 'Bong'. Thereafter multiples of 3 or 7 had to be Bing or Bong: '11, Bing, 13, Bong, Bing' and so on, with appropriate losses of lives. Chatfield's face, too, was a study!

Australia was in an interesting period of its history. The Australian economy was moving from the simple base on which its wealth had hitherto been erected – wool, wheat, cattle, agricultural goods – to the sophisticated and diversified condition we now see. A minerals boom – iron ore in Western Australia, bauxite, uranium, manganese deposits – was beginning. A transformation was under way.

This reached well beyond the economy, and deep into Australian politics and consciousness. In the past there had been general acceptance of very close ties with the United Kingdom. Australian national awareness is always said to have stemmed to a large extent from the First World War, the formation and exploits of the Australian and New Zealand Army Corps that fought at Gallipoli. But Britain was the Mother Country. Australia was a realm of the British Crown. The Governor-General, the Sovereign's Representative, as well as all but one of the governors of states, were British. Of course since the Statute of Westminster, which had regulated relationships between the British Government and the countries known (in what now sounds a patronizing phrase) as 'the self-governing Dominions', Australia had managed her own affairs and conducted her own international policy; but a close family relationship, even if sometimes (as in families) marked by domestic bickering and some mutual mockery, had been taken for granted.

All this was, perhaps, taken more for granted in Britain than in Australia – or, anyway, in some quarters in Australia; and it was changing. In the Second World War, as in the First, Australians had travelled to Europe, to the Middle East, had fought magnificently on war fronts far from home – as well as against the Japanese in Burma and Malaya and on seas and lands rather nearer their own direct interest. They had fought for the Empire and as part of the Imperial forces. But that British Empire which had formerly seemed an instrument of worldwide power, an institution worth supporting as a guarantor of security as well as a clan of blood-relations – that Empire had been ineffective when it came to confronting the Japanese in Asia and the Pacific. Australian perceptions of their security had by no means been co-terminous with British strategic priorities in the winter of 1941–2, after the Japanese attack which swept through South-East Asia, the Philippines and what is now Indonesia. It was the United States, above all at the battles of the Coral Sea and Midway, which had removed any direct threat to Australia. The Australians, I found, celebrated 'Coral Sea' week, a celebration of their deliverance through American victory. It was historically justified, it was fair, but to an Englishman it grated a little. Nevertheless I soon had to come to terms with the fact that it was to the United States – sometimes, no doubt, with a certain resentment – that Australians in matters of defence had learned to look. And the United States, whose shores lay on the same Pacific Ocean as Australia's, was a mighty market and instrument of economic advance. A large number of American servicemen had visited Australia during the war. For the British there was, in Australia, still a strong feeling, based on tradition and sentiment – a feeling stronger in some than others; but it was no longer a feeling also based, simply and naturally, on self-interest or the realities of power.

This sort of transition of national perception generally takes some time. It had started long before I arrived in Australia and it went on long afterwards. And some people were impatient for it to move faster: they thought Australia – or, certainly, Australian foreign policy – should be redirected to some extent away from the British and Western connection. They believed – and I agree with them – that Australia was part of its own

116

geographic region and that it should spend more attention on cultivating relationships with the nations of South-East Asia and the Pacific area than on burnishing some sort of post-Imperial or neo-European reflection. Perhaps the leading figure in Australian politics who took this view was the Foreign Minister, Richard Casey.

Dick Casey, later to be a distinguished Governor-General of Australia, embodied a certain paradox. More than most of his colleagues in Government – and certainly much more than his Prime Minister, Robert Menzies – he took what could be called a strongly and independently Australian line in policy even when – perhaps especially when – it could be criticized as being at odds with the views of Her Majesty's Government of the United Kingdom. He was, to a large extent, the originator of the sort of foreign policy Australia follows today. Yet in outward appearance and to some degree in tastes, associates and instincts he was more European, more British, than most Australians in politics at that time. With his clipped moustache, smart and rather formal bearing, he looked like an Englishman of an earlier generation. He had a host of friends everywhere, and a great many in England. He was, nevertheless, a great and independent Australian patriot.

So was the other dominant figure in politics, Prime Minister Robert Menzies. But Bob Menzies had very different views. A proud Australian, he was also vociferously proud of his British – and, in particular, his Scottish – ancestry. He seldom missed a Scottish celebration or occasion, declaiming Burns's 'Ode to a haggis' at Melbourne's annual St Andrew's Day party with huge enjoyment. He recognized that Australia was undergoing a certain inevitable change of course but he was sure that for the time being the closer and more loyally her destiny could be linked to Britain's the better for both countries. He was an articulate lawyer with a formidable intellect and he dominated his surroundings. Some have said that he crushed opposition, wouldn't tolerate disagreement. That was not, in my observation, true: but he was a tough fighter and a powerful orator to whom political enemies gave a pretty wide berth. There were murmurs of annoyance when Bob Menzies said, as he sometimes did, 'I'm British to my bootstraps', but the murmurs were subdued. He had vision. He loved Winston Churchill, and in a way he belonged to a more heroic age in which Churchill, too, had preferred his part. Bob Menzies had a robust wit and a very quick one. In the House of Representatives he was unsurpassed, and on a political platform he was hard to match. 'I wouldn't vote for you if you were St Peter himself,' an ancient virago yelled at him when he was speaking once in his constituency. 'If I was St Peter, madam,' Bob Menzies shot at her, 'you would not be in my electorate!' He was a true friend to Britain, for which I often had reason to be grateful: a great Australian first and last; and one of the most outstanding men I have met in life.

It was predictable that these two, Menzies and Casey, were often at odds. Menzies thought Casey somewhat too much the diplomat and civil servant, too exact, too correct. Casey reckoned Menzies was a swashbuckler, overexuberant – and too uncritically pro-British. There were difficulties for me in their relationship, for a High Commissioner is accredited to a Government and thus formally to its head, unlike an Ambassador, whose accreditation is to a Head of State but who does business with the Foreign Ministry. A High Commissioner, of course, also has dealings with a Foreign Ministry but was at that time likely to have a more personal relationship with a Prime Minister than would be normal between an Ambassador and a Sovereign or President.

These difficulties lay in the future. Before sailing in the Orient liner *Oronsay* I did as much homework as possible about Australia, talked to everybody I could on its personalities, politics, customs and economy, and prepared my mind as much as one can on these occasions. I saw a great many prominent Australian businessmen and bankers as well as diplomats, and listened as hard as I could. My preparatory period ended with an interview at No. 10 Downing Street. I supposed that the Prime Minister, Anthony Eden, would say a wise word or two about Australia, Britain and the Commonwealth; or, perhaps, about South-East Asia. On the contrary, he never uttered a sentence on any such subject. He spoke of nothing but the Middle East, and talked obsessively about the problem of Nasser,* Egyptian adventurism and the Suez Canal – which Nasser had nationalized, to general consternation, in the last week of July. I left the Prime Minister certain that he was determined on some sort of dramatic action. Of course I knew contingency plans were in preparation but I knew nothing of their scope or immediacy. Eden was nervous and his manner was neurotic. It was easy to see he was a sick man. It was October 1956.

The Carrington family sailed – Iona and I, three children, a governess, and the staff of six we had been told would be necessary for the house in Canberra which was to be our home; we had been advised that domestic staff were unobtainable in Australia and thus had to be imported. The accuracy of this last advice was demonstrated immediately after arrival. A fortnight after reaching Canberra four out of the six left us for better paid jobs. One of them had been my mother-in-law's cook whom we had, I suppose, pinched. She was pinched from the pinchers and no doubt it served us right.

The Suez Canal being closed by the Middle East crisis, we had to go round the Cape and the journey was a long one. Having reached Australia it thereafter took a considerable time to get to our destination. We arrived at Perth in Western Australia, and travelled in sequence to Adelaide, Melbourne and Sydney before finally arriving in Canberra. Each of these cities was the capital of one of Australia's states. In each there was a Governor, representing the Queen, on whom a formal call had to be paid. At each call the ceremonies usual in those days had to be observed with bowing, curtsying and so forth. And, as I have said, each Governor (except in New South Wales, Uncle Charlie's old fiefdom) was, by nationality, British. It was a different Australia, although only thirty years ago.

At Melbourne we arrived on the day of the Suez operation – the Anglo-French invasion of Egypt. In Moscow Khrushchev† had made a belligerent and threatening speech. It didn't seem entirely impossible that my first task in Australia would

* Gamal Abdel Nasser, Prime Minister of Egypt and virtual dictator.
† Nikita Khrushchev, First Secretary of the Communist Party of the Soviet Union.

be trying to negotiate Australia into the Third World War. Meanwhile it was also the day of the Melbourne Cup, the great November social event in that city, when the world gathers at Flemington racecourse. I was advised about the essentials and the protocol, and my morning coat was excavated from the bowels of the ship so that we could appear in proper order. We then went by motorcade to the racecourse. Arriving thus, with much ceremony, we were greeted by a tall and immensely distinguished gentleman in a grey morning coat. I bowed, as at each of these occasions, and Iona curtsied. He turned out, however, to be not the Governor but his Military Secretary, who was greatly disliked by everyone in Melbourne. We had, not for the last time, got it wrong; although much to the amusement of the onlookers.

In Sydney the Governor – a delightful Australian general, Sir John Northcott, the only Governor we met who belonged in origin to the country – asked us to stay the night. It was, of course, Uncle Charlie's house and we were photographed under my family's coat of arms – all past Governors' arms were carved on a verandah which ran along the front of the house. The house itself had a magnificent view of Sydney Harbour. The famous Opera House was later built immediately below the garden.

And from Sydney we drove to Canberra. The High Commission Rolls Royce – a vehicle wildly unsuitable for much Australian travel – was sent to Sydney to take us on the last lap of the journey to what was to be home for three years. The car was green. The chauffeur's name was Paddy Coyle. He had once been a sergeant in the Irish Guards. His uniform was also green – bright green. Half-way between Sydney and Canberra Paddy Coyle opened the glass partition between driver and passengers. He turned and threw a question.

'Do you like me uniform?'

I could feel that the topic was loaded. 'Well, what's wrong with it?'

'If you put me in a field,' said Paddy with emotion, 'the cows would eat me.'

We appreciated that before any other matter claimed

attention it would be necessary for us to get him a new uniform: so we did. He was a marvellous man with a huge sense of humour, and he made our Rolls Royce journeys as agreeable as could be. I remember one journey, sitting in the back with Dick Hull, who was visiting Australia as, I think, Commander-in-Chief Far East. He started to speak of some rather secure nuclear matters. I indicated Coyle's back.

'Sh!'

Dick had clearly got things to impart so I wound the glass partition shut.

I called out, 'You can't hear me can you, Paddy?'

'Not a word, me lord,' came the comforting reply!

Sometimes Paddy reverted sharply to his days as an Irish Guards sergeant. He was furious when the students of Perth University, on a visit of mine to Western Australia, had tied tin cans and rattles under the High Commission Rolls and (only discovered on reaching Government House) had chalked 'Just Married' in letters three foot high on the back of the car's boot. Paddy, supremely unamused, wanted to turn round and put the lot in close arrest.

I knew that Canberra was a small place (in those days it had about 35,000 inhabitants); and I knew that as a purely administrative capital it had a preponderance of diplomats, officials and politicians, together with those who could be persuaded to attend to their needs, although there were also some graziers, who had been part of Canberra before it became a capital city. I was, however, unprepared for the fact that one could drive through it without realizing one had done so. Much has changed, but in those days there seemed to be remarkably few buildings, and those few separated by miles of open space. Traffic was minimal. I used to ride to my office every morning. My younger daughter, Virginia, used to accompany me and take the horse back. By 1956 there were few capital cities where that sort of thing would have been practicable. The climate was delightful – never unpleasantly hot, and with a cold winter redeemed by plenty of sunshine. In the Australian spring – the British autumn – Canberra was covered with blossom, the mimosa (called, I think regrettably,

121

'wattle' by the Australians) was in flower and the place was beautiful. For our first seven months it never rained and the sun shone. One gets bored by this, of course, and I started to say I would never again complain about the grey skies of England (I started to complain, my family told me, a fortnight after ultimate return). All in all, Canberra was a most agreeable place in which to live.

Our house was six months old and had only just been occupied by my predecessor. I don't know what he thought of it – he was, I was given to understand, different from me in every conceivable way so his taste in architecture and furnishings might reasonably have been supposed to differ as well. In fact the white, green-roofed house (which resembled a golf Club House or Dormy House in the Home Counties of England) was well laid out and convenient. The furnishings, however, were appalling. This was a Ministry of Works responsibility so there was no reason to grumble at my predecessor, except insofar as one can arrogate to oneself a certain sanction in these matters: but grumble at what we found we certainly did. The interior looked like a bad parody of a tourist-class lounge in a P & O liner. Legs of chairs, made of light beech wood, stuck out at an angle. The drawing room carpet was dark brown with lime green stars and stripes woven on it: and everything else was as bad or worse. All this was new – and enormously expensive – so what we could do to change it was very properly limited. We had brought a few things with us, but our house's interior did not present to our guests a proud example of British workmanship and design.

Some years later I found myself in Buenos Aires. The British Ambassador showed me his house which was being done up at the time by the Ministry of Works. The Ministry's representative was there, and we were introduced to each other, neither, I think, catching the other's name. I asked if he'd done up many houses. He said he had, and the one of which he was proudest was the High Commissioner's house in Canberra. 'It was beautiful,' he said, 'until people called Carrington came and ruined it.' He spoke with feeling. Perhaps he had heard my name after all.

It was soon clear that, perhaps apart from the British and Americans, the diplomatic world of Canberra was not over-burdened with business. It was a small society, much of it extremely nice, but little of it overworked. In that sort of society questions of protocol and procedure tend to loom unreasonably large, and offence is given and taken as a way of passing the time. The social round can be tedious and repetitive. Iona and I were by no means expert at precedence – made difficult in Australia by the fact that there were three different precedences – the Commonwealth (of Australia) list, the Governor-General's list and the list in each state. It was hard at first to know whether we had got it right; and more often than not the word got back that we had erred. I suppose my lack of diplomatic training told. I used to say as we sat down to one of our lunches or dinners:

'I'm sure we've got it wrong. You remember, I expect, the Governor of Bermuda who found a lady annoyed about pre-cedence. She said to him, snappishly, that she supposed it was difficult to get such things right, and he snapped back, "Those who matter don't mind, those who mind don't matter!"'

This was intended to disarm, and certainly placed obstacles before those wishing to take offence. But there were many pitfalls. On one occasion the Greek minister was not invited to another nation's celebration. On complaining, he learned that this was because the British High Commissioner had opposed it, at a time when we were 'oppressing the people of Cyprus'. What had happened was that the host's staff had asked the advice of my staff as to guest list, the latter had noticed the Greek minister's name typed twice and had, tidily, scratched it out once. So he was scratched entirely, and the matter took a little repairing.

There were other problems beside precedence, familiar to many an apprentice diplomat. The guest of honour at our first dinner party was the Sultan of Perlis, in Malaya. The Federated States of Malaya were still under British tutelage and the Sultan, on a visit to Australia, was thus within my province. I had given strict instructions that he was to be served no wine, and Iona had been categoric to the cook about leaving any sort of pig off the menu. The system failed. The butler started to pour wine into the Sultan's glass. The Sultan recoiled violently and waved it away. The butler – as new as we were – then poured a colourless liquid into his glass which turned out to be neat gin. Then the savoury arrived – scrambled eggs on toast for everybody else but, specially for the Sultan, angels on horseback. I don't think the poor man enjoyed himself.

We got better at it. We got more used to the intensity of our own entertaining – I recall that in one February, mercifully not a Leap Year, we had twenty-eight dinner parties. Iona took it all in her stride, and I do not remember her ever echoing the British Ambassadress in Rome who, three years earlier, had entertained me to lunch at the Embassy together with Signor Fanfani. When Fanfani, a long-serving Cabinet minister, left he thanked her and she said, 'Oh, don't thank me! It's my job!' Job or not, we got used to it. And we got more used to dressing up in formal clothes and driving through what appeared to be open countryside to dine with a neighbour in the city. The most exacting as well as the most enjoyable occasions, however, were when we would drive, I in white tie, tail coat and decorations, Iona in her tiara, all resplendent in the Rolls Royce, steered by Paddy Coyle, to the residence of another of the very few outstanding men I have met in life: the Governor-General, Field Marshal Sir William Slim, later to be created Viscount Slim of Yarralumla.

Bill Slim had been Governor-General of Australia for three years when we arrived. His reputation as a brilliant soldier and a plain-speaking, forthright man had preceded him and the Australians had welcomed him with open arms. They soon started to wonder about the forthrightness. Australians flatter themselves on their no-nonsense frankness, their contempt for soft-saying; they are not always pleased to be on the receiving end of the same treatment, if not expecting it. In his first years there was a good deal of surprise at the unflattering remarks the Governor-General aimed at anything or anybody in Australia he regarded as below par. The story has often been told of how, when visiting the (charming) Governor of South Australia, Air Marshal Bobby George, Slim was given a motorcycle escort which he thought scruffy and ill-disciplined. At the end of the day the escort commander asked the Governor-General if he would like to inspect them, which he did; and if the Governor-General would care to address them, which he also did. It was during my time in Australia and the word soon got round. 'I have misjudged you,' Slim said. 'Until I inspected you I had thought you'd not cleaned your motorbicycles. I now realize you have cleaned them with your uniforms!'

That sort of thing can lead to soreness and scars. With Bill Slim it didn't. He had extremely high standards, and he reckoned it was part of his duty to Australia to set them and insist on them. The least pompous of men, he was nevertheless determined that everything with which he was associated should be done faultlessly. That was owed to the Crown, and to demand less was to insult Australia by accepting second best. He had a magnificent sense of humour, but it was a mistake to presume on it. He could be formidable, although even he was at a loss when entertaining at Government House Mr Diefenbaker, Prime Minister of Canada. Diefenbaker was accompanied by his brother. He mounted the steps to shake hands with his host, the Queen's Representative dressed in the uniform of a Field Marshal, baton in hand, five stars on his tunic; and was followed by the brother, Elmer Diefenbaker, who took Slim's hand and enquired, 'Name again?' Slim glared at him.

'I'm the Governor-General, you bloody fool!'

But Bill Slim was soon recognized by Australians for what he was – a truly great and humble man, utterly bent on doing his duty by them and by the job, fearless in word and action. By the time we arrived he was venerated by the people of Australia for the strength of his character, the obvious honesty of his purpose and the direct good sense of his speeches.

To Iona and myself he – and his immensely competent and delightful wife, Aileen – were kindness and helpfulness personified. Government House was run in a way it would be impossible to better. We were young and inexperienced, and although the Governor-General couldn't appear to be treating the British High Commissioner preferentially, he used to say, 'Come along in if you ever want advice. Come in by the side door.' And I did.

A month after we arrived was our first Australian Christmas and we went to Christmas dinner at Government House – with all the children. Virginia was ten, and not one to mince her words. It was a large party of all ages, but one of those silences occurred where, for a moment, nobody spoke. People used to say, tritely, 'An angel's passing overhead.' On this occasion no angel but Virginia broke the silence, loudly, to one of the ADCs. We all heard her.

'Do you know who Daddy hates most in Canberra?'

One of my staff had failed to impress me favourably, and I'm afraid the family knew it. Before Virginia could explain this, naming names to the Governor-General's dinner table, Sally Shaw, our friend and governess, gave her a sharp kick under the table which produced pain and silence. After dinner, however, Aileen Slim organized a game of hunt-the-thimble for the children. One of the guests was an old lady, a distinguished poetess who was deaf and had an ear-trumpet. Virginia, getting the thimble, stuck it down the ear-trumpet. I don't know what the Governor-General thought but it didn't seem to affect our relationship.

Bob Menzies, too, was exceptionally kind and welcoming to us newcomers. He was warm, friendly and hospitable, often inviting us to his house (which was near ours) and dining with us, alone or with others. He was an extremely entertaining companion. With his physical bulk, his brilliant blue eyes and heavy eyebrows, his extrovert personality conveyed confidence and power. When I first called upon him formally to present my credentials he was in his room at the Parliament House, a room leading off the Cabinet room. Between the latter and the Prime Minister's room was a small ante-room where ministers used to have drinks before Cabinet – a proceeding remarkably different from that before a British Cabinet, where ministers and civil servants stand about in the passage outside the 10 Downing Street Cabinet room like boys about to be called into the headmaster's study for a collective rebuke. It was three o'clock in the afternoon when I presented to Bob Menzies my official papers from Anthony Eden. He looked at me with a good-natured expression.

'Will you have a martini?'

Dry martinis go straight to my head and I have always avoided them like the plague. It was, however, no moment to refuse – no diplomat yet, I was at least confident of that. I thanked him.

Menzies led me into the ante-room, took from a cupboard an enormous jug and poured what looked to me like a whole bottle of gin into it, to which he added a thimbleful of French vermouth and started mixing the martini. He handed a large tumbler of it to me, soon insisting on topping it up. I wandered unsteadily out of the Parliament House, part of my mind speculating what the doorkeepers and sundry onlookers thought of the sight of the new British High Commissioner staggering down the corridor at half past three in the afternoon.

Slim and Menzies liked and admired each other but sometimes found each other difficult. There was between them at times the friction which can arise between 'simple' soldier and 'devious' politician. Curiously enough it can arise most sharply where the soldier is as intelligent as Bill Slim – yet would suddenly strike Menzies as simplistic, because of his no-nonsense directness; and where the politician has the integrity and stature of a Menzies – who would yet sometimes vex Slim by what appeared out-of-character changes of tack and accommodation to circumstances. Each was what he was; and each was very, very good.

It was predictable that over the Suez question Menzies and his Foreign Minister, Casey, would take opposed views. It was natural to Menzies to be, as he saw it, loyal to the British and to take – as he also saw it, perhaps with a certain anachronism – a world strategic view. In this view – particularly seductive to one who, like Menzies, had played a lead part in the Second World War – the stability of the Middle East was threatened by Nasser's adventurism. The Middle East was, by this set of assumptions, a crucial centre of Commonwealth sea and air communications – the 'route to India' argument, familiar in earlier days of Empire, had not been totally expunged by Indian independence. To Menzies, that the Suez Canal mattered was self-evident, and that it could only function securely if external powers, primarily the British, were dominant in the area (albeit indirectly) was an article of faith. And then, of course, there was the oil. I doubt if Menzies fully shared Eden's obsessive identification of Nasser's ambitions with those of Hitler, but he was not out of sympathy with the idea that Nasser's behaviour demanded an exemplary response. To Menzies the British – and the French, and, for the matter of that, the Israelis – were fighting the civilized world's battles and having the guts to fight them sufficiently early. And then the gradual diplomatic isolation of Britain aroused in Menzies the pugnacity of the friend, the champion. Certainly Menzies, a highly experienced and intelligent man, saw the many facets of the problem, but these were his instincts.

To Casey the question looked quite otherwise. Casey was personally charming. He also had a gifted wife – small, dynamic, full of fun and sharp as a needle. An adventurous lady, she used to fly her own aeroplane until well into her eighties: I believe that the Royal Australian Air Force more than once had to scramble an aircraft to rescue her when, at a later time, as Governor-General's wife, she was flying with determination in quite the wrong direction. She wrote well, she drew well, she was an enchanting person and Casey was a most likeable man. But over Suez Casey, unlike Menzies, took a view entirely opposed to that which I was instructed to argue. He thought the whole Anglo-French adventure a mistake. He felt, keenly, that Australia's influence among neighbours in South-East Asia could be diminished by too demonstrative a pro-British stance. He reckoned American hostility would mean that no forward policy of the kind Britain had launched could long be sustained in the Middle East; the thing could not be carried through. In all this Casey was right. Ultimately the issue settled into some sort of grumbling background, while accusations abounded. Eden resigned and Macmillan became Prime Minister.

For me the matter, despite my instructions, was confused. I had no moral feelings against Government policy – I took the pretty widely accepted view that Nasser's conduct was bad for Britain, bad for what might be called the image of international law – but I thought the British and French military action injudicious. The Suez operation was based on false premises. First, Nasser was not Hitler, and the analogy drawn by Eden was grotesque. Hitler had pursued and had announced his intention to pursue a policy of European domination, and made clear that his preferred path was war. Nasser stirred up a good deal of domestic unrest in neighbouring Arab states, was a dedicated nationalist and thought that outsiders, and particularly Britain, had played a malign and patronizing part in Arab and Egyptian affairs for too long; he was, like Hitler, a personal ruler and a demagogue. But he did not threaten the peace of the world unless the reactions of others accomplished that for him. It was inevitable that, sooner or later, the Arab peoples would struggle for more independence and thereby more self-respect. Oil enabled this ambition to be satisfied, and Nasser articulated it. Of course it was true that Soviet aid and influence was at that time strong in Egypt, but it was an exaggerated deduction, to put it no more strongly, that this meant Nasser was in the Soviet pocket and that the Russians were about to get a stranglehold on the Middle East. With our experience we should – and many did – have known better.

Second, Britain and France conspired to play a part on the world stage which was out of harmony with their respective strength in world terms. Sometimes forward policies, even small wars, can still be conducted nationally; and have been. But the Middle East with its oil and Egypt with its international waterway – to say nothing of Islam with its worldwide communities – were of self-evident and significant concern to everybody; and, most certainly, to the United States and the

Soviet Union. To bring those two together in criticism of Britain wasn't British diplomacy's finest hour. It was done, moreover, at exactly the moment when the Soviet Union was engaged in bloodily suppressing a spontaneous anti-communist people's rising in Hungary. The unctuous and strident humbug of Khrushchev's condemnation of Britain could barely drown the sigh of relief he was simultaneously emitting, that we were distracting the world's attention from the Red Army in Budapest.

It was, thirdly, a foregone conclusion that British influence with the Arabs – arguably a waning asset for some time – should be almost entirely destroyed by an expedition which could be described as an Imperialist attack on legitimate Arab aspirations; which was, demonstrably, too feeble to attain any clear military object; which, all could see, had to be stopped because other nations and particularly America demanded it; and which – sin of sins – was launched in covert but obvious collusion with Israel. Suez made it impossible for our Arab friends to show their friendship, and the known fact of that friendship seriously weakened their own domestic situation in some if not all cases. Fourthly, and I will make it lastly, for this whole subject has been treated by others to the point of tedium, nobody seemed to have a consistent idea of what the whole thing was intended to achieve. Of course it was by no means obscure what Eden *hoped* to achieve: he hoped to topple Nasser, and he supposed that a military operation would lead to the Egyptians repudiating Nasser and cheerfully restoring some sort of *status quo ante*. But to the soldiers, ordered to clear a corridor astride the Suez Canal (after extensive aerial bombardment of Egypt), the political aim of operations was confused and improbable – a confusion not mitigated by one official explanation that the British and French troops were 'putting out a forest fire' (fighting between Israel and Egypt) which it didn't take great perception to deduce we and the French had largely started. For those, like myself, charged with explaining British policy, the task was made somewhat heavy by the difficulty of understanding it ourselves. It has often been suggested that, having launched this ill-fated

130

adventure, we should have 'seen it through' – and that, however secretly, the Americans and others would have been gratified by our success despite professed outrage. Maybe. But we had just, after a difficult and protracted negotiation, got out of Egypt, given up the Canal Zone bases. Now we looked as if we contemplated going back in, with no clear idea of how we could get out again one day. I do not for a moment believe that had we 'seen it through' – in the sense of prolonged occupation of a part of Egypt – our own people or allies would have found the burden long acceptable. The advantages are hard to perceive; and the odium and diplomatic penalty would have been unchanged except, of course, very much for the worse. Our policy would have been defensible only if really thought through; the cost, including the international cost, counted; and the means consistent with a quick and successful military decision leading, as is the object of all war, to a better peace. None of this applied. A good many of these reflections derive from wisdom after the event, but it is better than none at all.

Canberra in those days was an indiscreet place. Politicians and Pressmen lived during the week in hotels, and there was only one decent hotel at which they used, very naturally, to meet and drink. Gossip abounded and there was every opportunity for mischief-making. The leader of the Country Party (the Government was a coalition of Country Party and Liberals) was Arthur Fadden. He was a capable, popular, sociable man: and he was Treasurer – that is, Finance Minister. Fadden used to talk in the evenings a good deal more than is wise for a Finance Minister; and the more convivial the hour the more he talked. On one occasion he was known to have let out secrets about the forthcoming budget. He was so well-liked that nobody took advantage of this to bring off a scoop and do him down – an experience somewhat different from that of Hugh Dalton, a Labour Chancellor of the Exchequer who had committed a similar but much more trivial indiscretion in London some years before.

Others, too, were indiscreet. Dick Casey himself kept a diary, and was known to write it up every night of his life. I soon discovered that if I gave him some particular and particularly confidential piece of news from London, or showed him a 'top secret' telegram I thought he should see, the content was transcribed that evening in his diary; and next morning he circulated his diary widely in Canberra. This way of doing business was inhibiting, to say the least. It led me, inevitably, to do as much as I could direct with Menzies. But in those days, particularly when the Suez business had died its ignominious death, there were few very difficult matters to disturb relations between Britain and Australia. The sense that Britain's position was of diminished consequence had been there from the beginning, and probably received an impetus from Suez: but it corresponded to a perception whose long-term accuracy could hardly be gainsaid. We did, undoubtedly, count for less in the world than our more robust Australian friends liked to believe, and were less an oracle of wisdom than once we had fancied. I cannot say that London gave evidence of taking much trouble to correct this. I was informed, in the usual way, of what other diplomatic posts were thinking, by being on the distribution list of other Ambassadors' despatches; but these came by sea, so that I did not exactly have my finger on the pulse of British overseas intelligence. This had its compensations. I remember reading a despatch from our man in Paris. 'I have just had luncheon', I think it ran, 'with an old, broken, disappointed man who knows that never again will his country turn to him in its hour of need . . .' There was more in the same vein, written after a visit to de Gaulle at Colombey-les-deux-Églises. By the time I read the report the General was triumphantly installed in the Élysée Palace.

Australian politics were not, of course, confined to Canberra. In that vast land, activity in the states' capitals tended to be of more interest to the ordinary Australian; and in some states government was subject to pretty frank comment as to integrity and effectiveness. Australians, born democrats, relish the privileges and are not immune to the hazards of the electoral system. In Queensland, early in 1957, I paid a visit during a memorable political storm. Queensland had for a long time been governed by the Labour Party. All Labour Members of

Parliament had to take an oath that they would obey the directives of the party executive – an unelected body which had, as it happened, fallen almost entirely into the hands of extreme left-wing trade unionists, not reckoned to be representative of the ordinary voter. They called the tune.

The State Premier had come to office and flourished with the support of this system within his party. On the day I arrived, however, he had decided that a particular party executive directive was most inconvenient: and had declared that he could no longer accept so undemocratic a state of affairs. He was promptly dismissed from the Labour Party, together with his inner Cabinet (except for the Deputy Leader, who deserted him), whereupon he formed a separate Labour Party! I was told in Brisbane that this disarray did not mean the Opposition (Liberal by name, in fact Conservative) would triumph at an election, since they were so incompetent – to say nothing of the gerrymandering of boundaries which were such that 5000 votes elected a Labour Party candidate while it needed 35,000 to elect a Liberal. None of this was regarded as particularly curious or unique to Queensland: and now that I have lived longer and seen more, I realize that perhaps it wasn't, and isn't, a peculiarly Australian phenomenon. The system, furthermore, would one day break in Labour's hands.

On that same Queensland tour we went by Paddy Coyle's Rolls to Cairns on the Cape York peninsula and drove south to Brisbane down nearly a thousand miles of largely unmetalled road, an experience which seemed about to shake the Rolls's body off its chassis and induced me to replace Paddy at the wheel to give me something to hang on to for a bit. We drove thus into Rockhampton, to be met by a rather surprised Chief of Police who had the job of conducting us to a civic reception in our honour. At this, however, the Mayor was clad in shorts and shirtsleeves, so protocol was not very strict in Rockhampton. After it was over the Chief of Police surprised me somewhat by asking, rather conspiratorially, 'What did you think of our Mayor?'

I said something anodyne.

'At the last election,' the Chief of Police told me in a grim voice, 'that man drove down Rockhampton High Street with his mistress, in the mayoral car. His wife stood on the pavement and shot him twice in the stomach as he drove past.'

'Good God,' I said. 'What happened?'

The Chief of Police sighed. Then he said simply, 'Trebled his majority!'

I have said that we counted now for less in the world, but we could still count for a good deal; and here the performance of our business community and our exporters was important. I travelled as much as I could throughout Australia to try to put the case for Britain, to talk to as many people as possible, to argue the underlying strength of our economy, to reassure everyone I met about the vigour and resilience of our country. In my three years there was no corner of Australia I failed to visit, and it is a big place. But I confess that my efforts were often hard going. British business, I discovered, was inclined to take the Australian market for granted. Some British enterprises had done very well, but British manufacturers seldom bothered to take Australian customers' needs into account – it was a case of, 'Here is our product, take it or leave it.' As an example, General Motors had by now largely cornered the Australian motor-car market – yet in the immediate post-war years it had been forbidden to import American cars. The British had the ball at their feet, and threw the game away. There was immense opportunity for British risk capital – capital was the crying need of Australia, while resources abounded. Some British responded: but not enough. British businessmen – even so recently as my time – sometimes tended to be patronizing, and to irritate thereby. And by these attitudes – which began to change, for the better – we sometimes lost business. And we sometimes lost friends.

The travel itself, however, was of great personal fascination. Around Canberra the graziers were invariably kind and hospitable, and we would stay with them, ride over their properties and increasingly learn to love the country, with its brilliance of light and sky, the smell of the eucalyptus trees, the sense of space. Australian landscape, so utterly different from any European landscape, casts a spell all of its own. And further afield there was great variety of experience. We toured the exquisite Tasmania. We went north, south, east and west. I stayed on one property in Western Australia which was the size of Belgium. There was, of course, no fencing, no visible boundary on such estates, estates extending to millions of acres in which the 'home paddock', where there could be some control over breeding, probably extended to 50,000 acres, and where as many as three-quarters of the calves originally branded might never reach the meat market. The distances, the dependence on radio doctors, on radio education, the scale of farming enterprises, the vastness of all – this was magnificent and absorbing. In the north-west much was still primitive and seldom visited by outsiders.

The wild life and bird life, the wild horses, donkeys, camels (brought from Egypt by a perfectly comprehensible Australian theory that they would feel at home in much of Australia, and then turned loose), the exotic birds never seen elsewhere – all this gave one a sense of adventure. We would be housed in hotels as primitive as the land itself. I went to a place which boasted one hotel – a bar along the whole of the ground floor, and the upper floor divided into two rooms, one for men and one for women. The sanitary arrangements could be described as limited. Australia gave an exciting feeling of a new land, still in process of discovery and development – rapid development. Everything was happening fast. Minerals were being discovered and extracted (with little difficulty), and railways were being rapidly created for the major task of taking product to port. Australian energy and enterprise were admirable. The sensation must have been similar in America a century before. People were living rough, remote lives. In one place I was taken to the local cemetery – no stones, no concrete but bare brown earth and graves edged with broken glass from beer bottles. Some places were lawless: there was still some cattle rustling.

Conversation was sometimes unpredictable. At one Western

135

Australian town I heard Iona, sitting with the Mayoress in the back of the car, say, 'Have you any children?'

'Yes,' said the Mayoress. 'Two. But unfortunately they are only four months apart.' After a pause she added, 'But you have to take them when you can get them.' We never straightened that out.

But if some parts of the north-west were primitive, others stunned with the sophistication – and wealth – that flourished in such isolation. The first thing to strike me in one house I visited at the heart of a huge property in 1959 was that week's London *Economist*, flown from Perth like everything else to the private airfield of the (very cultivated) proprietor and his wife. Distance and logistic problems had been conquered, and an elegant way of life flourished. At the same place, after dinner, I was invited to get into a boat and shoot a crocodile.

'I've got a torch,' my host said. 'I'll shine it around the billabong and if you see two little red things shoot between them. You'll have hit a crocodile between the eyes.'

I was armed with a twelve-bore shotgun, and no. 2 shot. I soon saw two little red things, did as I was told, and scored a hit. A small aboriginal boy jumped over the side of the boat to get the crocodile – not a task I would have relished. Those crocodiles are only about six feet long but I would not have volunteered to share the billabong with them. As the boy jumped and the boat listed, my host's torch illuminated an enormous kangaroo on the bank.

He yelled, 'Shoot it! It's been doing a lot of damage! I've been trying to get that bastard for a long time!'

I again did as I was told, and again I scored. I may not have been the most skilful High Commissioner in diplomatic history but I doubt if any other – or many people – have bagged with a right and left a kangaroo and a crocodile.

I visited the ranges at Woomera and Maralinga – there were major nuclear tests in the autumn of 1957 – tests which have become matters of certain retrospective anxiety, unforeseen by anyone at the time. At the time I was chiefly impressed by the logistic triumph. The country – Maralinga is on the edge of Nullarbor Plain – is flat, with red soil, absolutely no vegetation and neither corner nor hill for over three hundred miles. In this immense emptiness, where summer heat reaches extraordinary heights, a village of aluminium huts with every modern convenience had been constructed. The whole operation struck me with its efficiency.

Woomera, too, was an impressive place – a prosperous township where women were allowed to accompany their menfolk, and about four thousand people lived: and like Maralinga, both complex and efficient.

We went to Papua New Guinea, where I marvelled at the Australians' task – one they were, I believed, tackling extremely well. The world was largely ignorant of the primitive innocence in which the people lived, a people among whom cannibalism still existed, but a people friendly, charming and vulnerable. The only common language between tribes was 'Pidgin', that curious and appealing version of our tongue in which 'Run' becomes 'Throw away leg', and I, as British High Commissioner, was 'Mrs Queen mark he belong'. Much of the country was unexplored.

Missionaries were much in evidence. Some of the work they did among those remarkable people, people clad in bird of paradise feathers, was no doubt admirable: but, like many others before me, I found the multiplicity of sects and the interdenominational rivalry unattractive: and to the natives it must have been at the least confusing. Converts were freely pinched by one church or sect from another. There were exceptions to this – and some of the missionaries' achievements in education were impressive; but I found myself wishing that Christianity had been presented to Papua New Guinea with greater solidarity. This has, after all, often been achieved elsewhere. All in all, however, the Australians did a fine job in Papua New Guinea, and I am grateful to have witnessed it for one fascinating fortnight in the days before decolonization.

Sometimes I travelled beyond Australia. Because I was a diplomat who had once been a minister, the British Government used me as their representative at various international conferences. All too often these conferences were spectacular wastes of time but they had their moments of entertainment. At one such – a meeting of the Economic Commission for Asia and the Far East in early 1959 – I sat astounded (if one can be astounded by an experience which was so wholly predictable) that so many people could talk to so little purpose, without relevance to what had gone before, so incomprehensibly and for so long. When my turn came I delivered a sharp attack on the Russian delegation who had been uttering pernicious nonsense, and I was surprised to see their leader clapping enthusiastically. His companions on either side then grabbed his arms and forcibly restrained him. On another and earlier conference occasion the same Russian delegate, Mr Firyubin, attacked me at the reception each delegation had to give to colleagues during the proceedings. This was the Soviet reception. I was drinking whisky. Firyubin eyed me:

'You are not drinking our national drink!'

I admitted it.

'Since 1947', Firyubin proclaimed, 'we Russians have been making Scotch whisky!'

I felt depressed, anticipating a lecture on how the Soviets had invented Scotch and how great was their output: but Firyubin peered at me, lowered his voice and said, 'But it was disgusting!' and then passed on.

Conferences came in all shapes and sizes. This was still in the days of Empire – the first African colony to gain independence received it only in the year I reached Australia – and Britain had a large number of direct responsibilities all over the world. At big assemblies such as the Eden Hall Conference in Singapore British High Commissioners and Ambassadors would assemble from every country between Pakistan and Japan, with Governors of British colonies throughout South-East Asia, and Commanders-in-Chief of the various commands. I had sat in Canberra and read their despatches and telegrams. It was interesting now to observe them and assess them. Some clearly spoke with knowledge and authority. The reputation of others was shaky: I recall the

Ambassador to Laos who had shipped his Continental Bentley to that country, apparently unaware that there were, at that time, only a few miles of motorable road.

It was, for Britain, an entirely different world, so close to us in time yet now so extraordinarily remote in sentiment. Malcolm MacDonald had been Commissioner-General in South-East Asia, and thus used to chair such conferences – a remarkable man. But one of the most notable participants was his successor, Robert Scott, a barrister by training, who had joined the China consular service, had been taken prisoner by the Japanese in 1942, and had been senior British civilian prisoner in the notorious Changi jail. He had dominated his surroundings and his captors by the quiet force of his personality, and was one of those deeply impressive human beings who emerge triumphantly from that sort of experience without bitterness or detectable mark upon the mind. His goodness and courage shone for all to see.

One of my first international conferences was a meeting of the South-East Asia Treaty Organization – SEATO – which was held in Canberra: an unsuitable venue for such occasions because of the shortage of hotels. It took place in my first year and was interesting to me for the novelty of the experience and the fact that we were still, so to speak, in the shadow of Suez. I met John Foster Dulles there for the first time. The American Secretary of State struck me as dour but agreeable. He also seemed, contrary to some impressions, particularly friendly to our country.

At a dinner party at our house Casey called across the table to Dulles: 'What on earth did you mean by saying that no American soldier would ever stand shoulder to shoulder with a British or French soldier again?' Dulles's remark, in the aftermath of Suez, had made quite a stir.

'I'd been testifying,' Dulles said. 'I'd been testifying for two days, each of seven hours, before the Senate Foreign Relations Committee, sitting under arc lamps and in front of television cameras. The only thing that surprised me was that I didn't say something much sillier, much sooner.'

On the whole I found Dulles humourless, but I liked him.

He appeared, however, a man working under so demanding – not to say intolerable – a system as to find he had time neither to read nor to think.

Several conferences took place in Malaya, a land I find particularly beautiful and visited several times from Australia. At that time the campaign to save Malaya from the communist insurgents was not long over, and we had come to regard the country as firmly in the British orbit – for in those days we thought, still, in terms of a British orbit. I doubted that this would continue long. 'In the next four or five years,' I wrote home in February 1958, 'events will make it impossible for the Tunku [Tunku Abdul Rahman was the benign and respected Premier of the Federation] to be quite so pro-West as he is at the moment and sooner or later it is likely that a more neutralist Malaya will emerge.'

Later rather than sooner – I did not reckon with the Indonesian 'Confrontation' which threatened the integrity of Sarawak and Sabah after the British left them to be incorporated as East Malaysia: a 'Confrontation' which drew in British troops for a protracted campaign that only ended with revolution in Indonesia. This unforeseen event prolonged British presence and influence in Malaya, but the ultimate out-turn has been much as I supposed.

There was travel, there was a certain amount of international representation and negotiation, there were incessant speeches, there was tub-thumping for Britain's economy and prospects, there was friendship, there was sport. I remember a race meeting at Adelaide – I loathe horse racing above almost all else but it was obligatory to go. One horse entered was named 'Lord Carrington' – rather a successful horse as it happened. I was introduced to the owner and asked the inevitable question.

'I wonder why you've called your horse "Lord Carrington"?'

I thought I might get some myth connected to the pious memory of Uncle Charlie: even a half-forgotten murmur of Grandfather Rupert perhaps. The owner looked at me without expression.

'Well, his dam was Lady Carrington!'

And there was, of course, cricket. I watched one Test Match at Adelaide and at the Governor's dinner party that evening fellow-guests were Donald Bradman and Brian Johnston, the cricket commentator. Brian was an old friend, having been in the 2nd Grenadiers with me. He started to rally Bradman about Australian umpires and about one particular umpire's decision that afternoon: an English batsman had been given out controversially. In general the English performance on the cricket field was deeply depressing while I was in Australia. It was rather like that of some of our businessmen. The fielders didn't seem to think it worth seriously trying.

'I can't understand how he can have given him out,' Brian said. 'He doesn't know the rules of the game! He can't have played cricket in his life!'

Bradman got angry. He raised his voice sharply at Brian across the table.

'Hasn't played cricket! He played for South Australia! He played in several Tests! In fact,' he roared, 'he'd be playing still, if his eyesight hadn't failed!'

There were also a great many visitors. They were very welcome – those from England brought us news of home and injected a new vitality into what, it has to be admitted, can become a jaded and repetitive diplomatic circuit. Official visitors to Australia abounded, and if they were British I had the duty and the fun of looking after them. The Queen Mother came to Australia when we were there: and, inevitably, conquered all hearts and made my job significantly easier than before her visit. Princess Alexandra came on her first such official visit and so delighted everybody throughout a fortnight that the Australian Press Corps (a notably hardbitten and critical bunch) presented her with a bouquet of red roses at her tour's end – an unprecedented gesture and wonderfully well deserved, for she was enchanting. Artists and performers came – it was a joy to welcome Margot Fonteyn in 1957. Politicians came – some showing tact and sense, a few less so. Some were accompanied by children, also variable. The son of one such

British visitor was at an Australian university and joined his father for the trip. I heard an Australian remark to him that it was often difficult to remember names.

'I never have that difficulty,' the young man answered, 'because everybody knows me!'

Not all visitors enhanced life, and a British journalist who used an Australian tour to denigrate Britain did disproportionate damage. But, by and large, we were lucky in the people we entertained. Of these the most outstanding political success was Harold Macmillan.

Macmillan had become Prime Minister when Eden resigned, a sick man, in the aftermath of Suez. His visit to Australia and New Zealand took place at the end of 1957. I had been attending the huge Eden Hall Conference in Singapore and arrived back in Australia to be greeted by a banner headline: 'British Prime Minister snubs Australian Minister'. Macmillan had not been well during his journey, had found it difficult to sleep and had taken a sleeping pill which knocked him out at his first Australian appearance. In fact he had only been staging in the middle of the night through an airbase in Queensland en route to New Zealand which he was visiting first, but his drowsiness was at once fastened upon by the zealous and iconoclastic Australian Press. It would have been easy for his staff to defuse the incident by telling the facts, but they didn't. I soon found that – as generally but not always happens with trivia – the matter quickly faded from public memory because of the admirable impression the Prime Minister made thereafter.

At first I was uncertain of how his visit would go. He stayed at Government House but I accompanied him everywhere. In those days the visit to Australia of a British Prime Minister – and this was the first ever – was a significant event and wherever Macmillan went huge crowds turned out. He was – at least at that time – a shy man, a shyness which I believe was the true inward man, disguised by an assurance which had not yet flowered. When he got out of an aeroplane he would potter over to the waiting crowds behind the barrier and say in a rather nervous voice, 'Hello, hello! I bring you greetings from the old country!' It was hardly charismatic, and did not initially seem to be of the stuff of which Australian triumphs are made. But every day in Australia, by my observation and that of others with him, his confidence expanded, and although he never entirely lost the habit of suddenly winding down the window of Paddy Coyle's Rolls Royce, waving to an empty street and saying, 'Hello! Greetings from the old country!' he gradually scored an increasing and impressive success.

We travelled as widely as time allowed. He was quick to spot local habits and turn them to laughter with a graceful reference in a speech. In Melbourne he arrived during what they called there the 'five o'clock swill' – the pubs closed at six and one used to see the citizens, on their way back from leaving offices at five, sitting behind sixteen or so schooners of beer on a pub window ledge, downing them before closing time. Arrival in 'the swill' guaranteed for the Prime Minister a cheerful and noisy reception as he drove from the airport, and he noted the fact and its reason in a typically witty allusion in a speech thereafter. Lady Dorothy Macmillan, of course, was extremely popular. A completely unselfconscious person, her disdain for appearances and her natural friendliness endeared her to all; and that did nothing but good.

Welcome though the visit was, because a British Prime Minister was showing his face in Australia, Macmillan himself was largely unknown. Eden, of course, had possessed an international reputation. Churchill had been a legend. But nobody had heard of Macmillan, and they didn't know what to expect. 'They' exaggerates the point. Menzies knew well. 'If it had been my choice,' he said to me, 'Harold Macmillan would have been the man.' Menzies approved.

I wanted Macmillan to meet businessmen, those who were making a success of Australia, as well as politicians of all persuasions. I gave lunches or dinners for him at clubs in Sydney and Melbourne – Harold Macmillan always relished the atmosphere of clubs. He enjoyed himself greatly. He was increasingly extrovert and agreeable to everybody, intelligent, entertaining and the best of company. He hated those dinners

143

coming to an end. It took Menzies to get him from one party to a civic reception in Melbourne Town Hall. I had done my best, with a respectful nudge or two.

'I really think we ought to go.' The civic reception was about to start. Macmillan was due to make a speech.

'Nonsense,' Macmillan said. He poured himself another glass of brandy. When I tried again five minutes later he said angrily, 'Go and tell the Lord Mayor I'm drunk!'

I enlisted Bob Menzies' support. That great man tapped Macmillan on the shoulder and said, 'I'm going to the Town Hall. I expect you to be there in three minutes!' Three minutes later I followed this up. The Prime Minister got to his feet, wagging his head irritably and saying, 'Very well, I'll go, but Churchill wouldn't!' His visit was extremely popular and the general view of Britain and its Government was correspondingly enhanced.

Next year was to be election year in Australia, and no political leader was going to neglect any advantage which Macmillan's visit might procure. I wanted him to see the Opposition leader, the Labour Dr Evatt. Evatt said he would like to talk privately, so I left Macmillan's side – to discover that the wily Evatt had filled his room with every political journalist and television cameraman in Australia. They started filming and noting as Macmillan entered and they continued for twenty minutes, until Evatt summoned the director of Macmillan's tour – who had, of course, also been excluded – and added innocently, 'By the way, is this all right?' But Macmillan was too old a hand to be surprised by any electoral tactic and I believe he thoroughly enjoyed it all, rascality included. In the event the election at the end of 1958 was extraordinarily dull. No party, no leader, seemed to advance any coherent political philosophy, or even to know whether the party possessed one. Programmes were presented, packed with wild promises and nakedly composed on the principle of expediency – on what, from week to week, might attract votes. The Liberal Party, and Bob Menzies its leader, on the whole stood aside from this auction, themselves offering no sort of explicit policy but relying on the phrase 'Trust honest Bob'.

Menzies probably reckoned that in an Australian election activity and declamation can seldom win votes and can more probably antagonize and arouse suspicion. He won, hands down: and I was greatly relieved.

We were sad to leave Australia in October 1959. We had come greatly to love the country. To a degree I had not anticipated when first going there, I had come to look on it as a second home. I even contemplated buying a property there. I still hanker for that a little, and I know exactly where it would be, although I am afraid I would see it too seldom. But one thing, perhaps paradoxically, was borne in on me in Australia: the fact that we in Britain are a West European nation. Distance, geography and a history which reaches back through centuries of shared European experience are realities not sentimental abstractions. Despite the affection I had found for Australia, I realized in a more positive way than hitherto that I was and am a European.

We sailed, finally, from Sydney in a Dutch ship, the *Oranji*, and planned to stop in Singapore and thence take a holiday in Cambodia, and among other things visit Angkor Wat. The Commander-in-Chief of the Far East Air Force, Paddy Bandon, was proposing to take us in his aircraft. On the first leg of the journey the captain of the ship came up to me. We were not far from Jakarta.

'There's a signal for you in cypher.'

'What cypher?'

'My own private cypher,' he explained. 'I've never used it before in thirty years at sea! It will take some time to decode.'

After a while he returned with the signal in clear. It was from Harold Macmillan. The Conservatives under his leadership had just won a General Election in fine style. The signal had the effect of changing our plans and cancelling our trip to Angkor Wat. It read: 'Will you become First Lord of the Admiralty Query Come straight home.'

145

CHAPTER 7

The Admiralty

Some of the caricatures of civil servants which have appeared in books or on screen in recent years have been most amusing, producing reminiscent chuckles from those familiar with Whitehall. They are, nevertheless, caricatures and anybody who has served as a Government minister recognizes – albeit with enjoyment – the fundamental distortion, a distortion, I accept, necessary to the art of theatre or fiction.

In these caricatures the civil servant is determined to frustrate the will of ministers, by courteous, ingenious and constitutionally proper means, if the ministerial will or policy threatens the cosy and established Civil Service consensus, the bureaucratic inertia, the *status quo*.

All this is great fun, and there's something in it sometimes: but it is, nevertheless, a distortion. I have almost always found British civil servants, anyway in the higher reaches of the profession, to be models of what such men and women should be – intelligent, selfless, knowledgeable and fair-minded. Of course they are in the job of making Government function smoothly – and this may lead them to counsel restraint from some of the wilder policies which can take a minister's fancy and upset the business of administration. Of course they have to adapt to ministers of sharply different and ostensibly antagonistic political colour – and thus the civil servant learns to avoid the sort of emotional involvement with particular policies which can make objectivity difficult or anyway suspect. And of course, being individuals of sense and experience, they form their own views on what's best for the country in general and their own Department in particular, and often these views don't find favour. But in all this they preserve, from my observation, both integrity and loyalty despite what must frequently be trying circumstances; and every Cabinet owes them a great deal. The few exceptions to this tribute should not be allowed to diminish it. There are rotten apples in every barrel.

One of the best of civil servants in my personal experience met me at London Airport on that autumn day in 1959 – I had left Iona in Singapore to follow by sea and had flown home. Patrick Nairne was to be my Private Secretary as First Lord of the Admiralty, and was already a very skilled practitioner. He was only two years younger than myself, an accomplished artist, a lively minded, energetic and articulate man of great charm. Later in life he was to be Deputy Secretary in the Ministry of Defence with me; and later Permanent Secretary in another Department. In another incarnation, as Chancellor of Essex University, he conferred on myself, his former minister, an honorary degree.

Pat started straight away to tell me the problems of the Admiralty and it was clear they were not inconsiderable. I had, of course, seen a good deal of them from my earlier work in the Ministry of Defence: but now the perspective was different. I had witnessed Harold Macmillan's frustration at being overlord of some robustly independent Service ministers, petty princes in their own domains. Now I was one of the petty princes. The First Lord of the Admiralty had once been a member of the Cabinet. This was so no longer, but, like the Secretaries for War and Air, I held what was called Cabinet rank and had direct access to the Prime Minister if desired. We three Service ministers were a cut above the junior ministers in other Departments, the Ministers of State. We had an overlord still – Harold Watkinson, Minister of Defence – but we each had an historic and powerful Department of our own. And of the three, the most historic was mine.

The Boardroom of the Admiralty, in the older, seventeenth-century, part of that delightful building, was a glorious room in which to do business. Perhaps there is a subconscious prejudice current that decisions appropriate to a modern and technological age can only be taken efficiently in rooms devoid of ornament or character, soulless and disinfected. I don't share it. The Admiralty Boardroom, of majestic proportions, had an overmantel carved by Grinling Gibbons. A huge semi-circular bight had been scooped from one end of the Victorian table at which we sat, so that an earlier Civil Lord of the Admiralty, immensely fat, could reach his papers on the table. The weathervane on the roof oscillated a needle on the wall map of the Channel, so that generations of Boards of Admiralty could see when the invasion winds were blowing from France. Next to the chimneypiece was a small white plug on the wall denoting the exact height of Nelson – I think five foot two inches: immediately after his time this had set the height standard, and no smaller entrant was allowed into the Royal Navy. The room exuded history.

Beside myself there were two civilians on the Board of Admiralty. Ian Orr-Ewing was Civil Lord, a politician, and a minister who, like me, had come and would go. The other was the Permanent Secretary, John Lang. Lang was a man in his early sixties at that time and had served all his life in the Admiralty, except for a spell with the Royal Marine Artillery during the First World War. He was one of the most, if not the most, astute civil servants of his generation. In Whitehall his name was a household word for getting his own way. He was a master of bureaucratic manoeuvre and when he judged it necessary for the navy he was also a master of procrasti-nation. He had a hiding place in his office – said to be under a loose floorboard under the carpet although that may be apocryphal – where he used to bury any file which contained an insoluble problem in the run of correspondence: after a while, he told me, and after the usual puzzlement over where the files were, these problems used to solve themselves or die an unmourned death. I never learned whether that floorboard was investigated after his ultimate departure. John Lang ruled the Civil Service roost with a rod of iron. Among the serving officers in the Admiralty the Admiral's word was law, exactly as on board ship, and among the civilians John Lang's writ ran in just the same way.

The Sea Lords outnumbered the civilians on the Board and

their senior was the First Sea Lord, Chief of Naval Staff. Their discipline, too, was absolute, their voice united. Before meetings of the Board of Admiralty the Sea Lords used to meet to coordinate their approach to the agenda. I have no doubt that the unanimity thus achieved owed a good deal to the personality of the First Sea Lord. One too feeble or unnecessarily abrasive would, I expect, have had a discontented, albeit outwardly united, team. On this side, too, I was ultimately lucky. Just before I arrived Dickie Mountbatten had given up the post of First Sea Lord after four years in office and had moved to be Chief of the Defence Staff, a position he was to hold until 1965. His successor at the Admiralty, Sir Charles Lambe, was a highly regarded sailor who impressed me very favourably and immediately: but unfortunately Charles Lambe died after a heart attack within a very short time of my assuming office. It was my responsibility to name his successor.

I regarded Caspar John – whom I had known well, before I went to Australia – as the best candidate. He was both outstanding and interesting – outstanding because of his personal and professional qualities, interesting because he embodied a dichotomy. A son of Augustus John, he had his share of his father's Bohemian and uninhibited attitude to life – although having, by his own witness, mixed feelings about that father. With the other half of himself Caspar was a disciplined naval officer, with the sternness, the touch of rigidity, which that implies. He was a thoughtful, firm and far-seeing man, literate and excellent company. His wife, a talented sculptress, was highly entertaining. As well as sculpture, she loved racing. She reflected more the Bohemian than the Service side of Caspar's personality and I suspect she often found uncongenial the duties associated with the latter, but she always played her part nobly, turning up at meetings of naval wives with a copy of *Sporting Life* sticking out of her shopping basket. Dinner parties with the Johns – they had a house at Barnes – were splendid and unpredictable. A party might be formal, the First Sea Lord doing his duty most elegantly; or something a good deal more mixed, with unexpected guests and lasting until three or four o'clock in the morning.

I owed Caspar John gratitude for something beside professional service. We had no home in London, and when I first arrived I put up at the Turf Club, then in Clarges Street. The First Lord had, in those days, a 'tied' house that went with the job – Admiralty House, a huge place with five or six drawing rooms. It was a most awkward house to contemplate as a London home in the second half of the twentieth century – it was heated at public expense but there was no provision for cleaning and so forth. Domestic problems as well as expense would have been great. Luckily, at about that time it was decided that No. 10 Downing Street was to be refurbished and that while this was going on the Prime Minister would occupy Admiralty House. That suited us well (Harold Macmillan told me later that he much preferred it to No. 10, after sampling both) but it left us unhoused, and here Caspar John's courtesy and wishes were helpful. The Johns decided that they wanted to remain in their house at Barnes, so that a flat normally made available to the First Sea Lord would be untenanted and ours if we chose. The flat was in Admiralty Arch, on the left-hand side if entering Trafalgar Square from the Mall. We moved in, and were there throughout my time as First Lord.

It was a comfortable flat: its only drawback was noise. Approaching Admiralty Arch from the Mall, car-drivers change gear downwards: noisily. Noise was incessant, and to open a window in the flat carried a penalty for those within. Nevertheless it was an agreeable place to live. It had originally formed the nursery wing (it was on the top floor) of the First Sea Lord's house which in earlier times had been the whole left-hand part of Admiralty Arch. Dickie Mountbatten told me when dining with us that we were sitting in his nursery: his father, Prince Louis of Battenberg, had occupied the house when First Sea Lord.

Thus, living pretty well 'over the shop', I started work in my little kingdom of the Admiralty – started work, as must be obvious to the reader, with considerable pride. The sea and the navy have a very especial part in British history and I had

always wanted to have some connection therewith. I have described the Boardroom: my office, too, had splendid associations. I worked in the room in which Churchill had sat at the beginning of two world wars, with the same furniture — including a bookcase panel he kicked with rage, the repair marks still showing. The room, with its fine octagonal table, had a glorious view over the Horse Guards Parade. I loved it.

I was less enamoured of the First Lord's uniform, which (again said to derive from Churchill's time, and his dislike of visiting ships dressed as a civilian) I wore on sea-going and such-like occasions. Churchill had invented it. There was a reefer jacket with black Admiralty buttons, and a peaked cap with the Admiralty fouled anchor. I donned it without enthusiasm. Jim Thomas told me that he had once worn it when unveiling the War Memorial at a Royal Naval Hospital and as he was about to pull the string had overheard one of the bereaved, sitting nearby, whisper hoarsely to her neighbour, 'How very democratic of the Royal Navy to allow a sick berth attendant to unveil this memorial!'

In the House of Lords I was not only First Lord of the Admiralty but spokesman, more often than not, for each of the three Services and for Defence generally. I would present to the House (and justify) not only the naval but the army and air estimates as well. I introduced the annual Defence White Paper. All this was admirable experience, and my previous duty as Parliamentary Secretary had prepared me. It also helped offset the parochialism which was endemic in any office of that kind, where Service Departments were competitors as well as colleagues — and often a great deal more so. And it brought me, straight away, back into the chief questions which were dominating our defence policy. I made my first parliamentary speech as First Lord in November 1959. I spoke not about the navy but about the British nuclear deterrent; and in the following years I made a great many speeches about it.

I have already described the place of nuclear weapons in our

thinking, and my own views upon them since that moment in 1952 when the world first learned of the American hydrogen bomb. I was convinced that these frightful instruments of destruction could inhibit the chance of all-out war, could reduce the possibility of aggression itself. I never imagined that they would be the sole answer to the prevention – or waging – of major war but I was convinced they were a major component. There must be, between East and West, what has come to be called a balance of terror, which, since these weapons could not be disinvented, might produce its own sort of fearful stability – just conceivably a more durable stability than the balancing power combinations of earlier times. Since the Soviet Union was and would remain a major nuclear power, nuclear weapons must be in the hands of the Allies – which initially meant the United States. Less universally accepted, however, was the proposition that Britain must possess her own.

Attlee's Labour Government had made the original decision to produce a British atom bomb, after the Second World War; and after the achievement of the United States in making the terrible leap to the fission weapon, of immensely greater power, Churchill's Conservative Government made the decision for further development – we would have our own hydrogen bomb. This would have to be developed nationally, and without the sharing of American know-how which was now inhibited by United States legislation on nuclear information, known as the Macmahon Act. Britain's first H bomb was tested five years later, while I was in Australia. It was to be delivered by a new generation of RAF bombers, the 'V' force.

By the time I came home, however, the Soviet Sputnik had demonstrated what seemed a Russian breakthrough in missile technology, and the fear had taken root that our deterrent force might ultimately be incredible because of a missile threat to the launch airfields: aircraft themselves, too, were apparently becoming more and more vulnerable to missiles, both air and surface launched, and it had become increasingly questionable whether our delivery aircraft could reach their

targets – already assumed to be in the area of Moscow. This had led to the concept of a nuclear missile launched by rocket: the British deterrent ultimately to succeed the V force was to be such a missile, launched from an underground site. A British warhead and a British missile: Blue Streak.

Right from the start there were those who regarded a British deterrent force as irrelevant (because inadequately strong), unnecessary (because the American armoury sufficed) and/or immoral (because of its awful and indiscriminate effects), and these arguments resurfaced each time there was debate about the practical decisions which needed to be taken. Our policy was, on each occasion, reiterated. We believed in the inevitability of the nuclear dimension as an element – the key element – in deterring war. We believed for a variety of reasons, which I will discuss later, that there should, if humanly possible, be a British part in this. And we believed that this necessitated continuing development and expenditure – expenditure which we had little difficulty in showing would make only marginal difference to our conventional forces if diverted thither. In my first speech to the House of Lords as First Lord in November 1959 I told them that the Government's underlying policy had not changed (it was known that Blue Streak was in technical difficulties). Throughout the ensuing few months I had to temporize about what British nuclear force would ultimately succeed the V bombers – whose life, I emphasized, was good for another ten years – but I always stressed that we were remaining in the business. In March 1960 I spoke cautiously about the possibility of a Polaris solution, a submarine-launched missile. A month later I was able to tell the House that Blue Streak had definitely been cancelled. It was still an open question what we would have instead.

What we were to get instead started a chain of events which added a new dimension to the debate. By an agreement negotiated at Bermuda in 1960 the United States agreed to sell us a stand-off air-delivered missile, Skybolt, which would enable our V bombers to launch their weapons from afar, thus avoiding Soviet air defences. The deal could significantly prolong our bombers' effective lives. From henceforth, however, we would be dependent on American development and American goodwill. Added to those who said our nuclear deterrent force was inadequate or unnecessary or immoral there now, therefore, was a new class of critic who said that it had also ceased to be independent.

I had to deal with these criticisms at least once a year when the Defence White Paper was presented, and on other occasions such as periodic debates about NATO. On the question of adequacy – people would ask how so comparatively puny a force could impress the mighty Soviet Union – I found and find a certain lack of imagination in opponents as to just how immense was the damage fission weapons could cause. Of course our V force had only a fraction of the power of the United States or Soviet Union, but it could still eliminate more of the latter (provided the weapons got through) than a sane Russian statesman could conceivably regard as a fair price to pay for any sort of benefit of conquest. On the question of morality I adverted always to the horrors of conventional war. It was absurd to talk as if there was something desirable about returning to that: men were capable of unimaginable cruelty and wickedness to each other without the aid of nuclear physics.

On the point of necessity – that everything needful could be satisfied by the American armoury – one always had to proceed delicately. I said in January 1961 that the Soviet Union 'might miscalculate' that America might not risk her cities by using nuclear weapons in response to an attack on her European allies, and that this was one argument for our own deterrent force. This was always the crux, of course. It could be expressed as a Soviet miscalculation, but everybody appreciated the dilemma of an American President invited to threaten Moscow while knowing that the immediate response could one day be the destruction of Washington; to threaten Moscow, furthermore, because Russia had invaded Europe, the United States secure behind the Atlantic barrier the while. Plenty of people said that whether or not it was credible the Russians wouldn't believe it and the Russians could be right.

The point had to be handled with some diplomacy because it was easy to provoke charges of 'failing to trust our American allies'. Trust didn't come into it: in such Domesday circumstances Governments can only be expected to be concerned with the survival of their own people. And on the point of independence the fact was that the force, however armed, was and would continue under our own control.

In answering these various criticisms of our nuclear arsenal we were helped by the fact that the United States approved of it, and had agreed to sell us Skybolt. Describing it as our 'independent contribution to the nuclear deterrent' (for it was always important to stress that it was the whole power of NATO which was needed to deter), I said in the House of Lords in March 1961:

> It has been challenged at every level of consideration: on purely military grounds, that it is an unnecessary duplication of the American deterrent: on economic grounds that we cannot afford it: on political grounds that it is a barrier to disarmament; and on moral grounds, that it is iniquitous to use it.

I said that our force was devastating and effective; that the United States welcomed it, as creating (in Soviet eyes) a greater dispersal of centres of decision, a greater certainty of retaliation (this was the 'Why should an American President risk his cities' argument, in veiled speech); that it increased British influence with both the Soviet Union and the United States – this, perhaps unprovable, argument has sometimes been turned against us, to suggest that successive British Governments have maintained our nuclear force for impure motives, a suggestion I cannot understand since foreign and defence policy essentially has to be about the obtaining and management of influence; that it was thoroughly economic, in terms of the infinitesimal conventional strength which could accrue from cancelling our nuclear outlay; and on the moral point – and I seldom failed to stress the horrors of conventional war – I also asked why there was morality in sheltering beneath the United States' nuclear umbrella. Few of our critics wanted that umbrella taken down and thrown away.

I don't think a great deal of the basic argumentation has changed at the time I write. I still believe, as I believed in those debates in the early sixties, that there is no morality in subscribing to a strategy which involves America in having a nuclear potential one rejects on moral grounds oneself. I still think that a comparatively small force, such as the British must necessarily be, is entirely credible because of the almost incredible degree of destruction it could inflict (and this is now infinitely greater than in the days here described). I still think that *in the ultimate*, were we threatened by nuclear blackmail – 'surrender or be utterly destroyed' – a force under our own control is a more credible, perhaps the only credible, counter; that it, alone, would enable us to say, 'I don't believe your threats – look what we could do in response!' I still think that the entire nuclear dimension, although it may not be a rational and certainly can't be the sole counter to conventional aggression, *by its own terrible existence* must act as an inhibiting factor on anybody contemplating that aggression: the stakes are very high, the consequence of miscalculation appalling.

There remained, however, the practical question of how best to give effect to our policy. Skybolt would be ours, ours to control; but Skybolt placed us for the first time as customers of America rather than independent manufacturers – and customers are dependent on suppliers.

In 1962 the United States cancelled Skybolt development.

We declined an offer to take over that development. By then, and for a number of reasons, we were moving towards preference for a submarine-launched system – and not least of the reasons was the fact of American belief in it and the state of American development. We had been considering Polaris for some time – I had been questioned about the possibility in the House of Lords as early as October 1960. The cancellation of Skybolt was decisive. At a meeting in 1962 with President Kennedy in Nassau in the Bahamas, Macmillan concluded a deal on very favourable terms. It would take a little time, as the V force was phased out of service, but the British deterrent would be based on a rocket produced in the United States and launched – with British nuclear warheads

– from British-built submarines. Thereafter the Royal Navy would be responsible for the independent British nuclear deterrent. Its independence lay not in origin of manufacture but in the fact of control. We assigned our V bombers and later our Polaris force to NATO, but that was a matter of the coordination of targeting policy with Allied Command Europe. We never relinquished our independent right to control it, and nor could we.

The Americans were very conscious of the inherent logic behind European doubts about American will to exchange nuclear devastation with the Russians. They were frank about it. Their armoury was primarily intended to deter a Soviet strike against the continental United States. How not? There is nothing new or irrational about this. It led the Americans, at about this time, to float the idea of some sort of Allied nuclear force – multinational manning of delivery systems or something of the kind. I was generally discouraging about this and pointed, in the House of Lords in January 1961, to the difficulty of combining the instancy of response which a credible nuclear force must possess with the complexities of control by a multitude of nations. Control, after all, was the key to credibility. A deterrent force had to be controlled by some power in whose will a potential enemy could believe: it didn't matter a damn who, or of what nationality, manned the system. The multinational force idea lingered on for a while – until pretty well the end of my time as First Lord, in fact; and into the era which followed the Nassau agreement to acquire Polaris.

In addition to the question-mark over the credibility of decision-making which such a force might raise there was also, inevitably, scepticism over whether various nationalities could be combined in an effective crew – scepticism I shared, and which, in fact, subsequent developments (for example in NATO airborne early warning systems) have, I'm glad to say, disproved. Pursuing this point, however, in March 1963 Monty, with characteristic delicacy, asked the First Lord in the House of Lords,

'Does he not understand that the whole question of

157

multilateral mixed-manned forces is utter and complete poppycock?'

I made a polite reply.

British defence policy still recognized worldwide responsibilities, and in presenting Defence White Papers as well as the estimates for each of the Services I generally found it necessary to stress the fact. It was not only a question of current operations – these had been reduced in number and scope since my previous time in the Defence Ministry. The Malayan communist emergency was over, the Cyprus situation temporarily stilled by recent agreement to establish the island as an independent republic within the Commonwealth. Trouble in Aden was yet to come, as was a rebellion in Brunei which led to a confrontation between Indonesia and Malaysia lasting several years with Britain playing a major part. But present or imminent conflicts were one thing: quite another was the degree to which our Forces should or should not be shaped and equipped for these 'small wars' as well as for their obviously most important task of self-defence by contribution to the NATO Alliance. Had we, in other words, still a world role, and if we had, what preparations should be made to meet it, in planning the long-term structure and armament of the British Services?

In those days, more than a quarter century ago, it seemed clear that we had indeed such a role and must be ready to play it – and the next few years justified the assumption, an assumption which applied to all three Services. Speaking on the army estimates as late as May 1962, and stressing the inter-dependence of the Services, I said that the first and most vital part of the army's role did not begin and end in Europe: we seemed at that time to be needing to fly battalions in all directions at the drop of a hat, and it was essential that we had enough of them (the end of conscription put a strain on army manning about which the Government, quite justly, was often under pressure) and that they should be suitably equipped and prepared. It was, in those days too, necessary to remind Parliament from time to time that our interests and our military tasks were reflected by membership of Alliances outside the Atlantic area: the Central and the South-East Asia Treaty Organizations, CENTO and SEATO. If Britain were to impress these allies with her sincerity in participation, she had better demonstrate the capacity. In reiterating that we had this worldwide role I also took the opportunity whenever I could to show scepticism about the proposition that even major war would be over in a matter of weeks if not days. I had always felt this; and although I had to defend the concept of 'tripwire' still, the concept of conventional East–West operations doing no more than 'forcing a pause' before escalation to a nuclear level, I nevertheless derided (in presenting the naval estimates in 1962) the idea that major war would *certainly* be a 'push-button, nuclear affair, all over in a matter of weeks if not days'.

The Royal Navy was deeply involved in the debate about the proper spread of our responsibilities. It was still comparatively large. There were naval bases round the world, in Gibraltar, Malta, Aden, Singapore and so forth. It might be thought that of all Services the navy is the most versatile, in that a ship is a ship wherever sailed: the same self-sufficient weapon system moves and fights, or is ready so to do. But the crucial issue, which dominated much of my time at the Admiralty, was the question of air support for the fleet. If we were to have a navy capable of operating worldwide it had to be supported by aircraft, operating overhead and worldwide. This, we reckoned, meant a new generation of aircraft carriers, and enough of them. We had a fleet of four, and from a limited defence budget we reckoned we needed three carriers operational. It meant a considerable investment in one particular facet of one particular Service, and we acknowledged it: but the painful memories of those occasions in the Second World War when lack of air support had led to the avoidable loss of capital ships was very vivid to the generation of admirals who sat in the Boardroom of the Admiralty with me.

There was an alternative solution (for the decision to replace our carrier force would involve huge expense). The official view of the Royal Air Force was that the fleet could be better and more economically supported from island bases, by aircraft flying from ashore. There were, or there could be developed, a number – allegedly a sufficient number – of such island bases, and the planned generations of future aircraft could reach out from them to cover our ships wherever they might be. It was said that islands, unlike aircraft carriers, couldn't be sunk. The 'carrier' and 'island base' policies were set against each other and the Dark Blue and Light Blue proponents of each spent much time drawing circles on maps of remote oceans, proving what aircraft could or could not perform – and how reliably throughout the year, for ships need refit and islands don't.

The 'carrier battle' was a fierce one and went on a long time. My own view was that we needed both carrier- and land-based aircraft if we wanted to deploy naval forces as widely as we then assumed necessary. Speaking on the air estimates early in 1962, I said that I believed: 'Air bases and aircraft carriers are complementary one to the other, and both are essential if we are to deploy our military forces round the world.' That was what I thought and think. It was an expensive conclusion, but there is no way that one can shrink from the operational implications of a strategy because it is expensive. One can change the strategy, but if one deploys forces one cannot plead poverty as an excuse for not giving them air support. The question was examined incessantly, and generally with acrimony. Hugh Fraser, Secretary of State for Air, told me that the whole business made him ill, he so loathed the bitterness and unseemliness of the quarrel. I think that a number of air marshals could hardly go to sleep at night without making sure there wasn't an admiral under the bed, and vice versa! In all this Caspar John tended to be a moderating force. He was perfectly certain that our carrier force needed replacing, but he believed in care and courtesy in arguing a case. On the whole I think the professionals in the air force argued their points more compellingly than those in the navy. I remember Peter Fletcher as a particularly brilliant advocate.

Compromise was sometimes suggested. At one point the

Chief of the Air Staff, Tom Pike, asked whether we might not have the best of both worlds and combine island bases with a less expensive sort of aircraft carrier. I was attracted by this idea, and I think Caspar John also liked it – provided, of course, that it would work, and that these more economical ships (because of the genesis of the idea they were referred to as 'Pike ships' in the controversy) would be sufficiently robust and sophisticated to do the job. The Naval Staff were convinced they would not be: they argued with a wealth of detail that only the best would be good enough if it came to a fight, and after comparatively brief discussion the idea died.

I suspect we were mistaken. The best, particularly in the business of defence, is so often the enemy of the good. I used to suggest to the Naval Staff on other topics that we should investigate the possibility of cheaper and less sophisticated ships – and more of them. Sophistication inevitably led not only to basic expense, but to additional cost because it usually involved design change during construction, technology having evolved since the start of the project. It seemed to me that the older ships in the navy tended to have too many accretions, afterthoughts during construction which perverted the original design by the admirable Royal Corps of Naval Constructors. The Naval Staff answer, and there was force in it, was usually that we already had a Second Eleven Navy because of the financially constrained slowness of the replacement programme. If, they said, 'we *plan* a Second Eleven Navy we won't, in the end, be given any more of it: we'll just have a smaller Second Eleven Navy. And to match the new-style Soviet Fleet we need a First Eleven, anyway!' Maybe. I defended in Parliament the principle of quality rather than quantity, but I remain of the view that some of our specifications have been too extravagantly pitched – and it doesn't only apply to the navy. The difficulty lies in doing sensible and economic things about it in mid-project. And most ministers find themselves in mid-project.

In the end the carrier issue went to Cabinet. I was experiencing, from the other end of the telescope, the limited authority in such matters of the Minister of Defence. Our minister,

Harold Watkinson, was a tough, incisive man who knew what he wanted to do. He was a good person to work with: but in matters of this kind his power was limited. The whole matter was referred to Cabinet, and in July 1963 I was able to tell the House of Lords that Her Majesty's Government had decided on a three-carrier force. The lives of HMS *Eagle* and HMS *Hermes* were to be extended (the Naval Staff had explained to me that the bottom was about to drop out of *Hermes*, and replacement rather than extension was vital: in fact she performed competently, as far as I can judge, in the Falklands War, twenty years later). *Victorious* and *Ark Royal* were to be succeeded by one new-built ship, to enter service by the early 1970s.

Before the early 1970s, however, we ourselves had been succeeded in office by a Labour Government and the replacement carrier was cancelled. It had been incidentally delayed, in my view, by Treasury procrastination. It is a feature of our system that Treasury officials can frustrate a decision of Cabinet by the device of asking questions and requesting further information – all within their constitutional right – so that delay may eventually lead to the reversal of policy. This may seem somewhat at odds with my earlier encomium on civil servants, and to some extent it is.

The First Sea Lord, David Luce, resigned over the carrier issue (I am leaping forward to 1964, our first year of Opposition, yet to come). So did Christopher Mayhew, the Labour Navy Minister. He disagreed with the strategy which necessitated carriers but he was convinced that if we retained the strategy we should retain the means to carry it out.

We ended up, of course, with no island bases, no carriers of the type envisaged, and precious few worldwide commitments, so that arguably our policy would have been ultimately anachronistic. That assumes a lot, however. It is an uncertain world, and despite the fact that the Treasury expects the Services to justify every programme by reference to a known commitment or an existing deployment, it remains true that the unforeseen tends to happen. This argument about the unforeseen is sometimes condemned as a request for a blank cheque. Of course it cannot be allowed to become that, but there has to be, in defence planning, a certain humble awareness of how wrong *most* strategic forecasts have historically proved.

There was a great deal more to the navy programme than the aircraft carrier debate and the question of Britain's future deterrent. We had a major ship-build under way. I was able, a few months after taking over, to say, 'The total tonnage now launching is rather above the average of all the years since the war.' This was satisfying as far as it went.

We were also about to build our first nuclear-powered submarine. These 'Fleet submarines' were to have a remarkable range and the capacity to remain for a very long time submerged. They represented a technical revolution. The revolution was to be accomplished with American help, as to know-how for the nuclear propulsion unit, a delicate constitutional matter for the Americans. The key to this help was in the hand of an American admiral who exercised great personal authority in the United States as far as the whole nuclear area went. His name was Rickover.

Admiral Rickover was feared throughout the American Navy for his dynamism, his extreme ill-temper and his legendary contrariness. He blew hot and cold with very sudden alternations; and hot was fierce. It lay much with Rickover as to whether we got what we wanted in the matter of nuclear propulsion. He came to London and I was advised to do my best with him. Caspar John was away. I invited the Rickovers to dinner, together with the Second Sea Lord and one or two others. I thought the evening, which threatened to be stodgy, might be lightened by the addition of David Eccles and his wife, since Rickover was said to be interested in education and David was Education Minister (for the second time). I also invited Freddie Birkenhead. Son of the great and greatly entertaining 'F. E.' Smith and possessing not a few of his father's characteristics, he would, I thought, help the party go. Rickover mattered.

Second Sea Lord, the Rickovers and Freddic Birkenhead all arrived together and together squeezed into the very small lift which ascended to our flat over Admiralty Arch. Rickover turned to the British Admiral during the lift's journey.

'Admiral, I would like to tell you that I think your navy is second-rate!'

The Second Sea Lord understood very well the object of the evening and remained commendably restrained.

'How very interesting, Admiral.'

Freddie Birkenhead, who knew nothing of Rickover or of his significance, heard this exchange with a good deal of patriotic indignation but he didn't comment. The lift arrived. Freddie had, I think, been to another party before coming to us; perhaps to more than one. He said nothing throughout dinner but as the ladies left the dining room afterwards he turned to Rickover. There was a well-known portrait of Nelson above the dining room fireplace. Freddie uttered for the first time.

'Admiral, you bear the most astonishing physical resemblance to Lord Nelson.'

There was something in this; their features were not unlike, and Rickover preened himself somewhat. Freddie went on, however, to say, 'But, alas, with *none* of his other virtues!'

We joined the ladies. Freddie sat down next to Mrs Rickover and addressed her.

'Madam, you are a decadent American matriarch!'

This was unprovoked aggression. Mrs Rickover had said or done nothing offensive. Rickover took it all very well, but when I finally took him down in the lift he said pensively,

'That was a very funny Earl you had to dinner!'

Nevertheless, we got our nuclear propulsion agreement and the Americans were most generous and helpful about it, enabling our Fleet submarine programme to get going a great deal earlier than would otherwise have been possible.

There were plenty of problems, all interesting. There was the perennial problem of the dockyards – whether we had too many, whether they were managed economically. There was the equally perennial problem of officer recruitment. At that time the gap was beginning to show between the traditional education of the naval officer – and we still had many early entrants, people of splendid character and sterling devotion to the Service – and the ever-increasing demands of a highly technical navy. Weapon systems, communications and everything else became more sophisticated every year. We decided that it was necessary to raise the academic qualifications of an aspiring officer in the Service. We moved with a good deal of self-questioning in this matter, not from the often-pilloried British mistrust of brains and excessive regard for what is called 'character', but because simple observation showed that first-class academic and scientific aptitudes don't necessarily mean that a man can lead other men: and leadership still matters. We were looking, of course, for all-rounders, for intellectual and moral qualities together; but we'd had too little of the former. We adjusted the entry system to help this point, but we tried to do it in a way which still made possible the exception, the boy or man who failed to shine academically but who had the obvious character and personality to lead. I remain certain that the navy needs him and that we were right. Furthermore, my observation of other professions since those days has inclined me to believe that we are not short of brains, but we are often short of the qualities which enable people firmly but harmoniously to lead. It is not only in the Forces that these matter. Command, Bill Slim once observed, is a different art from management. The latter can be cerebral, technical, organizational. The former must have something inspirational about it.

Visits were, as always, enormous fun. The Naval Secretary to the First Lord, a Rear Admiral, generally accompanied him on these occasions. The one longest with me was Frank Twiss, who later became Second Sea Lord and, after retirement, Gentleman Usher of the Black Rod in the House of Lords so that we always saw a great deal of each other. He had been sunk in the war in the Java Sea and been for a long time a prisoner of war of the Japanese, one of the few such I know who survived that intensely disagreeable experience with spirit unimpaired despite obvious physical suffering and wear. He looked frail but was indomitable. He had a splendid and sardonic sense of humour and wherever we travelled he seemed to find a fellow ex-prisoner of the Japanese. They generally used to go out to dinner together, a sort of old boys' reunion; and next morning Frank Twiss always looked greener and frailer than ever. We visited the United States Navy together once, and flew from shore to the deck of an aircraft carrier. Our aircraft had on the side in huge letters 'COD' I remember, and I also remember that we landed with a terrific bump. As I got out and approached the Guard of Honour, bugles ringing out, I heard Frank Twiss say loudly, 'Now I understand what COD stands for – Crash on Deck!' It was not, I think, a popular remark. After dinner the Admiral told us that the whole crew, all ranks, had to jump six feet from a stationary position every morning, a sort of mass levitation. Back in the quarters allocated to us – I think the Admiral's day cabin – Frank Twiss, Alistair Jaffray and I discussed this with astonishment.

'We must have misheard him,' I said. 'One *can't* jump *six* foot from a stationary position! Very few, I think. Let's try!'

So we all tried, with laughably inadequate results and were still trying when the Admiral walked in to see we had all we wanted. It was impossible to explain our activity to him.

It was during that trip that I first met John Connally, Secretary of the United States Navy and later Secretary of the Treasury and a presidential candidate. In a later incarnation, when I was Defence Secretary, we had to deal with each other quite often at the time when the bankruptcy of Britain's Rolls Royce brought problems to America's Lockheed.

We visited the French Navy – a wonderful trip to Toulon and Brest. In Brest the battleship *Richelieu* had been converted into an accommodation ship and I lunched on board. As I was walking to the wardroom I saw sticking through the bulkhead the head of an unexploded fifteen-inch shell.

'What's that?'

166

My escort smiled. 'That', he said, 'was fired at us by HMS *Hood*. It didn't go off!'

Then I remembered that *Richelieu* had been shelled by us during the unfortunate affair at Dakar in 1940! I looked more closely. Round the shell had been set an oak plaque. On it was inscribed, '*Honi soit qui mal y pense.*'

On another visit, to the United States Pacific Fleet, I was entertained by an American admiral in his house. After several very strong drinks a stunningly beautiful lady joined us.

'Lord Carrington, may I introduce my wife.'

A few minutes later we were joined by another stunningly beautiful lady, identical to the first in looks and hair style, and wearing identical clothes.

'Lord Carrington, may I introduce my wife's twin sister, who lives with us.'

Some drinks and dinner later I said boldly to my host that it must be confusing to have these two indistinguishable beauties under the same roof with him. He considered, and then said, simply, 'That's their problem!'

CHAPTER 8

Choppy Water

As everybody knows, British Governments run into patches of choppy water from time to time, when the ship doesn't answer to the tiller, when nothing goes right, when Parliament and party ripple with unfavourable rumour and when every morning seems to bring to the British people a fresh newspaper headline suggesting ministerial incompetence, disarray in Cabinet, immorality in high places or something of the sort. Any administration, of any political colour, is vulnerable to this sort of thing when it has held office for some time – and the longer the time, the more inevitably vulnerable, because an extended period of power tends to breed a certain combination of fatigue and complacency. Governments become accident-prone. Publics get bored and hanker for change. Oppositions, if they're any good, recognize the moment and exploit it. The media, very naturally, flourish on such occasions. They are, essentially, entertainers – they have to be, or nobody would twist a television knob or buy a newspaper; and only a humbug would pretend that scandal is not first-class entertainment. That it is often also false in the impression conveyed and cruelly unfair in its effect on individual lives counts little. It never has.

As far as I was concerned, our patch of choppy water began in 1961, when the Conservatives had been in power for nearly ten years and Macmillan was in the fifth year of his premiership. He had ridden smoothly over some quite testing ground: as early in his time as January 1958 the Chancellor of the Exchequer, Peter Thorneycroft, had resigned with junior Treasury ministers over the direction of economic policy – described in a legendary phrase by Macmillan as 'a little local difficulty'. He had established a very firm and definite personal place on the international scene. We had experienced few diplomatic disasters, and on the whole the lives of people at home were more prosperous than they had been – a consummation Macmillan always placed near the top of his commonsense list of priorities. Then, in March 1961, he made a statement in the House of Commons. There was to be an Inquiry by a High Court Judge, Sir Charles Romer, into a recent case of espionage at the Admiralty underwater weapons establishment at Portland. I made a parallel statement in the House of Lords.

Ever since the first Bolshevik espionage and counter-espionage apparatus was formally established by Dzerjinsky in 1917 the Soviet Union has spent enormous resources, time, patience and ingenuity on placing spies and agents of one sort or another in foreign countries – by definition hostile to the Communist Fatherland, in Soviet theory. These countries must, according to Marxist-Leninist dogma, remain hostile because of their fundamental character, regardless of the disposition of particular Governments at particular times: it is historically inevitable. This theory of predestined hostility between systems, furthermore, is quite independent of 'correct' relationships between states: independent, even, of temporary alliances, such as that between Britain, the United States and the Soviet Union in the Second World War. Indeed, from the Soviet viewpoint such alliances, by inducing a certain amicable euphoria in the non-Soviet partners, can offer particular opportunities for hostile penetration. All this has been the subject of exhaustive (if sometimes belated) description in a lot of carefully researched studies, as well as personal reminiscences of a more or less sensational nature and – not least – illuminating and entertaining works of fiction.

In these circumstances, and with Soviet espionage and penetration of Western agencies pursued with such plodding assiduity, year in year out, it is hardly surprising that the Russians score a certain number of successes, and that the game of trying to counter them is a continuous one, with counter-espionage also having its periodic successes. It is

169

ironic, however, that these latter successes in detecting spies or subversives invariably provide the occasion for maximum criticism of the authorities who have been spied upon, and who – sometimes tardily, sometimes not: the whole story is seldom told, even in court – have managed to catch the spies. We read a headline: 'Spy scandal. Whitehall probe'. If lucky, we may get, 'Spies. Minister may resign', a little later. A juster headline – 'Spy scandal. No Whitehall detection or arrest for thirty years' – would sell few newspapers.

Yet the battle is incessant and must have ebbs and flows. As water runs downhill, so will the Soviet Union seek to infiltrate, subvert, convert, spy, and place agents of influence in positions of responsibility in the non-communist world, seek to discover its secrets and affect its policy. To regret this is reasonable. To be surprised or shocked by it is naïve. Certain betrayals are, obviously, more damaging than others, but there is no end in sight to this struggle. Lenin, after all, made clear that until the final triumph of the Communist Revolution throughout the world the Soviet Union is in a state of undeclared war – but a war, in my view, which can be conducted alongside more or less normal if periodically frosty diplomatic relations between states; and which, I firmly believe, should not and need not degenerate into the sort of war in which whole peoples start killing each other. Indeed the relationship, given time, skill and patience can, despite Lenin, even become something more positive than the straight avoidance of war.

Meanwhile the battle goes on. Against this background a Russian with the assumed name of Lonsdale and a couple called Kroger had entered the United Kingdom with genuine Commonwealth passports some years before my time, and had set up a spy ring targeted on our Portland underwater weapons establishment, where they obtained employment. They were helped by an Englishwoman named Gee and by an Englishman named Houghton. We caught them. In my statement in the Lords announcing the subsequent Inquiry, I said, 'We should congratulate those who were concerned in catching the spies . . . not only did we catch those who were actually spying in this case but we caught the organizers.'

Nevertheless, I have no doubt that there had been at that time a certain laxity of security at the Admiralty. It was not accorded the importance it should have been, and although we were delighted to have caught the ring we could not contest the Inquiry's main findings, though we felt bruised by them and it was unpleasant; the Press attacked us pretty sharply and some headlines already proposed I should leave the scene. Sir Charles Romer found that there were 'certain defects in Admiralty organization for implementing security', as well as what he called 'specific shortcomings by individuals at Portland'. In other words, certain people had been less than energetic in the performance of their duty – but the system itself was open to improvement. We carried out a thorough revision of all security procedures, and we reckoned we had tightened things up a good deal. We appointed, for the first time, a Director of Security. I naturally told the Prime Minister I was ready to resign but he wouldn't hear of it. Romer reported that the Security Service itself had been efficient.

Then, in July 1962, we had a great shake-up of the Cabinet. It became known as the 'Night of the long knives', and political commentators have described the wholesale expulsion and reshuffle of ministers as one of the major milestones in the slow demise of Macmillan's Government. Iona and I were dining with the Rothermeres at Warwick House, together with a large party including a number of ministers. There were many rumours and much coming and going during dinner – and I recall that a number of the ministers who lost office were dining. I was sitting at the same table as Selwyn Lloyd, the Chancellor of the Exchequer. He went, and was extremely angry! Some, of course, were promoted. Peter Thorneycroft, who had left the Exchequer during Macmillan's 'little local difficulty' four years previously, returned to the Cabinet as Minister of Defence – he proved a most powerful advocate for Defence, an excellent minister and the one who oversaw that highly desirable transformation which produced, two years later, a unified Ministry of Defence and a Secretary of State with greatly augmented authority.

I stayed where I was – it was the loftier heads which had

been lopped. Shortly afterwards the Security Service again asked to see me. They said they had reason to believe there was another spy in the Admiralty: and a few months later they visited me again and told me they had discovered who it was.

A man called Vassall had joined the Admiralty as a temporary clerk at the age of seventeen in 1941. He had then been called up for war service with the Royal Air Force and on demobilization in 1947 had applied to rejoin the Admiralty. His application had been successful and he had served as a clerk in a number of branches. In 1954 he had been sent to Moscow as clerk to the British Naval Attaché. On return he had worked as a clerk in the Naval Intelligence Directorate; and had then been posted to the office of the Civil Lord as Private Secretary. The Civil Lord at that time had been Tam Galbraith.

On 12 September 1962 Vassall was arrested and charged under the Official Secrets Act with removing and photographing secret documents over a long period – 1954 to 1961. He had for a long time been Moscow's man.

Harold Macmillan had, of course, been kept informed throughout by the Security Service. This was his prerogative as Prime Minister. He knew there was a spy in the Admiralty Building itself, another spy still active in my Department after the rumbles of the Portland affair had subsided. I knew – and knew that he knew – that the culprit had been operating for years and it was with a certain pleasure that I went to the Prime Minister when the Security people told me they had nailed Vassall. I said that I knew he realized we had had a spy active for some time. I was glad to say we had caught him.

Macmillan sighed, 'Oh, that's terrible. That's very bad news.'

I was rather crestfallen. The Prime Minister sighed again.

'Bad news in a way, that is,' he said. 'It's when we find a spy that there's trouble, more trouble than if we don't. When one catches them it can be most troublesome!'

Naturally he wanted spies detected, but he appreciated with total realism that the publicity following detection and arrest would be damaging.

And so it was – damaging and painful. Some sections of the Press served the matter up with a rich sauce of innuendo and scandalous invention. Tam Galbraith had written a polite postcard to Vassall when on holiday and the imputation was that the Civil Lord had, by so unusual and intimate a courtesy (as described by the Press), given rise to suspicion of a guilty relationship. Vassall was a homosexual. Galbraith was hounded – Vassall having been in his private office, it was represented as inconceivable that the Civil Lord was ignorant of his treachery. There could only be immoral motives for not having exposed him. The wretched Galbraith, who may have been unduly tolerant of an ingratiating subordinate but was culpable of no more than that, felt that he couldn't carry on, and offered his resignation (he had by then left the Admiralty but was still in the Government as a junior minister). Macmillan accepted the resignation. I suspect he quickly regretted doing so, realized it had been bullied out of Galbraith by the Press and that it was unfair to accept it. I suspect, too, that this led him to move more slowly than he needed when another scandal hit us all in the following year.

The Vassall affair was one of the most unpleasant episodes of my political life. The Press, or some of it, gave me little peace and a good deal of the blows were well below the belt and entirely without factual justification. Some of it could be taken with a grin – one columnist asked how one could expect better from a First Lord of the Admiralty whose forebears had been moneylenders, so the successful old Smiths were resurrected to be slandered as well. But most of it was both false and infuriating. The *Daily Express* – beside the anticipated accusations of incompetence and calls for my resignation – published the libel that I had deliberately concealed from the Prime Minister that there was a spy in the Admiralty; in effect, an accusation of treason.

Everybody who has suffered this sort of thing knows how insufferable it can be, with every movement shadowed and with wife and children included in the persecution. Life has to go on. I remember having to attend a dinner of the Royal Naval Cinematograph Association — each year there was a dinner, the hosting of which alternated between the Admiralty and the great Moguls of the cinema world. In 1962 it was the Moguls' turn to entertain us and with characteristic frugality they had not only taken a restaurant on the Embankment but built out over the pavement a replica of *Victory*'s quarterdeck. Even more curiously, the route to the restaurant across quarterdeck was lined by girls dressed as the Tower of London's Yeomen Warders! Wearing the obligatory white tie, tail coat and medals, I knew that I would be photographed as much as possible in this peculiar environment; and, with some ingenuity, I managed to arrive without exposure to a single snapshot. When I had been given a drink, however, a photographer popped up from behind the bar. Frontpage headlines next morning gave the world the picture and the banner — 'Doesn't Lord Carrington care?'

The Prime Minister reckoned that, once again, there had better be a Committee of Inquiry, and yet another judge, Lord Radcliffe, presided over the Committee. Radcliffe had already conducted a review of Government security in the aftermath of the Portland affair and the discovery of a communist, Blake, in the Security Service itself. I had told the House of Lords in a statement in October 1962 that if the Committee found my Department to have been culpably negligent I would 'naturally accept full ministerial responsibility'. It didn't and I felt no obligation whatever to resign. I gave evidence before the Tribunal — which necessarily investigated the various scandalous stories propagated by some sections of the Press. I employed Counsel to represent me; Helenus Milmo was regarded as the best at the Bar in matters of libel and defamation. When I was in his chambers going through the case with him the telephone rang. It was the *Daily Express*, seeking his services to act for them in defence against what they assumed would be attack by me. I found that satisfactory.

Since the accusations against me had no foundation in fact, Milmo had a pretty easy time. Counsel for the *Daily Express* asked me, at the Tribunal, one or two desultory questions only. Then he said his clients would like to apologize to me. I answered, with all the coldness I could, that I heard what he said.

After the Radcliffe Report had been published and the whole wretched thing was over I went to the Prime Minister. I had been told that in an action against the *Daily Express* I would probably be awarded between £100,000 and £150,000 – a considerable amount in 1963. I thought it would be agreeable to extract this and give it publicly to the King George's Fund for Sailors. I asked Macmillan for his opinion. He shook his head.

'Not a very good idea.'

He went on to say that we were moving towards a General Election (mandatory before the end of 1964), 'And I don't think', he said, 'that it would be very sensible to get the *Daily Express* against us!' I understood, although not without a wistful thought or two for Uncle Charlie and his summary justice. I asked the Prime Minister's views, however, on my going for costs: these had been considerable. Macmillan assented. We put out a statement making clear that I had been advised a libel action would succeed, but that I was ready not to pursue it if the allegations against me were withdrawn in open court and I were indemnified completely. Helenus Milmo's and other legal bills, seldom modest, were most immodest on that occasion and I am glad to say the Press bore a good deal of them. The whole matter was disagreeable from first to last. The fact of Vassall's betrayal was odious, the misrepresentation and slanders were odious, and the protracted Inquiry in a different way was odious. It did no good, of course, to relations between Press and Government. The Press had been asked for their sources for their calumnies – a sensitive area always, and no doubt particularly difficult in this case since what had been published by certain journalists had been pure fabrication and no sources can possibly have existed. Two journalists from the *Daily Mail* and *Daily Express* were imprisoned for contempt of court, since they refused to give their sources. The Vassall business, inevitably, set the scene most prejudicially for the Government's next patch of rough sea.

In the summer of 1961 a force drawn from all three Services was sent to Kuwait in response to a request for support. The ruler of Kuwait had reason to anticipate an attack from Iraq and we had a treaty obligation to help. In the usual oven-heat climate of the Persian Gulf in July a Royal Marine Commando landed from HMS *Bulwark*, followed by substantial army and air force contingents – we deployed a brigade group direct from the United Kingdom and most of it had concentrated in Kuwait in six days. In those circumstances it was no doubt inevitable that some equipment – and some men – felt the strain of heat in a way that might have been avoided had troops been acclimatized more gradually or their equipment more specifically designed for the conditions and the weather. Amid the congratulations on Britain's prompt response, which had appeared to pre-empt trouble so that Kuwait survived intact, there was retrospective criticism and the suggestion that our forces might have been in no condition to cope if the issue had come to a fight.

The War Minister, Jack Profumo, was the target for most of this criticism, which took time to mature but was kept alive until well into 1963. Then it began to be whispered that the Press – and some of his parliamentary opponents, including especially George Wigg, a sharp Labour follower of army matters – were determined to bring Profumo down. The Kuwait business, insofar as any criticism applied, was one ostensible reason; but the real crux, it was murmured, was that the minister had an irregular private life, and 'security' was involved. In the summer of 1963 the Press started publishing a titillating sequence of revelations, including that a girl, Christine Keeler, who was briefly Profumo's mistress, had also been familiar with a military attaché at the Soviet Embassy. Profumo denied his part, in the House of Commons. Soon afterwards he told the House that he had misled them as to his own conduct. He resigned.

The stories kept the Press going for ages, and the circumstances of Profumo's peccadillo surrounded scandal with a rich coating of luxury and suggested corruption in high places, so that people could fantasize and disapprove to their hearts' content. One story attributed to Christine Keeler in the *News of the World* concerned no less than the President of Pakistan, and I remembered the occasion. Pakistan's High Commissioner in London, Joseph Yussuf, was a friend of ours who had been in Canberra when we were there. He was a very nice man but unduly fond of blondes, a weakness which had led to trouble in Australia and the considerable disapproval of the Governor-General. President Ayub Khan, on a visit to London some time before the Profumo business, asked Joseph Yussuf to arrange a relaxed weekend; and as part of this Yussuf telephoned Bill Astor, our neighbour, to ask if he could bring his President to lunch at Cliveden. We were invited also. After lunch on a beautiful summer's day Bill Astor asked Ayub Khan if he would like to swim. Iona and I said goodbye and went home, and the rest of the party went to the Cliveden pool where, we afterwards gathered, a number of other acquaintances were already swimming. One of them was Christine Keeler, and when the Profumo story erupted in 1963, the British public read something like 'The day I tickled Ayub Khan's toes in the pool'! Next morning poor old Joseph Yussuf found himself on an aeroplane flying to take up a new post in Afghanistan!

Profumo was a vigorous, talented minister, most able in pressing the army's case when it came to battles over priorities. Most of these, as I have said, were between navy and air force, but the army had its problems and Profumo was an able and dedicated advocate: it was no easy task to compete against him, as sometimes had to be done. In an age which, although not yet christened 'permissive', was mighty lax in its attitude to morals compared with previous generations, Jack Profumo nevertheless had his career ruined by indiscretion with a girl. It is odd how censorious the public is now presumed to be in such matters, and Prime Ministers have to take account of what they suppose – or the Press instructs them – the public feels. I don't suggest that the private conduct of ministers is of

177

no public interest because, obviously, it can affect their balance, their sense of personal confidence; and the possibility of blackmail can be a threat to security (although I regard the 'security' cry raised in the Profumo case as having been humbug from first to last).

Nevertheless we have come a long way since Disraeli ordered his supporters to say nothing at election time about a notorious adultery of the elderly Palmerston – not, as they first thought, from political chivalry but because, in Dizzy's words, 'If it comes out he'll sweep the country!' Jack Profumo paid a penalty which could never have been exacted by Melbourne or Wellington or Pitt – indeed the hypocrisy of the idea would have astonished them. It is, of course, true that he lied about it to the House of Commons. I accept the seriousness of this and its difference from lies in private life. Nevertheless people tend to lie at first about such matters, where others are concerned. Let those who have never tried to conceal some episode in their private lives throw the first stones at Profumo: I don't think he will be much bruised. By his selfless work for others after his personal suffering he soon, once again, showed the world the fine and patriotic man he is.

Macmillan, inevitably, was puzzled and injured. By his apparent innocence he made it easy for his political enemies to paint him as out of touch both with his colleagues and the times. And his readiness to hope the best about individuals – which, as I have mentioned, may have owed something to regret at having too promptly said goodbye to Tam Galbraith after the Vassall case – was derided as naïveté and as evidence of failing powers. Then, in the autumn of that year of 1963, Macmillan became ill, underwent an operation, would clearly take a long time to recover. He resigned.

I was extremely sad at Harold Macmillan's departure. He had always been kind and loyal to me, in bad times as well as good. I greatly enjoyed his quality, his technique, his grace in politics. I respected his principles, the things he was in politics for. I remember once lunching with him when the editor of

The Times had written a somewhat sententious leader to the effect that Macmillan's administration had corrupted Britain by excessively promoting ideals of material prosperity. Macmillan had been wounded. He thought the attack malicious and unfair.

He said to me, with a good deal of feeling, 'The reason we're in politics is to try to improve the standard of life of the people who elected us and appointed us to Government. That's the object – to improve their lives, remove drudgery, promote employment and so forth.'

I agreed. Macmillan continued, 'What they do when you make them more affluent, try to help them have more money – that's really their business, not mine. I'm not appointed Prime Minister to be a great moral leader. People have to decide for themselves. If they make bad choices, make a mess of things, it's very sad. But at least one should try to give them the opportunity to make a mess of things.'

The Conservative Party had never elected its leader. By tradition, the groundswell of opinion had always made it sufficiently clear on whom the mantle should fall – which meant, of course, who would have the confidence of the parliamentary party so that in the Commons (which is where it matters) the leader could animate, guide and when necessary dominate. Since Conservatives like being in office, the question also turns on who is thought most likely to attract the confidence of the country. Particularly in the run-up to a General Election, the leader needs to prove an electoral asset, to convey a sense of strong national leadership, to make people feel their affairs are likely to be in good hands. In most, although not all, periods of history the succession had seemed pretty obvious.

It was not in the least obvious in 1963. The Conservative Party was in power, so that the constitutional question was 'Whom should the Queen be advised to send for and invite to form a Government?' It was, of course, axiomatic that the advice would be to send for someone who would be acceptable as leader of the Conservative Party, but it is worth recalling the constitutional position; and that when, for instance, Churchill was asked by King George VI to form a Government in 1940 he only thereafter – having accepted the charge – procured his appointment to be Leader of the Tory Party. Now the party needed its leader – and electoral considerations loomed pretty large with only a year at the most to go. But Britain needed a Prime Minister.

The choice was further complicated by a recent Act which had allowed peers to disclaim their hereditary titles for life and thus to stand for election to the Commons if they chose. Names which until recently would have been debarred (although the Queen may send, under our constitution, for anybody she chooses there is general agreement that he or she must, in these days, be a Member of the House of Commons) were now on the list of possibles. Amid scenes of great enthusiasm at the Conservative Party Conference in October, Quintin Hailsham announced that he was disclaiming his peerage. His hat was in the ring. So, manifestly, were those of Rab Butler, 'First Secretary of State and Deputy Prime Minister' since mid-1962, and Reggie Maudling, Chancellor of the Exchequer. Alec Home, in the Lords, was Foreign Secretary and under the new dispensation was clearly also a starter.

I was away at the time, visiting Admiralty installations and ships in Hong Kong. It was the time of the Party Conference, and I generally tried to avoid conference – I had no constituency, I felt it no essential part of my duties to be there, I found the occasion usually uncongenial and it was often a good moment to be away, with little going on at home beyond the agitations of party. As it happened, therefore, I missed this exceptionally open and interesting leadership contest, which I regret. Mine would have been a spectator's role, but the spectacle clearly had some intriguing moments. Above all we needed unity. With the General Election no more than a year away, the country would be quick to detect and punish a divided party.

Rab Butler seemed to me the outstanding contestant from the Commons, and when I later got to know him a good deal better I was confirmed in my view that he was one of the most gifted and fascinating people I had ever met. Occasionally plain-spoken, more often Delphic, his calculated indiscretions and 'double-takes' have been interminably recounted and, to me, are eternally enjoyable. He had a marvellous nose for politics. He sensed better than any man what would and would not work. It was essential to engage his interest in a subject – then he would be superb: acute, dissective and very experienced. If he were bored he coasted, without much application or concern. It is hard to say whether he would have been an effective Prime Minister. I doubt if he would have been as decisive as the office often demands. His much-quoted aphorisms were cited as evidence that he was too equivocal and too supple to provide tough leadership. In the country Rab was said to lack charisma – and we needed a winner if we could find one. There was probably a touch of steel lacking in the Butler character, and although he was undoubtedly ambitious, even that ambition was perhaps short of the tinge of ruthlessness necessary to triumph. I suspect that he wanted to be Prime Minister – but that he would have ultimately preferred one day to look back on having been Prime Minister, savoured the office in retrospect more than the exercise of power at the time. Wise, judicious and an expert at the game of politics, he was less at home with the everyday leadership of a team, and there were undoubtedly many members of the parliamentary party whom Rab Butler failed to satisfy. Circumstances brought us together in the following year and he dwelt on the immediate past a good deal. He spoke of the leadership contest (as everybody thought of it) with sadness but not bitterness. He had by then become Foreign Secretary, and liked the job; and he liked his predecessor, now his Premier, Alec Home, although being Rab there were the usual ambiguities periodically uttered, just as (about Eden, earlier) 'he is the best Prime Minister we have' has passed into British political legend. Perhaps Rab Butler's approach to politics and even to his own career was a little too oblique, insufficiently forthright and hard – qualities now and then essential.

My own view on the leadership, all considerations of personal friendship set aside (and I liked them all, very much), was that Quintin Hailsham was the only man who might, just might, win a General Election for the Conservative Party. He had sat for years in the Commons where he had been an energetic, stylish and sometimes tempestuous debater, and, later, was one of the very few I have known who, when personally convinced, was capable of swinging the Lords from one view to another. He was a warm-hearted, somewhat impulsive patriot with a first-class brain: a lawyer, but without any of the pedantry or chilliness which are sometimes caricatured in lawyers. He was a highly enjoyable speaker. Like all men of idiosyncratic character he had enemies as well as friends, but he was never dull, he could inspire, he had enormous zest and I thought it possible that he might pull a somewhat disheartened party together and turn the tide.

In the event the choice fell on Alec Home. There was no minister and no politician I more respected. He was a selfless, sensible, reflective man and I knew that his judgement in foreign affairs – and, for that matter, in any sphere to which he devoted attention – was sound, clear and always decisive. When Alec Home made up his mind, which he did very coolly and rationally, he made his case with that sort of simplicity which is often more compelling than any amount of verbal acrobatics. I was confident that nothing could go wrong in the direction of our country with Alec Home leading it. As to his management of the Commons – and his effect in the country, who would get much of their impressions from reports of the parliamentary performance – I was less sure. Never having been in the Commons, I realized that my opinion was less valuable than that of old hands in that place. We had a very quick, adroit Leader of the Opposition in Harold Wilson, who would be and was quick to make all he could of Alec's lineage and consequential (in the Wilson thesis) disqualification from serious political work or understanding of the life of the ordinary elector. The thesis – that Alec was an aristocratic amateur, fumbling with the sort of economic or technological jargon of which Wilson was pseudo-master – was wittily marketed both in Parliament and out: I was uncertain how it would go.

When I got back from Hong Kong I found, therefore, a

new Prime Minister. At once he asked me to hand over the Admiralty to George Jellicoe and to join the Cabinet as Leader of the House of Lords. I was also to be No. 2 to Rab Butler at the Foreign Office, and formally Minister without Portfolio.

As things happened, Alec Home put such heart into the party with his calm good sense that we did a great deal better than anticipated when the Election finally came a year later. We lost it by a small margin, and it must have been a bitter blow to Alec, who had worked wonders and took defeat with his usual graciousness and generosity of spirit. Soon after it was over he instituted a procedure for electing the party leader, feeling undoubted dissatisfaction with a process which could leave ambiguities or wounds, and sure of the need for the more clear-cut device of election. When the party then chose Ted Heath (who had preceded me as number two at the Foreign Office, specifically charged with negotiating our entry into the European Economic Community, vetoed by de Gaulle), Alec served him both in Opposition and Cabinet with typical loyalty and a complete absence of bile, although there must have been inevitable pain. He always and only sought to do his best for Britain. No more honourable man has ever climbed to the top.

I thought Alec Home was right to be prepared to go, as he did and when he did. Not only was it desirable to change the system of selecting a leader but the Conservative Party is always vengeful towards anybody who fails to lead them to victory. Ungenerous in defeat, they blame the man or woman at the top. They would have carped and criticized had Alec stayed at the helm of the party in Opposition.

My first experience of the Foreign Office lasted only a year but it was a full year and a good one. Rab Butler was undoubtedly nursing personal regrets, although grateful for the Foreign Office; and he left a good deal to me, which I enjoyed.

The most difficult foreign affairs problem of the year was the question of Cyprus, and Rab put me in charge of it – from the Foreign Office viewpoint. Cyprus having been given independence as a new member of the Commonwealth after the recent, painful troubles, it was officially the responsibility of the Commonwealth Office, where Duncan Sandys was Secretary of State. There was a small hole in the wall through which I used to pass – we were both under one roof – to go from our Department to theirs. Both were intimately concerned.

Duncan Sandys was a very strong minister, with an inexorable will. He was deliberate, rather slow, and presided over our inter-Departmental meetings, which went on a great deal longer than I always thought necessary. He generally managed to wear down opposition through stamina and determination; and more often than not I think he was on the right side of the argument. The problem – which I do not intend to discuss exhaustively in this book – was how to reconcile the differing desires of all the people of Cyprus, their view of their own interests as well as the historic prejudices of Greece and Turkey, with what we regarded as the legitimate – but fairly minimal – objects of the British Government in the eastern Mediterranean. The situation looked menacing at the end of 1963, just after I first arrived in the Foreign Office. Widespread conflict between Greek Cypriots and Turkish Cypriots broke out all over the island and led to a massive reinforcement by British troops, who represented pretty well the sole coherent and impartial authority, until the United Nations Organization was persuaded to sponsor a peacekeeping force, deployed on a ceasefire line. A Turkish invasion often appeared on the cards of possibility, the mainland Turks resenting what they regarded as the unequal and oppressive treatment of their fellow nationals. I had attended a Cyprus Conference when with Harold Macmillan at the Ministry of Defence in 1955. Much of the underlying malaise was unchanged and would so remain.

I got to know a good many people on the international scene during that year – including, in the context of the eastern Mediterranean, Andreas Papandreou. He had been a university professor in California and had returned to Greek politics with the reputation, consequential or not I am uncertain, of being very anti-American and very left-wing. With these credentials he had joined the Government of his gifted, agreeable – and staunchly anti-communist – father. Whether the son's reputation deserved to be so questionable (from our and America's viewpoint) I was less certain.

As usual in my ministerial career, I did a good deal of travelling. The Vietnam War was in full flood and I went there and met most of the responsible people. The Commander-in-Chief, General Westmoreland, told me that the military position was so strong he was going to win the war in three months. While in South-East Asia I attended another SEATO Conference, an occasion familiar from my Australia days. The conference took place in Manila and was uninteresting and somewhat inconsequential. So, I am afraid, was SEATO. I remember the French Foreign Minister, Couve de Murville, speaking better English than I did but insisting, when it was his due, that proceedings should take place in French. He then rebuked (in English) the translator into English for an inadequate translation of his remarks.

It was an enjoyable year, enriched by first acquaintance with some delightful people. Rab Butler's Private Secretary was Nicko Henderson, a man of huge talents who has left his own inimitable account of those (and other) Foreign Office days. But perhaps the man who most impressed me during that year was David Bruce, the United States Ambassador in London.

David Bruce, a Virginian with a beautiful voice and superb presence, was a man of great accomplishments. He was immensely shrewd, very experienced, a person of enormous cultivation and knowledge, with perfect manners; and was as skilled a diplomat as one could ever hope to meet. I have watched him at conferences in difficult circumstances, when American and British ministers, as principals, didn't get on particularly well – I have in mind at the time Duncan Sandys and George Ball; and David Bruce's adroitness and intelligence at keeping the show on the road was a sight to see.

Yet behind all the loyalty and friendship and interest and enjoyment of that year I had become certain of one disturbing thing. There was – fairly or unfairly, and I think largely unfairly

– a great tide of feeling running against the Conservative Party. There was a feeling that too many of us were jaded, that we had run out of luck and ideas, that it was time for a change. We had sailed into choppy water two or three years before. It hadn't become calmer. In my last months in the Foreign Office I was pretty sure that only about one senior man of those who worked with me would vote Conservative.

My principal function was to lead the House of Lords.

The recent Act, allowing renunciation of peerages, had affected the character and composition of our House and would continue to do so. Some of our most noteworthy colleagues or future colleagues had renounced, in order to retain or recover seats in the Commons. Home and Hailsham had left us. Wedgwood Benn (Stansgate) never joined us. Hinchingbrooke (Sandwich) only joined us briefly, preferring a vain quest for another seat in the Commons he loved. Lambton (Durham) stayed where he was in the Commons when, much later, he succeeded his father. There were others. In the short term we in the Lords, on the Conservative benches, naturally found ourselves missing some of our stars. It was this development which left me as Leader. The top men had gone.

I have been asked why I, too, did not take that road and disclaim when it was first permitted. It was perfectly simple. I thought it would have been presumptuous if the whole Government front bench in the Lords disclaimed and went seeking constituencies. It was perfectly right for Alec Home and Quintin Hailsham. Both were old House of Commons men, both had the credentials to lead the party, Alec had actually become Leader and, since the Tories were in office, was Prime Minister. I had no desire whatsoever to lead the party or be Prime Minister – nor ever had. And I had no conceivable justification for thinking that any constituency would necessarily adopt me. In the Lords, however, I now had nearly twenty years' experience. I thought there was quite enough interest and reward in that place where I knew the ropes and had, perhaps, some service to give. I soldiered on.

Since 1951 the Conservatives had been in power, but despite our large majority there was always robust scepticism of Government policy bubbling not far from the surface of our House. Our function in the Lords, apart from the conduct of Government business and the rebuttal of formal attacks on Government policy, had been to enable peers of any persuasion to criticize particular actions of Government towards which they felt hostile, to call us to account; and it must be remembered that a significant number of peers sit on the cross-benches, facing the Woolsack, and take no Party Whip. We had, I suppose, had a comparatively easy time – certainly by today's standards – but there had been plenty of occasions which engendered heat. One such, well before my time as Leader, was the debate on whether Britain should have commercial television. This led to a furious argument between Salisbury and Hailsham (at that time on the back benches). It also contained a vintage row between Reith, whose knowledge and experience of the subject were as profound as his feelings (which was saying a good deal) and Woolton. Reith accused Woolton of everything under the sun. Woolton protested, looking like an angry turkey cock. 'If the cap fits,' Reith responded in his somewhat unctuous although melodious Scottish tones, 'let the Noble Lord wear it!' We had had some lively times and some vigorous debates. But when I became Leader there was a general feeling that the Government was in trouble and that a period of Opposition might once again not be far away. This was where I had come in.

The House itself had already changed, before the right to disclaim became law. In 1958 life peerages had been inaugurated – for both men and women – and the peerage was thus significantly expanded. The measure had had its opponents within the House, of course – Lord Glasgow was the most outspoken, basing his hostility on the shortage of lavatories and the inevitably greater shortage if some were to be converted for women. He had a point, but we got over it somehow. After the Life Peerage Act we also had a larger influx than hitherto of Members who had served in the House of

Commons. One consequence, I think, was that they found some difficulty in getting used to a House where there is no Speaker. They might have spent frustrating years with speeches in their pockets, never delivered because they had failed to catch Mr Speaker's eye. They found it an agreeable relief to join a House where they had licence to speak whenever they wished, and there was, I am afraid, no doubt that some excessively availed themselves of it. The consequence was that debates went on a good deal longer, we had the sort of pressure on the parliamentary timetable which the Lords' procedures, traditions and comparative brevity had precluded in the past, and we were sometimes within sight of losing that precious convention of the Upper House – that people seldom spoke unless they knew about the subject and had something to say. There had always, of course, been previous Members of the House of Commons who had been given or had inherited peerages; but in the past the more distinguished of them had seldom played a large part except under the accepted convention. The life peers, however, were designed as people who would be made Members of the Lords to do some work, as opposed to being sent there as a penultimate reward for good deeds done. Over the years this distinction has become somewhat blurred and too many receiving a peerage have tended to regard it as necessitating maximum verbal participation – a pity, I think, and incidentally leading inexorably to the presence of too many peers and too many taking part in overextended debates. At first the life peers gave a welcome shot in the arm to the Lords, but they also to some extent changed its character as a debating Chamber. As Leader I became very conscious of this.

I also became quickly aware that an old parliamentary hand could still take one down a peg or two despite what was now quite long experience and Cabinet rank. On one occasion we had decided that we should push the Government's favourable record more vigorously and stage a congratulatory debate in the Lords to get it some publicity. Alec Home had been given a hard time in some sections of the Press, and we needed to work strenuously in the run-up to a General Election about which few were confident. I opened a debate, congratulating the Government on the success of a recent Commonwealth Prime Ministers' Conference. I spoke of our own Prime Minister's experience, enthusiasm, belief in the Common-wealth and widely admired chairmanship of the conference. It was, I proclaimed, a personal triumph. I thought I did pretty well.

Lord Attlee rose. He had a reputation for terseness and asperity, and in my experience had earned them. Now he spoke for five minutes only. It was clear that he understood perfectly why we were having the debate, exactly what I had been trying to achieve, and the entirely political purpose of my congratulations. He saw through the device and in a few devastating sentences he destroyed it. 'The object', he said, 'was to give a boost to the Prime Minister of Great Britain,' and he coldly deplored the use of the occasion of a Commonwealth Conference and the time of the House of Lords for what he described as the personal advertisement of the Prime Minister. It was a splendid performance and I look back at it and admire, although I felt differently at the time. I remember, incidentally, that Attlee used the occasion to hope that the Government, in what he described as showing untypical warmth for the Commonwealth, had 'given up the heresy of the Common Market'! He was a bitter opponent of that sort of supranational-ism as far as Britain was concerned.

My leadership of the House at that time only lasted a year. In October 1964, after what Labour christened 'thirteen wasted years', the Conservatives lost a General Election and I was out of office. Henceforth I was to lead Her Majesty's Loyal Opposition in the Upper House.

CHAPTER 9

The Lords

People more distinguished than I have described the traumatic experience of losing office under the British political system. I suppose it should not have come as a surprise: the book-makers in 1964 had been confident of a Labour victory, as had most commentators and the majority of my friends – and most of us try mentally to prepare for the worst. Nevertheless, a surprise it invariably is – and a shock. Nobody, however sagely they talk, really expects to lose an Election. In the nick of time the electorate will come to its senses, we secretly reckon. Sometimes it doesn't.

And then, suddenly, there is no office, no crammed diary, no official telephone, no car, no Private Secretaries, no red boxes, no function. I have experienced this more than once and the sense of flatness never alters. One wakes the following morning wondering what on earth to do. A professional person plans, times, may even look forward to, retirement. The enforced holiday of a Minister of the Crown – of uncertain, perhaps infinite, duration – is an experience for which it is difficult to prepare. There is, of course, a certain compensatory sensation of freedom from responsibility and return to independence, but it soon wears off and the basic frustration of Opposition – the sense of powerlessness to do anything constructive – returns. One is in politics to be able to act, and there is little action in Opposition beyond preparation for the distant mirage of Government again one day – or beyond avoidance of the sort of political catastrophes which can make that day yet more distant. Our particular experience in October 1964 was the more poignant because we had been in office so long and through such changes. We all appreciated that

Alec Home had almost brought victory out of most unpromising circumstances, but it certainly seemed that Harold Wilson was riding the crest of a wave. He had a small majority but it seemed likely he would be able to hold it and increase it; and he did. We held a gathering of ministers with Alec at No. 10 to say goodbye – a gloomy, pre-lunch occasion. Then we dispersed.

I was lucky. From the beginning it was obviously likely that I would continue to lead the Tories in the House of Lords, so that I had a certain amount of specific activity to look forward to; and I knew from former days that it would not all be easy – harder in fact than leading the House. There was also, of course, the more general business of Shadow Cabinet.

A Shadow Cabinet can be a depressing assembly. There are no immediate practical decisions to take, of a kind which can produce a sort of cement to bind the building of an administration together. The decisions of a Shadow Cabinet are about attitudes to adopt rather than things to do – and debates about attitudes can as easily be divisive as unifying. On the instant, political level there was, of course, the parliamentary battle to be carried on; and discussion, at the tactical level, of the conduct of Opposition business in the House of Commons inevitably dominated much of Shadow Cabinet in the early days. Since I could do little about the Commons, I found Shadow Cabinet meetings generally tedious, with interminable arguments about what to think up for the next Opposition Supply day. Nobody cared much about what went on in the Lords unless (which was soon very possible) our activities became a nuisance to the Conservative Party official line: the Commons, rightly, are the important Chamber – sometimes, I think, the self-important Chamber, inclined to suppose Britain's favourite reading lies in the pages of *Hansard*. Parliament was reported more fully in the Press in those days: now we seem to get little but abbreviated accounts of rows and ructions; but even in 1964 I suspect the country minded little what it read about parliamentary business, day by day.

I could, however, observe and admire the rise of certain

191

reputations, even in Opposition, and here I must pay tribute to Willie Whitelaw, Chief Whip in the Commons. He was outstanding – as good a Chief Whip as the party has ever had. Ted Heath, when he first took over as Leader from Alec Home, was experienced neither in leadership of a team nor in high office. Whitelaw's moral and political support to him was decisive in establishing his authority. In the Lords, as Chief Whip, we had Michael St Aldwyn – a very wise old bird who understood our place and had the respect and liking of all sides in it.

A Shadow Cabinet has also, of course, to evolve sensible and coherent long-term policies. Opposition gives time for constructive thought. Governments tend to be so necessarily absorbed in immediate issues that they run out of both ideas and steam. I believe we Conservatives had run out of ideas and steam by the time of the 1964 Election, and a period of reflection in the wilderness was probably healthy. Nevertheless the contemplation of long-term issues, the strategic philosophy of politics, is not inspiring when the business of Opposition begins. One has, too recently, been in the actual driving seat and office seems a very long way away, consideration of it academic.

There were, I knew, likely to be challenges for me in the leadership of the Opposition peers: but I knew, also, that parliamentary duties would be insufficient to occupy me, and I wanted something else. I also believed that a period of Opposition should be used by any politician to learn about things of which he or she is ignorant. I was, therefore, gratified, albeit astonished, when a friend one day stopped me in a passage in the House of Lords.

'How would you like to join the board of the Australia and New Zealand Bank? And become Deputy Chairman, subsequently?'

I looked at him in amazement. 'But I don't know anything at all about banking!'

'The idea is you'd then become Chairman when the Chairman retires.'

'But –' I explained again my total ignorance.

192

All he said was, 'Oh well, it's quite easy, you'll soon pick it up.'

I thought it over. I was entirely unversed in banking, but I knew a good deal about Australia and quite a lot about New Zealand. If they really meant it, I thought I'd like to try. I joined the Australia and New Zealand Bank and almost immediately became Deputy Chairman.

I sat in the same room as the Chairman, Geoffrey Gibbs. The Gibbs family have considerable banking experience, and Geoffrey, no intellectual, was a splendid man with an extra-ordinary gift for doing exactly the right thing. I suppose it was judgement: it certainly seemed instinctive. But after a fortnight I realized I still didn't understand a word of what he was talking about. I tackled him.

'Look, you're paying me money to sit here. I don't under-stand a thing you're saying. I really can't go on like this.'

'It's quite easy, you'll pick it up.'

'No,' I said, 'that really isn't good enough. I've got to get down to learning properly.'

Thereafter he sent me on a course. I used to go to Glyn Mills twice a week and spend time being lectured, most excellently and kindly, by one of the partners. Gradually I got to know a little about it, although I have never been able legitimately to describe myself as a professional banker. My use to the bank was a certain knowledge of Australia and New Zealand; and although the bank operated chiefly in London I was able to travel to Australia once or twice a year, to maintain my contacts, renew old friendships, form new ones and form opinions. This was congenial. In 1967 I became Chairman.

In those days Australia had too many banks. There were six in every small town, and I soon saw clearly that there should be amalgamations, mergers, fewer and larger banks; and that the Australia and New Zealand Bank needed to grow. The only other British-based bank in Australia was the English, Scottish and Australian Bank. We decided to try to take it over – my first experience of that particular activity, and most interesting. We succeeded. The most difficult aspect – I expect this is true of all mergers – was at the human level. Each of the two banks reckoned it had the best team for a particular job, but what had been two jobs was now one. It took some years for the new bank to settle down but ultimately it did – and prospered exceedingly. Later – and I think perfectly rightly – the bank was patriated to Melbourne. It continued to prosper exceedingly. It has recently bought Grindlays.

A small percentage of the ANZ Bank was owned by Barclays Bank; and I was soon asked to join the board of Barclays. On three different occasions I have left Barclays, on becoming a minister, and have later been invited to rejoin. It is a splendid and civilized institution and my association with it is a source of much pride. I felt the usual diffidence at first. A colleague at the ANZ Bank reassured me before my first Barclays board meeting.

'If it's anything like the Midland,' he said, 'it's like High Mass without vestments!'

Barclays afforded me yet more opportunities to travel, because they put me on to the board of the overseas bank, at that time called Barclays Bank International. I visited parts of the world I didn't know, particularly Africa, and added something to a stock of knowledge which was particularly helpful when one distant day I became Foreign Secretary. I was lucky in receiving at this time another commercial invitation, to go on the board of Schweppes – later to become Cadbury-Schweppes. My previous 'overlord' at Defence, Harold Watkinson, was the Schweppes Chairman, and asked me to join them: like Barclays, I have also left and rejoined Cadbury-Schweppes on three separate occasions – another very happy association. I know some people feel that out-of-office politicians have little contribution to make to a commercial company, and of course they have no specialized knowledge of whatever the company is manufacturing or marketing, whether it be fizzy drink or financial services. But I have always found outside directors with some acquaintance with public affairs to be most welcome. I believe they can inject a certain breadth of experience and a different and perhaps sometimes more objective dimension into the formulating of company policy. One can, I think, contribute valuably

– not to running the business but to the making of the major policy decisions; and I humbly believe that sometimes I did. Furthermore the insights gained into the views of the financial and business community about politics and politicians have invariably been salutary.

Visits to Australia generally provided unscheduled entertainment apart from banking. On one occasion my visit coincided with one by Harold Macmillan, now in retirement, who was touring much of the world with his grandson, promoting the first volume of his memoirs, published in 1966. Macmillan had arrived by P & O liner, and held a promotional Press conference at exactly the same time that U Thant, Secretary-General of the United Nations, had flown to Paris on one of the periodic and unsuccessful attempts to negotiate an end to the Vietnam War. The Press were anxious to learn Macmillan's views on this. He expanded on the contents of his forthcoming book, and the journalists sought, without much success, to bring him to current political events. Minds failed to meet. Eventually an irritated newspaperman snapped:

'Mr Macmillan, do you appreciate that at this very moment Mr U Thant is flying to Paris and is seeking to end the Vietnam War!'

Macmillan inclined his head wearily. He murmured, 'How very good of him.'

It was undoubtedly the Macmillan we remembered! Macmillan's shafts delighted me right up to the end of his life. I recall sitting next to him during the enthronement of Robert Runcie as Archbishop in Canterbury Cathedral. Exceptionally ecumenical, the processing clerics were drawn from many religions and most Christian communions. Last, before the new Archbishop, came Cardinal Hume, looking magnificent. Macmillan's eyes followed the Cardinal intently as he moved up the aisle. Then he murmured to me, 'He looks like the landlord, coming to see whether the tenants have kept the place in order!'

*

At this time Iona and I, having a certain amount of unprecedented leisure, began modestly collecting things. Things for Bledlow.

We had started educating ourselves somewhat in Australia, amassing a collection of classical records and for the first time acquiring a good record player and becoming absorbed in music. We had more time to go to the opera which we both love. I had always been a compulsive buyer of books; now I had more opportunity to read for pleasure. Also in Australia, we had decided to learn something of Australian pictures. There were, during our time, some outstanding Australian artists – Dobell, Drysdale, Nolan, Boyd. We enjoyed them the more, the more we learned. And we decided to buy some pictures there, reminders of a happy chapter in life and embellishments for Bledlow in due course, our own personal acquisitions.

After our Election defeat in 1964, I also started to go to auctions at Christie's and Sotheby's, looking for decent pieces of late eighteenth-century furniture, which at that time it was possible to find at moderate prices – indeed I wish I had found a good deal more. Bledlow was bought by my family at the end of the eighteenth century and the house – which was lived in by the eldest son of the family while his father was at Wycombe Abbey – has a certain feeling of that era, although the original dwelling was built in the mid-seventeenth century. It is an architectural mish-mash. There was a Tudor structure in a field behind, and one John Banks pulled it down and built a new house in 1648. This was much altered, and most of the present building dates from about 1700. When I was doing something to the house and installing heating in 1950 we found a curious little cubby hole, a place that had been bricked up and to which there was no entry except from above; no doubt it had once been a cupboard, and the door sealed and bricked. Shining a torch down, we could see a pair of shoes – wooden-soled with leather uppers. I took them to the London Museum, asking for identification. They told me how extraordinarily nice of me it was to bring these and present them to the museum!

'What are they?'

'They are court shoes of the late seventeenth century.' They must have been placed there and abandoned not long after the house's original building, and before 1700.

We Carringtons acquired Bledlow from Samuel Whitbread and greatly altered it in about 1800, putting in late Georgian long sash windows. Later again the house was a school, and then occupied by a tenant-farmer until our own time, with farmyard immediately outside, a paddock, and certainly no garden. It is a house of agreeable proportions, its brick a particularly soft rose colour and having on most fronts a very satisfying balance between window and wall. Inside, the rooms are light and of modest size, and each new piece of furniture we found gave us pleasure. We started, too, to collect some watercolours in a small way.

I suppose the interest I discovered in this, so different, side of life, and the friends I made thereby, were to lead to a great compliment one day some years ahead, when I was invited to be Chairman of the Trustees of the Victoria and Albert Museum. The job, held until very recently, gave me enormous happiness. It was a total contrast from politics, banking, farming or business. It was by no means always easy – the buildings are falling down, there is never enough money, and the personalities who press their policies in the artistic world make politicians look like flabby-willed innocents. But it was always fun – and a privilege. It helped my induction as Chairman that the museum was directed by a man of outstanding talent.*

Our period in Opposition went on for nearly six years. I spent a good deal of it travelling, and not all my journeys were made as a banker. In December 1969 I went as an Opposition politician on a fact-finding tour to Nigeria where a war, described by some of the Press with gross exaggeration as the 'bloodiest civil war in history', was going on between the Nigerian Federal Government led at that time by General Gowon, and the breakaway Ibo province, seceding as an

* Sir Roy Strong.

independent state of Biafra, in the south-east of that huge country.

The trip, on which Miles Hudson, an old friend from Conservative Central Office, accompanied me, started badly, with uncertainty as to whether a carefully constructed programme (by our High Commission in Lagos) was going to survive in anything like its advertised form. The night before we left I had a message from the Prime Minister, Wilson, to the effect that General Gowon did not find my visit convenient. As I was going both to Nigeria and Biafra it was clearly a pity from the Nigerian point of view if I took back to the Conservative Party the arguments and versions of only one side in the war, and I made this pretty clear, but when we set out it was still uncertain whom we would meet and how much we would see. We had to change aircraft in Paris, and were met there with the news that no hotel room of any kind was available for us in Libreville, in Gabon, our first stop en route to Biafra; and that the chief Paris correspondent of the *Daily Express*, John Ellison, would be travelling with us. The *Daily Express* and I had had our differences in the past, but Ellison was a most agreeable man, and I knew that the Conservative Party leader – now, and for the previous four years, Ted Heath – wanted my visit to attract at least some publicity and demonstrate the party's concern with fact-finding and with Africa.

It was perfectly true that there was no hotel room in Libreville, a most unattractive town. There was, however, a delightful Anglo-French representative of the British Representative, a M. Robert Tyberghein, and he looked after us excellently. At about 9.30 in the evening we drove to an airfield, in a corner of which stood a deserted and decrepit-looking DC4 aircraft with a ladder hanging over the side. After half an hour the crew, two Frenchmen, arrived. They were to fly us to Uli airstrip, in Biafra, and we were told they were definitely flying 'for money' and not 'from mercy'. I was relieved. I thought it slightly more likely that they would be competent. The aircraft was loaded with sacks of rice and a good many cockroaches and weevils. And us.

We finally took off on what was meant to be a two-hour flight at 10 pm, and arrived at Uli airstrip – a widened road – at half past midnight. The airstrip had been bombed by the Nigerians during our flight and we had to wait until that was over. There were one or two formalities on arrival, including a request for a visa which John Ellison lacked – indeed he lacked any sort of papers but carried everything off with aplomb, saying that he would pay for his visa (2500 francs) on the way out. Escorted by a chief of protocol, we all drove into the town of Owerri, recently captured from Nigerian troops and now established as the Biafran seat of government. Next day we began the series of interviews which constituted the official part of our visit.

These interviews with the top people of Biafra culminated in one with Colonel Ojukwu, the Biafran leader, two days later. Each interview until the last followed a set pattern, starting with twenty-five minutes' abuse of Britain and the British Government for the attitude taken towards Biafra. Sometimes, as with General Effiong, Chief of Staff of the army, twenty-five minutes extended to fifty: abusive all the time. I sat through it, merely saying stiffly that I accepted none of the premises or conclusions put forward. It was not possible to walk out. Not in Biafra.

Ojukwu, with whom I had what he treated as an audience, was obviously highly intelligent, and made a cogent and effective speech, omitting the routine tirade against Britain – for which I was grateful since it was becoming wearisome. Equally obviously, he was extremely conceited. Every gesture was theatrical – he was surrounded by a clearly frightened entourage of sycophants. When he first entered the room where I was, he seated himself on some sort of throne, slowly took out a cigarette and lit it, then remained silent for thirty seconds before starting his remarks, fixing his large, intense eyes on us the while. His remarks lasted an hour. An act of some kind was clearly required from me in response, and I led off with a long, dignified and confident discourse about nothing very much.

After that our exchanges became rather more interesting. I

asked Ojukwu what his enemy in Lagos would tell me. 'They will point', he said, 'to the small size of Biafra on the map. They are mesmerized and seduced by the map.' Ojukwu was clearly motivated by pride, to a considerable extent: he would never accept Nigerian sovereignty. The people of Biafra were starving, as the world knew, but relief flights from outside needed the cooperation of his Nigerian enemies and he would not accept help on those terms. Ojukwu was less concerned about starvation than a European might suppose.

We were able to see some of that starvation during our short visit, and it was grim. We visited a Catholic mission run by an Irish priest, doing a wonderful job. 'I haven't time for religion,' he said. 'I spend my time trying to feed the starving.' Very pro-Biafran, he nevertheless recognized the faults of the strongly Catholic Ibo people, who were undoubtedly cleverer and sharper than their neighbours but who, time and again, had allowed these qualities to lead them into domineering arrogance; and thus into trouble. I talked at the mission about the Nigerian air-raids. Nigerian Migs had undoubtedly, on occasions, attacked anything moving in Biafra, pretty indis-criminately. One priest told me he had witnessed a raid on a Biafran market place from which the death toll was five hundred.

It was impossible not to have sympathies for Biafra. The Biafrans were maintaining some sort of fabric of civilized life under appalling economic pressure, and in confrontation with a hugely superior military foe. Law courts were sitting. Justice was being dispensed. Education was somehow kept going – children were being taught to write in sand. The postal service still functioned – we saw a postman, complete with bicycle and postman's hat! Their army, convinced of the rightness of the cause of Biafran independence, felt that it was doing bravely against the odds, and that it would never be beaten in the field – Ojukwu certainly held this belief. He thought the Nigerian Federal Government would sooner or later get bored with the war, and the Federation break up. Meanwhile he just had to hang on.

We visited a battalion headquarters at the war front, and

thence walked forward to inspect well-dug and well-sited trenches, with Biafran soldiers manning an odd assortment of weapons: the Nigerian enemy was visible about two hundred yards away. The Biafran divisional commander, trained at the British Cadet School at Aldershot, told me that everything was done according to British Army standards. 'The trouble is', he said, 'that the enemy, also trained in England, don't stick to the rules!' It upset him very much. From Biafra we flew back to Libreville, where, although an hotel bedroom was obtained, conditions were dirty and disagreeable.

It was now time to visit the other side, and after two barren days in Libreville we flew to Lagos.

I found our High Commissioner in Lagos firmly committed to the Nigerian side, and any suggestions of mine that Biafran morale appeared pretty good and Biafran determination unshaken were clearly regarded as evidence of brainwashing. The British Military Attaché gave an optimistic briefing on the course of the war and seemed a little put out when I told him my story of how General Westmoreland, in Saigon, had assured me victory would be his in three months. The British military observer, Colonel Cairns, later gave me what I suspected was a more realistic appraisal. He told me that any ordinarily competent army could defeat the Biafrans in a very short time. The Nigerians weren't and therefore hadn't. Battles, according to Cairns, generally took an inconclusive form. Every weapon was discharged in the general direction of the opposition, machine guns 'hose-piping' trees and not infrequently their own side. After about a quarter of an hour both sides withdrew rapidly, and later returned cautiously: the first to return claimed a bit of ground and the victory.

I found the senior Nigerian civil servants I met to be talented, capable people. The soldiers, too, were well-informed men – and particularly well-informed about British politics. This, indeed, had also been so in Biafra where the ex-Premier of the Eastern Region, a few days before, had said to me,

'Congratulations on the by-election results!'

'What were they?'

'A 10 per cent swing to you in Wellingborough, and 14 per cent in Louth.'

Not bad, for a besieged country the size of Yorkshire fighting for its life!

I thought General Gowon's move to redivide Nigeria into twelve separate states had been shrewd. It meant there were more jobs to go round than there had been before, and more consequential contentment – and local support. For Biafra to survive in the longer term it would have needed to be joined by the two neighbouring south-eastern states, and I was assured that no plebiscite in those states would bring them to join Biafra. Ojukwu would have needed Port Harcourt, to be viable indefinitely; and, unless by conquest, he would not get it.

My interview with General Gowon was as different as it would be possible to imagine from that with his opponent in Biafra. Gowon was a most agreeable, likeable man, modest, devout, manifestly honest, and neither so articulate nor so devious as Ojukwu. His instincts were pro-British. He wanted to help relief flights to Biafra – it was clearly in his political interest to do so, since Ojukwu was making a lot of capital from the world's reactions to pictures of starving Biafrans – but Gowon complained that whenever negotiations attempted to resolve the matter, he was required to make concessions prejudicial to his conduct of the war, and Ojukwu never. This, I think, was true.

Gowon began our interview by saying, 'You were at Sandhurst, weren't you?'

'I was.'

'So was I.' He paused thoughtfully and then added, 'That's the trouble with that fellow Ojukwu. He was only at Eaton Hall!' Eaton Hall was the Officer Cadet school in Cheshire for National Service rather than regular officers.

I returned to London depressed. Both sides in the Nigerian civil war seemed firmly dug into their positions. I could see few signs of hope for negotiation. The Federation of Nigeria might break up amid war fatigue and internal unrest, as predicted by Ojukwu, but it did not seem very likely. It was more possible, I thought, that Gowon could one day be replaced by others determined to prosecute the war more vigorously. I could understand Ojukwu's fears for the Ibo people, and I hoped that any ultimate out-turn would produce some sort of safeguards for that gifted folk. But I reckoned it was in the British interest that the Nigerians should win, should end Biafran secession. We had huge investments in Nigeria, including enormously valuable oil investments. We needed Nigeria stable and unified, not divided and at war. And it seemed to me that the best outcome would only come, however slowly and painfully, from Nigerian victory.

But my principal responsibility during these years of Shadow Cabinet and Opposition in the 1960s was to lead the Tory peers, and from the first I remembered and appreciated the example set me during my parliamentary novitiate by Bobbety Salisbury, and tried to follow the same broad principles. To lead the Tories in the Lords when there was a Conservative Government was a comparatively simple matter at that time, although there would always be some dissidents, or some who thought our policy inadequately robust. To lead them in Opposition, when they had a majority in the House and strongly objected to many of the Labour Government's measures, needed more delicate handling. Of course there was plenty of straight politics with little difficulty in producing a united party. The Prime Minister, Wilson, began by taking an attitude towards the Polaris project – that our nuclear armoury should not and would not be truly independent because of the American provenance of some of it – which I knew to be nonsense in logic and reckoned (and said) was a viewpoint advanced to placate the left wing of his own party, like much else. If we chose, our deterrent force would be entirely independent, because we would command and control it. But many issues were more controversial on our side.

I tried to apply the Salisbury Convention: and, like Salisbury,

I found the greatest difficulty lay in striking a proper balance between, on the one hand, giving my troops a taste of battle, allowing enough uninhibited passion to find voice; and, on the other hand, keeping them sufficiently minded that it was not our job to provoke a constitutional crisis, that the House of Commons had been elected by the people, that the Government had a majority in that House and that Government must go on. Both sides of the balance were necessary. We had to behave responsibly; but I couldn't expect our supporters to lie down and be silent when something to which they took strong and principled objection was being proposed. Plenty of them felt that their right and their duty was to protest; and they could protest both with their voices and with their votes. The former need not be discouraged, but the latter needed handling. On the whole, matters went tolerably well.

The most difficult issue was probably Rhodesia. Ian Smith unilaterally declared the independence of Rhodesia in the autumn of 1965. We were still getting used to Opposition, struggling with that sense of half-incredulous irritation which besets any party deprived of power after a long stint in office. A good many Conservatives sympathized with Smith, although I think that most regretted the course of events and foresaw little long-term good. In due course, however, the Labour Government accepted a United Nations proposal that economic sanctions be imposed on the 'rebel' Rhodesia. These sanctions were regarded as foolish by us Conservatives. We did not believe they would prove an effective way to bring about progress, they would poison the possibilities of negotiation, and they were known to be widely and successfully evaded. Sanctions had to be renewed annually by an Order debated in both Houses, and each year, therefore, there were all the makings of a first-class parliamentary row, with the Salisbury Convention strained to breaking point and beyond. Sanctions were formal Government policy, of course, but the British electorate had given no opinion on them since our General Election had preceded Smith's declaration. The Salisbury doctrine did not apply.

I believed, nevertheless, that it was right to get our people to abstain rather than vote against sanctions. It was perfectly true that these had not been put to the country nor formed part of a Labour manifesto – nor could they have been. But they were, by then, an important (albeit, as I thought, unwise) part of the Government's foreign policy. The Government could not shrug off a defeat on sanctions in the Lords: its credibility would have been destroyed internationally. It had a strong majority in the Commons. There would, in other words, have been a major constitutional crisis; and I could not believe that the British people would necessarily decide that the Lords had been right in their stance or right to provoke that crisis. I was sure that we should point out to the Government the folly of their ways over sanctions; but I did not believe it was the battleground on which to stage a major fight on the constitution. Our line, therefore, must be disapproving abstention. There were plenty who thought we were too weak, but I was completely unrepentant. It was, as time passed, more and more difficult to keep the Tory peers on course in this matter, and I understood why. I could sympathize, but it was my job to persuade them that there was a higher interest than impeding ineffective economic sanctions against Rhodesia.

The difficulty, therefore – and Rhodesia was only an example, although perhaps the most poignant example – was to make our views clear: to oppose, demonstrate against, often mitigate policies we disapproved of; but to keep opposition within bounds – unless there was an issue on which we manifestly had the feelings of the people of Britain behind us. But in all this it was also necessary to keep up the morale of our troops, to show them the enemy and encourage their combative instincts, to keep the fight going. It was not entirely unlike 1945. Experience of Opposition leadership, however, began to crystallize my views on House of Lords reform.

I had always been clear that the function of a second Chamber was threefold – to revise, improve and, on occasions where it could with prudence and propriety be done, reject and thus generally delay legislation; to initiate debate on issues of public concern; and to act as a final and essential blocking mechanism against extremism by a Commons majority of whatever political complexion, which might put our liberties and institutions at risk. I found myself thinking more and more about this last function. The other two – revision, debate, sometimes delay – were adequately dealt with by the existing House and they were not of such huge constitutional consequence as to call its composition too much into question. Of course there had always been grumbles, mostly though not exclusively from the political left, about the unrepresentative nature of the Lords and the iniquity of the hereditary principle in a modern legislature; but the Labour leaders in both Commons and Lords had been sensible and experienced men who knew the value to any administration of a second Chamber; such opposite numbers to me as Frank Longford and Eddie Shackleton were very sound constitutionalists. There was on the left – including the moderate left – a general sense that the existing House of Lords was an anachronism; but a good many privately thought it a useful anachronism, and few except the far left, single-Chamber men, the outright abolitionists, had any practicable ideas as to what one could put in its place. Nor, for that matter, had the Conservatives – many of whom also felt with unease that the *status quo* was difficult forever to defend.

But when I thought about the crucial part that the Lords might be forced to play in a situation of real danger – in the sort of situation, however far-fetched it might appear to recall it, which had overtaken the German Reichstag in 1933 – when I reflected that this, although it might never have to be invoked, was the ultimate justification for a second Chamber with power to restrain and to force a pause; then I realized, as I think I had always realized, that the existing composition of the House of Lords was not simply hard to defend in political theory – it was actually dangerous. A House which in effect appealed to the people by blocking the House of Commons had to have some sort of demonstrable authority. Our House consisted of hereditary peers, of first creations or of life peers; and, of course, of bishops. The first category were legislators because of the performance or fortune of their forebears: the second two categories were there on the recommendation of a Prime Minister – in effect they were nominees, however meritorious. I did not believe the House of Lords, unless reformed, could play what might be its most essential role in history: it could not play it with the necessary support of the nation.

My conclusion was not exactly novel. The preamble to the Parliament Act of 1910 referred to the problem of the composition of the Lords as being so urgent 'as to brook no delay'. Over fifty years later I felt the same, and nearly eighty years on I feel so even more. But the problem then as now was easier to state than to solve, for any change in the composition of the Lords which strengthened its position in the country – and it was that which was required – inevitably aroused the hostility of at least part of the House of Commons. A reformed House of Lords could and undoubtedly would use its enhanced status to play a more energetic part in the parliamentary process, and the House of Commons could feel diminished thereby, challenged in its authority as sole representative Chamber. There had always, therefore, been more disposition to grumble about the Lords than to agree on what should replace it. There were, of course, the extremes: the abolitionists who wanted a single Chamber and the traditionalists who would have no change. Most people, however, were in between, but organizing a consensus for reform was a different matter.

I was determined to try: obviously both main parties needed to be associated with the attempt and I welcomed a Government initiative which led to a sequence of talks. The Leader of the House was Shackleton and the Leader of the Commons was Dick Crossman. I was supported by George Jellicoe, my deputy, who had followed me at the Admiralty, and Iain Macleod held a watching brief for the Conservative Opposition in the Commons. The five of us were, I think, at least agreed on the basic object, on the framework of our conferences. We all wanted a second Chamber which could be recognized as having a right to play its proper and most important part in the constitution. We all thought that this was incompatible with a House consisting of inheritors and nominees. We all recognized that the existing House did its job perfectly well in practice – it was its theoretical basis which could be mortally attacked at the critical moment. And we none of us wanted that.

We came up with a scheme. As in all such schemes, each side knew that selling it to all supporters would not be plain sailing. Shackleton and Crossman reckoned they had come a long way towards us. They had their outright abolitionists to handle, but nevertheless they were prepared to back it. For my part I felt I could commend it to the Tory peers, although I knew there would be some powerful reservations.

A White Paper was published by the Government and in November 1968 the Lord Chancellor, Lord Gardiner, inaugurated the Lords debate upon it, and Jellicoe welcomed it for our side. The White Paper envisaged a two-tier House, with a voting strength of some 200–250 Lords of Parliament who would all be 'created' peers. They would be remunerated and there would be a retiring age. A committee – suggested as a committee of the Privy Council – should periodically review the composition of the reformed House, in which it was envisaged that in each Parliament the cross-bench peers would hold a certain balance between the proponents of party. Regular attendance – at not less than one third of our sittings – was to be a condition of voting. The House would have power to delay the approval of legislation passed by the Commons for up to six months, in order to give time for second thoughts.

There was also to be a second tier, the non-voting peers. These would be 'leading members of the community' (who might only serve for a limited number of sessions) and those existing hereditary peers who were not created afresh in order to serve as voting members of the reformed House. It was thought that their inclusion would give some continuity to our deliberations – and, of course, some were outstandingly expert in particular fields although probably only attending for occasional debates where their expertise applied.

Some authoritative attacks on the idea were launched in our debate, and some valid points made. I doubt whether our proposals would have lasted a great many years, and, as in all compromises, there were anomalies: but they would have begun a movement and most of our supporters reckoned that movement was essential and that it should be in this direction. Salisbury and Swinton, my old chiefs, among others, had strong misgivings. Bobbety Salisbury certainly did not support the hereditary element in our House by any appeal to logic: but he made the fair point that a voting House composed of the relatively illustrious would inevitably be an old House – the hereditary peerage enabled some young men to serve, and he pleaded for some fifty hereditary peers to be retained as full voting Lords of Parliament. Others argued that continuity was given some assurance by the hereditary peerage: a peer (like me, for that matter) could serve an apprenticeship, perhaps hold some sort of office, continue as a greybeard, cumulatively doing a long stint in Parliament and adding thereby to its corporate experience. Others pointed to the comparative normality of peers: we were a random selection, most of us undistinguished by particular achievements or ambition or popular appeal, and for that very reason had a certain claim to be representative (although in a different sense from elected Members). We were, in a word, ordinary because we were legislators by luck rather than by distinction, and that ordinariness could give us a certain empathy with our fellow citizens. And plenty of peers said, in effect and unarguably, 'Surely it works pretty well!'

I did not disagree with much of this. In my own speech I said, and meant, 'I do not think that any reformed House, whether it be elected or nominated, will be any better in composition than is the present one.' But I tried to bring the House back to the essential point – the weakness which the hereditary position of most of our Members produced for the whole House. A few months before our debate the House had, in fact, neglected my advice and reversed one of the annual Orders about Rhodesian sanctions. I referred to this – a touchy matter, of course – and said, accurately, '*All* public comment focused on the unelected, hereditary Chamber rejecting legislation.'

I knew that this was the critical point. If the country did not adequately believe in us we could not in the end do our job when it most mattered; and I had come to believe it might one day matter very much indeed. Since the powers of the Upper House were also covered by the White Paper, some (including Salisbury) disapproved of what they saw as a diminution of its formal authority. Others, however, felt our real strength was already minimal – because, or largely because, of our composition. I agreed with them. What mattered was less the House's nominal powers than the extent to which in the last resort the country would accept and support it as a bulwark of the constitution, and that depended on the country's perception of the Lords and, very definitely, on who they were. As it was, a good many peers resented what they felt as anomaly. Men who had recently played distinguished parts in politics and in the Commons couldn't swallow the enforced feebleness of the Upper House, however agreeable its atmosphere. 'It is damaging to our dignity', Rab Butler, now a life peer, said, 'and also to the British Constitution that when the Upper House, by a majority, makes a decision . . . its judgement will be reversed or else lead to a minor or major political crisis.' That was the crux and it turned, inevitably, on who sat in our House: here was the nettle and we had grasped it. There was also the purely political point that the White Paper put the Labour Party formally on record as believing in a second Chamber. In the Lords the Government won the vote approving the proposals by 251 to 56.

The proposals foundered in the House of Commons when the Government introduced them as a Parliament Bill three months later. Leading the attack and following each other hour after hour in a sort of point/counter-point, although their philosophies were generally and starkly opposed, were Michael Foot and Enoch Powell, a collaboration of left and right.

Enoch Powell's eloquence, his gift for the telling phrase, his limpid reasoning in the development of argument – all these were legendary. They had made for him a unique reputation, in print, on public platforms and in the House of Commons, where he was regarded with awe and a good deal of affection by friends and opponents alike. He was an extraordinary man. I remember him making a speech to the Party Conference of almost hypnotic beauty explaining why we should not remain east of Suez – we were no longer that sort of power, it was not our concern. It was exquisitely compelling. Conference gave him a rapturous reception. They then voted strongly that Britain should remain east of Suez. Whatever Powell's case, he had the reputation of expressing it with a clarity of language few could equal but which, on reflection, not all could understand or accept. It was a spellbinding, captivating talent.

Not having been at any time a Member of the House of Commons, the spell had never captivated me. The occasion of Powell's departure from the Shadow Cabinet into which Heath had brought him back (the 'Tiber flowing with much blood' speech, held to be exacerbatory of racial tensions which we all recognized) had impressed me unfavourably – not because I believed distorted accounts of what Powell's views were, but because we had all agreed, after discussion, the line which should or should not be taken and Powell, in my opinion, had gone against it – without dissenting to the faces of his colleagues. I was not surprised that he opposed our Lords reform scheme. Powell, behind his screen of formidable, almost pedantic, logic was at heart a romantic. He was a passionate believer in the distinctive tradition of the English Parliament, and he referred to the peerage as essentially a parliamentary peerage.

'The functioning and working peerage of this country during the last five hundred years has been an emanation of Parliament,' Powell said. He called the House of Lords a prescriptive Chamber – that is, I imagine, deriving from long usage and custom. He rejected with scorn the idea that a hereditary nobility, bearers of inherited titles of honour, could (as in every other European country) exist without a parliamentary duty and an inherited right to perform it. One can, of course, argue against the existence of such a nobility on egalitarian grounds but that was a different case. Powell said in effect that hereditary peers must be Lords of Parliament or nothing; and that nothing could replace them without absurdity and gross breach of our traditions. He objected strongly to the extension in the Bill of the principle of nomination.

'A nominated second Chamber,' he said, 'such as is implied . . . will not work, will not be tolerated and is unacceptable to the majority of Honourable Members.'

In the Committee stage he had a great deal of fun taking clause after clause to pieces. 'Where we are faced with so many absurdities,' he observed, 'it is difficult to find a rational line on which the division can be drawn.'

Michael Foot had equal fun – and equal stamina, for the Commons proceedings lasted a very long time. Professing a similar devotion to the traditions of Parliament, his starting point and his formidable qualities differed. Eloquent, like Powell, he was a demogogue as well as a brilliant pamphleteer; and like Powell he had admirers, however politically hostile, in all parts of the House. Foot's favourite predecessors were the men of the seventeenth-century Long Parliament who had waged war against the King and his ministers, and had led to the Protectorate of Cromwell and the abolition of the Lords (although it is often forgotten that Cromwell soon cre-ated a new Upper House, a Lords of his own, rewarding many of his friends thereby).

'I am', said Foot, 'in favour of a republic.'

He was, like Powell, also a romantic at heart, but one who romanticized left-wing causes and had some difficulty in perceiving evil to the left of him. He managed, at times with certain intellectual contortions, to harmonize revolutionary rhetoric with a sincere attachment to democracy. It was pre-dictable that Foot, like Powell, disliked the extension of nomi-nation and, consequently, of patronage which our proposals implied. Above all he saw nothing in the Bill, he said, which would alter – indeed it would perpetuate – the fact he most deplored, that, 'The constitution of this country is weighted permanently on the side of reaction.' And he ridiculed – and condemned – the basic rationale of the proposals, that there should be some power of restraint by a second Chamber on the House of Commons.

'How', he asked, 'could a constitutional arrangement be devised to ensure that when there is a Labour majority in this House there should be a Conservative check upon it in the other place, and when there is a Conservative majority in this House there should be a Labour check upon it in the other House? That is an extremely difficult constitutional puzzle . . .'

They both loudly mocked the mathematics which had led to a suggested size for our new House.

All this was enjoyable stuff, no doubt, but it was purely destructive and intended so to be. Like Powell, Foot objected to the basic premise of the Bill and intended to kill it. He wanted no improvement of the Lords: Powell wanted no change. At every point Foot implored the Government to reconsider their position: 'The longer the House discusses the implications of what is proposed in the White Paper,' he said, 'the more absurd it will become.'

Foot derided the expanded role suggested for the Privy Council; while, speaking of the proposed 'two-tier' character of the suggested Lords, where some peers might attend and speak but not vote, Powell observed, 'There is something obscene about the House of Commons, of all places in the world, summoning such a chamber . . . into existence.'

The outcome became very clear. 'Everybody except the Government', John Peyton observed wearily during the Committee proceedings, 'knows that this Bill is a lost cause.'

On 17 April 1969, Harold Wilson announced that the Government had 'decided not to proceed further at this time with the Parliament Bill'. He explained that the Commons programme was unexpectedly full with other business. That was that.

When I reflect on the episode, which I found most disappointing although not entirely surprising, I believe that we did not go far enough. Our scheme might have lasted a little time, but not, I suspect, long enough without leading to fresh dissatisfactions and renewed efforts at reform. Quintin Hailsham always held that it was difficult to tinker with the Lords – the attempt to replace a brick could bring the whole wall down; only fundamental change would work. I came to feel the same, but later. During the debate I said, 'No one can really suppose the House of Commons would consider for one moment a House of Lords which would be a rival to them,' and this, of course, had led me (and would, I am sure, have led our cross-party and inter-House conferences between front benches) to discard the option of an elected House, by whatever means. I believe I was wrong in principle. I am now convinced that what is required is an elected second Chamber. It would, naturally, need to be elected on a different basis and probably at a different time from a General Election of Members of the House of Commons – perhaps elected indirectly, perhaps by proportional representation. To command sufficient authority in the country, however, elected it should be; and without that authority it could fail the nation exactly at the hour when most needed. Such a Chamber's powers should remain limited: but they might include the right to compel a referendum if any fundamental change to the constitution were to be by the Commons proposed. I have not changed my view that the question is important.

Then, in the glorious summer of 1970, the whole of life changed again. We won a General Election. I had doubted whether we would bring it off and remember discussing with Willie Whitelaw the ineffably depressing prospect of another Wilson Government and its effect on Britain. I went down to Ted Heath's constituency to see his result and have supper with him. I doubt if he was confident of the result but he showed no worries – he is a particularly brave man. During the following June days he formed a Conservative administration. To my great surprise and pleasure he invited me to become Secretary of State for Defence.

In 1920, aged one, with maternal grandparents Lord and Lady Colville of Culross, and sister Elizabeth.

Rupert, 5th Lord Carrington, 'a stickler for the rules', and Sibyl, Lady Carrington, 'a gentle, sweet-natured person whose character tended to soften the sternness of my father's outlook'.

With Elizabeth in 1922. 'My boyhood was uneventful, happy and dull. My sister and I didn't see many other children.'

BELOW LEFT: Aged six. 'The sea and the navy have a very special part in British history and I had always wanted to have some connection therewith.'

BELOW RIGHT: At Eton, 1931. 'I was perfectly happy there but neither in academic nor in sporting ways did I shine.'

Bicycling to PT at Sandhurst, 1938 (on the right). 'One thing which has never left me – we knew how to change our clothes quickly: we were forever having to switch from drill uniform, to riding kit, to physical training order (white flannels, red and white striped blazer, pillbox hat) and back again in no time at all.'

At the Guards Chapel in London, 25 April 1942: 'I married Iona McClean, which is by far the most sensible thing I've ever done.'

The Grenadier Battalions being visited by
Princess Elizabeth, Colonel of the Regiment,
in Hove just before the invasion of France in
June 1944. On the Princess's right is
Lieutenant Colonel Rodney Moore.

Winter 1944 in Gangelt, Germany, with
Captain Edward Denny, Major John Trotter
and Lieutenant Geoffrey Sewell. 'We had
little idea of what we would find in Germany,
and were bemused by the comparative
normality of everything.'

The Manor House, south side. 'We moved into Bledlow in April 1946. We started to create a garden where none had been: a garden which has been a source of huge satisfaction and pride to us both.'

The 'white, green-roofed house (which resembled a golf club house in the Home Counties)' in Canberra, Australia, which was home for three years from 1956.

As British High Commissioner in Australia, on the terrace of Canberra House in 1957 with Rupert, Alexandra, Virginia and Iona.

A boat trip under Sydney Harbour Bridge during Prime Minister Macmillan's outstandingly successful visit in 1957: Sir Norman Brook, Lady Dorothy Macmillan, Iona, Harold Macmillan, Brigadier Edwards.

Robert Menzies *(left)* and Sir William Slim. 'They liked and admired each other but sometimes found each other difficult.'

As First Lord of the Admiralty (1959-63): ABOVE, wearing the reefer jacket and peaked cap uniform invented by Churchill; BELOW, transferring from one ship to another by jackstay.

Bledlow from the lawn: 'a house of agreeable proportions, its brick a particularly
soft rose colour and having on most fronts a very satisfying balance between window
and wall.'

As Leader of the House of Lords, 1963-4. 'I realized that the existing composition
of the House of Lords was not simply hard to defend in political theory – it was
actually dangerous.'

Walking on the farm at Bledlow, 1968.

With Ted Heath in the garden at Chequers in 1970. Also photographed are Victor Santa Cruz (Chilean Ambassador), Selwyn Lloyd and Lady Hartwell.

Rab Butler – 'wise, judicious and an expert at the game of politics' – in the garden at Bledlow.

Maltese Prime Minister Dom Mintoff's demand in the summer of 1971 for a new defence agreement with Britain 'began a sequence of negotiations which lasted eight months and introduced me to the extraordinary, the positively operatic experience of doing business with Mintoff.'

As Foreign and Commonwealth Secretary, attending the 1979 Commonwealth Conference in Lusaka with Mrs Thatcher who, 'despite the political aggravation and diatribes, was cheered'.

The final meeting at Lancaster House, 1979: 'the Lancaster House Conference went on for many, many weeks – indeed, until December – and was a tempestuous and testing time, as hard as I ever experienced.' Also at the table: Bishop Muzorewa, Sir Ian Gilmour, Joshua Nkomo, Robert Mugabe.

Zimbabwe independence celebrations at Government House, Salisbury, in April 1980, with Prime Minister Mugabe and Lord Soames.

With Chancellor Helmut Schmidt and Foreign Minister Hans-Dietrich Genscher in Bonn, February 1980.

October 1981: with Margaret Thatcher at the European Community.

As Secretary-General of NATO: a visit to President Mitterrand, September 1985.

A 'private' meeting with President Reagan at the White House in 1987. Others present included George Bush, Frank Carlucci, Caspar Weinberger and Howard Baker.

Defence

I took possession of the new (to me), unified and enormous Ministry of Defence, sprawling as it does between Whitehall and the Embankment, in the summer of 1970. It was, I think, designed in 1914 but not built until 1950 – for a different purpose. It is a dreadful building.

I was surprised as well as delighted with my appointment. Delighted, because much of my earlier career in Government had been concerned with defence issues, I had always been deeply interested in them and minded about them, and I thought I knew something about them – and a good many of the people concerned. Surprised, because it was unusual by that time to give one of the most important jobs in Government to somebody in the Lords; and the office of Defence Secretary is bound to be very important in any Government, not only because of the intrinsic importance of the defence of the country but because huge amounts of public money are involved. Furthermore to give an office of that kind to a peer when an administration is first formed is always hard for a Prime Minister. Someone in the Commons has been 'shadowing' Defence and there are likely to be disappointments. Anyway Ted Heath gave the job to me and I was highly gratified. I was supported by a strong team of junior ministers to deal with our business in the House of Commons. Two of them, Robin Balniel and Ian Gilmour, had once also been young officers in the Grenadiers just after my time, and there was much witty comment, not all of it favourable. Some doggerel verses circulated.

As on previous occasions I was admirably served, and by the sort of people who made business a pleasure. The Ministry

of Defence places what are meant to be the top echelon – Ministers, Permanent Under Secretary, Chiefs of Staff – all on the sixth floor of the building so that, at least in theory, they can move easily from one room to another without the barrier of mistrust or misunderstanding which – again in theory – even a short geographical distance can produce or exacerbate. It doesn't always work out quite like that. I occupied an agreeable, undistinguished room at this eminence, with an excellent view over the Thames and to the great curve beyond which towers the dome of St Paul's. I imported some pictures painted by the topographical painters on Cook's voyages of exploration which I'd had in my room at the Admiralty, and borrowed some pieces of silver from each of the three Services. The room had been bare of ornament.

On the military side I had a difficulty, indeed a tragedy, comparable to that which, years before, had greeted me at the Admiralty. The Chief of the Defence Staff was by now, in the centralized Ministry of Defence, a much more influential figure than the Chairman of the Chiefs of Staff Committee had been in the earlier times I recalled – at least in peacetime. He was, too, the Service officer with the easiest and most frequent access to the Secretary of State, the latter's most available (although not his sole) professional adviser. Mike Le Fanu, First Sea Lord since 1968, was just moving from the Naval Staff to take over this vital job. An ebullient sailor, with enormous character and exceptionally popular, he suddenly and tragically died. I had known and liked him hugely as Controller of the Navy when I was First Lord.

I asked Sam Elworthy, who had been Chief of the Defence Staff since 1967, to stay in post. A charming and cultivated New Zealander, he, too, was much loved as well as respected. He had been educated in England, called to the Bar and then had a brilliant career in the Royal Air Force, and I rate him as one of the most sensible men in any walk of life I have ever met. I first knew Sam Elworthy when he was Commander-in-Chief in Aden, and remember well that we both attended the celebration of Uganda's independence in 1962: which was also the occasion of my first encounter with his splendid wife.

It happened that HMS *Victorious* was in Mombasa, and going to Aden. The question arose whether the Commander-in-Chief's wife could properly travel thither aboard. The alternative to the comparatively short sea voyage was a laborious and time-consuming journey round a number of other points of the globe.

Sam made enquiries. The matter, he was told, would have to be referred to the Admiralty in London. It was. The signal came back that on no account would it accord with regulations that Lady Elworthy should be embarked.

I was not involved in this until Audrey Elworthy approached me, and told me in as trenchant a tone as I have ever heard exactly what she thought of the Royal Navy and in particular the Board of Admiralty. I loved her ever afterwards.

Sam Elworthy had been responsible for arranging – across a certain amount of difficulties – that General Steinhoff, the German flying ace, received medical treatment in England. He had been terribly wounded and lost his eyelids. Sam reckoned our plastic surgeons might help, and negotiated it – with high success: and Steinhoff ultimately became Chairman of the Military Committee of NATO. Sam's was in every sense a truly healing operation. It was invaluable to me that Sam Elworthy stayed on and he was undoubtedly one of the most successful of the post-war Chairmen of the Chiefs of Staff Committee. In 1971 he was succeeded as Chief of the Defence Staff by Peter Hill-Norton, a sailor with a splendidly salty flow of language, who was, in turn, succeeded in 1973 by Mike Carver, a soldier of high intellect. Both had outstanding ability. I was, as ever, lucky.

Labour had wrought some considerable changes in defence and our inheritance was very different from the one we had ourselves bequeathed six years earlier. In the area with which I had once been particularly familiar, our predecessors decided not to build a replacement aircraft carrier, and to let the carrier force run down. At the same time – and arguably restoring *post facto* a certain sense to this – Labour had decided to withdraw our military forces completely from the Far East and the Persian Gulf despite the fact that in the Gulf the states concerned had offered to pay for our presence. We were no longer to have a Far East Command, with a headquarters in Singapore; and we no longer planned to support the Gulf states by a small yet reinforceable presence in Bahrein. The implication had been clearly signalled – our interest in those areas would never again be underpinned by military means; or, if it were, it would involve new forces in a new situation for which it was certainly not planned to prepare.

There was no question of completely putting the clock back; we accepted much of the situation as we found it, although we had been, in Opposition, very sceptical of it. Particularly in the Persian Gulf, we Conservatives had reckoned a British military presence, however small, could be an influence for stability. The theoretic wisdom of the new dispensation was that equipoise would be preserved in the Gulf by the harmony and pro-Western sympathies of Saudi Arabia and Iran. Antipathetic though these two kingdoms were to each other (over certain issues), it was hoped they would, between them, prevent a dangerous vacuum of power developing. It had been Labour policy to develop, as far as they could, arms sales to further goodwill, particularly with Iran: and we took this a long way further, with some major cooperative ventures.

This meant cultivating the most cordial relations possible with the Shah, and when he paid a state visit to Britain during my time I knew that we should give him as good a personal briefing on defence equipment as could be arranged. The Shah was exceptionally well-informed on such matters.

He also liked to feel that he was being let into secrets, and we invited him to a session in the Chiefs of Staff room in the Ministry of Defence with curtains protecting every picture and wall chart, for the look of the thing. The Shah arrived to great applause from the clerical staff gathered in the hall and appeared for our presentation in high good humour. A senior officer from each of the Services spoke – a most eloquent admiral, a particularly lucid air marshal. When we came to army equipment the general was a cavalryman, with a characteristically full-skirted tunic and those bowed cavalry legs, sufficiently wide apart for one to insert the horse. The Shah interrupted him at one point.

'Tell me, General, how fast does that armoured fighting vehicle go?'

The general nodded and explained, in fruity tones, 'About the huntin' pace of the Beaufort, Your Imperial Majesty.'

I'm not sure the Shah was wholly enlightened. Later – in 1973 – I paid a visit to Iran in turn and again talked tanks and other things at an audience with the Shah. He no doubt had faults, like most of us – vanity, touchiness, a certain (probably necessary) ruthlessness and a progressively greater inability to detect when sycophants were concealing the truth from him. But of his aim – in which he had a considerable measure of success, too quickly forgotten – to improve the conditions of the people of his country there could be no doubt: and no doubt, either, of his intelligence and dedication. A heroic, and in retrospect a tragic figure, the Shah.

It looked, therefore, as if the principal pattern of Britain's military influence outside the NATO area would henceforth be training assistance, equipment sales and after-sales service, advisory support. It might be less exciting than the ability to launch expeditions beyond palm and pine but it could be more self-financing; and it didn't require carrier-borne air support! On the whole we accepted this, accepted that we must concentrate our defence on preserving our own homeland and in contributing whatever we decided to an essentially self-defensive Alliance. Defence had come full circle. It was not only to start but almost to end at home.

Almost – but not quite. In the Far East we decided to retain a small presence, based on a new Five Power Pact which we started to negotiate with Australia, New Zealand, Malaysia and Singapore. This engaged us to help, with whatever forces we could, if any of the Pact countries were in difficulties. It indicated that we had not completely abandoned our friends – pretty old friends – in that area. It wasn't a major defence treaty and none of the countries concerned thought of it as such – Australia and New Zealand by those days put prime faith in their pact with the United States, as I knew as well as anybody. But, at the time, the Five Power Pact was a signal that we in Britain had not shrunk to sole and solitary preoccupation with our own home concerns and domestic security, and I think it was worth negotiating. And as I was sent round to do most of the negotiating in a long Far Eastern tour in July and August 1970 it was satisfactory to believe in the task. I also went to India at about that time. I remember an interview with the Indian Defence Minister at which conversation dragged. In fact it dragged so much that it threatened to be over in about fifteen minutes, which I thought too little. The minister was a large and taciturn man. Rather desperate, I said,

'Tell me, what's the biggest audience you've ever addressed?'

He brightened, thought for a minute and said, 'Four million.'

I was rather taken aback. It didn't look as if we were going to have many easy and comparable reminiscences. I asked him how long he had talked to the four million.

'Four and a half hours.'

'You had notes?'

'Certainly not!' said the minister.

I decided our interview had probably lasted long enough after all. The incident came back to me years later when I received an honorary degree at Harvard, was initially greeted by a crowd of 30,000 on a beautiful morning, went into the Senate House, emerged later to deliver the Commencement Address: and found that the thunderstorm of the century had meantime hit Harvard and I was speaking to about one hundred disconsolate figures grouped under umbrellas.

There were, too, certain residual responsibilities, some loose ends which a previous historical epoch had left hanging untidily from the threadbare Imperial knapsack. One, which at this time gave little trouble but which would obviously require major policy decisions sooner or later, was Hong Kong. One, making small demands on Defence but always testing the ingenuity of the Foreign Office, was Gibraltar. One was in the Caribbean, where a British military presence was needed to deter any hostile moves from Guatemala against an independent – and coveted – Belize. And one, unique and never-to-be-forgotten, was Malta: of which more later.

In the nuclear area Labour had kept Polaris. A strong section of the Labour Party had opposed it but Harold Wilson, calling on his gifts for simultaneously espousing two mutually opposed attitudes with equally eloquent conviction, had explained to his party that it was not really an independent system, that there was no question of developing a replacement, and that it was too late to cancel it anyway. All that said, the Labour Government had then comfortably settled down with the newly commissioned Polaris force, although they cancelled a planned fifth boat, retaining four. On taking office, however, we immediately had to begin considering what should succeed our Polaris submarines. The hulls, we were advised, would not be effective after the mid-1990s – a quarter-century on. Should they have successors, with what should such successors be armed (or should our deterrent again be air-launched?) and what options were on offer? Wilson had declared Labour lack of interest in this issue (although I have no doubt their examination of the options would have been pressed ahead exactly like our own had they been in office): but we already needed to get studies underway. Twenty-five years in that business is not a long time.

It was necessary not only to examine the technical possibilities but to think again and objectively about whether and why we needed a national successor system to Polaris at all and what, operationally, it should achieve. On the first point I have written enough already in this book to show my own thinking. It had not changed and I was certain Britain needed to stay in the strategic nuclear business; apart from the question of American credibility, already discussed, I believed strongly that it would be unsatisfactory for the West and particularly for Europe if France were the sole European country to possess an independently managed nuclear force. I certainly never supposed that the British and French nuclear forces, whether separately or combined (and there were at that time frequent but tentative French hints that some sort of cooperation might be fruitful, an idea which needed handling with considerable caution), could in some way replace the American nuclear commitment to Europe. The idea, sometimes floated even then, was fantastic. Quite apart from technical considerations, the American commitment was the greatest earnest of American defence involvement, and it is that which counts. I remember Helmut Schmidt, whom I got to know well and liked greatly, asking me my ideas on the subject of our collaboration with the French. I think he initially regarded me with some scepticism. He had admired Denis Healey. Ultimately, however, we became friends. I shook my head to his query.

'Nothing will come of it.'

Schmidt nodded, and made clear that if we ever thought an Anglo-French nuclear force could be some sort of substitute for American we were sadly adrift.

'The Federal Republic', Schmidt said, 'is in NATO because the United States is in NATO. And if the United States forces, and above all their nuclear forces, were not here the Federal Republic would probably soon go neutral.'

On the second point – operational requirements – we were inevitably in the difficult business of trying to decide what would deter – a conundrum, because deterrence implies the induction of a state of mind in a potential enemy, and one has to make large and unprovable assumptions about his mentality and motives in the first place. But commonsense can be invoked, and it was our view that any nuclear system, in order to deter a (hypothetical) Soviet aggression, must itself be capable of inflicting (hypothetically) unacceptable damage on Moscow. We reckoned that Moscow, as the centre of the Soviet party and state system, was not a counter the Soviet Union would be prepared to sacrifice. And by 1970, when we took office, the Soviet Union had already developed formidable anti-ballistic missile defences round Moscow.

We thus needed, if we were to be credible, to show the ability to penetrate those defences; and before I left the Ministry of Defence we had set in hand a Polaris improvement programme – distinct from an ultimate Polaris replacement – which was intended to do exactly that. It was called Chevaline and it worked by flooding the defences with a system of decoys. I am glad to say that our Labour successors, albeit quietly, kept that work going after 1974. In none of this were any of us blind to the appalling consequences of a major nuclear exchange if that unthinkable event occurred. The scale of death and destruction would be almost beyond imagination, and there were plenty of voices raised to the effect that the world's climate, too, would be so changed as to eliminate much life on the planet. The object of our policy, always and all the time, was to help ensure it never happened: and I believed there was, regrettably, no way to do that except by seeking the sort of stability which comes from balance, so that nobody could possibly win.

We also inherited, as usual, a plan to reduce the size of the Services. I was very opposed to the sort of philosophy which reckoned we could exactly justify the number of ships, regiments or whatever by where they were currently serving – or expected to serve. In the first place our major defence commitment was contributory – to NATO. One couldn't deduce by some absolute criterion how large, or small, that contribution ought to be. Operationally and strategically the Alliance needed more forces in every sphere, especially if it was to give less prominence to nuclear weapons, as was already the urge. Who should produce these forces? Every nation had 'treaty obligations' and our own were complicated by certain specific national responsibilities inherited from the Second World War; but, in the last resort, every nation was judge in its own case. Our security, like the security of each Allied nation, depended on (greater) contributions: what should our own contribution be? How long is a piece of string?

The second factor which, in my view, made it futile to demand an exact rationale for their size and shape from any of the Services was the sheer unpredictability of international life. I asked how many operations in which British forces had been committed in the last twenty-five years had been anticipated. I think I was told that of thirty occasions two had been foreseen. All one can do is one's best with the limited resources the country reckons it can afford, keep one's word to allies, and be as ready for the unforeseen as can be managed – and, perhaps, be at least mentally prepared for a change of tempo, a real worsening of the international atmosphere, with all its implications. That was my philosophy. Defence is seldom about logical deductions from provable assumptions – it would be easier if it were. It is more a matter of making and mending and being careful with the margins. Defence commentators, far from responsibility, dislike this humdrum fact, but it is true!

In Labour's proposals to reduce the Services there were several which hit traditions hard. In the army a number of historic regiments were to be disbanded, amalgamated with others against their will, or reduced to token size. This sort of thing has to be done from time to time, but I formed the view that it didn't need to be done then – indeed, the trend should be in an opposite direction. Of course one can make the case – and some did – that any increase in manpower should be used not to retain historic regiments but to expand the size of the remainder: a unit below a certain strength is hopelessly uneconomic. I took the point, but at that stage I reckoned the army needed to feel that there was a change of course, that its traditions – and in the army tradition is more tribal and individualist than in the other two Services – were valued. There had been a lot of publicity about 'saving the Argylls' (the Argyll and Sutherland Highlanders had been scheduled for demise). The Regiment had run a pretty determined publicity campaign, not all of it welcome to the military authorities, to 'save the Argylls', with car stickers and the like. I thought that they and others should, in fact, be saved. A lot of people have taken credit for 'saving the Argylls'. It was I who was fortunate enough to save the Argylls! I also approved that the carrier *Ark Royal* should be run on, agreed with the raising of four more operational squadrons of Jaguar aircraft and planned to increase the Territorial Army by 10,000 men. We also confirmed that the Brigade of Gurkhas, whose future Labour policy had put in doubt, should remain in the army's Order of Battle. None of this was revolutionary but I hoped and intended that it should mark a change of direction. The need was there and the country expected it.

I had the advantage, of course, of being a Conservative Defence Minister. Conservative Defence Ministers are expected by their party to strengthen Britain's military posture – often to a ludicrous and unrealistic extent. Labour Defence Ministers, by contrast, are expected by their party to slash military expenditure and reduce Britain's military posture in response to a threat in which (in recent times at any rate) a substantial number of the party do not in the least believe. Both spend their time in office moving gently towards a more central position – the Conservatives under financial constraint, the Socialists, unless they are lucky, under pressure from menacing international circumstances or indignant allies to whom they owe money.

In my case I was first acclaimed by newspaper headlines saying that we had redeemed our pledge to strengthen Britain's defences, to reverse a dangerous trend; but I note, wryly, from my scrapbook a kind and congratulatory line from the Permanent Under-Secretary on having handled 'the proposed Defence cuts' with skill and success in Cabinet. I hope he was right. The note was dated May 1973!

My Labour predecessor at the Ministry of Defence had been Denis Healey. He had made a considerable impact on the Department, and, despite disagreement on aspects of policy, across the party divide I acknowledge my belief that most of Healey's impact was for good.

Healey had an excellent brain, a strong personality, a lively wit, and many qualities, of which intellectual zeal was certainly the most marked and consistency of position perhaps the least obtrusive. That said, he was a man of imagination and intelligence; combative and something of a bully by temperament but, at his best, in the first rank of European politicians since the Second World War. There is a very proper convention in British Government whereby an incoming minister (of one party) has no access to his predecessor's papers (of another party); but one did not need to see papers by or addressed to Denis Healey to recognize that he had dived personally into the most varied and abstruse – and technical – questions of defence with enthusiasm. He had made a great name for refusing to accept conventional wisdom without subjecting it to a sustained battery of his own examination. He had made people more thoughtful, more precise and more articulate. I daresay this was often unpopular. I doubt whether the experts' professional competence was higher because of Denis Healey's time as Defence Secretary but I'm sure their advocacy was improved.

I was certainly a very different kind of minister from Healey and I have no doubt that to the kind of person who enjoys speculative and intellectual gyration for its own sake I was something of a disappointment. I did not and do not believe in reading a great deal of paper which somebody paid and equipped to do so can summarize, in order to come to a conclusion. I respect logic but I have a certain regard for hunch. I recognize that experts differ with each other – nowhere more than in defence – but I believe that there are few strategic – or indeed technical – questions where the evidence points overwhelmingly towards one solution being right and another wrong, in the way that a mathematical proposition is demonstrably right or wrong. Generally there is a good deal to be said for opposing points of view; because they tend to turn upon assumptions about future hostilities which contain a great deal of speculation dressed up as quantifiable fact – and adorned by a certain amount of special pleading, more often than not. Each or all are defensible. It is a matter of balancing factors and selecting a sensible way. It is also a matter of deciding which of the experts themselves is most worthy of respect, judgement of men as well as their arguments. Some people are so dedicated to a particular cause, Service, strategic philosophy, even weapon system, that their advice, however competent and sincere, is too coloured by emotion to be taken without a good many pinches of salt. And scientists, presumed to argue from pure rationality, are sometimes even more emotional than others.

226

But defence is completely ineffective without contented and confident people manning the Armed Forces, believing in what they are doing and believing that their political masters believe in them. In this sphere I was keen to bring to the Services a certain atmosphere of calm.

'In the past six years', I told the Lords in February 1971, 'the Armed Forces have had more than enough of chop and change, withdrawal, retrenchment and reduction. The aim of the defence policy of the present administration is one of consolidation and stability.'

The Healey regime had produced turbulence – maybe much of it healthy, but at a certain level troubling. Healey could be abrasive and he enjoyed his reputation for it. That is sometimes effective, but on occasion the wounds produce not more efficiency but resentment at what is regarded as insensitive and uncomprehending behaviour. The Services had been subjected to so many harassing questions about their object, character, organization, methods of work and attitudes to the future that they were, I thought, in danger of excessive and debilitating introspection. They needed to be encouraged, and encouraged simply to get on with the job. Of course the long-term issues had to be faced and resolved but I wanted to remove the feeling of insecurity. I wanted to tackle the problems without implying that the whole profession of sailor, soldier or airman was in doubt. I wanted to reassure, and to decide the difficult questions backed by a less disturbed defence community. This could, of course, suggest a preference for cosiness and crunch-shirking. I had no illusions that we could afford that, but I thought we could improve atmosphere.

Consistent with this, one of the things I left alone was the existence of independent – or, rather, separate – Service ministers: Under-Secretaries specifically charged with overseeing each Service. Ted Heath and other colleagues wanted me to do away with them. We had a unified Ministry, and the Defence Secretary now had the sort of authority across the board which had so irritatingly eluded Macmillan and Watkinson in my earlier experience. There were, of course,

Service officers – Chiefs of Staff – as professional heads of each Service. Something as human and individual as an Armed Service needs an experienced and visible chief – and I knew better than to suppose that the Services resemble each other so closely that a man in a different uniform would ever be accepted as a qualified spokesman on Service (as opposed to strategic) matters for a Service not his own. But why did each Service additionally need a junior minister, I was asked?

I thought it right, at least for the time being, to keep them. I knew that the main business of a Service would be done by the uniformed Service members of a board – together, no doubt, with the senior civil servant. But after the turbulence to which I've referred I thought it undesirable that the Services should be deprived of a political voice special to each of them. The time might come when this was no longer important – I'm sure it now has. But I didn't think, in 1970, that it had come yet.

The security of Britain and the prevention of war meant participation in an Alliance – NATO. I have said that no absolute criteria can determine what contribution should be made by any nation to the Alliance, and that is true. Nevertheless it was impossible to avoid the sense that, in logic, the Allies could produce more in sum if there were to be greater specialization of role. Geography and history obviously suggested that the main burden of European defence on land be borne by the major Continental land powers, France and Germany; and that we British should concentrate upon the maritime area. To some extent, of course, this occurred – the British Army of the Rhine was small and among European nations the Royal Navy was and remains proportionately large. The principle could, perhaps, be developed further.

The difficulty was largely political and it was not new. There was a treaty obligation upon us to retain upon the Continent an army and a tactical air force of a certain size: but the political factor long preceded the formal commitment. To the nations of Continental Europe what matters most is always the security of their land frontiers; and what cements an Alliance is evidence of willingness to share sacrifice – evidence which implies total commitment. Our maritime contribution was and is significant in strategic – or, indeed, financial – terms; but it was beyond the horizon. What procured political mileage was, as always, evidence of readiness to stand and fight for the European homelands; to produce soldiers who couldn't sail away. The same – exactly the same – factors and pressures had existed before both world wars and nobody acquainted with European politics could suppose otherwise. The possibility remained, however, that in terms of getting best value for money role specialization within the Alliance could go further. In considering manpower, after all, one of the most populous nations in Western Europe lived within miles of the potential field of battle, and although there were other political reasons (beside those psychological points I have already mentioned) which must inhibit the idea of a Europe primarily defended by a German Army and a British Navy, we should, I thought, always be pressing further in that direction. 'Further', however, would never be very far. It was an area in which military logic had necessarily to be subordinated to political perception. And central to the argument was the position of the United States.

In that respect little has changed since my time as Defence Secretary. That America must be, and be seen to be, committed to the defence of Europe was a fundamental axiom of the North Atlantic Treaty: the nuclear element in deterrence made it vital, as did the whole world balance of power. This American commitment was, above all, signified by the presence in Europe of American forces, in whose ability to fight and win – together with their allies – the United States Congress and people were invited to believe. That, too, was fundamental. Anything which weakened it weakened the assurance of peace; and Britain had always to tread carefully to see that her own policy never contributed to that weakening. Every British Government had to take account of these underlying political realities, while trying, at the same time, to work towards the most cost-effective possible answers to the questions of who should do what for the Alliance, and to what degree.

It was not only Britain which needed, all the time, to take careful account of American sentiment in settling contributions to the Alliance. All the European nations – although their collective contribution, of course, far exceeded that of the United States – were vulnerable to American perception that they were exerting themselves inadequately. This perception – just or unjust – was and always will be used by those in the United States who wanted America to give up the business of stationing troops to defend Europe. The most vociferous of these in my day (and in Denis Healey's day) was Senator Mansfield. Senator Mansfield didn't simply think Europeans should do more – a perfectly tenable proposition. He thought, regardless of what Europeans did, that the United States should pull out. He was an isolationist.

Isolationism, however, was obviously nourished by any feebleness in Europe, and here I must pay tribute to Healey. During his time in office he had taken a lead in forming within NATO an unofficial party of the European members, known as the Eurogroup. The Eurogroup had its limitations. It could not be used to promote the cause of European armament cooperation, for instance, if only because France, having withdrawn from the military structure and Defence Planning Committee of the Alliance, did not belong to the Eurogroup. European defence collaboration had always been to some extent inhibited by the fact that NATO – an Alliance which spans the Atlantic above all things – must not be weakened by European visions of going it alone without America: while, on the other hand, the European Community (although it might one day, as I said in Parliament when we acceded in July 1971, have some influence in the economic and industrial dimension of defence) specifically excluded defence as an interest, under the Treaty of Rome; and rightly so at the time. Of course, nations which gradually over the years come together on economic and foreign policy are bound in time to align their defence policies – an essentially pragmatic process, as I told the Lords when pressed (often) on this particular point.

But the NATO Eurogroup had the modest but significant function of enabling the European Allies to coordinate the presentation of their policies (and spur each other on a bit) in order to counter the sort of American suspicions I have described; and Healey had played a major part in it. The Eurogroup used to announce each year what the European nations were doing for the Alliance and how much better it was than the year before, and sometimes it actually was. I don't think the Eurogroup could do much about such fundamentals as role specialization, but it had its uses.

Another NATO institution new since my earlier days in Defence was the Nuclear Planning Group: and this, too, had owed a good deal to Denis Healey who was an enthusiastic philosopher and advocate of the nuclear dimension of deterrence in those far-off days when he held responsibility. Here there had been a shift of emphasis.

In an earlier chapter I said that NATO strategy moved away from the concept of 'massive retaliation' and 'tripwire' at a certain point in time. This point had been in the period when we were in Opposition. When I became Secretary of State I found that after considerable debate the Allies had evolved a different strategy – different, at least, in theory. It was known as the strategy of 'flexible response'. In simple terms it meant that NATO would respond to any aggression 'appropriately'; confronting it, at least initially, with a direct defence rather than with the threat of instant and cataclysmic nuclear retaliation. Nuclear weapons, of all sorts and sizes, would continue to be part of NATO's (principally, of course, America's) armoury; but they would be used, in a deliberate essay in escalation, only if other means failed to halt aggression. This didn't make the basic dilemma disappear – that the Warsaw Pact could and no doubt would counter nuclear with nuclear, so that defence could become a pretty self-destructive affair; but it said, in effect, 'This, ghastly and even suicidal though it is, is what we *could* do, if pressed to the ultimate. Meanwhile, if you try anything you'll get hurt, and if you keep on trying we may, just may, all go to Hell together!'

This, I believe, was a good deal more credible than some of what had gone before. It was consistent with my belief that the simple existence of these frightful weapons was a hugely inhibiting factor on aggressive intentions, whatever the detailed logic: and it entirely matched my conviction that one can never be, and should not seek to be, too precise about exactly what measures one might or might not take in given circumstances. But, of course, to be more than rhetoric the 'new' strategy (it was more a development from than a break with the past) needed a stronger conventional defence posture than had been fashionable in NATO hitherto. The Allies struggled with this unpalatable reality; and are still struggling, not without success.

The strategy also made it desirable that the non-nuclear members of NATO should be fully briefed on nuclear developments; and thus the Nuclear Planning Group had been evolved as a forum in which discussions of that kind could be held. Membership of the NPG rotated. The new strategy inevitably brought pretty quickly into debate the stage at which, if aggression occurred, nuclear weapons might 'need' to be used (the need itself, of course, being the main subject of debate), what their capabilities and hazards might be, and what the effect on the enemy – and his response. The Continental nations did not want to be overrun by a Soviet enemy: but nor did they fancy having their territories subjected to intensive nuclear bombardment, described as 'tactical'! The difference between tactical and strategic has been described as turning chiefly on where one lives. The Nuclear Planning Group did little planning. It was a forum, but a useful forum.

Meetings of the Group also rotated, between different countries: and there tended to be competition as to which country could arrange the most splendid *ambience* so that the assembled Defence Ministers, when they'd finished talking about the end of the world, could enjoy something of it while it lasted. There were generally military demonstrations of some kind and, of course, entertainment. I remember one NPG meeting in southern Germany where we watched an excellently organized display by German paratroops, in the Bavarian Alps. We then went by special train to Munich's enchanting baroque opera house for a performance of *Entführung aus dem Serail*. The Nuclear Planning Group, Ministers and Chiefs of Defence Staff, were not a good party to take to a Mozart opera, and I recall Peter Hill-Norton grumbling throughout the journey to Munich and back again, while copiously refreshing himself from a pocket flask both during and after the performance.

The Nuclear Planning Group when meeting in Canada, after dull proceedings in Ottawa, was taken off in a Boeing 707 to be shown how big Canada is. We arrived in Calgary in impenetrable fog. We mounted a bus and drove to the foot of the Rockies, fog still completely opaque. There we had a barbecue, drove (befogged) back to Calgary and next morning flew to Hudson Bay (clasping the white Stetsons we'd been given) on another leg of the journey destined to show us how big Canada is. Cloud base on take-off was 100 feet, and we flew for nine hours in cloud, ultimately arriving back in Ottawa. For all we had seen, we might have been in Saudi Arabia. When the Group came to England I gave them lunch in the superb Council Chamber of the Royal Hospital in Chelsea, hired a brand-new river steamer and sailed them down the Thames to dinner in the Painted Hall at Greenwich. The band of the Royal Marines then beat Retreat. The whole thing may have been less ambitious than some but I think it was at least as successful.

A great deal of a Defence Secretary's time and attention is devoted to questions of equipment development and procurement. There had long been certain anomalies and discrepancies in the way the Services developed and obtained equipment. The affinity between military and civil aircraft development had made of the air a special case: the Controller of the Navy, with a long history of Departmental expertise, had made of the navy another special case. There had been a Ministry of Supply (which had always excluded naval procurement): there had earlier been a Ministry of Aircraft Production. And so on.

I thought that the Services and the country would gain if research, development, procurement and production of Service equipment were all handled by one agency within the Ministry, so that users and procurers would be subject to the same ministerial control. I asked for a study and recommendations from a distinguished businessman, Derek Rayner. When in Opposition, Ted Heath had had the idea that Government would profit from cross-fertilization between business and Civil Service, and that some leading firms would profit and the country would profit if leading industrialists were lent, for a while, to Whitehall. It didn't work in the least well when put into effect after our return to power. In the first place, few businesses want to send their best brains away for any length of time. In the second place the businessmen who tried the experiment found, somewhat to their surprise, that the civil servants they were intended to stimulate and broaden knew their jobs and understood the world a great deal better than they had been led to believe: and, I suspect, at least as well as they did themselves.

Derek Rayner was an exception and I was lucky that the Heath experiment gave him to Defence. He looked very hard at the whole procurement field and – with commendable speed – produced advice. As a result we set up in May 1971 a procurement executive within the Ministry, to handle all matters of procurement for all three Services. Research establishments – including in due course atomic weapons research – were brought together in the same way.

Procurement questions generally concern the fairly remote future. They may be urgent in terms of the budget and the costings, but as far as anybody watching can perceive life is going on regardless. This, however, was not quite the case in February 1971. Rolls Royce went bust. The Armed Services relied very much on Rolls Royce engines. So did a good many of the world's airlines. So did the American Lockheed Tristar aircraft which was designed by Lockheed for the Rolls Royce 211 engine – and if no engine appeared, Lockheed were in a lot of trouble. There was also a question of British prestige: as a general principle it is probably right that such intangibles should not affect commercial decisions, but 'Rolls Royce' is a name, a sound, which is inseparable, if only in a small way, from the reputation of Britain for appreciating, developing and producing articles of quality. Now we were advised that Rolls Royce was trading illegally. We decided that something had to be done by Government. I am confident we were right.

It was necessary to nationalize the company and to set up a new, publicly owned company (the motor-car division being excluded). All three of the Services depended greatly on Rolls Royce and I was put in charge of the operation. I never remember working harder. Peter Rawlinson was Attorney-General and on much of it we worked together. I got a good board together for the nationalized company – Arnold Weinstock, Kenneth Keith, who became Chairman in 1972, other industrialists and City men of distinction. They took some persuading and I'm not sure any of them enjoyed it very much but it got us through a difficult patch. Because of the Lockheed dimension I had to go twice to the United States – there was no doubt that Rolls Royce had seriously miscalculated the cost of the engine development for Tristar and this was the main reason for their collapse. I had to do business with John Connally again – he had been Secretary of the Navy when I was First Lord. He was a very tough character, but somehow we managed to get an agreement in the end. Lockheed were to go ahead and buy the RB 211 engine, the engine would be produced by Rolls Royce (new style) and the British Government would cover the finance required.

In the United States I also had to talk about it to Mr Dan Houghton of Lockheed. Later he got into terrible trouble over bribes. He bribed very widely. He bribed in Italy, he bribed in Japan. I'm afraid he didn't even give me lunch but I suppose this was less a compliment to my integrity than acknowledgement of the reality that we needed him more than he needed us. He was a delightful person. When it was all over I had dinner with him in Los Angeles and commiserated. He smiled sadly.

'Everyone was doing it.'

'Bribes?'

'Of course, it was accepted practice, and not only in the aircraft industry. The trouble was that I just got caught in the aftermath of Watergate. I was the scapegoat.'

In those days I also met Henry Kissinger for the first time. He was National Security Adviser and on my first visit to Washington I called on him. The security of national figures and the risks to them were in the news in a way which has since become all too familiar. Martin Luther King had just been assassinated. When I drove up to the White House I saw Kissinger's well-known silhouette through a window, illuminated, apparently signing a document.

We had never met before. When we'd shaken hands I said, 'You must be a very brave man.'

'Why?'

'You were entirely visible. If I'd had a rifle I could have got you with ease.'

'It doesn't worry me,' Kissinger answered, in that gravelly voice which became so familiar to me. 'I'm an intellectual. Only another intellectual would want to shoot me.' He paused before adding, 'And he'd never make up his mind to pull the trigger!'

I got to know Kissinger very well indeed. He was – indeed is – a remarkable human being. His love and devotion for the United States, his deep and intelligent patriotism, were utterly sincere; but his attitudes of mind and his understanding were thoroughly European, deriving from a German background and immense learning. I found him at all times a joy to work with because of the speed and originality of his mind, his flexibility and his enchantingly funny sense of humour. Henry Kissinger, too, had imagination. He thought big and he thought profoundly. He could be adept and tireless in negotiation but it was always against the background of a carefully reasoned and long-term political calculation. He was a great public servant.

I also greatly admired Kissinger's objectivity. In those days there was particular suspicion of the United States in Egypt –

indeed, throughout the Arab world, and it is unlikely ever to go very far away. Kissinger built bridges between that world and America and did so more successfully than anyone else. A Jew, he nevertheless disarmed Arab suspicion that his own breeding was distorting his judgement or his sense of justice – a remarkable achievement, and one that did him little personal good, for many difficulties and much abuse were heaped on him by the American Jewish lobby in consequence. They thought he had a duty to the Israeli side of the argument. Instead Kissinger was capable, always, of fairness and detachment. His 'shuttle diplomacy' in the Middle East achieved more – at least for a while – than anybody imagined possible.

Long afterwards – I was in Opposition – Kissinger was on a visit to London, and we arranged to meet at Claridges Hotel at three o'clock. He had a very busy schedule and was two minutes late, apologizing profusely for the fact. 'Henry,' I said, 'you've got a packed day and it's very nice of you to have fitted me in at all!'

'Don't feed my megalomania!' Kissinger returned.

Ultimately, in 1982, he asked me to join the board of a company he formed to give political, global advice to large companies who felt they needed it. All that I saw of him in that capacity confirmed my earlier view that he stood head and shoulders above most men in his knowledge and understanding of international affairs.

I paid many visits at that time. I seemed to go everywhere and meet everyone. A considerable slice of my life has been spent in the air. It was good to visit our one-time enemy, Indonesia, in February 1973 and to note the economic progress despite very serious difficulties. I remember one expedition to Yugoslavia. Tito expressed a particular wish to see me and I travelled in his luxurious special train to his hunting lodge in Bosnia where he was shooting bears. When I arrived for lunch he had just come in from shooting a bear and was most affable. Lunch was enjoyable – I had met Tito often over the years. On this occasion he smiled.

'Have I ever told you what Winston Churchill said to me?'

When I shook my head, he said, 'When I paid my state visit

to England Churchill was still very angry with me. He thought I had thrown in my lot with the Soviet camp in 1945, that I might be a communist but that I still owed something to England for what she'd done for us in the war.' Tito went on to say that Churchill made his disapproval extremely clear, not speaking to him and glaring his ill-feeling. 'But after lunch at Buckingham Palace,' Tito said with enjoyment, 'I drove away down the Mall with Churchill in his car. And he patted me on the knee and said in his inimitable voice, "I used to *hate* you, but now I *love* you!"'

I returned, too, to Australia and New Zealand early in 1973 on a trip which also embraced Kenya, Gan, Hong Kong and Fiji. Australia was now led by Gough Whitlam, and although he was personally urbane he made it clear that British interests and attitudes might from time to time be opposed, just for the look of the thing in terms of Australia's standing with the Third World in general and South-East Asia in particular. I had always understood and indeed supported Australia's determination not to appear anyone's satellite: but policy has to be based on genuine interest rather than facile attitudinizing and I hoped, without a great deal of confidence, that Whitlam's policy would not take Britain's friendship too much for granted. Whitlam's flirtation with ostentatious neutralism had led to a decision to withdraw Australian troops from the Commonwealth Brigade, based in Malaya. We did not welcome that decision.

Problems of resource allocation within Defence are perennial. They occupied us greatly then; they occupy my successors and will continue to do so. Disputes, difficulties, what the Press delights to call 'squabbles' – even 'bickering' (a wholly inadequate term) or 'rivalry' (too sedate a one) – between Services, between lobbies, between proponents of this or that equipment design; all derive chiefly from the problem of how to allocate money between different claimants, each with a strong case. I cannot shed any blinding illumination on this problem, but certainly one observation is due.

It is absurd to suppose that the strong and conflicting arguments which surround the question of defence resource allocation derive simply from stupidity or narrowness of mind. There is often Press comment (assuming the issues to be between different Services) on the lines of a necessity to 'knock their heads together'. This is to trivialize. One is talking of intelligent, professional men with reasonable points of view and with arguments which deserve consideration, not some sort of bluff impatience. It is also a mistake to suppose that the validity of one man's argument implies the falseness of his colleague-rival's (for where two men need the same thing and not less, they are rivals). Both may be demonstrably 'right' in argument – in the sense that, operationally, Britain (or NATO) may have a serious need for more or newer ships, tanks, aircraft or whatever, in order to play a desired part in dealing with an authentic threat. The question is which should be bought first, and which last or not at all. Of course in any debate part of the promotion of an argument lies in questioning and discrediting the claims of a rival argument – and, as I have said, in competition for resources all can be rivals. This discrediting of opposition – which, obviously, deserves careful attention – may or may not be convincing: its failure, however, does not mean that he who attempts it has not got a perfectly good case in his own field. More often than not, in my experience, one was dealing with conflicting claims which all had validity. One couldn't meet them all, but they were all sound. If it were otherwise, life would be much easier.

There is a further observation and I have already referred to it in previous chapters. The real cost of defence equipment has increased at a faster rate than ordinary inflationary pressures explain. We have, I think probably too often, simply accepted this as an inescapable fact of life, implying that we are all marching down an inevitable road to a world wherein we would in theory be defended by one ship, one tank, one aeroplane – each of unbelievable sophistication, quality and performance; and that inadequacy of numbers is something for a shrug of the shoulders, no more. That is nonsense. Cost growth chiefly derives from technological improvement:

sometimes it is vital, in the true sense that without it one would be unable to compete at all, one might as well give up, but I was unconvinced that this was so in nearly as many cases as suggested. In some – perhaps more than most dedicated professionals will admit – it is and was perfectly possible to 'make do', to repeat theoretically obsolete patterns at cheap cost, deliberately to reject innovation in order to save money for where it was truly needed and to have more adequate quantity. I remembered Harold Macmillan's regretful observations on how few steel-shafted clubs we might one day afford and how many wooden-shafted we should be careful to keep supple and retain!

We made progress in this matter here and there, but not enough. The truth is that whereas cost-equipment graph lines are always shown sloping steeply upwards, it is possible (in many cases) to keep them level or even in decline, as patterns become cheaper with repeated production. That involves deliberate choice, and mastering a scientific and industrial establishment dedicated to innovation:* as well as a military establishment spellbound by a Soviet threat perceived as ever-increasing, and, by the enticements of technology, increasing in every area.

Government allocation of resources between competing claims is, anyway, an intractable problem and it was not only my experience as Defence Secretary that made me wary of Treasury calculation and pressure. To anticipate, when I was Foreign Secretary I remember one of many occasions when all spending Departments had to trim their estimates – pretty drastically. The Foreign Office is a small spender, comparatively, but we had to save some ten millions. I grumbled away and I think got it down to six millions. That meant – it could only mean – reduction in funding for the British Council which spreads the word about Britain and British culture abroad: and the World Overseas Service of the BBC; as well as the closure of some consulates.

Soon, both within the British Council and the BBC, the

* And to a 'national' ethos in research, development and production which could form the subject of a book on its own.

240

tom-toms began to beat. Both institutions have very loud tom-toms. Soon their lobbies began to assemble. Both have very extensive and well-deployed lobbies. I suffered a good deal of obloquy and, of course, considerable pressure – some of it a little unconvincing, as when the BBC claimed a total number of Somalis known to listen to the BBC which I was able to explain greatly outnumbered the entire population of Somalia.

But something was done, and some millions were saved: and, I have no doubt, a little harm was done though perhaps not so much as pretended. And the financial consequence? On that occasion, in the out-turn, the Treasury figures were found to be no less than two *billions* awry! Yet to satisfy the bookkeepers' forecast, practical measures of a disadvantageous sort had to be taken.

Not all our financial problems were concerned with resource allocation to the British defence effort and Services. I made a statement about Malta in the House of Lords on 15 July 1971. It was the first of many.

The Island of Malta, awarded the George Cross for its corporate valour under German bombardment in the Second World War, possessed by 1970 little of the strategic significance which had once made it the base of the British Mediterranean Fleet. In modern times, with Italy and France our allies within NATO, Malta had no irreplaceable value. We had under lease certain military and communication facilities there; and these were of benefit to the local economy. We – and our allies – would not have welcomed a hostile Malta, ready to extend the hospitality of its harbour and airfield to a Soviet Fleet; and we had a traditional concern for the friendliness and prosperity of this essentially European island. But we were not prepared to pay more than a strictly limited price for the modest interests we had at stake. These interests, furthermore, were general and Allied rather than particular and British.

In Maltese eyes the rest of the world, and the British especially, were eternally determined to enjoy strategic advantages of immeasurable value in Malta for minimal outlay, negotiated from the islanders under what they believed were extortionate terms. As part of a protracted effort at getting more out of others, the Maltese Prime Minister, Dr Borg Olivier, had recently demanded a new defence agreement with Britain in return for substantially more money. The previous Labour Government had refused him. We, on taking office, offered a good deal – I think it was £50 million, 75 per cent of it in the form of an outright grant – in the hope that with this triumph on his colours Borg Olivier would win the Maltese Election which was to be held in June 1971. We wished for this; the alternative was likely to be much worse. In the event he lost by one vote and Mr Dom Mintoff became Prime Minister of Malta. Mintoff immediately demanded a new agreement – the proposed elements of which were in many cases unclear – within a month, plus a great deal of extra money. I was asked to go to Malta to discover whether there was any basis for agreement; and thus began a sequence of negotiations which lasted eight months, produced meetings in Malta (two) and Rome (four) and several in England, introducing me to the extraordinary, the positively operatic experience of doing business with Mintoff.

I will not enumerate the details, the successive bargaining positions, the sums of money discussed, withdrawn, increased and discussed again. Some impression of an often enraging and sometimes hilarious episode will suffice.

First, personalities. Dom Mintoff's personal style – perhaps his inescapable temperament – was to alternate between periods of civilized charm and spasms of strident and hysterical abuse. The most modestly phrased criticism, even when extended at a meeting he himself might have characterized as 'informal', 'unofficial', 'personal', would bring his voice to a shrill scream of temper in response. At times it even seemed that his mental balance was in danger and there were rumours that he was receiving psychiatric treatment from the same specialist as Colonel Ghadaffi of Libya, another somewhat unpredictable negotiator. On the other hand I realized that there was also calculation in every Mintoff mood. He undoubtedly knew that the British were saying to each other, among other things, that it could be counterproductive to push Mintoff on this point; that another small *douceur* might save his sanity and the negotiation. He was a man who could use that and every factor; and did.

Next, techniques. Mintoff's technique – his negotiating as opposed to his personal technique – was based on the military principles of shock and surprise. He liked to produce some sudden *démarche*, to throw everyone else off balance and start again on his own terms. Thus, when I was about to fly to Malta for the first time in July 1971 and we were already strapped into the aircraft, a message arrived on board that if I went to Malta Mintoff refused to receive me. Later – I having arrived and he having, in fact, received me and asked me to a dinner of almost unbelievable nastiness, I am unsure whether from some strange calculation or not – he suddenly said that no negotiation was possible unless the British Government preceded it by agreeing to all his demands (which were unprecedentedly large). Then there was the Christmas Ultimatum. On Christmas Eve 1971 Mintoff sent a message demanding that all British troops and facilities be removed from the island by 31 December; one week. We ignored it and he substituted 15 January. None of this was intended, of course; but it was the technique of sudden aggression, pretended ultimatum, emotional pressure. And it was mixed all the time with accusations – both official and personal – of meanness and bad faith. Yet, oddly enough, I formed the opinion that Mintoff, despite the impossibility of his behaviour, was a genuine patriot who wanted to do the best for his Maltese people and cared deeply about them. And through it all I liked him.

Then, allies. We involved NATO in the Malta negotiation. We reckoned it was an Alliance interest to get some sort of settlement and if that involved cash – and it did – we put it to our allies that there should be an Allied subscription list. The Secretary-General of NATO, Joseph Luns, joined me in the negotiations which took place in Rome. Having begun with the conviction that Britain in general and I in particular were being rather too tough with Mintoff (and that I was taking an inappropriately colonialist attitude), he soon changed tack when, after some fairly anodyne Luns interjection, Mintoff jumped to his feet screaming at the top of his voice, 'Shut up, Luns! Who the hell do you think you are? Are you God? I am not going to be treated like some Indonesian nigger!'

'I have negotiated with Sukarno,' Luns said to me afterwards, much moved, 'with Nasser, with Krishna Menon. But never have I met such a bastard!'

Then various allies – and Mintoff was adept at identifying them – thought they could help the cause by a little private negotiation on the side. The Italians, in particular, made a great deal of mischief, convinced that we should be gentler with Mintoff. The upshot, of course, was that whenever we brought him to the point of decision – of accepting or finally refusing a deal – he was persuaded by the Italians, or some of them, that a little more intransigence could still produce a little more money. There evolved a 'NATO package' – a financial package – and it was no easy task to keep some members from breaking ranks. The episode impressed me with the importance of never, if it can possibly be managed, admitting any other nation to a negotiation of this kind. Preliminary coordination is one thing, involvement in the negotiation quite another.

My final impression is of the necessity not to exclude or be surprised by the bizarre in public life. Public life can be, and is generally represented as, a matter of organized meetings, meals, discussions, protocol. Not with Mintoff. I treasure a memory of his visit to England, quite early in the saga, in September 1971: I went with him to Chequers. He appeared to be on best behaviour. In the Long Gallery, Ted Heath helped himself to a generous glass of brandy and said to Mintoff expansively, 'Now Prime Minister, what are your troubles?'

Mintoff outlined his troubles. He talked for one and a quarter hours. Heath nodded kindly and asked if there was anything else? Mintoff was taken aback, but repeated the catalogue of his troubles, changing them here and there and confusing matters somewhat: three-quarters of an hour, at the end of which Heath said, still very kindly, 'Ah! But I feel sure you would like to tell us more.'

Mintoff was flagging. He started gamely but petered out after thirty minutes.

'I think we had better now all go to bed,' said the Prime Minister, 'and we will meet again at 10.30 tomorrow morning.'

Next morning, we sat on a terrace in the rose garden, and Heath told Mintoff that he thought the best answer would be to try to get our allies to help; and to go for a new defence agreement, to be tied up in six months. Mintoff agreed, after barely perceptible hesitation: a document was drawn up and signed; and after lunch I went home feeling that the Prime Minister had done a remarkable job.

Two hours later the telephone rang at Bledlow. It was the Prime Minister speaking from Chequers.

'The most extraordinary thing has just happened.'

'Oh dear!'

'At 4.30, a short while ago, the front doorbell rang. Mrs Mintoff walked in.'

Mrs Mintoff was English, the daughter of a British admiral. I said rather feebly, 'They're separated.'

'I daresay,' said the Prime Minister, 'but he had asked her to meet him here. *Here!* To talk things over, over tea, with me!'

I admired Ted Heath's fine qualities, but I was sceptical about his suitability as a reconciliation counsellor of the Mintoffs over tea at Chequers.

'I managed to get them off fairly soon,' he said. 'It was all very embarrassing. I persuaded her to sit in the car with him, anyway!'

Mintoff came again to London. Some of our allies were particularly worried about his threatened *démarches* to various communist powers, including China, and despite all our efforts there were still whispers in a few quarters that we were being too harsh, and might by this harshness be jeopardizing the whole Western position. Mintoff at this penultimate meeting – it was March 1972 – was still desperately hoping for more cash. He mobilized those in British politics he described as his best friends – Tom Driberg, Barbara Castle and Tony Wedgwood Benn, as I recall. It was an unlikely background consortium with which to influence Ted Heath, but he listened to Mintoff sympathetically, Mintoff was abject and he in fact obtained a few concessions. A final agreement was prepared. Four days later the Italian Ambassador came to see me and explained that he had flown to Rome from London with Mintoff after his recent visit, that he 'had formed a relationship with Mr Mintoff which no one else had succeeded in doing', that he had previously misunderstood Mintoff and now appreciated his problems. He had then, with neither the money nor the authority, offered Mintoff a further £5 million – a debt which the Italian Government disowned with rage! The upshot of this meddling, of course, was that Mintoff postponed any decision on signing our agreement, managed to obtain half the extra £5 million from the Italians as an uncovenanted extra, and arrived in London again a fortnight later to sign on the dotted line before a battery of cameras. He was in an excellent mood, apologized for previous outbursts (particularly to Joseph Luns), drank champagne, smiled at the cameras and warmly shook my hand. Next week he flew to China and returned with £17 million and a button inscribed, 'I like Mao'! You had to hand it to him!

CHAPTER 11

The Tory Party

Throughout my time as Defence Secretary the Services were, as usual, carrying out far-flung as well as more domestic duties with their normal competence and commonsense – often in particularly trying and disagreeable conditions. We had always made plain, in Opposition, our dislike of sanctions against Rhodesia, but although we always stressed that we were hunting for a fair solution we could not unilaterally pull out of the sanctions we inherited, imposed by a United Nations resolution, without a disproportionate international row. We therefore played our part, while working as hard as we could for diplomatic advance; and our part meant maintaining a naval patrol at Beira to inhibit oil supplies by sea. There were other duties, few of which we would have chosen.

But the greatest nagging sore for the Services, and primarily of course for the army, was Northern Ireland. The army in Northern Ireland had and at the time of writing have a particularly difficult and disagreeable task. That sort of internal policing – which it inevitably became – in our own country was new to them. Every action was carried out in the glare of television publicity. Initially their equipment, training and habits of mind were all directed towards very different military scenarios. They had to learn, and learn fast.

They did so with what I regarded as astonishing speed and remarkable adaptability, living in squalid, makeshift conditions, abused by all parties, retaining a surprisingly high morale throughout as well as the good humour and objectivity which makes the British soldier what he is. No experience did more than Northern Ireland – I visited the army there about every two months – to impress me with the efficiency of the army compared to the one I once joined. At this hard and unpalatable sort of soldiering they became, I suspect, second to none in skill.

During our administration we experienced, on the political front in the province, a series of traumatic events. In March 1971 I had to repeat an announcement made in the Commons about the resignation from the Northern Ireland premiership of Jim Chichester-Clark. We introduced internment that year after painful Cabinet debate, and in September Parliament was recalled. In the following January 1972, demonstrations in Londonderry led to the shooting of a number of people by the army – on a day christened 'Bloody Sunday' – and to a report by Lord Widgery which exonerated the soldiers from misconduct or incompetence but – inevitably – did nothing to dispel myth. In fact the troops made what in any other country would be regarded as a pretty restrained effort in defending themselves. Three weeks after the Londonderry affair there was a bomb in the Parachute Brigade's Officers' Mess at Aldershot, with tragic results. And five weeks later I told the House that it had been decided to transfer most of the major powers relating to Northern Ireland security to the British Government. Brian Faulkner, who had succeeded Chichester-Clark, resigned. An extremely able man, on whom much hope had been placed, he felt the diminution of Stormont's authority put him in an untenable position. Direct rule – conceived as temporary and designed to exclude no ultimate solution whatsoever provided it enjoyed widespread support across the community in Northern Ireland – was imposed. I am sure that we were right to impose it.

Then, in July 1972, the army (greatly reinforced for the purpose) moved into a number of areas which had been declared as 'no-go' for police and army and civil law authorities alike; areas which, under the rule of the Republican gun, had in effect declared their secession. This could not be allowed for long and we were harshly criticized for allowing it at all: but we wanted to ensure that action, when taken, was swift, decisive and final. It was. I took the opportunity when announcing to the Lords what had happened to reiterate my pride at the honour I felt in being the political head of the army. I tried to do this as often as I could. Nobody who has been a soldier supposes that *Hansard* is the favourite reading of the troops but, especially in conditions like those in Northern Ireland, I think it helps everyone from general to private to know that people and Parliament support and admire. I must pay tribute, too, to the officers who commanded there with enormous skill and distinction – Harry Tuzo and Frank King come particularly to mind. They were outstanding. The 'internal policing' soon became a bitter anti-terrorist struggle, dependent on Intelligence and wise guidance from above as well as tough training at all levels. Urban terrorism is a more intractable problem than the fighting of a war.

Like most of my fellow-countrymen, I found the attitude of foreigners the most irritating facet of the Northern Ireland situation, be they American or European. I could not pretend to great personal knowledge of the province or its politics before going there on duty – I remember that an early visit impressed me most unfavourably with the bigotry – and insobriety – of a lot of the fairly senior people in Ulster politics whom I met. But I always appreciated that the mass of ordinary people there were disgusted by the criminality masquerading as nationalist struggle which had forced the Government to react as it did. Many foreigners, however, persisted in misunderstandings which were both ludicrous and provoking. They liked to regard the situation as a colonial problem – determinedly ignorant of the fact that the majority of the colonials were resolved to remain British and the majority of the mainland British would probably have been delighted to let their Irish compatriots settle their own affairs and devil take the hindmost. Against that background it was hard to sit down under the ignorant criticism of outsiders. It was we, the British Government, who were spending our taxpayers' money and earning obloquy in order to try to work towards decent arrangements for all parties. Later, when Foreign Secretary, I attended the European Parliament. Every sort of European party – fascists, communists, whatever – had representation there and they were no doubt used to some pretty rough politics at home. But when they first heard Ian Paisley and a few politicians from the Republic of Ireland exchanging shouted insults I had the feeling that they were beginning, with some surprise, to learn that the Irish situation was slightly more complex than they had supposed.

Problems like Northern Ireland – particularly Northern Ireland – tended to be depressing because of the vicious cruelty they generated and because one often had little sense of progress or improvement. But in much the largest part of my responsibilities my time at the Ministry of Defence was extremely happy. I do not claim to have brought about any huge revolution in defence management or British strategy and I had no ambition to do so. Our methods are well-tried and although some aspects – and I have mentioned a few of them – always needed a hard, clear look and here and there some temperate reform, the underlying structure was sound. Our system of mixing uniformed Service and Civil Service people within the Ministry's main policy branches was excellent. The sailors, soldiers and airmen brought professional aptitude, of course – but, more than knowledge, they injected a certain realistic atmosphere, a reminder that the entire building and its occupants existed to keep ships afloat, aircraft serviceable and up to date, and regiments of the army in good order; while the civil servants – many of long experience in the business of defence – brought continuity, administrative skill in running the Whitehall machine, and knowledge of the ways of Government. There was no need to dig this plant up by the roots. I pruned it a bit, did a little grafting, and tried to tend it. As for the Services, I visited them often and everywhere, and although I could never obtain for them all that they reckoned they needed, I believe I left them a little better, a little larger – and perhaps, a little happier – than I found them.

During my time I got my old friend Dick Nugent to chair a committee to look at all our landholdings – the Ministry of Defence seemed to have a great deal, not all of it perhaps necessary or rational and often giving rise to criticism. The committee reported in May 1973, and most of its recommendations were ultimately supported by Parliament: although action took place after I had given up office.

The major materiel decisions we took mostly, too, came to fruition long after I left the scene – that is the way of defence, with its long equipment lead times between research and production: but I was glad that we set in hand the improvement of Polaris and I don't think we wasted much money. The financial battle was always hard.

I was also glad that we had shown Britain had not become entirely self-centred, that we had not forgotten the rest of the world beyond the European and Atlantic area, beyond our own backyard. The Simonstown agreement, important for maritime operations in the South Atlantic and Indian Ocean, was periodically criticized, of course, because of the understanding – and joint manoeuvres – with South Africa it entailed. We always emphasized that it involved no sort of condonation of South Africa's internal policies; in Defence we believed in realism and pragmatism. One cannot conclude or maintain agreements only with people whose every attitude one supports.

But it was NATO that mattered most to us, and here I simply claim that we 'kept the show on the road' and demonstrated that we intended to play a marginally greater rather than a marginally smaller part than heretofore. It is a modest claim but a true one. NATO is a huge alliance and although its armed forces in sum are less than we would all like in order to be absolutely assured of security, they are, nevertheless, formidable. Being both huge and formidable they are not susceptible to dramatic revolutions during the life of any particular Government in any one of the member nations. Nor is NATO strategy. NATO seldom makes headlines – except when there is a row, generally exaggerated by the media. We did our duty by NATO, as was both our obligation and our interest: it constituted our own defence.

The day I left the Ministry in January 1974 was, for me personally, a miserable one. I was leaving friends and a job I loved. But, by then, new and mostly unwelcome developments had occurred; and I was particularly involved in them through another position I had somewhat unwillingly acquired. In April 1972 Ted Heath had asked me to be Chairman of the Conservative Party.

Every Cabinet is coloured primarily by the personality of the Prime Minister. Each Premier has a different style and induces a different atmosphere. The first Cabinet in which I sat was led by Alec Home. He was easy-going, urbane, very commonsensical and practical, and had little taste for speculative flights of fancy. He aroused considerable loyalty and where there is strong loyalty to a Premier within Cabinet that loyalty spreads laterally and members find it more natural to support each other.

Ted Heath was a different sort of leader. Certainly he attracted loyalty. A somewhat lonely man, he needed friendship, yet found it hard to unbutton himself to the affection of others; but those who knew him best were loyallest to him and I always found him an agreeable and happy companion, and at Chequers as well as Downing Street a charming host. Later, when his leadership was challenged, I had no difficulty in saying publicly that I thought the party would be best served if it retained Heath as its chief. In my view he had vision and a sense of history superior to those of any other claimant. Of course people said there was friendship as well as genuine calculation in my support, but friendship is a relevant factor in politics and particularly in Government. In a Cabinet there should be friendship, a sufficient degree of friendship in the atmosphere. It cannot work well otherwise.

Heath could, as Prime Minister, be abrasive and sometimes contrived to seem at the same time both touchy and autocratic. But in my experience Prime Ministers tend to become autocratic. It is probably necessary. They also tend, after a honeymoon period with their party, to be criticized for not listening to others – Heath certainly was. In my view this was untrue. He certainly listened. He may not always have been persuaded by what he heard – but that is the top person's prerogative.

He was an indifferent steward of his own time, sometimes

showing small capacity for concentrating on the right priorities, on always putting first things first. Nevertheless I had a high regard for Ted Heath and I believe that history will rate him as a Prime Minister, and his administration, a good deal higher than it does at present. He was delightful to work with. He was passionately devoted to his country, and he wanted to achieve specific things. He had no use for the game of politics as such – he was the sort of politician who is interested only in results and realities. He had a much broader view of what Britain could be than most leading politicians I have known. He had a strong, lucid mind. He was a man of wide interests and talents – sporting, artistic, cultured. He was extremely courageous. He had, when at the Foreign Office, led the way in devilling our negotiating position to join the European Community, an experience which had undoubtedly widened his understanding; and he was utterly convinced that in bringing Britain into the Community he was taking a step which was as essential as it was historic. He will increasingly be proved right. The Community was a great element in Ted Heath's political faith.

It is too easily forgotten, as well, that Heath was a tough Prime Minister, and a pretty harsh opponent if he thought Britain was being unjustly criticized. I recall a Commonwealth Prime Ministers' Conference in Singapore which we all enjoyed, albeit in my case from a distance, when Heath turned on a number of colleagues who were attacking us over the question of arms for South Africa. He silenced his attackers. He called humbug by its proper name. We had decided on sale of limited categories of arms to South Africa for external defence, and Heath defended it with spirit. South Africa, then as now, was a subject on which every country tends to unite in righteous condemnation, carefully abstaining, however, from actions which can harm its own interests and applying double standards with much emotion and little equity. Ted Heath was robust about that sort of thing. His problems were the same as those which have beset Margaret Thatcher in a later age. There was also a memorable occasion when Kenneth Kaunda of Zambia came to London in October 1970, again in order, he said, to explain how strongly he felt about arms for South Africa. I attended a meeting at No. 10 where both sides explained their (familiar) positions with courtesy and moderation and then dispersed to change for a small dinner, also at No. 10. While changing for dinner Heath turned on the television news and learned that on arrival at London Airport, Kaunda had told a news conference that he had come to Britain to appeal to the British people over the heads of their Government.

Ted Heath reckoned that if he, Heath, had made such a remark in Lusaka he would have been in trouble, and when we were reunited for dinner the mood was black. We sat down to dinner in silence. My early training had been that guests, however insufferable, had to be entertained and for the first two and a half courses I kept up a flow of increasingly feeble reminiscence, which met with African surprise, marked by animated giggling. Denis Greenhill took over from me and pursued, gallantly, the same line.

We moved in silence to the drawing room, and I said, desperation in the voice, 'We've had a very interesting evening.'

The Prime Minister spoke for the first time, and with menace. He addressed Kaunda.

'Very interesting! And what I don't understand is that we take full account of all your problems. We know you trade through Rhodesia with South Africa. You sell thousands of tons of copper to them. We understand it – you have to get power from Kariba Dam, and we make facilities for you to do so by intervention in the United Nations. What we do *not* understand is why you – whilst accepting all this from us – should totally ignore what we consider to be our own vital concerns.'

Heath then relapsed into silence. The effect on Kaunda was electrifying. His eyes rolled, he clasped his arms, he swayed from side to side, intoning,

'My God, my God, my God! Never did I think I would hear a British Prime Minister speak to me like that! My God, my God, my God!'

His entourage took their cue. They folded their arms and swayed in unison, murmuring, 'My God, my God! How terrible, terrible!' This lasted several minutes.

I tried an intervention, which sounded even feebler than it looks in print.

'The Prime Minister means, Mr President,' I said, 'that we all have our interests.'

The Zambian High Commissioner said that he thought it was time to go home, and the Prime Minister led his dinner party down the stairs, past the Cabinet room, to the door where they all passed into the night, no further word spoken. I don't think Kaunda loved Ted Heath thereafter, but I know he respected him.

Heath had, as Opposition leader, been identified with 'Selsdon' – a Conservative seminar had been held at the Selsdon Park Hotel, south of London, and the general tenor of what emerged had been a fairly assertive restatement of the virtues of capitalism and the benefits of free enterprise, in contradistinction to the creeping socialism we had, it was suggested, suffered in recent years under Governments both Labour and Conservative. It is simple, and often politically necessary, to produce emphatic doctrinal statements when in Opposition, statements designed to underscore the total change the electorate may expect from ousting a Government – and thus to appeal to that desire for a fresh start and a new direction to which everyone is prone from time to time. It is less easy – and often less politically sensible – to live up to the letter of such statements when back in office. On this occasion the Labour Government had been quick to stigmatize the outcome of our Selsdon seminar as the emergence of 'Selsdon man', depicted as archetypically uncaring and selfish in promoting the individual's devil-take-the-hindmost pursuit of material prosperity. Heath had never, in fact, been particularly dogmatic about any of this – his attitude to economic matters was essentially empirical. It is an attitude I share. I have described the Conservative Party publicly as 'never at its most attractive or most interesting or most useful when trying, out of character, to be ideological'.

Heath bore the 'Selsdon man' soubriquet with equanimity, but it made the Conservative Government particularly vulnerable to later charges of change of tack and loss of nerve when, in response to a rise in unemployment, Heath took a lead part in a reflationary policy – described as the 'dash for growth'. I don't think Heath was false to any principles of his own in the matter, still less was he in bad faith. He thought, and most of us thought, that economic policy should take account of existing circumstances and balance possible future ill effects (inflation) against present unhappiness (unemployment) by the introduction of judicious and undogmatic measures. Both from an electoral and a human point of view we believed at that time that unemployment above a certain level was intolerable. I don't think now that all our measures were perfectly judged; but nor do I think they constituted some sort of betrayal.

Heath probably appeared unsympathetic to the United States from time to time. He had become a passionate European, he minded deeply that Europe should regain strength by greater unity of policy and he recognized – and did not necessarily dislike – the fact that this might not always be palatable to America. He may not have been invariably tactful in making this sentiment plain but the wisest Americans undoubtedly saw and shared the sense behind the vision.

As Defence Secretary I found Heath sympathetic – he had served with distinction in the army in the war, he liked the Services and he believed in as strong a defence policy as we could possibly afford. The details of what it should be and where particular priorities should lie he and my other colleagues were disposed to leave to me, only pressing debate during the annual wrangles over Departmental allocation of cash. Defence decisions generally turn on technical detail nowadays, and few ministers outside the Department have the time or taste to involve themselves in that detail, although they will all share theoretic corporate responsibility.

*

It might be thought that Cabinet ministers, while not worrying themselves unduly about another Department's concerns, would nevertheless be greatly exercised about the running of the party, to which all belong and on whose general health will turn the question of how long they are likely to enjoy office.

It is not so. When our party is in Opposition the Chairman is a particularly important figure in the Shadow Cabinet. He has a high profile. His formal responsibilities may be the same as when the party is in Government but he is the chief builder of morale, the chief planner for the battle to come; and, of course, it will be an attacking battle, with the enemy – the Government – defending a record and able to be depicted as responsible for every disaster, every shortcoming in national life. In these circumstances every senior figure in the party is vitally interested in the plan of attack and the morale of the troops. The party's organization and health is crucial, and the Chairman has a great deal of support – of criticism too, no doubt, but certainly of support. I had seen this at first hand a few years previously when I had been asked to run a special fund-raising effort before the 1970 Election – £2 million was a good deal of money to get in the 1960s, and I had found the job both difficult and disagreeable, with its inevitable discovery of the unexpected generosity of some and the unexpected meanness of others. But it had enabled me to get to know most people in the upper reaches of the party and I had done so in Opposition, when everyone is eagerly concerned, and when everyone can be rallied to attack the foolishness, the incompetence and the policies of the Government of the day – and, with luck, to open their purses.

In Government all is different. The main difference derives, naturally, from the preoccupations of ministers with their Departments. They are – and rightly – chiefly concerned with their own formidable Departmental responsibilities, which keep them busy (and often much too busy) doing their own duty towards the running of the country. They don't have much time for the politics of the situation, whereas in Opposition they had all the time in the world. Inevitably, therefore, in Government they worry less about the Conservative Party; and about its Chairman, or his counsel. The Prime Minister tries to keep the political dimension before his colleagues, but no Prime Minister finds it easy.

But the Conservative Party worries about the Government – that is the other side of the coin. In Opposition the senior figures in the party have little difficulty articulating the feelings of the faithful – even the more extreme of the faithful. A speech is only a speech, and we all enjoy a bit of exaggeration, a witty cascade of abuse, a touch of rodomontade. But in Government, inevitably, caution creeps in and the Conservative Party starts to ask whether its leaders are still true believers, or whether they have been tainted by association with civil servants and other professionals assumed to be ready to dilute the faith. And it is probably inevitable in any party that the activists, the zealous workers, the people prepared to devote their time and energies to the organization, are also those on the more extreme wing. In this they are untypical of the voters generally. They are active, after all, because they feel more strongly than most of their neighbours. And the stronger people feel, the more they will be inclined to simplify, to paint issues as all black or all white, whereas most, as one knows sadly, tend to varying shades of grey. Disappointment at unpopularity (which may pass) or at by-election results (which may be equally transient phenomena) can make the activists intolerant and despairing, to an unhelpful degree. It is probably this which contributes so much to Liberal successes when Conservatives are in office. People look for what seems a tolerant middle way, repelled by the harsh language of vocal Conservatives feeling their backs to the wall. In 1972 this was an understandable if not wholly serious reaction – the Liberal Party stood for protest, and covered such a spectrum of dissent that it had no coherent policy at all, was completely implausible as a party of Government. But for a Conservative administration and a Conservative Party in mid-term trouble, it can be insufficient comfort to reflect that deserters from the party at by-elections tend to return to the fold when it is a matter of choosing the Government of the country.

All this means that in Government the Conservative Party has a great, indeed a greater, need for communication between the leadership and the body of the party, while most leading figures have less time, energy and interest to devote to it. Therein lies much of the Chairman's problem.

I do not wish, in this, to seem to denigrate the work of some Party Chairmen in Opposition, or to imply that their task was easy. Far from it. Woolton did a wonderful job rebuilding the shattered ranks of Conservatives after the demoralizing and unexpected defeat of 1945: I witnessed that, and greatly admired. Peter Thorneycroft did an excellent job. So did Tony Barber. But I reiterate that the task when in Government is both different and particularly difficult – probably Quintin Hailsham did it most successfully and most resoundingly between 1957 and 1959, a period when I was in Australia but which passed into legend. When in Government the party's supporters are prone to unease. All the mid-term – to say nothing of the more terminal – problems which beset any Government infect the confidence of its supporters in the country and of the people who try to enthuse them, organize, rally them. Even Quintin had found the going tough. I found it very tough indeed.

I accepted the charge with mixed feelings. Ted thought that I knew a lot of people in the party, that I had a good deal of experience, had been around a long time and was relatively senior. He obviously thought me a good choice. I doubted this. I was a hereditary peer, which makes things more difficult – although this had not, it was true, particularly handicapped some effective holders of the job in the past: nevertheless, I was always conscious that it was possible to say to me, 'What do you know about it? You've never faced a Selection Committee or fought an Election.' More importantly, I was extremely busy in the Ministry of Defence, with the additional time-load of international conferences, visits and tours which the post involved. I questioned whether the chairmanship should, ideally, be combined with one of the great Departments of State; and in the event the Ministry of Defence tended to think I spent too much time being Party Chairman, and the party officials certainly reckoned I devoted too many hours to being Secretary of State for Defence. I have not changed my mind on this – the combination is undesirable. Of course the party want, as Chairman, someone sufficiently senior to have the Prime Minister's ear, somebody in the inner counsels of Government, someone with status – that is natural, and to disregard it is to make the party itself feel disregarded, with bad consequences. But, I reiterate, combination with a major Department is bad for the party: bad for the Government; and bad for the country. Inevitably, however, I accepted. Most people feel they must do what a Prime Minister requests, defer to his or her judgement in such matters.

As so often I was lucky in my associates. My personal assistant within the party organization was Chris Patten, a brilliant young man, articulate, keen-minded and particularly nice. Sara Morrison, whom I had known for many years, was a power at Central Office with all sorts of ideas about the party, and fun to work with. Above all, Jim Prior, who was a Vice-Chairman. Jim, like I, had the problem of combining this office with a Department – he was Minister of Agriculture – but he was appointed to balance me as a Cabinet member in the Commons. He was an old friend. He had been Parliamentary Private Secretary to Ted Heath and very close to him in Opposition. He was an admirable colleague, reliable, likeable and wise. I regret that he has decided to leave the public scene.

I was, therefore, sure of working with a good team. It was going to be necessary. By the summer of 1972, party morale was pretty low. The rot had been started by the settlement of a miners' strike early in the year. The most devoted of our supporters thought the Government had bought their way out of trouble by giving in to industrial muscle – a circumstance which undoubtedly influenced us two years later when further trouble in the mines arose. There were other causes for our mid-term trouble within the party. Our economic as well as our industrial policies were regarded by some as flabby. There was a general feeling that the Government, under pressure, was conceding too many cases on which bold words had been uttered before and during the Election of 1970: that we were too often running away. By February 1973 there was newspaper talk of 'a party in crisis'.

We did our best for party morale. In particular we tried to improve the conditions and salaries of constituency agents, those people with a pretty thankless job on whom the organization largely depends. We had great opposition in much that we attempted – from within the party organization in general and from Central Office in particular. I am unsure why: like most organizations, Central Office did not welcome innovation but there was, anyway at that time, what seemed to me a wholly unacceptable degree of resistance and backbiting – the latter, of course, often touching the Leader of the party, the Prime Minister, personally.

I have also noticed that when Government and party are going through a bad patch there is generally a tendency to blame lack of communication and ascribe the lack to individual failure. People say, 'I'm sure the Government's doing the right thing but they simply don't explain it properly. They don't put it across to the country. That's why they're not as popular as they should be. In fact it's why they're damnably unpopular! And it's why our morale's low!' I am sceptical of this. Naturally, the message is sometimes conveyed with inadequate skill, or eloquence or conviction: but the hard truth is that if a Government loses popularity it is not primarily from a failure of public relations but because the Government's policies appear to be failing people in what they feel they have a right to expect. The policies may be eminently justified, but they don't give the impression of working – or working fast enough. The country is reported as being disappointed, the media fasten on a Government which appears to have lost its way, and party morale sags.

The Chairman of the party can't do a great deal, but he can do his best to show a cheerfulness he may not feel, he can try to enthuse those about him, he can work to see that the Government's achievements are described as widely and as convincingly as possible – and that the Opposition's promises and criticisms are deflated; and he can use his position in Cabinet to keep the reactions and mood of the party faithful well before his colleagues in general and the Prime Minister in particular. I did not find this a period of my life which brought great happiness or any strong sensation of success.

In 1973 the National Union of Mineworkers directly challenged the Government on the issue of pay. We had introduced in 1972 a statutory incomes policy, to put some sort of muzzle on what appeared a threatening level of wage-led inflation. I don't propose to argue here the merits and disadvantages of such a policy whether in economic theory or historic practice, but at the time it seemed to offer some sort of consensual way forward, which could reduce inflation by general agreement, and with consequential sacrifice equitably shared. No such policy is popular with trades unions whatever its hypothetical longer term benefits, but we had talked to their leaders at great length and although there were grumbles a certain moderation of inflationary settlements had been introduced, while unemployment remained comparatively low. The miners, with a large claim which went far beyond the Government's norm, were therefore on a collision course not with the National Coal Board (whose discretion was tied by statute) but with Government.

Then yet another Arab-Israeli war broke out, on 6 October of that year. The flow of Middle East oil was drastically reduced, to some countries being cut off altogether. The price quadrupled in the next three months. Energy supplies were at risk, and the negotiating hand of the miners in their dispute was greatly strengthened. It was decided to start a new Ministry of Energy – inevitably something of a crisis management organization. In January 1974 I was plucked from the Ministry of Defence to go and head it.

I went without enthusiasm. We were short of oil, participating in what amounted to a world crisis of energy; and our domestic coal stocks were running down. We were in confrontation with the National Union of Mineworkers, who clearly thought they could last longer than we could. Our national electricity supply and our entire industrial life was threatened. To conserve energy we had – before I left the Ministry of Defence – inaugurated a very unpopular three-day working week (production didn't greatly suffer, which may indicate something about industrial efficiency and productivity at that time): and the general atmosphere of a country in midwinter crisis, with cold pervasive and lights flickering, was demoralizing. As Party Chairman I knew – particularly in the light of what many thought a weak-kneed settlement with the miners in 1972 – that the Government would not be forgiven for a surrender. Our resolution was on trial and I believed that if we conceded the miners' case Conservative support throughout the country would be in tatters. As Energy Minister I soon discovered that we had little time.

I reckoned that if we were to survive the crisis we should have the country demonstrably behind us. That meant a dissolution and an Election – as soon as possible.

I made my view very clear, and simultaneously did what I could to start up a new Ministry, with new civil servants to bring together and a new place in Government to form and fill. For the weeks that this lasted I retain no affection. There were few decisions which could be made in the time. Government had, I remember, to take a view about nuclear power stations and the type of reactors needed, but in the end the view was taken by my Labour successors – Eric Varley and Tony Wedgwood Benn. These Departmental issues, which would in normal times have been interesting and were clearly important, were anyway dwarfed by the Western world's energy crisis. I attended an Energy Conference in Washington, with Alec Home. A great galaxy of Foreign and Energy Ministers had come together, with Henry Kissinger (brilliant as usual) in the Chair; and Alec Home managing to combine his splendid gift for the simultaneously conciliatory and robust in quieting a ferocious row between Kissinger and his French colleague. I met Al Haig for the first time at that conference, a man for whom I have a high personal regard. I sat next to him at a White House dinner at which Nixon – Watergate was at its height – made a speech which appeared completely spontaneous, was utterly right for the occasion and was delivered with impressive authority. It was a remarkable feat.

Departmental issues were also, of course, overshadowed by domestic political crisis. There seemed no hope that the miners would become less intransigent. Every suggestion for settlement foundered, and for its part the Government could not possibly concede. One proposal was advanced by the TUC on which the Prime Minister made a statement in the House of Commons on 22 January and I repeated it in the Lords. Leading members of the TUC had called on Ted Heath and suggested that if the miners were allowed to get their money on this one occasion it would be 'treated as a special case'. Some may be cynical at this – who could know what, in the event, would have been 'delivered'? Nevertheless we made clear, and I said in Parliament, that we did not question TUC good faith. The difficulty was that the miners' claim so far exceeded what was on offer – itself, we considered, treating the miners as a 'special case' – that to go further would have been offensive to every other worker who had so far shown restraint: or, alternatively, would have opened the floodgates. The proposal had to be courteously rejected. It might have solved the immediate crisis, I suppose, although I cannot believe it would have strengthened the Government's standing with its supporters. Meanwhile stocks continued to fall. The country was going to run out of coal and its economic life come to a halt. People would die.

I said to the Lords on 6 February, 'We are confronted today by one of the most serious crises in peacetime that any of us can recall,' and it was hardly an exaggeration. In the same debate I told the House that the NUM were now refusing even to talk to Government. There were, of course, voices to urge us to concede everything. As I said then, the line of least resistance has always had its advocates. We realized, of course, that however much people blamed the miners, they would undoubtedly take it out on the Government. Lives would actually be in danger, and in such circumstances Governments, who have constitutional power to act, inevitably bear responsibility and blame. With every day that passed I became more urgently convinced that if we were to tackle this business, this confrontation with a section of the community whose actions were putting the entire nation at risk, we must set the issues before the people. We could only do our duty backed by an electoral mandate. Jim Prior and my other closest associates in the party took the same view. I take it still.

I had first urged this view early in January – before I started the Ministry of Energy – but Ted Heath believed the moment was not ripe. He deferred asking for a dissolution until 10 February. There have been many criticisms of the timing of that 1974 General Election, ranging from those who – like myself at the time – reckoned it should be held as soon as possible to those who argue that it was unnecessary to hold it at all. Nobody, and certainly not I, has the right to be dogmatic in criticism of a Prime Minister in such a case. The Prime Minister has the sole responsibility. Timing, as in most things in life, is all-important. Ted reckoned that for the pie to be cooked, for the electorate to be ready to see it our way, they must be convinced that we as a Government had tried and tried again to reach a settlement, that we had been patient and conciliatory to a fault. He may have been right. At the time I thought we were hanging on too long, and I said so. Nobody will ever know what the upshot of an earlier Election might have been. As it was, it was held at the end of February and we nearly won it.

It is a mistake to try to run an Election campaign on a single issue. That single issue may have induced a Prime Minister to call the Election and clearly it has to play a part in the ensuing campaign; but a Government, inevitably, has to fight on its whole record. One cannot keep a particular matter like the miners' strike, however dominant, before the electorate to the exclusion of all else for the three or four weeks involved. It was, in 1974, necessary for us to fight on the broad front of all our policies – our statutory incomes policy, our general economic performance and so forth – and although we sought to emphasize that the main cause the country had to try was whether an elected Government should or should not subordinate the national interest to the blackmailing pressure of one influential section, our overall record at that time was not particularly popular and our opponents, with some success, sought to widen the debate.

Moreover, it was not easy to present the argument over the miners' strike with sufficient clarity at all times. The difficulty was that we had to give two impressions, and there was always the risk that they cancelled each other out. On the one hand it was necessary to show resolution, to convince that we had no intention of surrendering. Most people had, albeit without enthusiasm, accepted our incomes policy and a principle was at stake. On the other hand we wanted to avoid giving an impression of unreasonable obstinacy, of bloody-mindedness. If there were grounds for sensible and legitimate negotiation on detail, we wished both to be and to appear ready to explore them. The country was fed up with the miners; but it was always likely, we thought, that if people thought we were neglecting acceptable compromise they would also prove to be fed up with us, and show it at the polls. Orchestrating this, and keeping both credibility and unanimity, was never easy.

I don't intend to describe again the course of that Election. It has been done too often. The outcome was that Labour won four more seats than ourselves in a House of Commons wherein no party had an absolute majority. Ted Heath explored with the Liberals the possibility of a Conservative/Liberal coalition but nothing came of it – which I think just as well. I don't believe the electorate would have taken kindly to the two minority parties (in the immediate past being most abusive about each other) making common cause to form a Government and to exclude the majority party, however tenuous the majority was. Of course it can be done with constitutional propriety, but I don't think the circumstances were such as to make it politically healthy or wise in 1974.

I remain of the opinion that we needed to hold that Election, that the issues of principle were very important and that a four-year-old majority had to be reaffirmed, with sufficient national backing. Few campaigns are decided by one battle and it may even be that the long struggle to bring order to British industry was advanced, in the end, by that battle lost. For lost it was. The incoming Labour Government naturally conceded to the miners (and to the trades unions generally) all that was claimed, and then lasted five years until the force of economic events produced their own downfall in turn, in the middle of a raging inflation.

At the time, of course, we felt sore. Conservatives do not in the least like losing Elections and in the ensuing inquest every recent move and every recent decision came under fire. Ted Heath, as is the occupational hazard of Prime Ministers, had alienated a number of his supporters in Parliament who reckoned their virtues were inadequately recognized. His style of leadership was criticized, his tactics and timing in respect of the Election were castigated and his position was openly brought into question. Much of this was unfair, but it was the way of the party when beaten at the polls. As Chairman I received a good deal of adverse comment, inevitably. Ted Heath was entirely right to make a change, and to appoint Willie Whitelaw as the new Party Chairman. Parliament then ran on to October, when Wilson asked for another dissolution and proceeded to beat us again: handsomely, this time.

CHAPTER 12

Opposition and Party Leadership

I suffered once again the by now familiar psychological effects of moving from office to Opposition. I did my best to rally the Tory peers and keep the heat on Government: I was leading the Opposition peers once again. Once again I took up the threads of commercial and banking life as my former colleagues kindly invited me to rejoin them. I went, once again, on many rounds of visits – to Alaska, Japan and China in September 1975. In China although 'The Chairman' still nominally lived, the 'post-Mao' phase was effectively under way and I was impressed by the confidence and courtesy of Teng Hsiao Ping, at that time Vice-Premier. I went for Barclays Bank to the West Indies in September 1976; and met the leaders – interesting and colourful but in very few cases reassuring – of those territories. In all of them the economic prospects were depressing, and in most the problems of unemployment appeared formidable. Politically there were shadows: Guyana seemed well on the way to becoming a totalitarian state.

Val Duncan, a friend of many years standing, invited me, too, to join the board of Rio Tinto Zinc. This gave me a chance to learn something about the mining industry. It also gave me additional motive and opportunity to travel in Africa. The Pacific, also – I visited Bougainville, where my arrival co-incided with a unilateral declaration of independence! But Africa, particularly Southern Africa, led me to Namibia, to Zambia, to Mozambique. And it led me to Rhodesia.

Rhodesia had been living in the face of a good deal of international obloquy, expressed by United Nations-inspired economic sanctions which we had opposed but had not over-turned (insofar as our own observance of them went) when in Government. We always thought sanctions pretty futile, but they had constituted one of those occasions where to backtrack on a futility is likely to have worse consequences than to go along with it. I could, on visiting, observe how great was the futility, at least on the surface. Everything material man's heart could desire was being successfully imported to Rhodesia, clandestinely; or via South Africa. Every other car seemed to be a Mercedes. The Rhodesian Government had encouraged a lot of successful substitution. The only people who seemed to be applying sanctions painstakingly, and were certainly losing by it, were the British. When I went again to Rhodesia, much later, I sensed that sanctions were at last beginning to bite, as given time they must: but as an instru-ment for changing the mind of a people comparatively quickly, our disbelief in their efficacy was manifestly justified. Further-more we Conservatives had always had a fundamental objec-tion to the principle of handing the problem over to the United Nations. It was a British problem, however intractable, as I emphasized in my contribution on Rhodesia to the Lords in November 1974.

I was accused later, as the Rhodesian business developed and particularly in its often disagreeable aftermath, of being indifferent to the interests of the white settler population of Rhodesia. The criticism was made publicly and sometimes violently: or, more commonly, in private conversation and innuendo. Nothing could be further from the truth. I was always perfectly clear that the British Government had a considerable responsibility towards the white Rhodesians and their interests. They were a minority, a sizeable minority although in no way equating to the proportion of whites in South Africa, in a land which had been developed very largely by their own efforts – or by the efforts of those among them who had been there for some time. They were not to blame for the fact that fashions and perceptions in international politics had dramatically changed since the days when their predecessors had created a new country and named it after

Cecil Rhodes. They were convinced that majority rule on the basis of a simple count of black heads would produce chaos in their country – chaos, bloodshed on an increasing scale, and personal ruin. Their fear of black rule was generally represented abroad, impatiently, as a simple determination to hang on to a privileged position and lifestyle. There was something in this – Rhodesians were not the only people to believe with ease that general good is synonymous with private advantage! – but one could not possibly dismiss as fanciful the conviction that Rhodesia could inevitably go the way of some other black-ruled states. There were not many encouraging examples of these, and the pious hypocrisy of the diatribes some of their leaders uttered about Rhodesia's lack of democracy merely fuelled the white people's resentment, their sense of living in a world of dishonesty and doubletalk. Furthermore they reckoned the Soviet Union was exacerbating a good deal of the internal trouble which confronted them – undoubtedly true, as I acknowledged more than once in Parliament. Moscow's policy in Southern Africa was orchestrated from the Soviet Embassy in Lusaka, whose Ambassador I called on, from curiosity, on one visit.

I needed no persuading of all this. It was clear and comprehensible. When the white Rhodesians looked at some of their neighbours they saw tribal excess, cruelty and intolerance, economic ruin. They had committed their lives and fortunes to a country they undoubtedly loved. They felt it threatened by ultimate disaster. And they had come to regard this disaster as the consequence of betrayal. British Governments, they had always believed, had a duty to support them, to see sense, to take realistic stock of the consequences of black rule, to stick up for them internationally. Angry at London's refusal to see things their way they, or considerable numbers of them, had backed Ian Smith's defiant assertion of independence, and now they were surviving with a good deal of determination and success the rather fumbling efforts of the outside world, including Britain, to change their hearts and minds by pressure. The white Rhodesians were being defiant, resolute, somewhat backward-looking and certainly bloody-minded. In a word, they were being British!

I had two conversations at that time with Ian Smith. There was no doubt that he had shown considerable tactical adroitness in preserving his regime in the face of the hostility of the world. He had, illegally in the eyes of the international community, declared and maintained a state of independence, and he had managed this with no small skill. But my impression – reinforced later – was that Smith was not a generous-hearted or far-sighted man. I thought it mistaken to be unfair to him as some were: 'I happen to believe', I said to the Lords in 1977, 'that there is in some quarters ... a vindictiveness against Mr Smith and the white Rhodesians which is very much to be regretted.' But I nevertheless, as previously, urged the Tory peers not to oppose the sanctions Order. The truth is that Smith could, to my mind, have settled the Rhodesian business on terms offered in those days by Harold Wilson – terms better, from Smith's point of view, than those which events ultimately and inexorably dictated. He thought his position was stronger than it actually was – which can be fatal. He may have been influenced in this miscalculation by his Foreign Minister, P. K. Van der Byl, a man who managed to make enemies wherever he went.

But it was my concern for, rather than my indifference to, the white Rhodesians' situation which made me feel that my assessment of their interests was in this case better than their own. For I had believed for some time that their attitude was impossible to maintain indefinitely – and there was likely to be more hope of salvaging something if it were modified earlier rather than later. And as I, in Opposition, took my opportunities to visit not only Rhodesia but its neighbours, those who came to be called the Front-Line States, I became more and more convinced that Rhodesia could not exist for long without the acceptance of the international community and some sort of *modus vivendi* with the other African states: it was no act of friendship to the white Rhodesians to pretend otherwise. And the international community was not prepared to recognize a British colony, under unabashed white minority rule, which had unilaterally seceded from the British Empire and had no legitimate status in international law. Our

271

responsibility – and our best way of helping the interests of the white Rhodesians themselves – was to encourage some sort of development which would gain wide acceptance, and the goodwill, however grudging it might be, of Rhodesia's African neighbours. It was unthinkable in the 1970s that *any* British Government could cast the mantle of approval over an independent Rhodesia run by a small minority of its inhabitants, European in origin and white in colour, while the majority, African in origin and black in colour, had no discernible political voice. It may have been possible internally to justify that, as Ian Smith did, by saying everybody was happier that way, but for the rest of the world recognition must mean change. It must mean rapid development. To have argued otherwise would have seen Britain dangerously isolated in the world.

Furthermore I became sure, during those years in Opposition, that any such development must involve in discussion the leaders of the so-called Patriotic Front, Joshua Nkomo and Robert Mugabe, each with his own tribal base and conducting a guerrilla war. I was undeterred by the fact that both the American and Russian Ambassadors to Zambia agreed. The Russian Ambassador told me that Nkomo was not a Marxist.

'You are always so frightened of Marxists! He's a Capitalist!'

'Financed and armed', I said, 'by you.'

'Certainly!'

However that stood, the white Rhodesians consistently underestimated the genuine support which both these men had within the country. Nkomo was a pioneer of black nationalism and Mugabe, who had separated from him, had been his assistant. I became certain that there could be no long-term settlement without the involvement of both, and I spoke to that effect in Parliament. By then, during my travels, I had met most of the leading figures in the Rhodesian imbroglio and knew them tolerably well. The exception was Mugabe. Nkomo, Muzorewa, Kaunda, Machel, I knew. Ian Smith I knew. But only in later years did I encounter Robert Mugabe. A hardliner, he was not anxious to talk to a member of the Conservative Opposition and he made himself difficult to meet. He ran a disciplined team. I thought it a pity (and I may have been wrong) that the Front-Line Presidents insisted, as it seemed, that Nkomo and Mugabe were the sole representatives of the black Rhodesians: but that they were representative of large numbers I became ever more convinced.

The problem in Namibia was of a different order. Namibia was an area where South Africa had huge economic interests, and was naturally unwilling to see chaos. South Africa had held a United Nations mandate to rule the territory – once German South-West Africa until defeat in 1918 deprived Germany of her African colonies. The United Nations mandate had ended, and South Africa had tried to cobble together various amenable successor administrations, none of which had much, or sufficient, domestic support. South Africa thus had an economic as well as a security headache across her border, residual responsibility which had formally lapsed and a situation in which most moves she made were likely to increase her international unpopularity, already acute. The dual standard applied to South Africa was increasingly virulent, and I said to the Lords in April 1978 that I only wished, 'that the vociferous opponents of South Africa were sometimes heard to be condemning other evils just as bad and in many ways worse in countries whose systems they seem to admire!' This point was often with justice made but was, as ever, whistling in the wind. And there was, of course, the South-West African People's Organization – SWAPO – which, whatever the unforced support it could have attracted, possessed the dynamic of a revolutionary independence movement, at least in the rather haphazard sense in which such words can be applied to Southern Africa. South Africa reckoned a SWAPO-run Namibia meant a mess. A hostile mess.

I met the leader of SWAPO, Sam Njomo. We were both in Lusaka in Zambia. At that time his tail was known to be up. We shook hands and I said, 'I know that you think you are going to be President of the State of Namibia in a short while.'

He did not dissent.

'Tell me,' I said, 'when you get to Windhoek, what are you going to *do*? Are you a Marxist?' (He had that reputation, as most Africans in that situation so described themselves.) 'Or are you', I said, 'a Liberal? An African Nationalist?'

'I am a Freedom Fighter.'

'Mr Njomo, when you are a President you will have got your freedom. What do you intend to do with it?'

'It will be for the people to decide.'

'But you have said you intend to have an Election. What will you tell people about your policy, what will it be? Your people, if they are to decide, will need alternatives, need advice.'

'My policy', Njomo said, 'will depend on how long it takes and how difficult it is made for me to get there.'

It was a pragmatic, a revealing reply and at least it was truthful. Practical policy, decisions proper to government, can await the situation, whatever it turns out to be at the time. Meanwhile, the struggle is all.

It was in 1975 that the consequences of losing two successive Elections caught up with Ted Heath. Once again, in a crisis of the Conservative Party I was out of the country in Australia, so once again I missed the interest and excitement of what was undoubtedly a traumatic moment in the party's fortunes, the 1975 leadership election. Challenged as leader, Heath looked to his friends; and I was entirely ready to say that I thought he should be re-elected. I reckoned he had greater breadth of vision than any of us. In the event, Margaret Thatcher beat him and became Leader of Her Majesty's Opposition. I wrote to her to say that, as she knew, I had publicly asserted my belief that Heath should win, and I would perfectly understand if she reckoned I was dispensable from the Shadow Cabinet team: but that I would naturally be very ready to give her any assistance within my power.

Margaret Thatcher is a person of striking firmness of purpose and integrity of character. She has been caricatured in the way that strong personalities often are, so that the whole world reckons it knows them well, and likes or loathes according to preference, with few indifferent. Such characters, and particularly if they are politicians, arouse powerful reactions of adulation or condemnation, and Margaret Thatcher has had her share of both. It may be a defect in my temperament that I find it much more natural to like than dislike people I work with or for. I may be irritated by characteristics but I generally sympathize with perceived difficulties and challenges. I could see why people criticized Ted Heath, but I thoroughly liked him and admired him, and I regretted his departure. In the same way but for different reasons I came to like and admire Margaret Thatcher too.

Margaret Thatcher's attitudes are not far from the historic Liberal Party in England with its emphasis upon self-help and individualism. She calls things by their proper names, she is unashamed of any of her views, she has an excellent mind and well-reasoned opinions and she knows her strengths. Margaret, from the first day of leading the party, made clear that she thought and felt we needed to take a new direction, that there was no hope for our country unless inflation was destroyed by strict monetarist measures (whose efficacy I suspect she exaggerated, but I have no desire for an economic dissertation in this book), no hope unless the possibility and the will for individual effort and reward were revived among the British, no hope unless the power of the state were sharply diminished, particularly in economic affairs, and unless the function of the trades unions was restored to representing their members' interests (as opposed to dictating to Governments which economic policies the TUC found acceptable). In all this there was no doubt she had the mood of the country increasingly with her. In all this – or in the specific policies her philosophy indicated – she was particularly supported and inspired by the studies led by Keith Joseph, a much misunderstood man whose intellect and goodness of heart were equally great, but perhaps greater than was his power of communication with ordinary people, despite his enormous kindness. Under Margaret Thatcher the Tory Party took a decisive turn – described as 'right wing', a somewhat imprecise term; or towards 'conviction politics'; or in many other laudatory or offensive terms, according to taste. The mood was for classical economic theory, for the self-regulatory efficiency of market forces, for wider ownership of property, for personal responsibility and inducement, and for strong, patriotic commonsense in addressing all manner of issues. I suspect much of this – and I hope the best of this – marks a permanent shift of emphasis.

The danger of such attitudes is that they can be applied to issues beyond their reach. It may be estimable to feel in a particular way about a certain relatively uncomplicated matter – robust commonsense and moral courage may be exactly the qualities required. In other fields, and notably in those where foreign policy is concerned, they may not suffice. The prejudices of others are often tedious and irrational – and may be contrary to their own best interests, too – but where they exist they are facts: and factors. The heart may urge in one direction but the head, tiresomely, may indicate another course. In foreign affairs, particularly, one has always to calculate the consequences, and shun the self-indulgence of reacting as instinct may suggest.

It is to Margaret Thatcher's credit that on such occasions – of which, later, I was to observe several – her heart was generally compelled by her to yield, albeit grudgingly, to her highly intelligent head; and this not under pressure from others but because she, a woman of integrity, could weigh evidence, perceive (no doubt often with irritation) what course would turn out best and, against natural impulse, decide to follow it. That takes a great deal of doing, not least when one has to shed some old friends as well as previous conceptions along the way. Later, some of her more assiduous admirers were quick to suppose that her instincts (assumed as combative) would always be in conflict with the advice of the Foreign Office (presumed to be placatory). They may have sometimes supposed correctly, but they seldom appreciated that her judgement was capable of being superior to her – and their – instincts, and that genuine agreement could result.

There was always apparent, too, her courage – right from the start. To anticipate a few years, I remember flying with Margaret Thatcher to Lusaka, during a very tense phase of the

Rhodesian business to come. The British Government, and she in particular, had been vilified in much of the black African Press. I noticed Margaret had in front of her, on her little table in the aircraft, a large pair of dark glasses.

I said, 'What on earth are those for?' We were arriving during darkness.

Margaret answered very clearly, 'I am absolutely certain that when I land at Lusaka they are going to throw acid in my face.'

There had been reported some hysterical outbursts, using that sort of violent language. I laughed.

'You totally misunderstand Africans! They won't do anything like that! They may shout, but absolutely nothing like that. They're more likely to cheer you.'

Margaret stared at me.

'I don't believe you.'

At that moment the aircraft touched down. It was pitch dark and as we came to a halt we heard a great shouting outside. The doors were opened and Margaret descended first, into a sea of white eyes and white teeth which, like the shouting, were impossible to distinguish as friendly or otherwise. Next day the Zambian Press reported, most inaccurately, that a trembling Margaret Thatcher had deliberately arrived in the dark to dodge the demonstrations. On the contrary (and we had had little control over flight and arrival times: one never does), Margaret marched down the aircraft steps totally serene. No dark glasses. Kenneth Kaunda greeted her warmly, and they were all cheering her! Her apprehension had showed her inexperience and mistrust of Africa – soon rectified, as she met the African leaders and with few exceptions found them most agreeable people. But her demeanour, in the light of her fears, was remarkably brave; and that bravery, both physical and moral, was prominent from her first day as Leader of the Tory Party.

I travelled in those years as a politician as well as a banker and a businessman, for Margaret Thatcher had decided that she would like me to remain a member of the team: I led the Tory peers but had no other designated 'Shadow' responsibilities. I ranged widely. I went to Russia in November 1978 – a visit during which, not for the first time, I received one encouraging impression, viz. that Russian inefficiency is so general and seemingly endemic that they might not be quite such formidable opponents in war as our Intelligence Services proclaim. Every arrangement miscarried, every car reported at the wrong time and place. I had a long talk with Gromyko – geniality itself, but affecting to suppose that the next British Government (which he assumed, flatteringly, would be Conservative) would, under Margaret Thatcher, be bellicose in the extreme! As ever, I left Russia with relief at escape from so drab, sad and oppressive an atmosphere.

Often, therefore, I travelled half as a Shadow minister and half as a commercial person. To Canada and the United States in January and February 1979 I went part for Cadbury-Schweppes, part for Rio Tinto and a lot for the Conservative Opposition, meeting and talking in Washington where the talk among American *cognoscenti* was all of SALT II, whether the propositions being negotiated were or were not a good idea, and whether they would get through the Senate. My own view on strategic arms limitation was that Britain should, at least at that stage, keep carefully clear. It was so far a superpower negotiation, and we stood to lose a lot if we inadvertently acted so that either side could seem to be using us. When asked to talk about this I always stressed the European interest, however: Europe had a particular concern about Cruise missiles and Soviet SS20s.

Visits of this kind kept me in touch with the chief makers of policy around the world, and able at least to chat about the principal issues. Few of these were new since my last experience of office. A similar mix of banking and political enquiry marked my visit to South America, also in February and March 1979, when we went to Venezuela, Ecuador, Colombia and Brazil. On the whole I was able to live my philosophy of using a period in Opposition to see my own country from the viewpoint of others, and from as many different countries as possible, without the particular obligations of office.

I went to the Middle East too, at that time – to Jordan, Syria, Egypt and – separately – to Israel. I went several times to the United States. And I went often to our European allies, to Paris, Brussels, Bonn – and Berlin. I also went to Eastern Europe. On a visit to Rumania in June 1976 Julian Amery accompanied me and we had two hours' remarkably anodyne conversation with President Ceausescu. There tends to be something rather funny about watching the performance of a colleague trying to talk to a foreign statesman of decidedly hostile views with the dubious aid of an interpreter. Julian struck a chord which seemed to be aiming at the Churchillian combined with a touch of pseudo-Macmillan (his father-in-law), somewhat reminiscent of an elderly repertory actor called out of retirement! I intercepted a smile between Ceausescu and his Foreign Minister which implied that they, too, had caught the echo. I have no doubt that Julian, I expect with justification, could give an equally sardonic portrait of my own performance! It was not a comfortable or particularly enlightening interview and visit, and I reckoned the Rumanian regime in its internal policy was as bad as anything in Eastern Europe. But they periodically cocked a snook at Moscow in their foreign policy, which was healthy; and when I visited Bucharest again, some four years later, Ceausescu was critical in only thinly veiled terms of the Soviet invasion of Afghanistan.

Not all my political efforts were devoted to travel. In the House of Lords we had, from time to time, those problems with which I was so familiar of when and whether to defeat the Government, and yet be regarded as acting responsibly. On the whole I think we succeeded; and when we let ourselves go (as during the shipbuilding nationalization Bill) we had a good cross-section of peers with us, and could be seen not as pursuing a purely factional interest, but as seeking to stop Government improperly railroading a Bill through Parliament without proper process or discussion. We harried the Government ceaselessly, of course, on their defence policy. They had

– as ever, in the case of Labour – inaugurated a 'Defence Review' whose end-product looked like yet another reduction of our strength, and erosion of our Armed Services' morale. Our nuclear capacity they quietly left alone – in spite of the Labour Party Conference of 1973 having 'demanded the closure of all nuclear bases, British and American, on British soil or in British waters'. This particular idiocy had been shelved, but in other ways the Government did harm.

But time occasionally dragged. I do not relish Opposition.

Margaret Thatcher's qualities were rewarded in May 1979. We won by a handsome majority when James Callaghan, who had succeeded Harold Wilson, went to the Country that summer and Margaret Thatcher was then asked to form a Government. The Thatcher administration was born.

I didn't know what place in it Margaret would find for me. The Shadow Foreign Secretary, John Davies, had died and Francis Pym had taken his place. I reckoned I knew more about foreign affairs than any of them by now, although I felt for Francis, a personal friend, no sense of rivalry. There was, however, the nagging difficulty of membership of the Lords – Ted Heath had given me the Ministry of Defence in spite of it, but no Prime Minister can neglect it. On balance – and appreciating that Margaret Thatcher knew perfectly well that I was not a convinced fellow-devotee with her on all issues, since I was outspokenly cool on ideology – I thought it unlikely that I would be asked to take the Foreign Office. Without equivocation, however, I wanted it. It was the job I had wanted all my life, the summit of my political ambitions. I already had pretty clear ideas of some of the lines of policy I wanted to pursue. I was, therefore, delighted when invited to be Foreign and Commonwealth Secretary. And as counterweight to my membership of the Lords I was given first-class ministers to handle our business in the Commons – Ian Gilmour, in the Cabinet as Lord Privy Seal, was my number two, and I also had Peter Blaker, Richard Luce, Nick Ridley and Douglas Hurd, a splendid team. I took possession of that historic room, so often described (notably, brilliantly and recently by Nicko Henderson*), and, as most Foreign Secretaries have done in the first heady moments of independence, made changes to the pictures, importing two Zoffanys. I had enjoyed the fine view over the river from my room in the Ministry of Defence. I enjoyed even more this huge, sombre, archaic place with its even finer outlook across Horse Guards Parade. Ian Gilmour had the room once occupied by the Secretary of State for India, with its two identical doors side by side, so that two visiting Maharajahs of equal rank could enter simultaneously.

'Foreign and Commonwealth Office': the old Commonwealth and Colonial offices had been merged in the Foreign Office some years earlier. A number of Departments of State, notably the India Office, had once been responsible for Britain's Empire, but the Empire itself, the colonies, were in these days so limited in number as not to justify a separate Ministry and the nations of the Commonwealth were, without exception, wholly independent of the British Government and were running foreign and domestic policies with which London's only concern was as old friend, one-time mentor but now (in good times sympathetic) outsider. Problems, when they arose, were inseparable from the ordinary run of foreign affairs.

Many people find the present concept of Commonwealth an irritant. They are perplexed by an institution in which the Queen is acknowledged as head but is not sovereign in those Commonwealth countries which are republics: an arrangement which appears so distressingly different from the ancient ties of loyalty to King and Empire which brought men and women instantly from all over the world to make common cause with Britain in two world wars. They dislike the public wrangling, the virulent criticism sometimes voiced by certain Commonwealth countries about each other – but more often about Britain. They find absurd reference to a 'family of nations' of which much is bound together not by blood, religion or political allegiance but only by historic subordination to Britain – a period anyway often referred to by the

---

* In *Private Office* (London, 1984).

others in highly uncomplimentary terms. They remember that two erstwhile Commonwealth partners have actually gone to war against each other. They regard as odious the sanctimonious humbug which accompanies occasional utterances of certain Commonwealth leaders, with words like 'morality' and 'democracy' used as weapons of stricture by men whose regimes are distinguished by neither. They are provoked, particularly during periods of international tension, by what seems the self-important posturing of Commonwealth bureaucrats, representing – so it appears – little but themselves, and for high salaries. In sum they think the institution a sham, its virtues an illusion. Many Britons are, and are likely to remain, disenchanted with the Commonwealth, and no Foreign Secretary will find universal or automatic – or even widespread – support among his colleagues or their electors if he presses a somewhat different point of view.

I knew all this well. My own approach was practical rather than theoretical – or sentimental. The Commonwealth tended to make news only when there was a problem or a quarrel – it tended only to arouse reactions at times when those reactions were almost by definition bound to be mixed, and to contain a good deal of hostility. This hostility was the business of politicians, the words and attitudes of public men. Politicians, on the whole, feel most at ease if talking – even quarrelling – with other politicians. Politicians are apt to think that the opinions and comments of politicians, the interchange of politicians – and political commentators in the media – are the dominant, even the sole, indicators of relations between countries.

It is not so. At least as important are the feelings of ordinary people towards ordinary people of other nations. These feelings may be based on myth, outdated memory, comfortable (or hostile) illusion: but they all colour our politics, or should. For better or worse, to the British, Australians are Aussies: play cricket – more often than not, inconveniently well: 'stood with us' when the chips were down. They aren't like other foreigners. Whatever the constitutional theory, and however maddening particular British – and Australian – Governments are to their Australian – and British – counterparts, these popular perceptions have force and apply widely within the Commonwealth. They mean that Governments may differ sharply, but the area of their differences is circumscribed by the well-rooted emotions of peoples. There is a historic, human connection, and to recognize it is a practical not a sentimental matter; and despite the political aggravation and diatribes, Margaret Thatcher was cheered at Lusaka.

This factor varies a good deal from one country to another, but if one considers it – as it was my job to consider it – from the point of view of the British Foreign Secretary and of the attitudes between Britain and the numerous other Commonwealth countries, I doubt if this human connection is wholly absent from any of those relationships. There may be a particular bond where one is dealing with a nation whose population, or a large part of it, originated in Britain, but even here the relationship may not be straightforward. In many cases, after all, the origins of emigration were rooted in bitterness, whose aftermath was not affection but mistrust of Britain. The New England settlers, leaving an England whose current system they opposed, were enthusiastic rebels against the British Crown in the following century. True, this didn't happen in Canada, a refuge for loyalists from the American Revolution: but many Canadian settlers, such as the refugees from the Clearances in the Highlands of Scotland, had no great reason to feel affection for London. And so on. Ties of blood are not necessarily reflected in political affinity. Nevertheless kinship does imply a human connection.

I do not believe, however, that this human connection – and I regard it as probably the most significant element of the Commonwealth – is restricted to what is sometimes called 'The Old Commonwealth'. On the contrary it also exists, although in subtle and often confusing forms, between the British and those countries we once governed as aliens. The human connection here is generally complicated by historic memories of a very mixed sort. The impact of the British on India – and of India on the British – will be written about until the end of time, and written about, amid controversy, from many angles. Yet I do not believe that Indians and Britons, India and Britain, will ever be able to regard each other coolly and distantly as if their shared and often troubled past did not exist. We have seen too much together. There is a human connection. And even in the most unpromising circumstances – where, for instance, an ex-colony in Africa, ruled by a tyrant, an Amin, remains in the Commonwealth – the anomaly, even the outrage, is apt to be tempered by a good many amiable individual recollections of past responsibilities, former affections. Again, there is a human connection. The past has fastened it upon us. And politics is not all.

I understand those people who say that, in spite of all this, it is meaningless to give to the human connection an institutional form: that it fosters illusion and absurdity and actually exacerbates ill-feeling. I understand, but I do not agree. It would be a bad thing if the Commonwealth were to break up. Everything evolves, develops or loses momentum, dies if wholly useless, survives and discovers new vigour if genuine need exists. We should not be overpolite, or pretend, or sentimentalize over the Commonwealth. We should not talk of it as if it were something it isn't. It is not a power bloc. It is not a preferential trading partnership as once it was. It is not an Empire. It speaks with many voices, some of them intensely provoking from time to time. Yet it consists not of governments but of peoples; and those peoples have at *some* period in their histories been touched by similar influences, learned from some of the same books, played some of the same games, imbibed (and sometimes neglected) comparable principles of law and administration. Fought, at least once, under the same flag. There is a human connection, not contemptible because varied, uneven and intangible. I am not ashamed that the connection was created by and runs through Britain.

But the bonds of Commonwealth are loose. The Commonwealth is tenuous. It collapses – and is most vulnerable to cynics – if one tries to put too much upon it. The cultural sense of unity between Britain and the nations of Western Europe is much more profound, deeper, older, than anything within the Commonwealth *per se*. We and the ancient peoples of Europe have developed our institutions, our philosophy, our arts and our manners in parallel and in close community. We British have always been on the fringe but nevertheless an integral part of that Graeco-Roman world from which European consciousness derives. We can't alter that and it is fundamental – more than the past (but comparatively recent) fact of Empire or the present (and even more recent) fact of Commonwealth. Nevertheless one should not abandon an institution because it is not something else, something it cannot be. I was glad to become both Foreign and Commonwealth Secretary.

Margaret Thatcher evinced at times a distrust of the Foreign Office, a determined attitude that it didn't stick up for Britain and was softly conciliatory where the reverse was needed. I found that this sentiment was never far from the surface, and could erupt in impatient hostility unless ably countered – and sometimes even then. I knew that I would need as much patience and firmness as I could command. As for the issues, there were, I thought, three principal areas where something had to be attempted.

First there was the Middle East. There were a few hopeful elements, but menacing signs as well. I had watched, from Opposition, Henry Kissinger's efforts in that region with admiration, happy to be able to pay my tribute to him publicly, telling the Lords in December 1976 that 'He, an American Jew, uniquely won the confidence of the Arabs without losing the friendship of the Israelis.' But, since then, matters had again begun to look ominous in the Middle East. I always regarded it as one of the prime danger points of the world, a place where other powers could be sucked without truly willing it into a situation of confrontation impossible to reverse: a 1914.

Then there was Europe, about which there existed a very general and entirely accurate view in Britain that we had had a raw deal, that in our monetary contribution to the European

Community we were paying more than our due, and were, furthermore, already worse off than we were entitled to be and than most of our colleagues and competitors – the latter a disagreeable fact to admit in an international gathering, as had several times to be done.

Third, there was, of course, Southern Africa – Namibia: Rhodesia. And it was because of Rhodesia, likely to be the most intractable of our problems, that I reckoned my time at the Foreign Office was unlikely to be very extended. For over Rhodesia my views by no means coincided with those of an influential wing of the Conservative Party; and I was sure that unless we achieved some sort of breakthrough I would inevitably, perhaps rightly, and probably quite soon, be asked to make way for someone of a different mind. I gave myself about six months.

CHAPTER 13

Rhodesia

Some of my critics have said or implied I was indifferent to the personal destinies at risk in Rhodesia. This was true of neither myself nor any of us. Nobody doubted the importance of the Rhodesian issue in human terms. We were dealing with the lives and fortunes of people, many of them in origin British people, at a critical point in their history, and contrary to some impressions we were deeply aware of it and deeply cared. But Rhodesia's importance to British foreign policy was largely negative: it created a problem because it soured our relationship with other states but its own significance in terms of our economic or strategic interests was not large. Its importance, regrettably, was as an irritant – with the Commonwealth, with our European partners and with the United States, where the Carter administration for domestic reasons was anxious to woo black African goodwill. The reactions of others to our policy and position were often based on a good deal of ignorance as well as calculation, and they could, of course, be intensely provoking. But they had to be taken into account.

The consequence was that far too much of a Foreign Secretary's time was being spent on Rhodesia. Of course the Rhodesian issue was worth settling in its own right if that could be done; but I could not ignore its distracting effect on our foreign relations. There were many other areas – and I have mentioned two of them – where both our interests and the general peace could be more at hazard, yet the Government's attention was always being drawn back to the problems of Rhodesia, and I thought it essential if only for that reason that we should make another effort to reach a solution. A solution, to my mind, meant a settlement in Rhodesia which would end the civil war there, would command sufficient internal assent to do so, and would lead to recognition of an independent Rhodesia by the international community.

'It will be our objective', I said to the House of Lords as we embarked on the Rhodesian business, 'to achieve a return to legality *in conditions of the widest possible international recognition.'* That was the crux – and the problem. From my observations during the past few years I was convinced that such a settlement could only be based on some sort of universal suffrage (less than which other nations would criticize as a 'fix'): and that in the process the Patriotic Front leaders, Nkomo and Mugabe, would need to be involved. Successive British Governments had taken their stand on 'majority rule' as a necessary precursor to independence. It had to come. I was not unaware of the traditions of Africa and the ways – often bizarre to Western democratic eyes – whereby majority and consensus may be reached there. But majority rule, acknowledged as such by the world, had to come and not until it did could we pay enough attention to other things.

There were additional reasons for urgency. The civil war, the armed rebellion against the Smith regime being conducted by guerrilla forces of Nkomo's and Mugabe's Patriotic Front, was an appalling strain on Rhodesia's resources. This war had been going on a long time. It had claimed many victims, black and white. There had been plenty of tragedy and sickening atrocity – endemic in this sort of situation: warfare of that kind is always marked by disgusting barbarity, and Africa is no stranger to cruelty. The war had strained Rhodesia's economy and society to the limits, and in spite of a good many local successes for Government forces and some skilful military operations it was not being won. It was exhausting Rhodesia, and in this context that meant it was particularly exhausting the white Rhodesians. The sands were running out, and the South African Government, which had supported Rhodesia generously, was undoubtedly beginning to wonder if this situation and burden was doomed to last forever; and whether it could.

There had been very recent developments within Rhodesia

of considerable importance. In April 1979 an Election had been held under the auspices of the Salisbury Government in an effort to break the deadlock and win general international respectability. Nkomo and Mugabe (who had each spent ten years in prison under the Smith regime) had, although released, been allowed no part in the Election and had denounced it as a sham. The only black contender, who thereafter nominally led a Rhodesian Government, was Bishop Abel Muzorewa. This was described as the 'internal settlement' (Muzorewa was governing, with Smith firmly behind his right shoulder) and we were urged, particularly by the right wing of the Conservative Party, to acknowledge its validity and to recognize an independent Rhodesia. It would have been highly convenient if we had been able to do so. Alan Boyd was sent out by Margaret, when she was still Leader of the Opposition, to report on whether the Rhodesian Election had been full and fair; and he, a man of great experience and probity, a previous Colonial Secretary, reported that it had indeed been full and fair. What, our right-wing critics enquired, were we waiting for?

I was certainly keen to emphasize how far the Smith Government had come towards us and towards settlement.

'There has been a fundamental change inside Rhodesia,' I said to the Lords in my first speech as Foreign Secretary. 'There has been an election in which every adult man and woman has been enabled to cast a vote . . . there is now an African majority in Parliament,' and I took every opportunity to speak encouraging words about Muzorewa and to remind that these developments under Smith, who had not long before spoken of white rule lasting a thousand years, could hardly be shrugged off as insignificant or not marking progress. The trouble was that although the Election had been as full and fair as conditions permitted, Nkomo and Mugabe, with their factions, had not taken part; so that conditions had only permitted a vote for Muzorewa, as a black – and he collected what I am afraid was a great many more votes than he could have possibly scored in an open contest (ultimately – and I am not naïve about the effect of intimidation in African elections –

he received a derisory share of the vote when weighed against Nkomo and Mugabe). I was already, sadly, convinced that the 'internal settlement' was probably a fudge, in terms of the domestic support it really commanded. It was widely seen as a device to perpetuate the white man's rule behind an amenable and unrepresentative black front, and although this was by no means completely fair there was something in it. Above all – which for me was decisive – it could not possibly be sold to the international community. It has to be recalled that Smith's declaration of independence had been an unconstitutional act and his regime in consequence illegal – and thus difficult for the British Crown to recognize, even if sanitized, so to speak, by an appearance of democracy. The international community perceived the difficulty very clearly.

I asked David Harlech* to pay a series of visits, to form a view on who would be prepared to recognize the Rhodesian 'internal settlement' if we ourselves did. He reported that it would not be recognized by any black African state – Nigeria, very hostile to Rhodesia and carrying a lot of weight, was orchestrating this opposition. It would not be recognized by a single member of the European Community. There would almost certainly be an adverse vote in the United Nations. There would also be a likely break-up of the Commonwealth. The 'internal settlement' did not look as if it had a chance of achieving my main object – international acceptance of Rhodesia, as well as a cessation of fighting; and I reiterate that this main object was because nothing less could possibly be in the long-term interest of Rhodesians themselves. Black and white.

This assessment of the 'internal settlement' and of the situation was by no means unexpected by me, but it was awkward. I was determined that we should neither be nor seem to be unfair to Muzorewa; but I was reinforced in my view that no settlement made without the participation of the Patriotic Front factions could possibly stick. We had, however, implied – not spelt out but strongly implied – in our Conservative

* Lord Harlech had been a member of the Pearce Commission, sent out at an earlier stage to report on Rhodesian opinion.

290

Election manifesto that if the Rhodesian Election which had led to the 'internal settlement' was shown to be free and fair then we'd acknowledge it: I had not been Shadow Foreign Secretary at the time, but I and all of us had said, of Boyd, 'The Government will be guided by his conclusions.' Alan Boyd had now reported favourably, but I was still convinced we shouldn't acknowledge the 'internal settlement' and that it would be no act of friendship to Rhodesia to do so. My view was unpopular with my critics within the Tory Party but I was sure I was right. I was British Foreign Secretary, and my duty was to British interests and British standing, as well as against what I was entirely persuaded could not last long or really improve matters in Rhodesia. To have recognized the 'internal settlement' at that time would have led to embargoes on British goods around the world, rejection of British counsel and influence 'because of Rhodesia'; and within Rhodesia Nkomo and Mugabe would have done all in their considerable power to step up the insurrection – with Soviet and Chinese assistance respectively. The 'internal settlement' offered no solution. There had to be a better way.

I became determined to work for yet another conference. There had been previous attempts to find a way forward by international conferences. I did not disdain the attempt to keep America with us (our predecessors had worked up a series of Anglo-American proposals) but to involve too many people in a conference of that kind, striking attitudes, watchful of domestic reactions, and exchanging periodic insults, would be a mistake. Furthermore the previous proposals had been overelaborate, and had tried to address too many details, seeking to establish the exact methods by which an interim Government might work and under what supervision – whereas the first essential fence to jump was the question of principle, the question of the constitution: one must, I was sure, proceed from there and only from there to consideration of such details as how to organize a ceasefire and its aftermath. I was resolved that negotiation must be step by step, and be confined to those directly involved: in other words to all parties in Rhodesia and the British Government. But I knew that 'all parties in Rhodesia' must include the Patriotic Front, and that we had to persuade them to come – and persuade others, Smith, Muzorewa *et al.* to sit down at the conference table with them.

I also had to persuade the Prime Minister.

Margaret Thatcher had not particularly bent her mind to Africa. Her instincts were in line with those of the right wing of the party. Alan Boyd had reported, he was a man whose judgement was worthy of our respect, we had gone through the correct motions, why not stick out our jaws and get on with it, damning much of the world for its ignorant prejudice and its double standards? I had some spirited discussions with her.

In the end we came to see it in the same way. It was one of those occasions to which I've referred when her heart and basic instincts (which I don't think changed) were subordinated by her to what her intellect came to decide made political sense; and I much respected the process. When convinced of something like this she was, of course, a most able and indefatigable exponent of the line adopted. And it was no doubt reassuring to me, in a way, that we started our internal debate from opposite corners: it gave me a sense that the question had really been thrashed out, that some synthesis had been achieved. Meanwhile, we had to agree our practical policy and tackle the next and vital step: the Commonwealth Conference to be held very shortly at Lusaka. The timing of that conference produced another motive for urgency.

I had an excellent team in the Foreign Office working on Rhodesia: Derek Day, who went out to Salisbury until our main conference started in London, Tony Duff, Robin Renwick, Charles Powell, all first-class, dedicated men – I know that no institution but the Foreign Office could have produced such support and such skill. Tony Duff was particularly adept at taking soundings of what the various parties were thinking at times when it was necessary for me to keep a certain distance. But first, of course, we had to gain general acceptance of the idea of a London conference on the lines Margaret Thatcher and I had now agreed should be our object. It was to be a conference under my chairmanship and comprehending all parties, black and white, to the Rhodesian problem, however antipathetic to each other. If anybody – Smith, Muzorewa, Mugabe, Nkomo – refused the idea of such a conference it would be futile.

When persuading people to a meeting of that kind they – and their friends, who may be influential supporters rather than principals – need to feel that there is something in it for them, that it may turn to advantage, or anyway more so than abstention from it. By now Margaret and I needed no persuading: we were sure that the British interest demanded settlement of the Rhodesian issue and needed such a conference if it could possibly be attained.

Ian Smith and the white Rhodesians – he, perhaps, less than many of his colleagues – had somewhat tardily come to reckon that time was not on their side. Sanctions might be slow to bite and be triumphantly circumvented but they were not in the long-term interest of an independent Rhodesia, and the more thoughtful realized that one cannot forever live in a state of isolation from the international community, in the modern world. Muzorewa would take his cue from Smith. And behind Ian Smith was David Smith, his deputy and treasurer, a level-headed Scot who saw things very clearly, as did Peter Walls, Commander of the Rhodesian Forces, a good soldier and excellently sensible man of whom I formed a high opinion.

Joshua Nkomo wanted a settlement, and had a motive for participation. He was regarded as something of a father of the Nationalist movement, but he was getting on in years and he wanted to see some sort of results and attain some position in an independent Rhodesia. His own tribal following, the Ndebele, were less committed to the military struggle, the guerrilla war against Government forces, than were Mugabe's. Nkomo felt he would, in an independent country, enjoy prestige, a power base and a chance of ending up on top. He hadn't a great deal of time.

The black African states on or near Rhodesia's borders all

293

wanted a settlement, and although we were determined to restrict conference participation to British and Rhodesians, these states had their protégés and contacts and would certainly bring pressure; and those who were members of the Commonwealth would, of course, use that forum, and we needed their support. For Zambia Kenneth Kaunda, an emotional but fundamentally decent man, was desperate for a settlement. Nkomo's men (who were doing little fighting) based their operations in Zambia and their presence was unpopular, inconvenient and somewhat threatening since they outnumbered the Zambian Army; while in economic terms a restoration of Zambia's normal relations with Rhodesia was urgent. For Mozambique Machel – violently and immoderately anti-colonialist in earlier times but mellowing somewhat with experience – relied extensively on Rhodesian maize. The Rhodesian Armed Forces also periodically made incursions into Mozambique, whence Mugabe's men were operating. Machel wanted a settlement. He was fed up, he had plenty of enemies at home, and his internal problems gave him quite sufficient worries. For Tanzania, Julius Nyerere wanted a settlement provided it went the way he desired – in Mugabe's favour. Later, he made plain that he would not accept any outcome – which by then meant an Election – unless Mugabe won it. He would accuse us of cheating. A great preacher of democracy to the Commonwealth community, Nyerere sent his Foreign Minister to the ultimate act of Rhodesian independence months later. The Foreign Minister approached me.

'Lord Carrington, I knew all along that you were going to fix it so that Mugabe won!'

I looked at him without warmth.

He continued, 'But why by so much? Why did you make him win by so much?'

Nevertheless Nyerere, whatever his own particular interpretation of democracy, wanted a settlement. He thought the whole issue had dragged on long enough.

South Africa undoubtedly wanted a settlement, provided it was one compatible with her interests. The situation made a good many demands on her and did nothing to help her own

294

problems with the international community. The United States found the situation perplexing and tedious, with domestic as well as foreign policy ruffled by this small, extraneous issue which disturbed relations, normally harmonious, with Britain but which wouldn't go away. The European nations, too, found Britain's Rhodesian problem distracting, an irritant. It had nothing to do with them, it provoked their more left-wing critics to strike attitudes and make trouble; the sooner it was settled the better. The rest of the Commonwealth would support any reasonable effort to solve the matter, a matter on which their politicians tended to utter moralizing generalizations rather than advance constructive proposals based on reality. Nevertheless the Commonwealth could help or hinder – and we needed the help, because the immediate hurdle we had to leap was the Commonwealth Conference at Lusaka where the agenda was to be dominated by Rhodesia.

The one party who, I suspected, was not particularly enthusiastic about a conference or impatiently in favour of a settlement was the one who reckoned that the tide of events was anyway flowing his way; that his people would, given time, outlast their enemies (and rivals) in the military struggle; that he was comparatively young; that he need assent to nothing unless it provided certainty that he would emerge on top. Robert Mugabe.

Thus we came to Lusaka, and I have described how the Prime Minister's fears of personal animosity proved largely groundless and how she at once blossomed in the warmth of Kenneth Kaunda's friendly personality, dancing with him enthusiastically as she did at the first party. The Lancaster House Conference which followed was attributed by some to a 'Commonwealth initiative' in which Britain reluctantly concurred. That was nonsense. Margaret Thatcher and I arrived at Lusaka with perfectly clear intentions of what we wanted to achieve. We knew what we wanted and we got it. Margaret played the hand extremely well, and bore with equanimity a certain amount of predictable abuse from some of her Commonwealth colleagues, delivered at banquets as well as at meetings. She had a certain advantage in that she achieved surprise. Those present, or most of them, did not expect a Tory Prime Minister – and one whose reputation was well to the right – to be so forthcoming, so apparently ready to welcome all antagonists in the Rhodesian imbroglio to sit around one table in London. The United States administration, carefully monitoring proceedings, was also surprised – and for a while suspicious. But we got what we wanted. Some Commonwealth leaders were especially helpful: Michael Manley of Jamaica and Malcolm Fraser of Australia were keen and active. Somewhat less helpful was the announcement, to my fury, by the Nigerian Government of their nationalization of BP (Nigeria) on the morning the conference started! That said, I am bound to record that the Nigerian Foreign Minister played a full and constructive part in our proceedings and in helping us towards our aim. He had known nothing of the BP *démarche* and was somewhat taken aback when I gave him a piece of my mind in front of TV cameras!

The Lusaka conference thus moved towards the conclusion Margaret and I sought, and moved in an atmosphere of unexpected harmony. Matters had, of course, been undoubtedly helped by the Queen's presence to open the conference, which conferred on it a particular dignity and sense of occasion – and, indeed, happiness, despite the impending problems. The final communiqué conveying the Lusaka result and the agreement to hold a further conference of Rhodesian principals in London was almost derailed by Malcolm Fraser. His activities, exceptionally well-intentioned, had a way of being untimely. On this occasion he held a personal and premature Press conference about the Lusaka outcome since he wanted to be the first to announce the achievement in Australia. None of his Commonwealth colleagues except those privy to the communiqué's drafting (by a small inner circle, at a picnic in the gardens of State House) knew about it until Fraser gave its substance to the Press – including several English Pressmen – ahead of schedule, and there were difficulties! But they passed. The Lancaster House Conference was born.

*

I was not optimistic about the Lancaster House out-turn. I was confident we had been right not to recognize the 'internal settlement', to go for another conference, to get preliminary Commonwealth – and, on the whole, international – endorsement of the idea. But I thought it likely that the invited parties would come, and then create trouble at the moment they decided most favourable, break off proceedings, walk out, go away. In that case – if Nkomo and Mugabe decided to withdraw cooperation – everybody, including Smith and Muzorewa, would at least be seen to have tried, really tried. Their 'internal settlement' might still lack enough domestic support and their war would drag on, wretchedly, but we and with luck the rest of the world might be able to do more for them with a clear conscience. I thought this quite likely, and believed that this result, however imperfect, would sufficiently justify the conference. I hoped, of course, that it would not be like that: that the Patriotic Front leaders would not disbar themselves by quarrelling but would end by assenting to some sort of way ahead, some constitutional formula, some recipe for peace. Peace was the prize. But I was not optimistic. It was September 1979.

I decided to give separate dinner parties at the start, one for the supporters of the 'internal settlement', for Smith, Muzorewa and their followers; and another for the Patriotic Front. I knew that each party to the affair had assented to the conference because of a reasonable hope they might come out on top and I wanted to assess the atmosphere. I think, in retrospect, that I at the time underestimated the difficulties each of these sections and individuals had with the principle as well as the practice of sitting down with the others in conference. There had been bad things done in Rhodesia and much bitterness both among whites and those blacks loyal to the Salisbury Government; while, on the other side and at the second of my dinner parties, I was struck by the normality and poise of both Nkomo and Mugabe after their very long periods in gaol. Nkomo, of course, was a hearty, jolly man and his personality was extrovert. Mugabe was a withdrawn, intellectual figure. We had not met before. He had been allowed to study while interned, had got a first at university. His only child had died at that time and he had not been allowed to go to the funeral.

I remember asking him if he was bitter.

'Not bitter against people personally.' He added, 'But I am bitter against the system, the regime.'

Nkomo made clear that he shared this bitterness. And the regime, of course, was bitter against them.

When the conference started I had to greet them all in the big hall at Lancaster House. I had all the Press there. I kept my face expressionless. I knew that if I smiled at one or frowned at another – or smiled more warmly at one – Press comment would be vivid. As the conference progressed one thing hit me, which I had naturally realized but perhaps insufficiently estimated. All these people knew each other well. Rhodesia was not a large country and everyone active in its politics, however inimical, knew everyone else, whatever the relationship. During coffee breaks and the like this became increasingly clear, as did the fact that they didn't get on at all badly with each other! This observation reinforced my sense that we had been right to restrict attendance to Rhodesians and ourselves. I began to feel a little more hopeful. Furthermore, once the conference got going anyone who took an initiative to march out would have a progressively tougher time in explaining this to the world and to the UN. It was a card I could play with some confidence. They all – or almost all – had had an incentive to confer. And soon nobody wanted to be seen as the one to break things up.

I had my own domestic problems, as did they all. Lancaster House proceedings were for me interrupted by the October Conservative Party Conference at Blackpool, and the right wing of the party were out to get me. They reckoned I was a betrayer. The Monday Club organized a huge meeting with 'Hang Carrington' banners everywhere displayed and people shook their fists at me when walking down the street – they thought I was selling our people in Rhodesia down the river, conniving at their abandonment to the leaders of a bloodthirsty and atrocious terrorism. I knew that my address to the main

298

body of the conference needed to be persuasive and I have seldom taken more trouble with any speech's composition. I had to convince the party that what we were attempting – to get a settlement on reasonable and proper terms which would command general international support – was not only in the best interests of the British and the Rhodesians (all of them) but that no other course offered a decent chance of success.

My speech went well. The conference accepted – overwhelmingly – the proposition that if there was a chance of getting an agreement, settling Rhodesia, stopping the war and the bloodshed, we were right to seize that chance. The right wing suffered a setback. Their view was, in my perception, unrealistic. Oblivious of the irony of patriotic loyalists celebrating one who was officially a rebel against the Crown, they had fêted Ian Smith whenever possible, but it was not realistic to suppose that he or any other man could keep Rhodesia on track indefinitely without some sort of different approach. The Blackpool Conference marked a turning point because it marked the recognition of this fact by the main body of the Conservative Party. I felt considerable relief.

Back at Lancaster House I divided the agenda into different sections and I was adamant that the first of these must deal with a future constitution. I was not prepared to allow them to talk about other things until they had settled, with my approval, the constitution. They hated it, all of them! They wanted to ride off, amid shouting and tumult, in different directions. Next, I stuck their noses to the business of how to agree a ceasefire. They hated that, too, but on the whole it worked. We did the minimum in plenary sessions, with their opportunities for quarrel and attitude, the maximum in restricted negotiation behind the scenes.

The Lancaster House Conference went on for many, many weeks – indeed, until December – and was a tempestuous and testing time, as hard as I ever experienced. For much of that time I was the subject of ferocious verbal assaults from one side or the other, many of them made at Press conferences and generally accompanied by noise, rage – real or simulated – and innuendo. As ever, the most trying occasions generally took place out of the conference room itself. I remember having to keep Sonny Ramphal, Secretary-General of the Commonwealth, from interfering. Having been present at the Lusaka conference he thought, no doubt with the best of intentions, that he could help and had the right to try. He was mistaken, and I spent some time persuading him of the fact: totally committed to the Patriotic Front, he had no credibility as an impartial observer. Then various other Commonwealth Prime Ministers – I remember Kaunda, Nyerere – came to London during proceedings, to see how we were all getting on. Some were more helpful than others. Some, indeed, were the opposite of helpful. I remember, too, Ian Smith at one of the private rather than plenary meetings. He said to me, 'I think it's disgraceful the way you're handling this conference.'

'Why?'

'You're not attending to it. You're doing your other job as Foreign Secretary, and doing this as a part-time job, treating it as a part-time activity. And while you're doing so,' he added, 'hundreds of people in Rhodesia are being killed.'

I think I had kept my temper throughout some pretty provoking moments at that conference, but on this particular occasion it was touch and go. I said to Smith, 'Perhaps you might recollect that but for you nobody in Rhodesia would be being killed.'

I think it was a fair reply. Ian Smith went home shortly afterwards. It was not he but David Smith and Peter Walls who had been convinced that the white Rhodesians should keep at the conference, keep going. They were brave to do so, but I knew they were right. They hoped for a solution they could live with. So did I. The conference dragged on, looking like ending in failure more often than success. Nkomo and Mugabe, of course, knew that if they went home we should recognize the 'internal settlement', come what may. Although they would then denounce it again, and us again, it was becoming more difficult to revert to open hostility in the shadow of Lancaster House; and this was another strong card of mine. As such things do, the conference began to generate its own influence and atmosphere, so that everybody's mind started, imperceptibly, to adapt. Of course everybody – particularly Mugabe – was strongly determined on his own ends. But everybody, I suspect (even Mugabe), began to prefer the idea of settlement to the alternatives. Prefer it a good deal.

We reached agreement. There were some pretty desperate moments on the way to it, the usual disappointments, false alarms, false dawns and threatened walk-outs, but we reached agreement. I believe that critical to this was my determination to take matters step by step. On each step some of the parties demurred, saying they could not climb further without seeing entirely and exactly what stood at the head of the stairs. I refused to accept this. I was sure that previous attempts had failed through attempting overprecision too early, through framing complex plans of ultimate order instead of coaxing minds towards the resolution of the next practical, intermediate step in debate. Each step might be imperfect in logic, or even in principle, but it must be realistic – in the sense of not being a clear outrage to one of the parties and thus unacceptable.

The agreement set out a simple sequence – simple in concept, likely to be troubled in execution. There was to be a ceasefire: the guerrilla forces were to stand down, move to assembly points, accept disarmament. There was to be a reversion to the constitutional situation before the unilateral declaration of independence by Smith; and then there were to be elections in Rhodesia, based on universal suffrage, with all parties permitted to take part and with independence and recognition of a balanced constitution granted by the British Crown thereafter.

I was dreading the moment when I would have to announce that the first step would be the return of a British Governor, for although it was an inevitable consequence of our proposals for return to legality I knew nobody expected it and nobody would like it. The whites thought they'd declared for independence as irrevocably as the American colonists in 1776, and the blacks thought they'd been fighting for years for freedom 'from colonial rule'. Now I was telling them that the next thing they'd see would be a British Governor. I made the announcement at a plenary session.

There was a dead silence. It lasted a long time. It was broken by Joshua Nkomo. He looked at me enquiringly.

'Really? Will he have plumes and a horse?'

The whole conference dissolved in laughter. The day was saved.

I walked across from the Foreign Office to my old room at the Admiralty, overlooking Horse Guards Parade, a room now occupied by Christopher Soames, Cabinet colleague and minister in charge of the Civil Service. Christopher, ennobled and brought again into the Cabinet after his long and enormously distinguished service as Ambassador to France and as a European Community Commissioner in Brussels, was a very old friend.

'Would you go out as Governor to Rhodesia?'

Christopher said, simply, 'Yes, of course I will.'

It was a characteristic reply. He reckoned that if asked to do a thing like that it was impossible to say no, whatever the dangers — and there must be significant dangers — or the disagreeable and inconvenient aspects from both his and his wife's point of view. I found it a difficult moment when I saw them off shortly afterwards, kissed Mary Soames goodbye and wondered when and whether I'd see them again. It is easy to forget how uncertain everything seemed then in the Rhodesian business, and how great the turmoil. It was essential to have someone as Governor with Christopher's robustness, intelligence, and experience of politics. His 'don't care a damn' commonsense together with his wife's charm, courage and friendliness to all were exactly what the moment needed. Christopher could be relied upon to get priorities right, to see what fundamentally mattered in what would inevitably be a series of contentious situations. Being an old hand at politics, of course, he made it clear to me that I was sending him out at the wrong time! Furthermore he had a point, since when he agreed to go nothing had been finally settled. This didn't stop him devoting his considerable character and talents to making the thing work. None of us had any illusions about the problems facing us. Any settlement agreed at Lancaster House was a starting point, no more. The horses and jockeys, against all probability, had agreed to come under starter's orders, but there were plenty of fences to jump. Nasty ones.

There was also likely to be pretty dirty work between jockeys on the way round. Christopher's first and primary task was to rule Rhodesia while elections were prepared and took place. The level of intimidation of voters was expected to be extensive, and in a statement to the Lords in February I had to acknowledge that there had been 'large-scale intimidation of the rural population'. Intimidation was certainly not confined to any one faction, but the activities of Mugabe's followers, in particular, led to considerable revulsion, and there were many voices – not confined to white Rhodesians: some British civil servants felt the same – saying loudly that Mugabe's further participation in the Election should be forbidden. Christopher would have none of this. He was perfectly clear-eyed about intimidation but he saw without flinching that to disallow Mugabe's involvement would make nonsense of all we had been trying to achieve, and would place at probably fatal risk the international endorsement we had tenuously procured. The level of intimidation was not such, in his (or our) view, as to invalidate the result, a view he did not change. Christopher ruled that Mugabe's party would remain legitimate contenders. I am sure he was right. He – and his wife, and his exceptional deputy, Tony Duff – were magnificent from first to last. I had a direct telephone link to him at Government House in Salisbury and used it every day. Christopher's voice was so loud that, carried from Southern Africa, it boomed out of my open windows over Horse Guards Parade and made me feel the instrument was hardly necessary.

I cannot say that the Election's results – *pace* Julius Nyerere's Foreign Minister – were exactly what we had anticipated or that they gave to the British Government undiluted pleasure. I know that people say, and some said at the time, that the

Patriotic Front leaders must have known they could cope with an Election and manage to succeed, or else they would have refused our conference's conclusion. That may be, but such calculations, even or especially in Africa, can miscarry; and Nkomo, like Mugabe, had been absent or in gaol for a long time. The truth is that, all intimidation apart, it soon became obvious that the Patriotic Front had huge support. The mighty and enthusiastic crowds which welcomed both leaders gave a foretaste of what was to come. The experts were confounded. 'Informed sources', wise in the ways of Africa, told us that there was unlikely to be a clear-cut victory for anyone, that the votes would be divided between the Patriotic Front and Muzorewa. Intelligence, Rhodesian and South African, tended to think the same; it was said that a coalition might be cobbled together between Muzorewa and Nkomo, who got on poorly with Mugabe despite their nominal association. In the event the Patriotic Front, Mugabe in the lead, swept the board, with Muzorewa nowhere. I wondered how this result would be received. To some it would confirm their worst fears about the outcome of our policies, and to many in Rhodesia it would be thought to threaten life and livelihood. Politically, we stood to suffer a lot of criticism – a misconceived settlement, an inappropriate Election, a corrupt result, a betrayed kith and kin. I was unrepentant at our efforts but I can't pretend I was happy.

There could too, right up to the end, have been some sort of right-wing coup in Rhodesia, engineered to forestall the Election's result, and we owed it much to Peter Walls that this was not attempted. He was personally deeply disappointed at the outcome, and, like many, he resented and was provoked by the intimidation of which he knew: but he did his duty at all times with outstanding fairness and propriety. I had seen him quietly a good deal during the Lancaster House Conference, and valued him highly. He was not well treated in the aftermath of it all, but Zimbabwe owes him a lot.

The political repercussions were less severe than I had thought possible. The Election results may have been imperfect but they showed our dissidents within the Conservative Party that the Patriotic Front really did have the support of the majority of blacks, support it was much harder thereafter to discredit. There were certainly some right wingers in the party who would have liked to question that conclusion and defy the Electoral decision, but they now had less justification, weak ground on which to stand. Truth to tell, I think most people, whatever their politics, were by now relieved that the business was over. My conduct and policy remained resented by some and the resentment spilled over into other areas of politics, both then and subsequently, but I have yet to be persuaded that there was some better way which we ignored.

In this conviction I have been, on the whole, fortified by the magnanimity of Robert Mugabe. There have been disagreeable occurrences in Zimbabwe, and I have never concealed my dislike of them; but when one considers the aftermath of civil war in other African states, when one recalls the long years which Mugabe spent in prison, and when one reflects on his followers' expectations of the spoils of victory, it is not discouraging that at the time of writing there are still white Rhodesian Members of Parliament – including until recently Ian Smith – there is still a white minister in Government, there is still a handful of white civil servants, and Ian Smith still has his farm. The truth is that Mugabe, a highly intelligent man, needed the cooperation of all, including whites, to prevent the economy disintegrating. He had no ambition to be Prime Minister of a bankrupt country, and he was prepared to outface, where necessary, his own hardliners in order to keep his country on something like the rails. He had witnessed follies in other lands not far away, and he had no desire to emulate.

One of the trickiest on-the-spot problems was what to do about the considerable number of South Africans and the extensive South African military involvement. It had to be played by the Governor – and, for that matter, by Mugabe – with sense and without histrionics. Politically it could have been damaging too, because few people appreciated the size of the problem and the numbers involved. It went well, I think, and ultimately the South Africans cleared out without fuss having done a good deal in an unobtrusive way to make the Election logistically possible.

There remained the grant of independence itself. Christopher Soames was splendid immediately after the Election. I doubt if Mugabe was sure whether, even at that late stage, we would let him take over. Christopher had to win his trust and confidence, show him that we were sincere in wanting him to make a success of Zimbabwe (whatever we'd thought of him before). And Christopher achieved that confidence and that trust. Indeed he stayed on after independence for a few weeks as Governor, at Mugabe's personal request.

Iona and I flew out with the Prince of Wales for the ceremonies. At a great reception in a tent in front of Government House I saw Joshua Nkomo standing by himself. He was outside the enormous marquee, wherein all Rhodesians, of all colours and all parties, were gathered and were being entertained. Nkomo was standing, his appearance one of disgruntlement, his back to the proceedings. He had not been given by Mugabe the job in Government he reckoned should be his. Mugabe had once been much his junior. They had been rivals as much as colleagues: generally more so.

Laurens van der Post had come out with the Prince of Wales. I indicated Nkomo to him: back turned to the tent. Van der Post nodded.

'It is one of the customs of the Ndebele tribe.'

'What is?'

'When a member of the tribe has offended against the customs of the tribe, the elders form a line looking at him, he is standing in front of them. Then, very solemnly, they turn their backs on him. That is such a terrible disgrace that the culprit who has committed the misdemeanour runs off into the bush or throws himself into the river.'

He gazed at Nkomo.

'He has turned his back.'

The Rhodesian settlement and the emergence of Zimbabwe in the form it took will be matters of contention, I don't doubt, for many years. I hope people will not forget that the out-turn, however imperfect and even distressing to some, nevertheless marked the end of a particularly beastly war.

'For a war-weary country', I said in my concluding address to the conference, 'the prize is great.'

I knew that the prize, the peace, could still be delicate and elusive. There was blood on most hands – and certainly their owners would have hotly asserted, in all cases, that the shedding of it was amply justified. In such circumstances it is no easy thing to bring about a peace, however scarred, or a reconciliation, however partial and embittered. These observations apply to all, or almost all, who took part. I remember sitting down with Peter Walls in my house in Ovington Square about half-way through the Lancaster House proceedings. I said to him, 'You know, I look round that table at Lancaster House and it seems to me there's hardly one of them who isn't a murderer in one form or another!'

There were, I said, obviously exceptions to this exaggeration.

Peter Walls looked at me with some astonishment. It was clear he differed about my exceptions.

I went back once to Zimbabwe after independence. It was in February 1982, and the unease of many white people was predictable and comprehensible. The skilled white craftsmen were probably suffering the greatest reversal of fortune but I had the impression that adjustment to the new situation was highly commendable both in the countryside and in Salisbury – now Harare – despite the fact that the countryside had suffered the brunt of the war, and suffered the brunt of various outrages which occurred in the aftermath of war and often took an inter-tribal turn. Some white men, like David Smith, had shown great moral courage, serving in the Mugabe Government, stifling misgivings, seeking only to make things work. Others, I think, were intransigent, determined only to believe that the Ian Smith Government could have stuck it out and won the war; and that an independent, black-run Zimbabwe couldn't work and needn't have been tried. They were wrong. On the detail of the settlement I have some of the usual *post facto* regrets. On the strategy I have none.

CHAPTER 14

Europe

From the very beginning of the Thatcher administration much attention – and public interest – was devoted to economic policy. It had been the Conservative pledge that the Government's role in the economy would be dramatically reduced, that the frontiers of nationalization and state interference would be rolled back, and that individual enterprise, choice and responsibility would be encouraged and enlarged. Much was expected of us. Market forces would keep the economy in balance, provided that Government policy prevented excessive growth of the amount of money in circulation and kept sufficient check on credit. Central to this line of policy – and particularly harmonious with the Prime Minister's own beliefs – was the need to keep Government spending itself under more rigorous control than in the past; and a principal benefit of the policy was to be the conquest of an inflation which – for many reasons, by no means all of them under our predecessors' control – had reached insufferable levels and was producing a great deal of hardship and loss.

The measures we took from the very beginning were consistent with this philosophy, and although it took time, inflation was greatly reduced. Because, however, the world was also entering recession in the aftermath of the savage increase in oil prices of 1973 another consequence for Britain of this drastic exposure to classical economics was a sharp and continuing rise in the unemployment figures. Competition was hitting much of British industry hard, and the administration was determined that the uncompetitive should be no longer protected from disaster by easy credit or Government favour. Productivity and competitiveness had to be improved – and that meant among other things an end to overmanning, and the start of a tougher management style in a lot of places. Increased productivity meant smaller workforces – and world recession meant a harder climate for businesses to survive. But inflation came down and Britain's competitiveness began, with a good deal of difficulty, to improve.

When challenged to mitigate the painful effects of our policy – and in particular the rise in unemployment – by direct Government action, Margaret Thatcher used to denounce this as producing only chimerical benefits, short-lived and ultimately creating worse problems. We had, she believed, been here before. Spending the way into higher employment was an artificial and temporary expedient. It didn't work. The only sure route to more permanent jobs was via an expanded economy in a more competitive Britain. Anything else was palliative – and palliative inevitably leading to resurgent inflation and ultimately even higher unemployment. 'There is no alternative' was her reiterated maxim, and the phrase, 'TINA', was adopted and derided by opponents as epitomizing a dogmatic and uncaring approach.

I believed that there was, in fact, probably no alternative. There were no easy ways out of the mess of financial indiscipline, lax management, over-mighty trades unions, overmanning and excessive state interference which disfigured too much of British industrial life; inevitably, perhaps, under a Labour Government, in view of much of their philosophy and the source of their party funds. Under the Conservatives other ways to salvation had in the past been tried and one had to admit that, at least in the particular circumstances of Britain, they hadn't worked. In all this Margaret Thatcher had been more far-seeing than her critics and more so than the doubters among her colleagues, of whom I'd been one. I also believed, however, that some of our own side were too strident and insensitive in presenting policy. It may be necessary and sensible to act and only to act in a certain way. It may be essential to stand firm against a sentimentality which would make things worse tomorrow in return for a little popular easement today. But if people are actually suffering, actually losing jobs through no fault of their own, actually finding themselves in suddenly depressed industries because of economic waves well beyond their control and probably their comprehension, then I believe that a Government – and its supporters – should show that the human side of the process is a matter of concern and should take care to use words which reflect that concern. I don't think we always did so.

Our problems, of course, were general throughout the developed world and particularly throughout Europe, in differing degrees. And with Rhodesia moving towards some sort of resolution I was able to concentrate more personal attention on Europe and on our relations with the other European nations who, together with us now, composed the European Economic Community.

I have already said that it was my time in Australia which converted me to the idea of Europe as the true direction of British destiny. Looking from abroad, as I'd been lucky enough then to do, it was obvious that Britain had, or shortly would have, no Imperial or quasi-Imperial role left, and very reduced international authority as an independent nation without it. Today these statements seem pretty obvious, but they have taken a long time to penetrate and even in the sixties and seventies there were plenty of unpenetrated quarters. In every party. Dean Acheson's sombre aphorism that Britain had lost an empire but not yet found a role was still applicable to a good many British hearts.

There were two interrelated reasons for my conviction. First, of course, the nations of the Commonwealth had become used to fashioning their own political and economic lives in accordance with their own interests and without much reference to Britain: and rightly so. I'd seen this in Australia. Australia's market was clearly going to be very largely in Japan; and in consequence she would have to import Japanese goods. The same was true for the rest. Imperial preference was already dead or dying in 1956. It was foolish to suppose that the Commonwealth could have the sort of commercial cohesion Empire had once possessed. Later, when Britain joined the European Community, Australia and others made a great fuss – they were looking to their own interests which they fancied could be injured. They had every right to do so. But so did we.

The second reason for my conviction that our future lay in Europe was my appreciation – and, again, it seems very obvious today but was a great deal less so even a short time ago – that militarily as well as economically we were pretty small. We could, and I believed that we should, play a limited part here and there outside Europe: I had fought to retain for a while a certain presence in both the Middle East and South-East Asia – one should not be precipitate in these things, adjustments take time – but it was in Europe and the Atlantic area that our main defence interest lay and it was towards Europe that our chief political and commercial effort should be directed. That meant the European Community. We could, and we should, work to be influential in the European Community; and the European Community, if intelligently organized, had the size and strength to carry Europe's voice and experience to the world. That had long been my view.

But we had missed our tide. It was initially understandable. The politicians of the preceding generation had grown up – indeed I myself had grown up, but they had spent their adult lives – in a different world, a world in which much of the map was coloured red, with the British Empire regarding itself not only as in the front rank of world powers, but without peer. We didn't talk about superpowers in those days, but to one of Churchill's – or Eden's – generation it was barely conceivable that Britain should not have an independent and probably a dominant voice on every global issue. Churchill used to speak of three linked circles, and the image caught on and was widely used – the Atlantic circle, involving us with America; the European circle, as a group of islands near the European mainland; and the Imperial circle, deriving from our wide possessions. Churchill certainly had latterly a vision of a united Europe, and made a great and often-quoted speech at Zürich on the subject. But he made no suggestion in that speech that

Britain would itself be a part of that united Europe. On the contrary, Churchill – and Attlee, as I have already recalled, and Eden, and most of the first-rank British statesmen of those days – found unthinkable the idea of Britain as part of a broader European grouping. We were different. We were separate. The Channel lay between us and them. They consisted of ex-enemies – and the chief ex-enemy was the most dedicated advocate of the new grouping – or ex-allies who had been quickly subjugated in war and played an inevitably minor role thereafter, until liberated by British and American endeavour. We wished the club well but it wasn't for us.

This sort of thinking or sentiment was, I believe, comprehensible in our predecessors. It was a matter of the generations, of how people feel in their guts because of their earliest experiences and images. It may have been insular, nostalgic and obstinate but we could once afford to be insular, nostalgic and obstinate, or thought we could. It was all very natural.

It was also wrong. The British politician who deserved most credit for first perceiving where reality lay was Harold Macmillan. Macmillan showed understanding superior to his contemporaries. He was himself a man of that earlier generation of worldwide British power, and he liked to reminisce expansively about a bygone, confident age. He had fought in the First World War, in the aftermath of which British prestige stood remarkably high. His mind had been formed in the old times. But Macmillan, after some initial hesitation, saw clearly that our future must be in joining the European Community. He had vision much superior to Eden's and the rest in this matter. He wanted us in Europe and he wanted us in early, so that we could influence its evolution and its institutions from the beginning. Adapting Churchill's 'three circles', he believed – and certainly I believed – that our overseas interests, diminishing but still strong, and our particular relationship with the Americans which had been strained by Suez but which had a certain historic reality, meant that if we caught the tide we could be one of the leading nations in the Community – perhaps the leading nation. That was where the British future lay.

De Gaulle, as we know, vetoed that idea during the Macmillan premiership. There is no point in speculating on the General's motives and there is no denying that plenty of British speeches and attitudes at the time gave credence to the de Gaulle thesis that Britain was not yet, at heart, 'European'. 'Faced with a choice', de Gaulle said with a characteristic flourish, 'between Europe and the open sea, England will always choose the open sea.' Plenty of Englishmen would have echoed, 'Hear, hear': but the truth, if it was truth, was transient and regrettable. It assumed an Imperial sphere of influence which was already waning to the point of extinction. The consequences of this original exclusion and the friction it generated are with us still. The European Community was shaped without our voice being heard, and shaped to suit the interest and to advance or protect the economy of France. Of Germany to some extent; but primarily of France.

Macmillan felt this deeply. The mainspring of his foreign policy was broken. I recall his television appearance that evening, when he referred to the French veto. 'What has happened', he said with carefully modulated emphasis, '*is bad.*' He knew that it was bad for Britain and bad for Europe, and he said so. Macmillan suffered the blow not only as a politician but as a sensitive man of historical and cultural appreciation who felt profoundly European. In later years, including those when I was Foreign Secretary and after, he always particularly enjoyed playing the role of European elder statesman – he relished, of course, most of the parts he was called on to play and had the gift of getting the best out of all the ages of man. I remember his visit to Vienna at the anniversary of the signing of the Austrian State Treaty. Macmillan attended, together with other notables of earlier times. He received a great welcome. After the ceremonies I mentioned the name of Mr Muskie. It was late at night at the British Embassy and Macmillan was in expansive mood. Muskie was United States Secretary of State and I was breakfasting with him next morning.

'Muskie!' said Macmillan, in his best fading-away voice, 'Muskie! Isn't that the Senator who wept in public because someone loudly alleged his wife was an alcoholic? And thus failed to get the Democratic nomination?' He smiled malevolently and the British Ambassador, a somewhat pawky Scot, decided to show a bit of independence.

'That's not a very agreeable remark, Mr Macmillan, if I may say so. How would you like it if you were at a meeting in your constituency and someone from the back of the hall yelled out, "Lady Dorothy Macmillan is an old drunk." How would *you* react?'

'Ah,' said Macmillan, raising his voice strongly, 'I would shout back, "You should have seen her mother!"'

Macmillan took the de Gaulle exclusion of Britain hard. Nevertheless, we had returned to the battle, and at this point the mantle of Macmillan had been assumed by Ted Heath. It was Ted who negotiated for Britain in the Macmillan period which had so disappointing an outcome in our rejection, and his advocacy at that time and his mastery of detail were superb. Thereafter Ted never wavered in his determination that we should, ultimately, join – and join we did, during his own administration; and at just the moment when the oil price rise marked the virtual end of that surge of economic activity and prosperity which had attended the first, formative years of the Community's existence. The other members, the Six, had profited immensely, from membership and from boom conditions simultaneously. In consequence, while some of our people still said that it was a wicked idea for England to join, to scrap her distinctive historic identity, to place her ancient sovereignty at risk, others – or the same – said that we seemed to be getting precious little out of it in any case. It was a trying time for the dedicated Europeans.

And then, after the Labour victory of 1974, the Labour Government had held a referendum on our membership. I had taken as active a part as I could, sharing platforms with such convinced pro-Europeans of other parties as Roy Jenkins, David Steel, Shirley Williams. That referendum, thank Heavens, had gone right. Britain had voted sensibly and strongly. When I became Foreign Secretary I had no great knowledge of the other European statesmen with whom I would be dealing, no detailed knowledge of Europe or Community affairs. I had, however, conviction. It has often been contended that the Foreign Office, in its corporate wisdom, is exaggeratedly keen on the European connection. I disagree that there is exaggeration in this, and as to the keenness, I shared it and had developed it as early as any of them. There were, and there have continued to be, enemies of Britain's membership of the Community. For myself, I once described the Labour Party's (or some of its leading lights') wish to leave as 'a sort of national death wish'.

I needed my conviction. My first speech as Foreign Secretary to the House of Lords in May 1979 contained the sentence, 'Already the United Kingdom is paying far too high a share of net contribution to the Community budget.' I was in for a rough ride. Passionate European I might be, but British interests were going to demand vigorous and no doubt unpopular haggling.

It was shameful to have to admit it but we were now among the poorer members of the Community. Our gross national product was near the bottom of the list. Yet we were, when I took office, the only member country which was making a greater contribution to the Community budget than our receipts from it. In 1980 our net contribution, after receipts, was due to be something over a thousand million pounds and very much higher figures were projected. Callaghan had made some attempt to attack this system but I think half-heartedly and certainly without success. The reason for the increasing imbalance was, of course, the huge and rising sums spent on the Common Agricultural Policy.

This method of calculating and arguing – measuring contribution against benefit – infuriated the French. The principle of '*Juste retour*', they said, was not the idea of the Community. We were all members, we all had to contribute according to agreed criteria, what we received was assessed by different criteria, and so forth. Behind this opposition of principle – and we generally found ourselves pretty well isolated – was the less principled and entirely practical factor that the French and others were doing extremely well out of the existing arrangements. So were all the rest, in varying degrees. And that meant that they were doing extremely well at our expense.

The resultant rows went on a long time, and were at the heart of why the Community in effect stood still for several years. We couldn't possibly tolerate a situation in which Britain, because of the existing rules, looked like being a net loser, year after year. It was politically as well as economically inadmissible; and I still find difficult to understand the time it took for the other countries to see the point of our case, our cause of complaint. They knew perfectly well that if we left the Community – we had no wish to do so and it would have been a tragedy, but it was not impossible – the others would have to make good our contribution: all of it. I thought that our colleague members were curiously short-sighted. It was perfectly natural for them to argue, to bargain; but I couldn't accept their vigorous repudiation of the fundamental premises of our position. The matter went on tediously long, dominating Community business to the detriment of more constructive initiatives. Foreign Ministers and Permanent Representatives found their meetings obsessed by the matter of the British contribution. Everyone remained personally friendly – I thought that creditable, for the issue and the period was disagreeable and wearisome. I was keen to promote political cooperation within the Community – such cooperation was in its infancy as a concept and as yet wasn't unduly affected by 'the British contribution', but I realized that before one could apply energy and a whole heart to new initiatives this wretched matter had got to be settled, and better settled. Just as Rhodesia had intolerably monopolized British Foreign Office attention, so this question of our contribution to the Community budget was neutralizing everything the Community should be trying to achieve.

At this time the President of France was Giscard D'Estaing, and the German Chancellor was Helmut Schmidt. Both were keen on the European Council. Heads of Government had decided in 1974 to meet three times a year, and such meetings became called the European Council – a 'Summit'. The regularity formalized something which, as originally conceived, was to be an occasional get-together where Prime Ministers could discuss the really important issues, the strategy of the Community. Unfortunately it had become too frequent a function. An inevitable consequence was that knotty issues were now left to the European Council – were 'passed upwards' by Foreign Ministers simply because there was another body to which they could be passed. These knotty issues may have been difficult and time-consuming but they were for Foreign Ministers or other specialist ministers or their representatives somehow to resolve. That was what we were for. To introduce into negotiations the top people of all is a hazardous and not always successful move. Summits can disappoint. Prime Ministers do not always know more or speak more expertly than their Chancellors of Exchequer, their Agriculture Ministers and so forth. When detail was increasingly relegated 'on appeal' to the Council it didn't mean it was dealt with more knowledgeably, or business handled more expeditiously. I'm afraid the reverse tended to be the case. One should not involve the prestige of the senior office in any country unless there is clear advantage in so doing. Too often the result is simply that less and less is authoritatively handled lower down.

There was the additional – but not insignificant – difficulty that the President of France, as in the United States, is Head of State as well as Head of Government so that from the point of view of protocol he naturally entered the room last, had to have a hotel suite commensurate with his position and not that of a mere Prime Minister, and so forth. Trivia perhaps – but trivia which can detract from the spirit and even the achievement of an occasion. The European Council had been conceived as a meeting of top equals.

The British were also periodically troubled that well-publicized Franco-German accord – with the British clearly in the dock as 'difficult' – was tending to shut us out. I remember one of the Council's 'working breakfasts' at the time of the

Soviet invasion of Afghanistan. Helmut Schmidt had a date to visit Moscow. He addressed Giscard d'Estaing and Margaret Thatcher.

'Do you think I ought to go?'

Giscard spoke authoritatively. 'No, of course not. It would show great weakness at this particular time. It would demonstrate cracks in Allied unity. We must stick together over this.'

Schmidt said he understood. A week later the Foreign Secretaries were meeting at the Villa Rosebery in Naples, a splendid house next to the villa which was once Sir William Hamilton and Emma's in Nelson's day. Jean François-Poncet, the French Foreign Minister, suddenly left us, with what looked like embarrassment. We discovered he had gone to join Giscard, and that Giscard had just flown to Poland to meet Brezhnev in Warsaw.

Before dinner I found myself strolling on the terrace with Hans-Dietrich Genscher, the German Foreign Minister.

'Having regard', I said, 'to your close relationship with the French, I imagine you knew Giscard was going to Warsaw.'

Schmidt had cancelled his own visit to the Soviet Union, on Giscard's decided and uncompromising advice.

Genscher said, 'No!' rather abruptly.

We continued strolling. I pressed a little.

'Surely there must have been *some* communication? Giscard can't have gone off without any consultation, with you Germans above all! At a time like this!'

Genscher made clear that this was exactly what Giscard had done, and after a few more lengths of the terrace I said that I had always assumed the Franco-German relationship to be so close as to make this unthinkable.

'And the personal relationship between Giscard and Schmidt! I thought that was so close, too! It's almost unbelievable!'

Genscher stopped his strolling and looked at me angrily. 'That's what Helmut thought!'

As far as the row over the British contribution was concerned – and it overshadowed my first eighteen months as Foreign Secretary – the introduction of the European Council into the debate meant that the row was conducted largely by Margaret Thatcher. She is no bad hand at conducting rows, and on several occasions – I remember particularly a session in Luxemburg and another in Dublin – the Prime Minister made herself exceptionally unpopular, bluntly saying, 'I want my money back', language which sent shudders down many a Continental spine. She had a strong – and entirely justified – feeling that Britain was the victim of deplorable inequity: she had more determination than most of those with whom she was negotiating; and she was not temperamentally averse from showing the British people at home that when it came to outfacing foreigners she was in the first league. There is no doubt that her colleagues in the European Council did not look forward to the next round with her, and although one can always argue and hope that gentle persuasion may outperform vigorous assertion, there's no proof that it is so. I have little doubt that Margaret's firmness and intransigence were the key factors in getting us a proper settlement: but I cannot pretend that the resultant atmosphere made all our foreign relations easier to conduct.

Ultimately, but with British implacability by now well advertised, the matter of the British contribution was yet again sent to the Foreign Ministers to try to settle. We met in June 1980 for an unbroken twenty-four hours and finally reached a three-year agreement which gave us as much as we could at that moment possibly hope. Agreed ceilings of £370 million in 1980 and £440 million in 1981 meant that we would receive a rebate of £1570 million: and unless a radical review of the system (and we had achieved recognition that such a review must come) had been completed, the same easement would extend to 1982. I doubt if Margaret was particularly pleased with this but half a loaf is better than no bread, and the question of the British contribution was reduced to manageable proportions. We had taken an important step towards a durable resolution, which was achieved after my time.

*

The key institution within the Community is the Commission, sitting in Brussels. It plays the central role. It provides, as it were, the machinery of the Community's government. The President of the Commission and his Commissioners are thus people of authority – indispensable authority. Without that authority nothing at all would happen. The Commission is answerable to the Council of Ministers, that is to the representatives of the individual Governments of individual sovereign states, meeting together and corporately providing the Commission with its legitimacy and its support.

Because the Commission is important the Presidency of the Commission is important, and during my time it was held, with distinction, by Roy Jenkins. He rightly expected to be treated like a senior minister and he upheld the dignity and enhanced the efficiency of the Commission at all times. He insisted on attending European Council meetings. He understood the limitations of his office, the limits to the Commission's powers and, indeed, the limits to the present span of the Community's authority; but everything he did he did well. I once asked him what he intended to do when he left Brussels.

'Oh,' Roy said, 'I'm going to go home to start a new party.'

We were sitting next to each other at one of the many Community lunches. I said I thought that would be difficult to get off the ground. Roy agreed with me.

'But,' he said, 'I'm so disillusioned with what has happened in the Labour Party that I'd never forgive myself if I didn't give it a try.' It's been a brave try.

The power of the Commission is essential to efficiency and decision-making, and the responsibility of the Commission to the representatives of national Governments, sitting as a Committee, reflects the fact that Europe is not a state, or an empire, but an assemblage of independent and sovereign states. In the last resort, what happens is the responsibility of the Governments of those states, and their electorates can turn them out.

This matrix of relationships reflects reality. It is not easy to fit into it the European Parliament. A Parliament implies a political entity within which it has its function; a function of consultation, financial control perhaps, protest perhaps, veto perhaps, legislation perhaps – and all or any of that implies the exercise of a certain power.

Such power only makes sense in relation to a political entity which is itself some sort of sovereign realm. The British Parliament has a part – in our case, of course, the dominant, the sovereign part – in the government of the United Kingdom; but there has to be a realm called the United Kingdom, with legitimate authority over its citizens and with the legitimate right to conduct relations with other realms, to conclude treaties, settle disputes, even make war. No realm, no Parliament – or no Parliament with perceptible purpose beyond that of the talking-shop. I'm not saying that there have only been Parliaments of unitary states: I know that there have been (and in Europe) Imperial Diets and so forth – assemblies at a higher level than that of the state as modernly conceived. But the Imperial Diet presupposed an empire, in its own sense a realm. The European Community is not an empire, nor a realm. It has no head. It has no sovereignty. It is in its own way a political entity, but it satisfies few of the criteria which the existence of a Parliament implies.

Yet the European Parliament exists – exists as a talking-shop, much other than which it cannot be until or unless a realm, an empire, a genuine federal polity called Europe emerges. I understand why the European Parliament was invented. In many ways I think the invention was healthy, because discussion and international personal relationships must only advance rather than hinder the evolution of Europe. I have already observed that the European Parliament, exposed to the remarkable antics of some members (including some of our own), has an educative effect which is probably desirable. Nevertheless I find anomalous the idea of a European Parliament, with directly elected members, struggling to behave as if it were a sovereign Parliament in a sovereign state. For the truth is that the European Parliament, although full of aspiring politicians interested in Europe, cannot have power. True, it has a little power over the budget and it has theoretic power to dismiss the Commission – and even those powers are an anomaly. If they were vigorously exercised they would, indirectly but very quickly, bring the European Parliament up against the authority of national Governments, supported by national Parliaments. And national Parliaments are the Parliaments of realms. They do have power.

It would be as unacceptable as unrealistic to try to alter this power-equation. It could only be altered were Europe as a polity to evolve. In the meantime I didn't, and don't, believe that the 'decisions' of so diverse an assembly as the European Parliament could be allowed greatly to impinge on the policies or the actions of nations.

My scepticism about the European Parliament by no means implied pessimism about the evolution of Europe, perhaps institutionally but certainly politically. At present this could only come through the action of Governments, but come it would, and from the first I was anxious to promote political cooperation, so that the European nations would increasingly form the habit of discussing and where possible coordinating their external policies. Of course there were questions on which total identity of interest might not exist – the members of the Community are commercial rivals, after all, and they also have the habit of electing Governments of widely differing political colour. But nothing but good could come of the attempt to harmonize views about and at the least to discuss the agitations of the world, from a European standpoint. Taking the lead in this is never easy. The smaller European nations look upon France with a certain awe which is, in terms of European history, entirely comprehensible. They do not find it natural to take strong positions which may seem to challenge the French – although it is sometimes highly desirable that this should be done. As to the larger nations, I once said to Helmut Schmidt, 'You Germans are strong, numerous, prosperous! Why don't you take more initiatives in Europe?'

He looked at me very seriously. We happened to be dining with Roy Jenkins, at his home in England.

'Scratch a European and you will find dislike of the Germans.'

I demurred, and Schmidt said with some grimness, 'You were never occupied!'

We made some progress. There could be no question of a united European foreign policy – and, indeed, the very idea foundered on the fact of divided sovereignty which I have already discussed. But there was certainly the possibility of a concerted foreign policy, of the foreign policies of the member states having been discussed in principle before the event and designed to push in the same direction. In April 1980 we managed to coordinate our words and attitudes towards Iran – it was the time of the American hostage crisis. In a 'Venice Declaration' in the summer of 1980 we published an agreed text on three particular plague spots – Afghanistan, invaded by the Soviets; Lebanon, in a state of blood-stained chaos; and the Middle East, where besides reaffirming the integrity of the state of Israel we specifically – and I think for the first time in that way – recognized that the Palestinians, too, had rights. We achieved agreement that on certain such issues we would accept that one spokesman – the Foreign Minister of the country holding at the time the Presidency of the Community – would 'speak for Europe' in the United Nations. I am sure that this, small and procedural though it may seem, was a valuable step, an indication to the world that Europe, rich, large and highly populated, was capable of one voice – the voice of a considerable community, stronger and louder in unison than would be the voices *seriatim* of twelve medium-sized nations. Coalescence *does* produce a certain virtue. In June 1981 I said in the House of Lords that 'the very existence of such a grouping of like-minded countries is a support for the principles of freedom and democracy'. I am sure that is true, intangible though it may be. Political cooperation between the nations of the Community has been strengthening throughout recent years, has come to be taken for granted as a major factor in the conduct of foreign policy, and I am delighted to have had some hand in the process.

But in spite of progress here and there, we always had a good deal of dissatisfaction surfacing over lack of advance in the institutions of Europe, lack of movement forward of the European idea. Some of the smaller countries would like to see a genuinely united Europe. Some of the bigger countries would like to see a more closely federated Europe. Towards the end of my time, there was concern at the sense of standing still, a concern particularly felt by Germany, and to some extent by France.

I would never dismiss the idea of institutional evolution in the Community – indeed I was confident it would happen one day – but I suspected that the day might be pretty remote and could not be hurried. Meanwhile I was sceptical of further blueprints for advance. It was perfectly true that the Treaty of Rome itself had emerged from a blueprint, an organizational idea spelled out; and that the imagination and genius of Jean Monnet, Robert Schuman, Konrad Adenauer and others had led to a blueprint, to a plan, to the genesis of the Community. But having got as far as we had, I thought the Community should settle down, that new institutions or forms should grow within it organically, should evolve. We all know that an idea bears fruit when its time has come, then one can't stop it; whereas before then one can't promote it, however intrinsically wise or desirable. I didn't think that the time had come for major institutional advance within the Community. That time, I believed, was only likely to come and be seen to have come when most members agreed on the shape and spirit a new Europe should adopt, and when their own domestic opinions had considerably advanced. Movement could only be in the direction of greater unity, of some sort of federation, of acceptance of a higher sovereignty than that of the present nation-state. I didn't believe many of us were yet ready for it.

Nor did I regard this tragically. Convinced European that I am, fully persuaded that the European nations must increasingly harmonize their voices, coordinate their policies, combine for economic benefit and external influence, I nevertheless believe that because a polity like Europe is developing slowly we should not grow impatient. Attitudes, all the time, are modifying. People are, little by little, changing, coming to think in somewhat different ways. The impotence of the small nation-state in international affairs has long been evident: it is becoming more and more evident now, to more and more people, and affecting their way of looking at politics. We should reflect, not with complacency but without frustration, on how much has been achieved. I feel about it as I have already written of the recovery of post-war Europe and the healing of sores; how remarkable, forty or even thirty years ago, would have seemed what we have already built, imperfect though it still may be.

The Presidency of the Council of the EEC rotates between nations and is held for six months. It came to the United Kingdom during my time as Foreign Secretary and it meant occupying the chair at meetings of Foreign Ministers. I enjoyed this and found it educative as well as tiring. Like any Chairman, one has to listen carefully at all times. And one has to know the rules.

Sometimes – and it was symbolic of the progress we had made in political coordination – the President of the Council had to personify the whole Community in some international negotiation or representation. Not much happened during my own tour of duty – except for the question of Afghanistan. I went to Moscow to tell the Soviet Government what we in the European Community were united in thinking of Soviet actions. We had agreed to propose a two-stage International Conference on Afghanistan.

Nothing much was expected to come of this and nothing much did. It was a *démarche* that had to be seen to be made, and that was that. Gromyko, Soviet Foreign Minister with the longest service as such on record, listened courteously to what I had to say; and then described the Community's proposal as unrealistic. I then asked him, among other things, whether he did not find it appalling that out of a population of nineteen million Afghans, three or four million were now refugees in Pakistan as a consequence of the Soviet invasion.

Gromyko responded politely.

'They are not refugees,' he observed, 'not refugees. The Afghans have always been a nomadic people!'

I detected no trace of any emphasis whatever in his remark. No resentment. No irony. And certainly no concern.

CHAPTER 15

Middle East

I believe that these days a Foreign Secretary must travel. Everybody does a job in his or her own way, and I plead guilty to wishing to go to places with which Britain has relations, often delicate and difficult relations, seeing and sniffing the atmosphere for myself, meeting face to face those with influence in other nations' foreign and domestic policies and forming the sort of opinions which follow personal contact. Our representatives abroad and their staffs compose admirable telegrams and despatches. Far more often than not we staff our Embassies and High Commissions with perceptive and sympathetic men and women who, generally in an astonishingly short time, come to know a great deal about the inner sensitivities as well as the external attitudes of the people to whose countries they are accredited.

I can recall occasional slips, naturally. I once broke down, or rather my aircraft broke down, in Pakistan en route to Australia. The High Commissioner kindly helped the time pass with a beach picnic. I asked him whether the country was stable.

'Splendid,' he said, 'really splendid!'

The Pakistan Prime Minister was replaced by a military coup during my flight to Canberra. This was some years earlier, and I reiterate that any British Government is, generally, well-informed by its professionals abroad. Nevertheless, nothing can replace a touch of on-the-spot contact and impression and I not only wanted to see as much as possible of foreign countries for myself; I wanted also to meet as many as could be managed of the British who were representing us and serving us. I had always enjoyed talking to people working expertly in their own field. I had met as many as possible of our Service working within the Foreign Office itself, going round section by section in the first days. I also wanted to see as much as I could of our Missions abroad. On the whole they were, and always have been in my experience, very good. There have been exceptions to this encomium – unimpressive diplomats, insensitive, opinionated wives – but the exceptions have been and I suspect remain rare.

This, of course, had to be combined with the frequent, more or less formal, meetings with colleague Foreign Ministers, or meetings of Heads of Government with Foreign Ministers attending – all of which have been greatly multiplied by modern communications and air travel. And there were sometimes occasions nominally ceremonial – like a Royal visit – on which the Foreign Secretary might be in attendance *de rigueur* but during which a good deal of less formal but useful business could also get done. There is no doubt that I travelled a great amount during the three years I was Foreign Secretary; and, inevitably, it was often undesirably exhausting. If anybody thinks I travelled too much, some journeys unnecessary, I doubt if he has been Foreign Secretary. I believe that I travelled, on the whole, to good effect: but good effect which could seldom be measured and will never be exactly recorded. Mood, impression and personal influence can be neither quantified nor proved.

My travels were generally accompanied by Iona. Such is the convention, and it is essential. The usefulness of being able to share human impressions with the person one knows best is beyond price. Then there is a wife's independent contact and conversation while one is segregated in conference – contact and conversation with the wives of one's foreign hosts, with less 'official' people who will have been corralled to help with the sight-seeing which probably balances one's own formal discussions, very importantly with British Embassy or High Commission staff families whose lives may well be lonely or tedious or dangerous – all this gives a Foreign Secretary an added perspective; and he needs it. There is also the more selfish point that on travels which can be extraordinarily tiring and sometimes exasperating the presence of one's partner provides an essential safety valve, reassurance and prop. Iona was all this and more. She also had exceptional powers of observation.

Not only Iona accompanied me. There were generally spare seats in the aircraft and I sometimes tried to get some business-men to fill them, selling for Britain. On one occasion we went to South America, and filling some spare seats were George Jellicoe, George Nelson, David Montgomery and Eddie Rothschild.

I had to explain to our rather bemused hosts that George Jellicoe was not in the Royal Navy. Nor was George Nelson. David Montgomery was not a soldier. The only one who had some professional connection with an illustrious namesake or progenitor was Eddie Rothschild. Our hosts continued to look puzzled. Of my colleagues Eddie Rothschild was, I think, the best pleased. On another occasion several accompanied me to the Far East and we were received by the King of Thailand in his northern capital. I remember that we had rather a scramble to get changed and attend a banquet at the palace surrounded by formalities and the somewhat feudal trappings with which Thai Royalty is charmingly decorated. Indeed, I remember the distinguished leaders of British industry, impeccably dressed above the waist, all huddled uneasily awaiting their trousers which were being cleaned and pressed and were late in being returned. One of my commercial colleagues was a forthright and entertaining Cockney, but at the banquet he found him-self, frustratingly, between two Thai ladies who spoke no English. At the end he muttered to me, 'I'll tell you one thing! I'll never bother to go to a Yul Brynner film again!'

Iona, more often than not, kept a diary record of our journeys. I note from it that between October 1980 and April 1981 we went together to some eleven countries for more or less extended visits. In October we accompanied the Queen on the Royal visit to Italy, which covered a great deal of Italy and Sicily, as well as including Governmental discussions in Rome and audiences in the Vatican, where the Pope's extraordinary personality dominated. Ceremony, however splendid, and business, however intractable, is always light-ened by humour in Italy, that delightful country. I remember President Pertini, aged eighty-four, presenting some two hun-dred official guests to the Queen and afterwards observing in an audible aside to Prince Philip, 'How old they all are! Wouldn't they look awful with no clothes on!' Then he con-gratulated our (very pretty) interpreter on her looks and asked for her telephone number.

Thence, still with the Queen and Prince Philip, we sailed to Tunisia for a similar mix of ceremony and business. Still in October, we flew to Hungary, and from there travelled to Poland where, at the time, a demonstration of Western interest was particularly important. I met two First Secretaries of communist parties on the same day, since I had a session in Budapest with Kadar and later that day met Kania, head of the Polish communists. Even later on the same day Kania flew to Moscow, summoned for what some people anxiously fancied might be the fate of the Czech, Dubcek! There was a good deal of speculation that the Soviet Union might reckon Warsaw had been insufficiently vigorous in dealing with dis-sent, and I think there was relief when Kania returned next day. Poland was thawing a little, like most of Eastern Europe – thawing nervously, unevenly and with eyes cocked in different directions, attempting little by little and no doubt inadequately that near-impossible reconciliation between ideological purity and practical economic advance. Iona told me that a senior Polish minister surprised her by observing, 'You can't expect people to work hard or take initiatives in a nationalized indus-try!' Quite so.

January 1981 found us in Morocco, and from there we flew to Egypt for conversations with President Sadat. Sadat at that time had faith in the ability of the Peres Government in Israel to come to some sort of settlement with the Arabs. He believed that Saudi Arabia and Jordan should be associated with his long, difficult peace negotiation by the end of 1981, perhaps – but not yet. Sadat was an impressive man of great charm and geniality whom I had met before and always liked. I told him I had admired his instant hospitality to the Shah, when the latter appeared after his fall friendless in a once welcoming, even sycophantic world. Sadat shrugged. What else, he asked, could one do?

We had two days in hand after the Egyptian visit and booked cabins on a Nile steamer, through Luxor. It was necessary to keep in touch with London in case of crisis and the Embassy in Cairo had detached a young man to keep communication with us by driving along the bank sufficiently near our boat. The Ambassador was with us.

At about eleven o'clock one evening some apparently urgent message came through. The young man motored up and down what might in other conditions be called the tow-path and eventually saw what he supposed was our boat.

The problem was to make sure and to make contact. For a better view he climbed a railway signal – the railway also runs along the Nile bank – and struggled on to the crosspiece: it was one of those old-fashioned signals where the crosspiece was up when no train was in sight and lowered sharply to 130° from vertical when a train appeared. He sighted our boat and was satisfied that it was the right one, despite the Egyptian night. At that moment a train came into view and the signal crosspiece was lowered abruptly, sliding him to the ground. Then he and my secretary who was with him found and pinched a rowing boat and rowed into the middle of the Nile. As the steamer approached they shouted, 'Stop!'

Nobody paid the smallest attention. Full of resource, the young man said to my secretary, 'Scream!'

She told me she was anyway petrified and she screamed with a will. The steamer eventually stopped. The young man climbed aboard. He was wearing tweed coat and deerstalker hat. He delivered the telegrams, lifted his hat, descended to his rowing boat and disappeared into the night.

Returned from Egypt in February 1981, we flew almost immediately to Washington for one of many, many such visits, of which the first as Foreign Secretary had been with Margaret Thatcher in President Carter's day – Christmas 1979 and a huge, friendly party at the White House, extremely well done. Some of the principal singers from the Boston Opera Company were in Washington and came to sing: and periodically some wretched guest was dragged on stage to join in 'The Twelve Days of Christmas' or something of the sort. The chief soprano from Boston was a majestic lady, tall, dressed in black and wearing a pince-nez. She sang a Berlioz aria, splendidly. As she reached a particular high note she was interrupted by a terrific crash. Cy Vance, United States Secretary of State, had fallen through his little gold chair: had the soprano's eyes been laser beams he would have died on the spot. This time, in 1981, the Prime Minister was visiting President Reagan and, as so often, I was struck with how generous-hearted and decent he was, how desirous to do good things. That was not, I recall, a visit during which Margaret Thatcher was exuberant in her praise of the Foreign Service and I had to remind her of its competence and virtues on more than one occasion.

In the next month, March 1981, we flew to Pakistan. President Zia was another ruler who had had an uneven press; a likeable man of great warmth, he was always agreeable to do business with. Then, later in March, we found ourselves in Hong Kong, already exercised about the longer-term future; and thence travelled to China, to Japan and home. China was already moving out of the shadow of Mao Tse-tung, but it is a long shadow.

With most of these countries – and I have given these six months in some detail to indicate the intensity of travel pattern at times – there were problems of one kind or another. Problems deriving, often, from the past, whether recent or remote; or problems rooted in anxiety about war and peace, about the relations between superpowers and power blocs and our perception of them; problems primarily about trade, perhaps East–West trade; or problems, as in Hong Kong, about the future. I believe that I in every case had a better understanding of these problems after personal visits. I had always been well-briefed, but it is impossible to visit a place and not to learn more than can be assimilated from the written word, however good the writing. And friendliness, personal and genial contact, also helps, although its effect should not be overestimated. On the whole the Foreign Secretary's job is to

improve rather than worsen relations with other Governments, provided it can be done without detriment to British
interests, realistically conceived. There were, and will persist,
certain sore places in our international relationships, but one
can always try to keep the sore from becoming too angry, and
journey round with a small pot of balm.

Gibraltar had been one such sore. I reaffirmed – as most of
my predecessors had reaffirmed – to Parliament, in January
1981, that 'Her Majesty's Government would never agree to
Gibraltar passing to another sovereignty without their [the
inhabitants'] freely and democratically expressed wishes' – a
quote from the preamble to the Gibraltar constitution. 'Nothing', I said, 'could be clearer than that.' Belize had been
another such sore. Guatemala had certain claims, and Belize
– hovering on the edge of independence – was nervous of
those claims. We reached general agreement with Guatemala
on Belize in March 1981, and thus the sometime colony of
British Honduras received independence. And with Spain we
worked for, and to some extent achieved a certain amelior-
ation of the situation, which would preserve Gibraltar's essential position while being not inconsistent with Spanish feelings
and pride. I negotiated an agreement at Lisbon with
the Spanish Foreign Minister in 1981 which would, I think,
have satisfied those conditions; unfortunately it was not
put into effect for some time owing to political difficulties in
Madrid.

One of the most difficult constitutional exercises, I'm sure,
is to manage (as a colonial power) a condominium. We had a
condominium with France over the New Hebrides in the South
Pacific. At one moment the New Hebrides were suddenly
shaken by some internal troubles and needed the help of their
protectors. Some French gendarmes were despatched. Then
some British Royal Marines were despatched and the French
objected. Some eight weeks later objections had been succeeded by relative harmony and joint Anglo-French military
action restored the situation. Nevertheless, I do not recommend condominium. There are too many anomalies. If an
inhabitant of the New Hebrides was arrested for an offence by

a French policeman he was tried under French law, if by a British under British law! De Gaulle visited on one occasion. Passing the (rather splendid) residence of the British Commissioner on a rocky island he observed, 'I see the British have their Gibraltar!' He was not one to let any troublesome allusion escape without reference.

All these things could periodically ruffle the waters, but unless we or others were astonishingly ham-fisted they could not become truly dangerous. Different in kind was the question of the Middle East.

I had first spent some time on the problems of the Middle East during the Heath Government, when I was Defence Minister. We had tried to be ostentatiously neutral when the Arab-Israeli Six-Day War broke out, and the neutrality took the form of not helping Israel with the provision of spare parts for British-supplied weapons. This had led to a good deal of hostility from the Jewish community in Britain, and at a large rally at the Coliseum I got a pretty chilly reception. I recall seeing Henry Kissinger at about that time and he had clearly found the Europeans hard to deal with and their attitudes far from commendable. He told me how frustrating he found it to cope with a Europe that had so disunited a voice: some were trying to support the Arabs, fearful for oil; others were pro-Israel; while others – and we aspired to be of their number – genuinely tried hard to be neutral. It was all, Kissinger said, unimpressive: however it is fair to record that his even more frustrating experience was, as he much later told me, when the Europeans were united – and united in a way America disliked!

A journey to Saudi Arabia also at that time as Defence Minister had been memorable because it was arranged I should be the bearer of a personal letter from the Queen to King Faisal, a letter which I had persuaded Buckingham Palace to ask Her Majesty to sign. On the first evening, at the Embassy in Jedda, I was given this missive in a sealed envelope by Robert Andrew, my Private Secretary. I held it up to the light on some idle impulse. As far as I could see, it had no written beginning, nor signature at the end.

Next morning the Ambassador, I and our advisers discussed The Letter. The consensus was that for me, at an audience, to hand the King an unsigned letter would be gravely discourteous. We decided that we must steam open the envelope to see whether, in fact, the Queen's signature was or was not appended.

This took a long time – until after lunch, in fact! I think the Embassy staff were probably inexperienced at steaming open letters. When the operation was complete we saw that the Queen had indeed not signed.

We considered the options. Forge the Sovereign's signature? Write something else and pretend it was never meant to be signed? (This presented the difficulty that no Windsor Castle writing paper was to hand.) Forget the whole thing? Ask advice from Buckingham Palace? (This would, disagreeably, involve explanation of why we'd steamed open the letter.) After considering some other, even less attractive, possibilities we decided to telegraph Buckingham Palace saying that it had been thought necessary to open the envelope in order to provide an Arabic translation, and, noticing that the letter was unsigned, we wondered whether this was the Queen's intention or not.

A tart reply from Buckingham Palace arrived a few hours later to the effect that the Queen had not intended to sign it, but that we should not hand the original to King Faisal. Instead, a copy should be submitted, with a covering letter from myself. There was unanimity among all present that this represented a cover-up for Palace incompetence! I cannot remember whether it was on the same visit that I handed over the statutory gifts demanded by protocol (the Foreign Office cash allocation for such being notoriously mean) and solemnly received in return a number of objects including a beautifully polished, large and heavy wooden case. On opening it I found it to contain a machine gun, well-oiled, and one hundred rounds of ammunition.

I explained it at Heathrow. The Customs officer reacted with propriety although with what seemed at the time insufficient imagination.

'Have you a firearm certificate?'

I told him no, and that he had better keep the machine gun. I asked him, however, what he planned to do with it. He knew the answer.

'There's a hole in the sea, off the Isle of Wight. Unwanted firearms are dumped there. It's deep, so they can't foul fishing nets and so forth!'

It seemed all right. He added, 'It's the same hole where they put down admirals, that ask to be buried at sea.'

Then, when in Opposition after the Heath Government's fall, I had included countries of the Middle East in my journeyings. Saudi Arabia again – a less sophisticated place than today; Jordan, where I had a particularly high regard for the courage and record of King Hussein to whose friendship and statecraft amid huge original and continuing difficulties we all owed a great deal; Syria – I respected President Assad of Syria as a level-headed man, although he had undoubtedly mortgaged Syria to Soviet influence, not, perhaps, with much enjoyment. Everywhere I was treated most courteously and frankly. The Arabs had and have an intractable problem, and they did not themselves create it.

That problem is the expropriation of Palestinians from their homeland. I was invited to visit Lebanon during those years – Iona and I were asked to go there by the Lebanese Ambassador to London, M. Nadim Dimichkie. The troubles in Lebanon had not broken out then. Beirut was one of the most delightful places in the entire Mediterranean. I was in Opposition, a comparatively private person.

We stayed at a very beautiful hotel on the harbour. All was green, peaceful, Beirut luxurious, sophisticated and sunny beneath a cloudless sky. The Ambassador's brother-in-law entertained us – a very rich and very charming man who happened to be a Palestinian. His family had lived in Jaffa since the second century AD: they had introduced the oranges! Now, over seventeen hundred years of continuity had been broken and he was a (very wealthy) exile. He spoke without bitterness, but he made gently clear that in his view the Palestinians had a grievance; and he didn't need to emphasize that, unlike him, for most of them the grievance was compounded by material loss and actual suffering.

On the same visit I met a number of university professors, also Palestinians. Moderate, civilized men, who would not have been out of place in any Oxford senior common room, they felt very strongly on this matter of Palestine. And to exacerbate the original fact of Israel and fact of exile and expropriation, there was now the forcible incorporation into Israel of the West Bank of the Jordan, in the aftermath of war. I appreciated very vividly that the Palestinians – historically among the best educated and most intelligent of the Arab peoples – did not lack skilful and persuasive advocates for their cause among the Arab nations; most of whom, of course, also harboured large numbers of Palestinian refugees.

It was in Syria on one such visit that, when dining with Khaddam, who became Deputy President – my host was very full of British colonial misdeeds in the past – somebody whispered in my ear that 'Arafat would be prepared to see me'. As I have said, I was more or less a private person, so I agreed with interest; was bundled into the back of a car; and soon found myself passing through the sandbagged entrance to a block of flats in the outskirts of Damascus where Yasser Arafat, leader of the PLO, was waiting for me, supported by his scruffy, tommy-gun-toting escort.

Arafat's manner was half-ingratiating, half-threatening on that occasion, and I didn't take to him. But whatever my impressions of Arafat, I formed and retained the view that the Palestinians had not only a case but a strong case; and that there was something in the often expressed Arab view that the Christian and European peoples expiated their guilt for centuries of sporadic anti-Semitism, anti-Semitism culminating in an enormous and horrendous crime, by creating Israel – at the expense of Arab peoples, themselves Semitic, who had never evinced anti-Semitism in any form. As to the strategic issue, I once in Syria visited the Golan Heights, then occupied by Israeli troops. My Syrian hosts asked me whether, in their place, I could feel safe with an enemy entrenched on this feature, dominating the approaches to Damascus.

But I also went to Israel during that time in Opposition; and from Israel I also visited the Golan Heights. My Israeli hosts also asked me whether, in their place, I could feel safe with Syrians occupying the heights and the whole of Israel extended before them. To neither host was there a sensible or consolatory answer. And my sense that the Arabs – and in particular the Palestinians – had a case in this long, bitter quarrel was balanced by my understanding of the problems, the fears and the historic memories of the people of Israel. It was impossible not to be impressed by Israel. The country had been made productive and fertile through the energy, the talents and the inspiration of the Jews. The achievement had been prodigious. And to balance the indignation of the Palestinians over Israeli occupation of the West Bank of the Jordan was the undoubted fact that the borders of a Palestinian state on the West Bank would be about eight miles from Tel-Aviv. Israel would have no depth at all; I doubt whether she will ever willingly give up the West Bank now, unhappy though the situation remains.

These various visits over a number of years both as a minister and in Opposition had convinced me that negotiation must be attempted. It might or might not be that we British should have some part to play in it – we could hardly plead lack of historic connection, since modern Israel largely owed its existence to our own initiative, a fact the Arabs seldom ignored: while Britain had held the Palestine Mandate from the fall of the Ottoman Empire to the birth of Israel. Not only had we a certain moral involvement, we had also an interest. For I was sure that the Middle East would continue a place of danger, one of the few places which could, if all went wrong, bring external powers into confrontation. We had an interest in preventing that if it could be done.

But rather as I had been persuaded, ultimately, that we had to involve the Patriotic Front in the Rhodesian negotiation, despite the hostility of many who had suffered from them and hated all they stood for, so I was sure that the Palestine Liberation Organization had to be involved in any settlement. It might be impossible. Some were, entirely fairly, stigmatized as terrorists. Some might never concede one point from the extreme, ultimate demand for the elimination of the state of Israel. The Israelis might refuse, in any circumstances whatever, to talk to them. But at that time the PLO, like it or loathe it (and a good many moderate Arabs, as well as Israelis, loathed it: especially in Jordan), represented the majority of Palestinians. They could not be ignored. If there were ever to be any sort of productive negotiation it must include them.

That was the sentiment with which I arrived at the Foreign Office. I told the House of Lords in my first year as Foreign Secretary that there could be no Middle East peace until Israel recognized the rights of the Palestinians and until the Palestinians – including the PLO – recognized the state of Israel. The Foreign Office has often been accused of being intemperately pro-Arab. In my experience this is nonsense. Of course there is only one British Ambassador accredited to Israel and a good many stationed in Arab countries, so that there is at any one time more paper circulating in the Office bearing the imprint – and no doubt sometimes reflecting the sentiments – of Arab capitals than of Tel-Aviv. There is more widely diffused experience in the Foreign Office of Arab nations than of Israel. But, that said, I never found in the Foreign Office anybody who would not strongly and conscientiously defend the integrity, independence and legitimate concerns of Israel. We had plenty of periodic difficulties with Arab sensitivities and they were as quick as the Israelis to suspect us of hostility. Some incidents may have started in triviality but could blow up unhealthily. I remember the television programme 'Death of a Princess' which was regarded by the Saudis as intolerably and inaccurately unfriendly – indeed they asked the British Ambassador to quit Riyadh. The incident demonstrated the sad irresponsibility of some entertainment media in a free society, with programmes made regardless of their impact on British interests.

The fact that most of our Service could nevertheless

understand the Arab viewpoint, could sympathize with Palestinian grievance and could regret the more intemperate Israeli actions from time to time did not prove bias. It demonstrated objectivity, and it was wholly consistent with British interests, which, above all, demand harmony not discord in the Middle East.

It remains a pretty unfulfilled demand and there was certainly little harmony in the area in summer 1979 when I became Foreign Secretary. A number of extraneous factors of considerable significance were affecting the situation – whose underlying reality, as I have said, lay in the unhealed sore of Arab-Israeli conflict. There was the rise of Islamic fundamentalism, which had found violent expression in the overthrow of the Shah and which was causing explosive polarization throughout most of the Arab lands – polarization between 'moderates' and others, but by no means eliminating conflict between different 'immoderates', as was soon evident in the Iran–Iraq war. There was the dramatic rise in the oil price, which hugely exacerbated the difficulties of the industrialized world and appeared to give to the Arab countries – or some of them – greatly increased international bargaining power. And very soon we were to have a Presidential Election in America (November 1980: but Presidential Elections cast a long shadow before and there were few initiatives from the Carter administration, nor were likely to be).

In these circumstances the Europeans decided – and I felt it wholly right – that Europe should try to agree a policy towards the Middle East and should be active in the matter. There was always a real danger of war breaking out again. The United States were having a sabbatical, and moderate Arabs, in particular, needed to see that somebody, somewhere, was alive to the problem and wanted to help. Hence the Venice Declaration to which I've already referred, and which strongly affirmed our loyalty to the existence of Israel but – I think for the first time – explicitly recognized that Palestinians, too, had rights. No European minister was foolish enough to imagine that European intervention could somehow solve intractable Middle East problems, but in these matters one should always look for and advance chances to strengthen moderate and conciliatory forces and elements, in whatever country they may be. I think the Venice Declaration made a modest contribution to that.

The major factor in the Middle East, however, is always the attitude of the United States. That does not mean that America is always right, or should be invariably placated, but no initiative can proceed far without American involvement. The Carter administration – and, indeed, their Republican opponents – disliked the Venice Declaration. They disliked our reference to the necessity for the association of the Palestinians with any negotiation. The Jewish lobby in America is powerful and many of them clearly thought the Europeans were minded to betray Israel and sell out to terrorism. They were wrong – and something not dissimilar to the Venice Declaration was adopted by the Reagan administration a few years later. At the time, however, and for some years, there was division between the United States and their European allies over Middle East policy.

I believed American perceptions were faulty in this matter. They tended – one should always avoid blanket generalization: there were many strains in United States thinking and policy, as in European – tended to underestimate the difficulties which 'moderate' Arab states and their rulers had in remaining 'moderate', whether on Israel or anything else. Americans were apt to take the view that these people depended on the United States, couldn't do without them, didn't need much humouring. I, on the other hand, reckoned that these same 'moderates' needed to show their peoples that moderation paid: paid possibly in material terms, but paid very definitely in terms of results in the great struggle for an equitable settlement with Israel over Palestine. If moderate rulers were unable to show some sort of progress in the international sphere from time to time they would ultimately be succeeded by a more extreme and demagogic sort of style, whether fundamentalist Islamic or whatever. It wasn't in our interests that that should happen. It wasn't in America's interests that that should happen.

On the other side of the coin, of course, the Arab states were pretty well unanimous in reckoning that the United States was too gentle with Israel. The Arabs thought America could and should exert legitimate pressure on Israel – Israel with its enormous economic problems, its dependence upon America for viability, security, almost all. In fact this dependence was so considerable that it made almost impossible pressure of the kind the Arabs desired – most of the time. America was wholly committed to Israel's independent existence, and to cut off economic support would destroy it. Americans knew it and Israelis knew it. And Israelis knew Americans wouldn't do it. Short of that extreme and (it must generally appear) unthinkable step there was not a great deal of graduated pressure that could be applied, although I believe there were occasions (the invasion of Lebanon by Israeli forces was one) when the tide of world opinion ran so strongly against Israel that the United States might have brought decisive influence to bear. If they had turned tough with Israel then, instead of trying to settle the Lebanese problem by more direct intervention, they might have brought all parties to the negotiating table, and perhaps moved on thence to the issue, the fundamental issue, of Palestine. At its most vulnerable to criticism American policy has allowed itself to be excessively dictated by Israel, and when Washington cautiously (in 1981) welcomed a certain Arab *démarche* – Saudi Arabia for the first time acknowledging the existence of the state of Israel – Begin soon brought the United States back into line. The atmosphere had been improved in some directions by Henry Kissinger's valiant efforts to build bridges between Israel and Sadat's Egypt. I doubted whether 'Camp David', a genuine and courageous attempt to improve relations in the area, could ever get beyond a certain point because it didn't deal with the crux issue, Palestine.* But in the autumn of 1981 Sadat was murdered.

I flew to Egypt for the funeral – we had just returned from Australia. The Prince of Wales represented the Queen and I represented the British Government. Jim Callaghan was also

* When Golda Meir heard that Sadat and Begin were nominated for the Nobel Prize she said gruffly, 'Should have been an Oscar!'

of the party. It was a strange affair. The funeral procession formed up on the parade ground where Sadat had been shot, and began with a large reception, drinking coffee and other things somewhat lugubriously in an enormous tent. Thence – without organization, briefing, ushers or the like – we moved to follow the coffin, and His Royal Highness, Jim and I found ourselves in the middle of a shouting and gesticulating *mêlée*, surrounded by people of whom not one seemed to know where he was meant to be going. Without discipline or order we reached some stands and sat down, to find that we were facing in the wrong direction. We then found that we were sitting among bloodstains; and it was explained that we were sitting in the actual place where the President had been shot.

I have referred to an Arab *démarche*, cautiously supported. This took the form of a Saudi 'eight-point plan', and for the first time it, at least implicitly, recognized the right to existence of Israel. It coincided, more or less, with discussion about whether the European nations should – with the United States and at their request – contribute to a peacekeeping force in Sinai, to monitor the Camp David agreements between Egypt and Israel, and in particular the withdrawal of Israel's troops from territories captured from the Egyptians in war. The Arabs in general were unconvinced that this would be a particularly good idea without a more comprehensive arrangement which, at the least, acknowledged the unresolved problems of Palestine and the West Bank of the Jordan. To them 'Camp David' might suit Israel and Egypt but left the main issues untouched. Now it seemed the Europeans were going to underwrite it.

The United States Government in general and Al Haig in particular were keen on European (including British) participation. I had reservations. We were ready to help but I understood the Arab viewpoint. Then came the Saudi 'eight-point plan' which at least attempted to nod in the direction of all the chief issues of contention. If the Europeans supported it they would be seen to acknowledge the existence of the problems – and the Israel–Egypt accord, helping to solve at least one of them, could go forward.

When we welcomed the Saudi initiative, however, we were immediately and trenchantly criticized in Israel for so doing – despite the progress towards recognition of Israel it implied. Haig took the view that our support for the Saudis had been specifically designed to procure Israeli hostility – and thus get the Israelis to say they didn't want us in any peacekeeping force: specifically designed, that is, because he thought we were anyway reluctant to take part. The consequence of this sequence of accusation and counter-accusation was to bring European-American, and in particular British-American relations to a somewhat chilly condition, in which Haig in a series of speeches and interviews implied that this sort of behaviour could make the Americans (undesirably, as he made plain) think twice about their contribution to European defence. It was a bad patch: I came in for a good deal of personal criticism from the Americans – I had welcomed the Saudi plan not only as British Foreign Secretary but as, for the time being, President of the EEC Council of Ministers.

I understood the American viewpoint. They feared that this, to them, somewhat tangential Arab initiative could lead to deadlock over the implementation of the Camp David agreements, demanding as these did an acceptable (to both Israel and Egypt) peacekeeping force in Sinai. The Israelis attacked the Saudi plan as a 'betrayal' of Camp David and the Americans, after cautiously welcoming it initially, quickly came to see it the Israeli way. We – British and Europeans – were attacked for rocking the boat. The Americans felt that they were holding the main responsibility in the matter, that they were becoming increasingly isolated and that we Europeans were unhelpfully striking attitudes on the sidelines. Some harsh things were said. My own view remains that the Saudi initiative represented limited, modest progress; that Israeli opposition to it was excessive; and that it deserved support.

*

My policy towards the Middle East caused a number of people both in Britain and the United States to regard me as anti-Israeli. I made no secret of my belief that something must be done about Palestinian rights on the West Bank of the Jordan, perhaps some sort of demilitarized self-governing zone, with Israeli security wholly safeguarded. I never disguised my conviction that the PLO would have to be involved in any negotiations leading to long-term settlement. We, as a Government, declared our support for UN Security Council Resolution 242 which required the evacuation of lands occupied in the last Israeli victorious war. None of this was popular with the partisans of Israel (it is fair to say that America also backed this Resolution, and one of her chief objections to our desire to involve the PLO in negotiations was the latter's refusal to accept it – also embodying, as it did, recognition of Israel's right to exist). I was invited to speak to a large Jewish audience at Caxton Hall in London. I was heartily booed; interrupted incessantly; and barely given a hearing. People refused to shake hands with me – it was Rhodesia and all that once again! In New York some very angry representatives of the Jewish community came to see me to castigate me for the Venice Declaration. It was clear they had no idea what was in it and when I took them through it clause by clause they couldn't find much wrong with it – apart, of course, from the assertion that the PLO must somehow be involved in any settlement if it was to stick.

My reputation for being anti-Israeli was strongly fomented by the Israelis themselves. Both they and the Jewish lobbies in Britain and America tended to regard as an enemy anybody who accepted less than a hundred per cent of their view, anybody who saw another. Shamir, then Israeli Foreign Minister, and the Prime Minister, Begin, continuously spread the word of how hostile I was. I had to put off two visits to Israel where I would not have been welcome. When I eventually got there, in March 1982, I did, however, see most of the top people, culminating with Begin himself.

I had never felt warm towards him. I understood Israel's fears and insecurity. I sympathized with past Israeli sufferings.

I greatly admired present Israeli achievements. I respected Israeli courage, talent, determination and patriotism. I was wholly dedicated to Israel's right to exist. But I could not regard Israel as having a monopoly of right, nor the sentiments of the Palestinians as without justice. No good can ultimately come from blindness to all causes but one's own. Begin's obsessions with the crimes committed against his people were perfectly understandable but in a statesman of international significance they should not have been allowed to induce something close to paranoia. I remembered how Begin, on a visit to England, had once lunched at 10 Downing Street, and turned to Margaret Thatcher:

'You are responsible for the death of two million Jews at Auschwitz!' Margaret looked somewhat astonished. I suppose she had been aged about thirteen at the time in question. 'You are responsible! Because you didn't bomb the railway line!'

Begin was living in the past: the frightful past of genocide, and the (to him) heroic past when, as a member of the Stern Gang, he had done his no doubt murderous bit against the British in Palestine. On that occasion in March 1982 we had a tough hour's meeting, as I tried to persuade him to some sort of progress towards a settlement over the West Bank, a settlement with the Arabs. He looked at me fiercely and banged his hand on the table.

'Never, never, as long as I live, will I negotiate with the PLO! They are terrorists!'

I nodded. 'We have been decolonizing and dismantling our empire for a good many years. It's a fact that a lot of people we considered terrorists – not unreasonably – turned out to be quite responsible people when they got power and office.'

Begin looked unimpressed and I said, 'Look at Kenyatta in Kenya!'

Begin still looked unimpressed.

'Give or take a bit, what about Makarios in Cyprus? And then, to give another example –'

I was about to cite Robert Mugabe. Begin interrupted me, saying, 'Not me, I hope!'

For the first time I found myself almost liking him! But

during the whole period before that encounter the knowledge that I was suspect in Israeli eyes had made me especially keen to visit them when I could, and try to disabuse them of the idea that I was an enemy. This keenness was to have a curious and unhappy consequence.

CHAPTER 16

The Falklands

I recall a luncheon at Chequers very early in my time as Foreign Secretary, during which I raised the question of Argentina and the Falkland Islands. The inhabitants of Argentina, almost regardless of their political views on other subjects, were convinced that the Falkland Islands – to them the Malvinas – lying several hundred miles off their eastern seaboard, are by nature and geography a part of the Argentine homeland. The inhabitants of the Falklands – British settlers or descendants of British settlers over the last 150 years – were equally convinced that sovereignty is essentially over people rather than land, and that they wished to remain subjects of the British Crown. There are no indigenous or native people. I had experienced the strength of Argentine feeling long before, during a visit Iona and I paid to South America in 1965: and, of course, the Falklands issue had periodically surfaced in Cabinet during my previous and various ministerial incarnations. The question had a long history, and in recent times every British Government had needed to face it in some degree.

There had been a considerable measure of continuity in British policy. In 1967 the Labour Government stated that Britain would be prepared to cede sovereignty over the Falklands to Argentina if the circumstances were right – and the circumstance which mattered was that the wishes of the islanders should be respected. Discussions were opened, and were continued by Ted Heath's Conservative administration three years later. These, and subsequent, negotiations, however, were always conducted under a number of constraints. First was the intransigence and emotion of the Argentine

claim. To them this was a matter of national dignity so fundamental that compromise would always have a difficult passage.
Second was the known position of the islanders. They were
in origin British, they felt British, and they regarded Argentina,
its language, its traditions and its *mores* as intensely alien: the
sense of alienation was intensified by the accession to power
of the military junta in March 1976 although it was always
there – Peron, and other rulers in Argentina, were viewed by
the Falklanders with pretty impartial disfavour. Third was the
reaction of the British Parliament to any proposals for change:
both sides of both Houses tended to look on these with enormous suspicion, regardless of which party was in Government.
Parliament reckoned that negotiation was intended to lead to
surrender – of the liberties and allegiance of an inoffensive
British people, albeit eight thousand miles away and number-
ing under two thousand.

It was never a promising atmosphere in which to seek
advance by diplomacy, and plenty of people reckoned that it
was inept to try. The truth was, however, that the basic,
underlying situation was flawed. I was entirely satisfied with
the strength of our position in law: our title to the islands
was good, although Argentina argued the historical case with
complete conviction. But the eighteen hundred Falkland
Islanders depended on Argentina for pretty well everything,
particularly communications. It was, in those days, impossible
to reach the islands by air, or postal service, except by courtesy
of Argentina. Argentina was a country with, in other respects,
a long tradition of friendship with Britain, and to maintain a
very small colony (in terms of population) a few hundred
miles offshore from the Argentine coast and several thousand
from our own in the face of irreconcilable Argentine hostility
made little sense to successive Governments in London. The
Falklands represented no vital strategic or economic interest
for Britain, and although nobody had questioned that the
islanders' views on their own future must carry proper weight
it was clear that the only long-term solution to make sense
must be one leading to peaceful co-existence with Argentina;
while anybody could see that a protracted posture of defence

against Argentina – if it were allowed to come to that – would be so intolerably expensive as to be an aberration of defence finance and priorities. There was not, I think, much underlying difference between successive British administrations that our dispute with Argentina must ultimately be a matter of negotiation. They had the emotion. We had the interest. We had to try.

Previous attempts had not got far. London had always formally stated that no settlement would be imposed on the islanders against their will, and a number of possible negotiating positions had, over the years, been discussed – always on the 1967 basis that Britain had no fundamental as opposed to practical difficulty over the question of sovereignty. The first idea to be mooted – predictably rejected by Argentina – was that of a 'sovereignty freeze'. Under this we would seek to discuss such practicalities as improved economic collaboration while agreeing to set on one side the sovereignty dispute for a given period of years. The trouble with a 'sovereignty freeze' was that while to the Falkland Islanders it was, not unnaturally, the preferred option (if anything had to be done at all), to the Argentinians it was simply a British device to put off dealing with the most difficult issue, procrastinate the problem away.

Which indeed it was, although not necessarily to be dismissed on that score.

Then there had, some years previously, been talk of a condominium – an idea which, as I suspect for the best, never got far. And there was discussion of 'leaseback'; a solution whereby Britain would cede sovereignty, thus satisfying Argentine pride, and would lease the islands from Argentina for some extended period, during which administration and almost all else would remain British. All these possible negotiating positions were mooted against a background of Falkland Islands mistrust and Argentine impatience with what they saw as British prevarication, as refusal to recognize a just claim. But they were also mooted against a background of Falkland economic decline. The dispute was not good for the islands. The only outcome to make sense must be one which would, somehow, restore goodwill.

At regular intervals during those years, under British Governments both Labour and Conservative, there had been Intelligence assessments of what Argentina's policy was likely to be in given circumstances, and of whether – in view of what seemed to Buenos Aires lamentable lack of progress – there was likely at any time to be some sort of Argentine military intervention. The advice generally received was that provided Argentina believed Britain was negotiating in good faith, military rather than diplomatic action was highly improbable – advice which was tendered pretty well until the last day, but which was inevitably modified somewhat by what was thought to be the unpredictability of the junta regime. There was never doubt in any British Government's mind that Argentina could, if she chose, mount a major military expedition. Two things, however, were consistently believed about that. First, it was always reckoned that we would have warning – in the sense of a progressive deterioration of the situation. Second, it was recognized that although we should – and did – make plain that we would meet force with force, nevertheless the commitment to deploy such military strength as would actually deter – in the sense of demonstrably making an attack unlikely to achieve even initial success – would be impossibly onerous and expensive. In November 1977 our predecessors had temporarily deployed a submarine and two frigates, standing a thousand miles off, in case a particular patch in the hot–cold sequence with Argentina turned nasty. The deployment was as far as we knew covert; as such, it could not have played the slightest part in deterrence or anything else at that time; and I have no evidence to support the suggestion subsequently made that the Argentines may have been given some warning through a discreet channel.

The situation we inherited in 1979 was, as previously, one of Argentinian impatience, with all options seeming intractable. The impatience, however, was sharper than hitherto, and the internal troubles of the Argentine regime were unlikely to soften it. A mission led by Lord Shackleton on behalf of our Labour predecessors to see what could be done for the

Falklands had been greeted with indignation in Argentina, where it was represented as evidence that the British still regarded themselves as ruling the islands for ever; while the mission's most publicized, and in retrospect most significant, recommendation – that the Falklands airfield's runway be lengthened so that long-range aircraft could cross the Atlantic and fly direct – was turned down by the British Treasury.

I return to my luncheon at Chequers in 1979. Convictions of the kind the Argentinians held are facts of politics. They are often inconvenient, and when one disagrees with them in logic they tend to seem unreasonable prejudices rather than views based on evidence and interest. But they have to be taken into account. They matter. I was under no doubt that the issue of the Falkland Islands must continue to be a proper subject for negotiation with Argentina, and that we should not simply let matters lie.

That luncheon party, however, showed me that this might become one of those cases – which, as I have said, she was always ready to scent and challenge – when the Prime Minister suspected a defeatist Foreign Office of finding ways to appease a foreign Government. I scouted any suggestion that I contemplated surrendering our position – I had myself spoken vigorously to the Lords in the past on the matter of the Falklands and Argentinian claims.

I knew that negotiation would be hard and often appear fruitless, since there was little common ground between the perfectly understandable resolve of the islanders to remain British and the passionate determination of Buenos Aires that these islanders (however governed) were inhabiting Argentinian territory. Nevertheless I was sure we should do what we, and our predecessors, had consistently tried to do – find a way forward. There are times when it may be necessary to say, in international affairs, 'I don't mind what you think: I'm not going to talk about it.' There are (a few) times when it may even be necessary to add, 'And I'm never going to talk about it.' This did not strike me as such an occasion. Sooner or later it would be better for all parties if some accommodation could be reached, some equitable formula found which could reconcile the islanders' interests and loyalty with the tradition and pride of Argentina. It would, I knew, take time.

Such long hauls are not uncommon in diplomacy. They need great patience, and skill of a kind which our professionals, at their best, display to an outstanding degree. They need determination. One cannot negotiate if the other side believes that mere obstinacy – let alone force – will triumph in time. But they need underlying goodwill – a certain shared belief by principals, behind what will probably be strong and passionate language, that agreement is a desirable goal and that the other side probably has a point of view, albeit misguided. Above all, such long hauls need communication and a certain degree of good temper. At every stage there will be domestic critics quick to raise accusations of weakness on the one hand or unseemly bellicosity on the other. As in the case of Rhodesia, it took a certain amount of persuasion before we all in Cabinet saw the matter through roughly the same spectacles, and before I could, with my colleagues' support, send Nicholas Ridley on his first visit to the Falklands in July 1979.

Nick was the Foreign Office minister in charge. The background to his visit was continuing British adherence to the principle that any change in their status must have the islanders' consent; and our awareness that Argentine impatience was mounting and that for many reasons – largely domestic – they might force the pace in the not too distant future. The safety valve must be negotiation; but there has to be some basis of negotiation, and Nick was empowered to discuss certain options as well as the general situation with the Falkland Islanders. It was alleged much later that we took little notice of the Falklands situation until it was on a disaster course, and that earlier attention might have averted trouble had we not been, or supposed ourselves to be, too busy with other things. That is nonsense. The first Ridley mission took place within weeks of Margaret Thatcher forming a Government and of my taking office.

Nick Ridley, a highly intelligent, able and imaginative man, did not have a reputation for being on the leftish or unduly pacific wing of the Conservative Party, and his observations on return were as robust as they were sensible. The consequence was that in September 1979 I minuted my colleagues with three possible alternatives in our attitude to the Falklands. These alternatives were self-evident. We could adopt an attitude of 'Fortress Falklands': 'We're not going to talk any more, we're going to stick it out forever, and we're going to be strong enough in the area to defy any attempt at coercion.' Or we could seek to negotiate further about practicalities, economic cooperation and so forth, while declining to consider any concessions whatsoever over sovereignty. Or we could decide to be prepared to negotiate over sovereignty, while still stipulating that the islanders' agreement to any change must be a paramount condition.

At this point I should give my personal view. I regarded 'Fortress Falklands' as an unreasonable object of policy. It might be thrust upon us by Argentine behaviour (it has been) and I always made entirely clear that if force – believed unlikely – were ever used by Argentina in furtherance of the dispute we would use force in return, however reluctantly. But the expense and logistic difficulties argued themselves, and in a defence budget which I understood with as much personal experience as anybody it was absurd to suppose that our main, NATO, priorities would not soon be adversely affected. I could not believe that successive British Governments would *ad infinitum* tolerate a Fortress Falklands policy. Nor would their electorates. We should act so as to avoid that policy becoming necessary, and we should certainly not choose it.

The option of seeking to negotiate while conceding nothing on sovereignty might be forced upon us – in effect it soon was forced upon us – by our commitment to respect the wishes of the Falklanders, as well as by British domestic political hostility to change. I regarded it as dangerous, nevertheless, and in a further minute in October 1979 I told my Cabinet colleagues that such a policy meant that we must live with a serious

354

threat of Argentine invasion of the islands, sooner or later. Argentina had the capacity to invade, and was unlikely forever to tolerate the *status quo*. This toleration could, I thought, be stretched provided we showed willingness to discuss the future as if change were at least possible. Our refusal to do so would mean living with a menace – or that the islanders would be living with a menace – which would not go away.

My own preference, unequivocally, was for the third option – preparation by the British Government to negotiate the issue of sovereignty and to find a way forward, however difficult. Of the possible constitutional devices already described, I believed some sort of leaseback arrangement might, just might, be negotiated with Argentina and become acceptable to the islanders. It had been mooted before, and by it Argentina would obtain formal sovereignty over the islands while simultaneously agreeing to lease them to Britain for a long period of time, perhaps a hundred years. There were those who said that this was to create a Hong Kong problem, to lay up trouble for our successors a century later: I doubted if the world would look the same a century later. Leaseback, to my mind, offered the best bet, if we were to be ready to discuss sovereignty at all; and if we weren't, we were forced back on the other alternatives, of which the second would lead to confrontation sooner rather than later, and the first would raise a bill which successive British Governments – and the British Treasury – would be highly unlikely to find tolerable for long. I thought leaseback the best solution if it could be negotiated. It was a very big 'if', but I have not changed my mind.

I found little support for leaseback among my colleagues. The general reaction was that this would, ultimately, mean selling the Falkland Islanders down the river. I thought this reaction took too little account of the adverse consequences of the alternatives, and I decided that my best course was to keep on trying, thinking, and, as I believed, educating. The case for leaseback might prove more persuasive over time; and meanwhile it would be important to keep some sort of negotiations going with Argentina – of a fairly meaningless kind, perhaps, but time, again, might adjust that.

Further talks with Argentina, proposed by me in January 1980, started in April; and by July I had been able to secure Cabinet agreement to Nick Ridley paying a second visit to the Falklands. He was, furthermore, empowered to discuss with the islanders a number of different options, by now familiar to my readers: these included the concept of a 'sovereignty freeze', and the idea of leaseback. My colleagues had agreed to these parameters. Leaseback was on the agenda.

The Falkland Islanders, predictably, wished for a 'sovereignty freeze'. The Falkland Legislative Council passed a resolution in the following January, 1981, in which it was agreed 'that Her Majesty's Government should hold further talks with the Argentine at which this House should be represented and at which the British delegation should seek agreement to freeze the dispute over sovereignty for a specified period of time'. This was unlikely to get us far. The Falklanders disliked all our options and in their reactions they made that very clear. I think the more far-sighted, however, recognized that Argentine hostility and economic stagnation were connected conditions which it was legitimate to seek to change. Meanwhile in December 1980 Nick reported to the House of Commons.

His reception was hostile. He was told that there was in the Falklands deeply felt suspicion of British politicians and of the Foreign Office. He was told that any leaseback proposals weakened our title in international law. He was told that the Foreign Office had wanted to get rid of the Falklands for years – a mischievous misrepresentation. He was told that there was a considerable British interest at stake, in terms of the future of the South Atlantic – an implausible exaggeration. He was asked, in effect, that we should break off negotiations with Argentina, 'to advise the Argentine Government that the matter is closed'. He was asked why the Foreign Office could not leave things alone.

A fortnight later the matter was raised as a debate on the Adjournment, in which any idea of leaseback was described as 'totally unacceptable' in view of the impossibility of relying on Argentina's undertakings. Nick again spoke up for commonsense, for the long-term interests of the islanders in a *modus vivendi* with the Argentines. He got little support. Hostility emanated on the one hand from the Labour left, which expressed outrage at suggesting concession of any title to a right-wing fascist dictator: and, on the other, from the Conservative right which regarded it as unthinkable that any British territory should ever be ceded to anyone, if British subjects lived on it, regardless of the guarantees given. The former were remarkably bigoted and the latter were narrow and nostalgic. Those of both parties who saw some sense – indeed inevitability in the long term – in what we were trying to do, sat on their hands and said little. It wasn't a promising atmosphere in which to take matters further and when I minuted my Cabinet colleagues in January describing the islanders' reactions as disappointing, I knew and they knew that we had been left with little room for manoeuvre. The Government's critics had conspired to make diplomacy near-impossible.

In these circumstances I could only hope that time and reflection would encourage better sense and meanwhile try to keep lines open to Argentina. Buenos Aires had rejected any idea of a 'sovereignty freeze' and there was clearly a danger that an impasse of this kind could and would lead in the end to outright confrontation. The Intelligence assessments took the same line as hitherto – indeed they had been unchanged in essentials over the years. There was little risk of outright military action against the Falklands provided Argentina supposed there was a chance that the British Government would ultimately be prepared to negotiate about sovereignty. It must be increasingly difficult for Argentina so to suppose, since we were faced with apparent immobilism among the islanders, an immobilism which could not fail to draw encouragement from the Government's critics at home; while the Government, faced with this, had always made it clear that we would do nothing without the islanders' consent. The outlook was stormy.

In the summer of 1981 Argentine impatience was visibly mounting and we had a certain sense of sands running out. I was criticized later for not at that stage making a further effort to persuade the islanders – and Parliament – towards a more flexible attitude; and for not launching a public and active campaign to educate opinion. Had I thought such an effort might succeed I would certainly have done so; but the political realities at the time were such that it would have proved counter-productive. The best hope, I thought, was to try gradually to persuade colleagues as events went forward and presented their own logic. In taking this line I drew some support from continuing Intelligence estimates that there would be a build-up of tensions, an escalating situation, before any outright military adventure were tried by Argentina. It seemed reasonable then, and I still believe it was reasonable, to suppose that we had a little time.

But to make use of that little time the dialogue with Argentina had to be kept going. In September 1981 I saw the Argentine Foreign Minister (subsequently replaced) in New York, explained our position in terms which I hoped were both conciliatory and firm and invited the Argentinians to put forward their own proposals. The ball was thus kept in the air. In September, too, Richard Luce succeeded Nick Ridley as the responsible minister – and was equally admirable. In December General Galtieri became President of Argentina.

General Galtieri, even more than his predecessors, needed some sort of diversion to unite a discontented and long-suffering Argentina – long-suffering from its own brutal misgovernment – and a more strident approach to the question of 'The Malvinas' was always likely to be popular. Agreement, or patience, in dealing with us would, from Galtieri's point of view, remove the need for such an approach. He had inadequate motive to come towards us, and we had offered him little incentive to do so. The odds against crisis had shortened.

Nobody was in much doubt about this, and while I still hoped we could persuade both the British Parliament and the Falklanders towards a more far-sighted position it was important not to encourage Argentina to suppose we had lost our resolution. Diplomacy, in these circumstances, has to be buttressed by deterrence which had, of course, been the position of successive British Governments. Deterrence has to make plain to an adversary that to carry the argument by force of arms won't work; but it has to be made plain in a way which doesn't simply constitute a challenge, make it a point of honour to maintain hostility. It was always recognized that Argentina must not be given the temptation of occupying the Falklands, or part of them, unopposed. On the other hand complete deterrence – the deployment of a force strong enough to defeat an attempt at invasion – had always been regarded as excessively expensive and disparate to the interests at stake. The Chiefs of Staff considered the matter in September 1981 and, once again, assessed the requirement of complete deterrence as a huge one. It would take time to assemble such a force: it would mean our other priority commitments would be neglected (a situation which couldn't be allowed to last long); and – a factor given weight in the Intelligence assessments – it might provoke the very adventure it would be intended to deter.

But there are degrees of deterrence. A balance has to be struck. Our answer, and our predecessors' answer, was to deploy a small force of Royal Marines on the islands, and to rely upon their presence as evidence to Argentina that any rash adventure automatically meant dealing with some of the forces, however small, of the British Crown and thus throwing down a challenge we would undoubtedly take up. There was also HMS *Endurance*, an icebreaking ship of the Royal Navy which was kept in those waters and acted as support. *Endurance* had no great war-fighting capacity, but she was there, and her presence served to underline the message. Deterrence at that modest level says, in effect, to a possible aggressor, 'Don't try anything on. If you do we shall hit back, and in such a way that any early success you might obtain will be totally overshadowed by your subsequent defeat.' That is a perfectly appropriate defence posture in certain circumstances; and one such circumstance is if confronting a possible adversary who lives many thousand miles nearer the disputed objective than oneself.

Deterrence, however, can fail. Obviously it can fail if the potential aggressor does not believe one has the resolution to do what is necessary. It can fail if one's military capacity is seen to be defective. And it can fail if the potential aggressor simply gambles, miscalculates both one's resolution and one's physical ability; and gets it wrong. Our policy in the Falklands was based on deterrence. To 'militarize' the islands, in the form of a large enough garrison of troops and aircraft to defeat invasion, accompanied by a major maritime presence in the South Atlantic, would have been disproportionate to the object – unless we had been gifted with such prescience that we could assemble and move such forces exactly at the time and by the time they were required. In which case it may be presumed they would have succeeded in the object of deterring and returned home. And what then? And might they not, as the Ministry of Defence at the time contended, actually stimulate and advance the timing of hostile action?

There was, at that time, a Defence Review, one of the myriad through which I have lived: one recommendation was a reduction in expenditure on the Royal Navy; and one consequence of that would be the withdrawal of *Endurance* from the South Atlantic. This worried me; and I wrote on several occasions to the Defence Secretary, John Nott, to ask that the Ministry of Defence should reconsider this decision. I said it might send the wrong signal to Buenos Aires, where the Argentine newspapers had fastened on it as evidence that Britain's commitment to the Falklands might be weakening. The question was raised in Parliament, where my concern was supported by a large number of voices. But economic considerations were allowed to prevail. I doubt whether words of mine, at that juncture, could have been more effective than they were, however often I had written or argued. In the context of the time it seemed, on balance, defensible.

In the event, *Endurance* was not in fact redeployed – the landing on South Georgia saw to that. But it was known that the British Government intended that she should be, and it was the intention which mattered. How much it mattered remains debatable: on reflection, I doubt whether this proved a decisive point.

One element in deterrence is military presence. Another can be the power of rapid reinforcement. I have already referred to the Shackleton recommendation that the Falklands airfield runway be lengthened – a long and expensive proceeding which the Government of the day declined. It was said by some afterwards that such a construction might have tipped the scales of deterrence. That may be so. I don't know what the effect would have been. I certainly know, however, that during the earlier years the beginning of such a construction would have scuppered attempts at negotiation then in progress – which does not necessarily prove the idea wrong, but at least makes comprehensible the British Government (of Harold Wilson) decision not to build it. In default of such an airfield we had either to maintain indefinitely a large and wildly expensive military presence and a sizeable fleet eight thousand miles away; or seek to deter, by a token presence and by the clarity of our language.

Deterrence is very dependent on information. If one rests one's policy on being able to react to actual aggression with a vigorous and painful counter-stroke, one needs to have sufficiently early warning, not necessarily to reinforce and defend (which may by definition be impracticable) but at least to mobilize opinion, prepare that counter-stroke and make utterly clear that one is not bluffing. That takes time, and makes warning crucial. Given sufficient warning one may still be able to take steps which, while perhaps not able to pre-empt an initial assault by one's adversary, will at least show one means business. And the more warning one has, the more competently one can handle the essential political and diplomatic steps to gain maximum popular and international support. Warning matters. Our advice was that if there were a decision for invasion we might get very little actual warning of the decision and the hour; but that there would be preliminary indicators, in the sense of a deteriorating situation over a period. With this we had to be content. As a defence policy for the Falklands we had always chosen deterrence. Deterrence was the only sane policy. But, as I have said, deterrence can fail: and if it fails one is faced with the options of surrender or war. In the Falklands it failed. We had war.

Throughout the first months of 1982 we had continuing Intelligence reports that an Argentine attempt to invade the Falklands was unlikely in the near future, despite the cold diplomatic climate, the sense that there was a volatile situation in Argentina and hints (clearly inspired) in the Argentine newspapers that if negotiations 'failed' a military solution might be inevitable. We had throughout the previous years had a good deal of this sort of thing and there was no particular reason to suppose the situation might not still be contained or defused. A good deal has since been made of the fact that Argentine planning for invasion had started immediately Galtieri assumed power. That is totally unsurprising. Argentine claims would have found outlet in Argentine contingency plans throughout the period and Galtieri's advent to power no doubt gave them a fillip. We never doubted Argentine capability: what we had to decide was whether or when Buenos Aires would decide to turn a plan into an operation of war – and what to do about it beforehand.

When the whole business was over, the British Government commissioned a report presided over by Lord Franks on exactly what had happened, on who knew what when, and on whether they might have done something more or different about it. The Franks Report was published, it set out all the events, developments and reactions in exact detail and I don't intend to recapitulate. We knew the situation was dangerous but our Intelligence reports gave no indication of any basic change. Lord Buxton, who knew South America well, paid a private visit in February, saw a number of influential people in Argentina and came away impressed that invasion itself was unlikely. Our Embassy in Buenos Aires, although naturally wishing that some basis for negotiation could be found, was far from alarmist. Nevertheless I minuted the Prime Minister, also in February, that the Argentinians were getting tougher. We should keep a dialogue going, without prejudice to our position on sovereignty, but we were in for a difficult and hazardous time. I have seen it alleged that I never, before the subsequent invasion, told my Cabinet colleagues that the situation was dangerous, with no 'give' on sovereignty by ourselves – or by Argentina. The allegation is nonsense.

The islanders, meanwhile, who regarded leaseback as effectively 'dead', were united in favour of a 'Fortress Falklands' policy: while it was clear that any move in that direction would mean the end of any possibility of talking to Argentina. We held some conversations with the latter in New York at the end of February. They went not too badly – perhaps better than one had any right to expect. And, judging from Argentine reactions, better than the hawks of Buenos Aires would have wished – but there was precedent to suggest that one needn't take too alarmist a view of that. The ball still seemed to be in the air.

I have, naturally, asked myself often whether – given that we had now no room for diplomatic manoeuvre at all – we might have averted disaster at that time by sending to the area a substantial maritime contingent. To succeed in deterring, it would have needed to be substantial and overt, and although we later deployed a submarine followed by a second to the South Atlantic I am sceptical of subsequent Argentine comment that a submarine known earlier to be on station would have put them off. It would have had to be a sizeable force, and I doubt if such a decision could have been sensibly made at that time. With hindsight, of course, it appears the merest prudence, but we didn't know for certain there was going to be an invasion, we reckoned that such a deployment might actually precipitate matters, and we also knew that even if it successfully deterred (a thing impossible of proof), it couldn't be maintained indefinitely. I do not believe it would have been a rational decision. Had the deployment been ordered after a certain date, of course, it couldn't have made the smallest difference.

At the same time I worked to enlist further United States

support. The United States Assistant Secretary of State concerned with Latin America, Thomas Enders, was due to visit Buenos Aires and I asked Al Haig for his good offices; and this was promised. I remain unsure how much Mr Enders managed to do, but in mid-March he reported that the Argentinians had not discussed the Malvinas situation with him in terms of threats, and he had not received the impression they intended to do anything drastic. We received the same impression from our Embassy in Buenos Aires, whence the telegrams referred always to the necessity and possibility of a 'civilized solution'. Meanwhile in Parliament we took every opportunity to make plain that we had no doubts about our sovereignty, that we had no doubts about our duties to the islanders, and that we would discharge them.

In the middle of March 1982 we had the affair of the scrap-merchants. A Buenos Aires scrap-metal merchant named Davidoff had obtained a contract to salvage equipment from disused whaling stations in South Georgia (a generally uninhabited and distant appendage of the Falklands, and under the same colonial administration). After a preliminary visit in December 1981 aboard an Argentinian Navy icebreaker – a visit which had raised the temperature in Port Stanley since the ship had not obtained clearance to enter South Georgian waters, although Sr Davidoff had written his intentions to our Buenos Aires Embassy – a party sent by Davidoff returned and landed on South Georgia on 19 March. Again, Davidoff had notified our Embassy of his intentions, but the party – thought to contain military personnel – was suspected, not least by the Governor of the Falklands, Sir Rex Hunt, of being a cover for a deliberate Argentine adventure. No proper immigration clearance had been obtained, nor contact made with the commander of our Antarctic Survey Base on South Georgia. The Argentine flag was reported to have been run up. It looked like a try-on.

We made it clear to Argentina that these men must be taken off, and we directed *Endurance* towards South Georgia to take them off if they hadn't already gone. We were, I recall, considered by the Embassy in Buenos Aires to be acting excessively. We were warned against 'spectacular reaction to a piece of trivial misbehaviour which could do lasting damage to the whole structure of our fruitful bilateral relations'! Be that as it may, we told Parliament that we had no intention of tolerating this development; and later agreed that an Argentine ship could, if it chose to arrive in time, take over the illegal immigrants from ourselves. Nevertheless the incident, trivial and even absurd though it might appear, was a bad augury. The Argentine Navy was known to be the most 'hawkish' element in the country, and its commander's voice in the military junta was strong; and South Georgia looked like an Argentine Navy gambit. On 24 March I had to minute my Cabinet colleagues that negotiations with Argentina might be at an end, and that we could not exclude the ultimate possibility of military action. Certain Argentine ships were at sea and it seemed possible that they would actually seek to intercept *Endurance*.

Another corollary of the worsening situation was that we might find the Falklands cut off, isolated by Argentine action or non-cooperation; and this, as well as a diplomatic offensive against us in the United Nations and elsewhere, was always regarded as a probable first hostile step – and far more probable than any instant military initiative. To deal with these non-military measures if they came demanded contingency planning and, in the event, money. This needed endorsement by the Treasury and I recall a dusty response from the Chief Secretary, Leon Brittan. There was no objection to planning, but there could be no money from the Treasury Contingency Fund! That was on 29 March.

The previous day, I had again addressed Al Haig. I said I thought things were going from bad to very bad. I hoped the United States would counsel caution on Argentina. The influence of America, after all, was likely to be a major factor – perhaps the only applicable factor left – in restraining Galtieri from folly if Washington chose to exert it. On the same day I flew to Brussels with Margaret Thatcher for a meeting and we were able to discuss the latest Falklands situation en route. Argentina's reaction to the whole South Georgia incident – or, rather, to our own reaction to it – was so hostile that it was hard to believe the situation wouldn't worsen, although at what pace it was impossible to say: there were no serious indications of military action being imminent. I had intended to fly direct from Brussels to Israel which I had a longstanding arrangement to visit, but in view of the Falklands situation I returned next day, 30 March, to London and made a statement to the Lords about the Falklands, South Georgia and the general position. We had already sent one nuclear-powered submarine and that day agreed to send a second, in order to help counter any aggressive Argentine naval moves, still assumed not to be imminent. I wanted to send a third, but the decision was deferred.

I also received a return message from Al Haig relayed by Edward Streator at the American Embassy in London. The Americans, it said, were concerned about the dispute between two nations who were both friends. Restraint all round was urged. The United States would not take sides.

I reacted sharply to this, and told Streator that we had supported American policy in Sinai, had supported it in El Salvador: that this support had not been particularly willing, nor wholly consistent with our own better judgement, but we had given it; and now we expected a better response than this not very friendly message, equating our case and position with that of Argentina. I'm glad to say that I had, on 1 April, a much more helpful letter from Al Haig.

I considered sending the responsible Under-Secretary in the Foreign Office as a personal emissary to Buenos Aires; I felt that, somehow, communication must be reopened. The Ambassador, Mr Williams, resisted this, pointing out that the arrival of an official – as it happened, junior to himself – would imply that he was being disowned. His instructions, he said, had been pretty tough and he had carried them out loyally. He was concerned that it would undercut him and his credibility if we dealt through anyone else. I did not overrule him.

366

Our advice that day – 30 March – was that some sort of Argentine military initiative might be expected some time during April. There was considerable Argentine naval deployment (ostensibly, maritime exercises were pending). In addition to the two nuclear-powered submarines of our own ordered to the area, we considered the deployment of some seven surface ships, currently near Gibraltar, but decided against. Their timeliness was impossible to assess and their efficacy in a major confrontation had to be set against the possibility of their provoking a pre-emptive implementation of the action they were intended to deter. If Argentina were contemplating an adventure a credible deterrent force would anyway have to be larger. There was still no positive indication that Argentina intended major military action – at least in the near future. And the following day (by which time I was out of the country) the Joint Intelligence Committee assessed that the South Georgia incident had not formed part of any deliberate Argentine plan. It was, the assessment ran, unlikely that Argentina would choose any 'extreme option' in the immediate future.

This last assessment was modified, however, later that day (31 March) by a report that 2 April had been fixed as the 'day of action' by Argentina – the first indication of serious and imminent danger we received. By then, on 30 March, I had flown with Iona to Israel. That I would not have done so had I believed that British territory was about to be invaded, or had Intelligence assessments pointed to that beyond doubt, is self-evident – although, of course, I remained in touch at all times and able to return in five hours.

I have already said that I was particularly anxious not to miss any chance to go to Israel, where my reputation and consequently that of the Government was one of hostility to them, a reputation which, while it lasted, meant we could do little good. There was, too, a great deal of talk at that time of Europe and America seriously falling out over the Middle East, and cancellation of my journey would, I thought, serve only to confirm such allegations. The Middle East always appeared to me as the most dangerous arena in the world and diplomacy there the most urgently required, whatever the discouragements.

I believe the visit was not unsuccessful: I believe that, despite my arriving with the reputation of having two horns and a forked tail, they ended by seeing that Britain was genuinely seeking to help a settlement along, and not trying to undermine Israel. I saw not only Begin but Shamir, Peres, Rabin and Sharon – with whom I had a long time and who is a man of presence, style, energy and determination. It's unlikely they agreed with all I said, but I think my visit did something to repair our relations.

There was, however, no time to consolidate any impression made. On the Wednesday evening – 31 March – I was asked to return to London. I have been criticized – very naturally – for making the journey at all, and of course with hindsight I wish I hadn't.

On Thursday 1 April I was back at my desk. Certain British forces had now been put at notice. On Friday 2 April Argentina invaded the Falkland Islands. On Monday 5 April I surrendered to the Queen at Windsor my seals of office as Foreign and Commonwealth Secretary.

It was a difficult as well as a painful decision and it was entirely my own. There was a good deal of pressure on me to remain at my post. I was grateful for the confidence and kindness this implied but I could not agree that it would be right. It was a great additional sadness to me that Humphrey Atkins, Lord Privy Seal and my number two in the Foreign Office, as well as Richard Luce, decided they should go as well.

As to the responsibility for the invasion itself, in the sense of having left undone something we should have done which would have pre-empted it, I could not with honesty and soul-searching feel much. To have prepared and sailed the sort of military force which could physically have prevented invasion, which could have defeated the attempt, was not a decision it was at any time rational for the Government to have taken before the event on the information they possessed. Had it, by some extraordinary stroke of intuition, been taken – say in late February – it might well have prevented an invasion in April, but we would never have known that there was to have been such an invasion: there was no conceivable argument by which such a force could be kept in the South Atlantic indefinitely: the Argentines would certainly have refused to negotiate 'under the threat of force'; and the subsequent withdrawal of the force would have exposed us to precisely the charge of 'sending the wrong signals' to Argentina, that must be the principal case to answer in the circumstances that actually occurred.

On the question of wrong signals, I will add only this. The right signals, for us and for previous British Governments, were to my mind to combine a clear readiness to negotiate with an equally clear determination to defend the islands if need arose. We could perhaps have done better on both counts in the areas I have touched upon; but I think that the fundamental difference between us and previous British Governments of either party was not in the signals we were sending, but in the fact that we were faced with a Government in Buenos Aires determined on action whatever the realities of the situation.

As to whether we might – or British Intelligence might – have discerned earlier the actual intention to invade, I doubt it. Plans, even detailed plans, are one thing: firm decisions quite another. It was rumoured afterwards that American satellite Intelligence had disclosed everything, and been rejected by us – rumours without a breath of truth. Lord Franks and his colleagues opined that from mid-March we were inadequately sensitive to a change and hardening in Argentinian attitudes. I believe that we were fully aware of this change, and appropriately disturbed by it: it was the background to my appeals to Al Haig. Nevertheless it doesn't appear that the junta's final decision to invade was taken until very shortly before the event, and there was force, however mistaken with hindsight, in the argument that overreaction could precipitate a crisis while calm might defuse it.

Stories which were later given currency that we in the Foreign Office ignored warnings from our Embassy in Buenos Aires were totally without foundation. The basic criticism levelled at us was, of course, miscalculation – we miscalculated that the Argentinians would invade. Certainly we did: we miscalculated Argentine folly. And history will record that the fundamental miscalculation was General Galtieri's.

It was not a sense of culpability that led me to resign – a subjective judgement, of course, but one which was later to find confirmation in the Franks Report. The logic of my resignation was different, and I had two principal reasons, one general and one more particular.

The general reason was my sympathetic understanding that the whole of our country felt angry and humiliated. I felt the same myself. British territory had, without warning, been invaded. There were hysterical outbursts in Parliament and yells of 'betrayal', and although these were inaccurate and offensive they were understandable. Inhabitants of a British colony – men and women of British blood – had been taken over against their will. Diplomacy had failed to avert this. Military reinforcement had not been tried. Deterrence had been exposed as a bluff. Our hand had apparently been called. There was never the slightest doubt that, with Margaret Thatcher at the head of the Government, we wouldn't take this lying down, and we didn't. But the first shock and fury were felt throughout Britain, and in those circumstances – with people very naturally turning on the Government and accusing it of mismanagement – it is right, in my judgement, that there must be a resignation. The nation feels that there has been a disgrace. Someone must have been to blame. The disgrace must be purged. The person to purge it should be the minister in charge. That was me. I was also very aware that my membership of the Lords was at that moment an embarrassment to the Prime Minister, and a weakness. In the Commons Humphrey Atkins was first-class, as was Richard Luce, but when there's a real political crisis it is in the House of Commons that the life and death of Government is decided and I bitterly regretted that I could not face that House at Margaret Thatcher's side.

The more particular reason was my awareness that the Government was in for a hard time and that my presence would make it not easier but harder. We were now assembling a task force and sailing it to the South Atlantic – an action with which I wholeheartedly agreed. During the time it would take – a matter of weeks not days – it was going to be difficult to keep Parliament and country sufficiently united behind our actions, and unity is essential in war. My departure would put a stop to the search for scapegoats. It would serve the cause of unity and help turn the eyes of all from the past to the immediate future. With John Nott, I had attended a fairly disagreeable meeting of the 1922 Committee and although nobody shouted for my resignation I knew that within the Conservative Party itself my remaining in office was not going to help the Prime Minister with her own supporters.

The rest of the Falklands story has nothing to do with my own. I'm glad to say that I was mistaken in thinking, as I did for a little when the Task Force was at sea, that we might be isolated in the international community if it came to a fight, as now seemed certain: that aspect went pretty well – and we won the fight; militarily and – at the time – politically. But the problem of the Falklands has not reached its ultimate, and will not do so until the day – difficult now to discern – when Britain, Argentina and the Falkland Islanders themselves can all agree on an honourable, sensible and peaceful way ahead.

My resignation was an occasion of very great sadness to me and to Iona. I loved the Foreign Office. I admired the men and women of the Foreign Office and felt it a privilege to work with them – they were outstanding, and in my experience their quality exceeds that of any other Department – and any other Foreign Office. They are periodically objects of suspicion to their more belligerent fellow-countrymen, who too easily forget that the aim of diplomacy is to make friends, advance peace and commerce, and influence people; and that is the way to promote British interests. I enjoyed my work hugely and the day I left that enormous and inconvenient building abutting on Horse Guards Parade was probably the most sorrowful I had known. Any politician, however, learns to be

371

philosophical in some degree, and to accept reverses as well as occasional blessings from the run of events. Bitterness of any kind is wholly inappropriate and I never felt it. The anger of the British people and Parliament at the Argentine invasion of the Falklands was a righteous anger, and it was my duty and fate to do something to assuage it; the rest was done by brave sailors, soldiers and airmen, too many of whom laid down not office but their lives.

CHAPTER 17

The Alliance

Politicians are often asked why they do it, what impels them. Answers can range between the highfalutin' and the incredible. Honest answers must include the element of enjoyment: basically, in spite of the exasperations, the alternations of overwork and disappointment, the often frenetic lifestyle and the not infrequent abuse – basically, despite all this, politics is fun. I will have failed as an author if I have not conveyed at least here and there in this book that much of my political life has been highly satisfying.

I have never disguised that it is office that has satisfied rather than the game of Parliament or party. It is office which gives the chance to do things, to steer things perhaps very slightly, almost certainly very gradually, and, sadly, often most impermanently, towards what a person believes right. But politicians are often asked, too, not only why they live the life they do but what it actually is that they believe right, what they want for the country? They are invited to generalize. And because politics is inevitably concerned so much with immediate issues – in politics the tactical, in military terms, tends to overshadow the strategic – politicians are apt to flounder somewhat when pressed beyond the sort of platitudes we can all trot out if occasion demands.

I can certainly flounder. I am not all that keen on ideology – and one is talking about ideology, belief, fundamental attitude. I am a pragmatist. I have found all my life that the gulf between what is theoretically desirable and what is practically attainable is so wide that it is sensible to concentrate almost exclusively upon the latter. Certain courses of action can, of course, be wrong in principle: one rejects them. Others are right in principle: one considers them. Choices are, however, generally confined to few alternatives, and they are normally fewer than most observers pretend.

But there are choices, and to make them one has to have some guiding principles beyond pure expediency. My own guiding principles as far as the domestic condition of our country is concerned can be stated simply, and no doubt emerge very obviously from these pages. I believe in the maximum amount of individual choice, enterprise and personal liberty which can be contained within the limits of an ordered society. I regard liberal capitalism as efficient and benevolent in its effects. It beats all other systems at creating wealth, and distributes it widely, although here and there the undeserving (and how does one infallibly describe them?) may take, for a while, more of the cream from the milk than they should. It produces incentives to compete and excel. I regard its opposite – state socialism – as pernicious in an exactly opposite sense. It is inefficient. It promotes shrinkage rather than growth. Obsessed with equity of distribution, it neglects to encourage – and then, futilely, seeks to direct or bribe – enterprise. It expands bureaucracy.

Nevertheless the role of Government is not only necessary but can be honourable, and in the pursuit of liberal capitalism and the personal liberty with which we associate it, we should not neglect or denigrate the power of the state – and its generally very honourable servants. The state has an absolute obligation to help those who suffer through circumstances genuinely beyond their control. The state should not cushion from life the feckless and the idle but it should recognize how powerless many individuals are in the modern world in the face of enormous – and international – economic forces. The ex-unemployed Guardsmen I once commanded were not feckless. They were not idle. They despised layabouts and what we called skivers. They wanted a decent and dignified living, a fair day's wage for a fair day's work. They respected skill and were keen and quick to acquire it, given the chance. In the then prevailing conditions, only the state could have helped them, and hadn't. Only the state could have created or helped to create economic circumstances which would have been favourable to the recovery they needed. I profoundly believe in circumscribing the power of the state; it does some things supremely badly – like trying to run industry or make sensible commercial judgements; but I also profoundly believe that the power of the state is nevertheless needed, and always will be needed, to create favourable conditions for necessary developments which private enterprise will be loath to do and can't be expected to do. Some things and some changes are so fundamental, perhaps so capital-intensive – and these days so inevitably European in their implications – that only the state can lead. Business can follow. Banks can follow. But for leadership there has to be political as well as economic vision transcending commerce, and it is the leaders of the state who must possess that vision.

This is a beneficent, an honourable and in my view inescapable role of the state and conditions my attitude towards it. I regard it as a traditionally Tory attitude. It may be stigmatized as paternal, but why not? We are, or should be, a family. I don't find paternal an offensive word.

As to the external relations of the state, it must again be very clear from this book that I believe in a strong defence policy. Again and again I have found that weakness in defence leads to flabbiness of will and non-existence of influence. At its ultimate, of course, it leads to war, because a potential aggressor may suppose that the will to resist has disappeared and that he can take risks, win the fruits of war without the risks of war. He may miscalculate in that supposition – in the case of the Falklands he did miscalculate, although I don't think we led him into doing so; it was, put simply, that Galtieri, like Hitler, got the British all wrong. But certainly an ostentatiously weak attitude to defence will mean trouble sooner or later: while a strong defence policy will mean peace, relative influence and self-respect.

But strength isn't everything and I also believe deeply in the necessity to see the point of view of others, and to try to see how others look at Britain. This is sometimes rather disturbing but is an essential exercise. One must make very clear that one is – or one's country is – a force to be reckoned with, to be treated with dignity, not to be pushed around, hectored and ignored: but one must also understand – without necessarily sympathizing in the least with – the perceptions of others, their particular traditions, experiences, fears and prejudices. We all have them, and to look at ourselves from outside can help that necessary and sometimes humbling discovery – what our significance as a nation really is and really is not. For arrogance and insensitivity come too easily to a people which holds an inflated view of its own rights and importance. Proper pride is entirely desirable; but I believe that any state – particularly Britain, with its extraordinary transition from offshore archipelago to maritime and commercial empire and back again all within three centuries – needs to possess a very clear vision of its relative size, its powers and limitations, its place in the world and the combinations which can maximize rather than minimize its security, prosperity and effect. In the case of Britain this means, by my conviction, membership of a European Community, so that we can play an essential and with luck influential part on our Continent; and it also means a transatlantic Alliance designed to ensure that never again will the New World be indifferent or stand detached from the fate of the Old.

I thus am an opponent, and a vigorous opponent, of those who cherish a nostalgic and absurdly grandiose image of Britain's modern destiny. I am an opponent of those who resent or reject our place as a European nation – a great European nation. I detest insularity. And I am equally an opponent of the unfeeling, the inwardly callous however smooth-spoken, the hard-hearted people in politics, the cynics. I have been in politics because I have enjoyed it, have loved my country and wanted to contribute to governing it. The simple ideas I have spent much of the time trying to promote are those of the fortunate sharing responsibility for those less so; and of our nation, vigorous to defend itself if attacked, seeking harmony and genuine understanding with others in a world where Britain – a good-natured, good-tempered and good-mannered Britain – has a limited but still significant and honourable role to play.

It was with satisfaction that in June 1984 I became Secretary-General of NATO. The two years after my resignation from the British Cabinet had been spent, like previous periods in Opposition, amid a certain amount of commercial activity: among other things I was for a short while Chairman of GEC at the invitation of that most enjoyable and remarkable man, Arnold Weinstock. But this time I was not, of course, in Opposition. As far as politics went I was in limbo, and I won't pretend I didn't miss it, or a good deal of it. I joined a company started by Henry Kissinger to provide advice on international affairs and trends for large-scale commercial undertakings who felt the need of it, but nothing compares with actual responsibility, and the invitation in 1984 to serve the Alliance to which I'd devoted a good deal of time and thought and in which I strongly believed was, in the main, welcome. 'In the main' because it meant a good deal of upheaval in life; and it was a new departure to become an 'international person' – a transformation I had witnessed in others but was now to experience myself. I decided that it would not be proper to play any part in the British Parliament while serving NATO.

NATO's headquarters is in Brussels – or, rather, in the outskirts of Brussels at Évère, near the airport. A large building, purpose-built for both political and military staffs, was run up in an astonishingly short time by the Belgians, when NATO was given its marching orders from France by de Gaulle: the organization's headquarters had previously been in Paris, just as the Supreme Commander's headquarters, now at Mons in Belgium, had originally been at Versailles. The Belgians had responded to the situation of a homeless Alliance with speed, hospitality and warmth, and the hospitality and warmth were given additional emphasis by the fact that the headquarters of the European Community was already based at the Berlaymont building in the heart of Brussels itself. The Belgians, as hosts, have been remarkably long-suffering. I am told there are about 40,000 diplomats in Brussels, and a country like ours has to maintain an Ambassador to NATO, an Ambassador to the EEC and, of course, an Ambassador to Belgium, each with an appropriate staff. To this host of foreigners the Belgians are patient, agreeable and understanding and we all owe them a great deal more than we always recall.

And Brussels was a most pleasant place in which to make a new home. It was a very different Brussels from that I boasted having helped to liberate forty years before. There were huge underpasses, there had been demolition of pleasant old buildings, erection of new – and by no means always sightly, *comme partout* – blocks, and a somewhat feverish atmosphere in place of the earlier calm of a small but historic European capital, or the chill of occupation which I had witnessed overtaken by the thrill of liberty. Yet Brussels has a grace and charm to which its guests soon succumb, if they have any sense. NATO is lucky.

We took over the house of my predecessor, Joseph Luns, and then moved after some months to another, which suited us better. It was at the top of the Avenue Louise, that long, elegant way running from the Avenue de la Toison d'Or (which marks the city wall line of ancient Brussels) up to the Bois de la Cambre – itself bordering the Forêt de Soignes with its superb beeches, giving Brussels a lung of many, many square miles at the edge of the city itself, and enabling it to breathe the air of open country in a way which I think is unique among capitals. We spent frequent weekends flying to and from England and Bledlow. Life and commitments at home continued – not least the Victoria and Albert Museum whose Chairman I had become. And, inevitably, my job at NATO itself meant almost as much travel as when I'd been Foreign Secretary. But Brussels was our base, and we enjoyed it.

I had, of course, had a lot to do with NATO in my various Defence posts and as Foreign Secretary. I had always firmly supported it – the Alliance, spanning the Atlantic and committing America to the defence of Europe, is the keystone of our own security. I had attended countless NATO meetings. I had, however, never had much to do with its mechanics. Nobody understands much about the organization until having to deal with it internally.

The Secretary-General presides over the two top political committees – the Council and the Defence Planning Committee. The Council consists of the Foreign Ministers of the Allied countries and the Defence Planning Committee comprises their Defence Ministers. These – the ministers – meet personally about twice a year at what are known at Évère as 'the Ministerials'; but for most of the time these committees meet in the form of the Permanent Representatives – the Ambassadors: who are acting, of course, on the instructions of their Governments, Foreign Ministries probably leading in the case of the Council, Defence Ministries in the case of the DPC. It might be thought that the same body of men meeting under the same Chairman as two different committees could periodically simplify their proceedings by considering only one agenda. This, however, would be to overlook the position of France.

There are certain popular misapprehensions about the position of France. When de Gaulle withdrew French forces from the Integrated Military Command structure of NATO – the forces which, assigned by the various member nations, would operate in war or crisis under the several NATO military commanders – he emphatically did not withdraw France from the Alliance. The French position has always been that France is very much a member of the Alliance, would certainly play her part in accordance with the obligations of the Alliance. France, therefore, has her seat at the NATO Council. What de Gaulle did was to announce – for reasons which successive French Governments have continued to find sufficient – that French forces would not be assigned to a non-national command. I shall not discuss the logic of this, in French eyes, beyond making one point which may have more cogency than non-Frenchmen always comprehend. De Gaulle believed that if the French are told their security is the concern of another, rather than their own undiluted responsibility, they will tend to do nothing. If they are told that it is up to them and that they can rely on nobody else they will bestir themselves, hackles up, pride aroused. Who am I to dissent? And certainly France achieved a consensus about defence right across the political spectrum, which remains an object of legitimate envy to many of us from other countries. The upshot was the decision that French forces would act on French and only French orders, that NATO integrated institutions should depart from French soil; and thus France left the DPC. But she did not quit the Alliance, nor give up her seat at the Council.

The Secretary-General takes the Chair. He sometimes keeps the peace. Where Allies fall out – and the histories and fiercely differing viewpoints of Greece and Turkey meant that Allies sometimes did fall out, sometimes dangerously – he has to do his best to use the corporate effect of the Alliance to defuse the situation. He often has to utter NATO's view to media, to visitors, or to non-Allied nations. He – or rather NATO – is served by an International Staff, to which the nations send, as a rule, excellent men and women of considerable ability; just as the Permanent Representatives are generally people of experience and authority, so that the level of discussion and debate tends to be high. But the Secretary-General has no executive power. He cannot take initiatives, or give instructions to anybody actually to do anything, unless it be to a member of his personal staff to produce a paper. He can only act as the servant of an institution which operates by consensus. Everyone has to agree.

It could not be otherwise. NATO could not function for a day if its senior committees worked by, say, rule of majority; so that some nation could be outvoted and then be expected to conform. It wouldn't conform! NATO has to run by consent, and for it to move in any direction sixteen people, acting on independent national instructions, have to agree. To get sixteen people of different nationalities, backgrounds, and (as they often reckon) interests to agree needs a lot of persuasion. And it takes a lot of time. Having come from a number of jobs where it was possible to decide, to order, to act, I experienced undeniable moments of frustration. But, of course, the organization works – and could only work – because its members believe in it and want it to work. NATO's fundamental objects – the security of Europe and the Atlantic area against a potential threat which all perceive – are not matters of contention. There were in my time, and there will continue to be, disagreements about the right action to take, the right responses to some Soviet initiative, the right balance of power within the Alliance, between Europe and America in particular. There were painful differences between certain member countries, differences which could destroy unanimity and make progress difficult. But there is, overall, goodwill in NATO, without which it would founder.

In small things as well as large the necessity for consensus produces problems. An important post on the International Staff may become vacant. It demands to be filled by a candidate of quality. It also demands to be filled by a candidate who is not from countries A or B, who filled the last four such posts – and who now present by far the best qualified two candidates. NATO staffing as well as NATO policy can absorb a good deal of time, and on every occasion when such a job is on offer each NATO Ambassador visits the Secretary-General to explain that his country is underrepresented on the International Staff, and that he has the pleasure of now proposing an outstanding, no doubt the only outstanding, name. Language matters too. NATO has two official languages – French and English – and although Northern Europeans tend to find French not too difficult, English often comes harder to the Mediterranean members, and it is important to see that they are not unjustly penalized thereby.

From the first I was determined to have a multinational Private Office with a British nucleus. But the Deputy Secretary-General was a senior Italian diplomat and I made him very much part of the inner circle. The Assistant Director of the Private Office had traditionally been American: that was just what I wanted – a young and brilliant public servant was sent from the State Department. We also added another Assistant Director post, filled for most of my time by an excellent Dane. We thus had a fair mixture, and regular meetings with senior members of the International Staff –

381

including an academic 'Sovietologist in Residence' whom I brought in as something of a free wheel inside the bureaucratic machine – broadened it still further.

So we didn't only think and behave as Englishmen. I remembered that when Pug Ismay was sent out as the first Secretary-General of NATO, Churchill addressed him: 'I realize you're now about to be an international man! You have to be impartial between countries! I realize that – but there's NO reason why you should be opposed to British policy!'

No particular reason, certainly; unless it were to be wrong! But there were always two temptations. One was to take the British side too easily, too naturally – especially since I was particularly familiar with the argumentation. To avoid that was not difficult, because of the obvious impropriety of failing to do so. The opposite temptation was to be overcritical of my own country. In the effort to be objective one had to think oneself into other positions carefully and sincerely. Some of those positions might be antagonistic to the British view; and it was possible to end by wondering at the insensitivity and lack of comprehension of the British Government. That, too, could be overdone – and during my time at NATO the British really behaved rather well!

The problem of NATO is the problem of success. We have had peace in Europe for over forty years, and if we consider the implacable ideological hostility of the Soviet Union to Western values, as well as Soviet (and Russian) historic readiness to use force in furtherance of policy, that is not something to take easily for granted. One of my generation remembers the weakness and devastation of a demoralized Europe after the Second World War in a way which is mercifully remote from the experience of our juniors. We recall what seemed direct challenges – over Berlin, in Korea – which summoned us to surrender or resist. And we reflect with gratitude that, led by the United States, the European nations combined to resist. It is probably simplistic to say, 'NATO has preserved peace'; that makes a lot of assumptions about Soviet intentions at particular times which are equally difficult to prove or to deny. But what I find demonstrably true is that NATO, by its combined efforts, has produced a certain balance, a certain Western strength and confidence, which cannot have failed to inhibit any temptation to adventurist Soviet policies at least in a westerly direction. I think it was Palmerston who said that Russian expansionism is like water running downhill. Checked, it may find another way; but it can be checked. To check it requires adequate strength and evident will. NATO provided both, and continues to do so. It will be a long haul – the Russians think historically, and they take a long view.

It is this long view, as well as the very success which NATO has achieved, which makes life difficult for Western Governments. Time has brought new generations to the stage. History which to me seems recent is to them remote. The idea of unrelenting (and expensive) confrontation often appears to them a poor way of ensuring peace. To the Soviet Union this confrontation is a natural, historical condition, preached by Lenin, with his doctrine of irreconcilable hostility between systems – theirs and ours. To the historically minded Russian, too, it may not be particularly bizarre: Russia has long felt remote, underpopulated, congenitally suspicious of strangers, threatened at some or many points of her immensely long and vulnerable land frontiers, simultaneously chosen by Providence to fill a messianic role and challenged by hostile unbelievers. To the patriotic Russian, as to the communist ideologue, a centuries-long condition of hostility and military confrontation is not offensive. It is even natural. But to the inhabitants of prosperous Western democracies the need for NATO and its paraphernalia, the cost of military budgets, the language of threat and response, can all seem both inappropriate and distasteful. Periodically there is a crisis, awareness sharpens, a gust of fear blows through Western societies, NATO is popular. More often – and mercifully – life seems pretty calm. Commonsense probably persuades majorities most of the time of the underlying rationale of deterrence, of the truth that it is the weak not the strong who tempt an aggressor; but substantial minorities protest that arms themselves create the possibility and thus the risk of war. They resent the cost and they query the need.

The consequent 'peace movements' have, of course, largely based their protest on the existence of nuclear weapons, and the refusal of the West to dismantle its nuclear armoury or commit itself to a 'no-first-use' strategy. I have written plenty in this book to show my own views on all this, and they certainly didn't change when I became Secretary-General of NATO: but I recognized that not all those who were anxious about nuclear weapons were strident (or covert) left-wingers, playing the Soviet game – which, of course, was and will remain directed towards weakening the West and procuring a favourable shift in what they call the correlation of forces. Nor were they all idealistic but unrealistic zealots, living in a world of their own imagining, remote from the hard facts of life. There were plenty of both these categories; but there were also a good many people, particularly in the Northern European countries – Britain, the Low Countries, Scandinavia, Germany – who were concerned about what they thought was the drift of events, and who, at least at some points, made common cause with the more intractable visionaries of the peace movements, so-called.

There were reasons for this latter development – this certain unease among the normally sane. The first was the decisive breach with the Soviet Union which had followed the invasion of Afghanistan. This had been an entirely just reaction to an outrageous Soviet act, but as time went on people forgot the outrage of the act and simply found themselves living with the breach, the hostile Western reaction; and, as people will in the West, they started to question whether it was all one-sided. They saw what appeared an icy atmosphere between super-powers, thought to be accentuated by the Reagan presidency; they fancied the idea of supposing that America might share responsibility with Russia for the freeze. Such a fancy induced a sense of broadmindedness. It was subtly flattering. It was also obscurely consoling. Broadminded onlookers don't risk getting hurt. Yet it was natural – politically predictable.

Other circumstances had, in recent years, contributed to the same rather nervous and questioning trend. There had been events in Poland, where at times the communist regime appeared to be in considerable difficulties and people spoke of a Soviet intervention – and wondered what the West might do and how it ought to react. And there was the issue of intermediate-range nuclear missiles. The Soviet Union, in the late 1970s, had deployed a large number of SS20 missiles, manifestly targeted on Western Europe, and the United States – urged by the Western European nations themselves, let it be remembered – had proposed to station missiles (Pershing and Cruise) in Western European countries to restore some sort of equivalence. This deployment was represented – adroitly – by Soviet propaganda as itself an escalation of the 'arms race', rather than (as it was) a response to Soviet action. But the propaganda was not unsuccessful, Western Governments found themselves objects of a sustained protest campaign of 'anti-Cruise'; and the resultant waters were soon so muddied that a number of perfectly well-meaning people began to feel confused and anxious about the course of events.

To the considerable credit of the European nations concerned, these deployments took place, restoring a certain balance: to have stepped back from them would have marked a significant Soviet political victory and would have done the cause of deterrence – and peace – no good at all. But the atmosphere was one of rows and animosity; and, inevitably, the Soviet Union exploited the unease among Western populations with a good deal of skill. In parenthesis, here, I question whether the 'twin-track' element of the 1979 Western policy was particularly wise. By it we had announced that we would deploy Cruise and Pershing missiles if, by the end of 1983, agreement had not been reached with the Soviet Union to withdraw or dismantle their SS20s – or stick to a limited number which we would match. I doubt if the Alliance would have agreed with the deployment of Cruise without some such *démarche*, so it may have been inevitable; but the upshot was that for the intervening four years the Soviets could keep the issue before Western publics, could affect our policy. Declarations of that kind tend to be two-edged. The fact remains, however, that once the deployments were made most of the rows stopped; and the Soviet Union started seriously to negotiate.

One must, therefore, stand firm. One must take as long a view as one can. But I thought there was another truth we shouldn't lose from sight, a truth whose importance the rows about Cruise – or about anything else for that matter – emphasized. There is nothing foolish or faint-hearted about people fearing war, longing for peace and pining after better East–West relations, however elusive. This emotion is only likely to be counterproductive if people, electorates, feel about NATO that there is no parallel diplomatic effort being made for peace and understanding: parallel, that is, to the search for security through an adequate defence effort. If people believe NATO Governments are genuinely seeking to diminish tension, if they can see that sincere and sensible efforts are being made to reduce the enormous number of (particularly) nuclear weapons in the world – and you don't have to be a strategic expert to suspect that we could have a stable balance between East and West with only a fraction of the present arsenal; then they will support intelligently argued defence programmes. But if all they can see is a build-up of arms devoid of diplomatic effort, their support for the Alliance withers. This places a great premium on communication. To proclaim it is perfectly in line with the objects of the Alliance, whose true aim has always been to seek a more relaxed East–West relationship, consistent with the security of both sides.

The principal job of the Secretary-General, I thought, was to do his best in this field – the field of communicating, as far as could be done, with the peoples of the Allied nations; of explaining NATO's purpose and philosophy; of emphasizing the need for its strength, its achievement in underwriting our security; but also of reminding people that NATO should always be seeking ways forward towards better relations and better understanding. Communication meant getting out of the office, travelling as widely as I could, and appearing where possible on television.

The perceptions of NATO populations, however, are largely conditioned by their view of how the United States is managing the superpower relationship. All that I've written about nuclear weapons – Cruise, Pershing, SS20s – has to be taken against the background truth that these are American weapons or Soviet weapons; and where I've written of efforts to reduce tension it is American–Soviet efforts and tension with which people are chiefly concerned. It was, therefore, the resumption of the Geneva talks on reduction of nuclear weapons – as well as the meetings between Reagan and Gorbachev – which primarily helped NATO back on course after a somewhat confused and unpopular period, however unjust the confusion or irrational the unpopularity. And that brings me to the transatlantic relationship, the difference in perception between the European members of NATO and the United States; a difference of which I've already written a good deal, but which must always absorb a significant amount of a Secretary-General's time.

This difference in perception is fundamental. When a European is asked his view of the critical problem of East–West relations, the underlying challenge to NATO, he will say, 'the divided Continent, of course. Central and Eastern Europe are now part of an alien world. An artificial line runs through a divided Germany. Europe has been brutally transformed, and our frontiers with it. That is my preoccupation; and only a very short motoring distance down an excellent road are the armed forces of a huge, menacing and alien power.' But the same question put to an American would elicit a response about the various problems affecting United States–Soviet relations throughout the world. The difference between a Continental and a global point of view is fundamental – and natural.

The difference can make both parties quick to scent insensitivity in the other. Americans often feel that Europeans are inward-looking, preoccupied with their own security and too narrow in their appreciations, that Europeans disregard the fact that much of what happens in the wider world is of as much moment to Europe as to the United States; and of this the Middle East has always been an example. Europeans, on thc other hand, recognize American responsibilities on a wider stage but can be quick to resent what seems an occasional lack of consultation and consideration when the Americans choose to act upon it. Europeans, for instance, were very ready to see that the United States' quarrel with Libya affected them all; although not strictly in the designated NATO area, the Mediterranean is the unifying element in the Southern Region of Allied Forces Europe, and in a matter closely affecting Europe they were dismayed at what they thought was a cavalier American attitude towards consultation over the bombing of Tripoli. The Americans, on the other hand, asked for help at that time from a number of nations, and were angry and astounded when some refused. They thought such refusal cowardly and unfriendly. The Europeans, or some of them, thought the request precipitate and ill-conceived.

Yet on this occasion – not unique but certainly a cause of strain – the Alliance ultimately recovered its good temper, and relations between Europe and America were restored with no lasting damage done. The reason was that which I described as the secret of NATO working at all – the fact that everyone wants it to succeed, recognizes its importance, believes in it. Furthermore the United States has generally taken immense trouble with the briefing of its allies on matters where it is carrying the main, and immense, responsibility: George Shultz and Caspar Weinberger have both been outstanding in this respect. I suspect, perhaps a little unkindly, that the only times when consultation has failed have been when United States actions have taken the United States themselves somewhat by surprise! Anyway, the few occasions where there has been justifiable complaint serve to highlight the majority where it would be impossible to fault America. The arms control negotiations are a case in point – the American negotiators, men of enormous expertise and experience, have consistently kept their NATO allies closely informed at every stage of the game. Another example was the President's briefing of heads of NATO Governments after the Geneva Reagan–Gorbachev meeting. Ronald Reagan's personality was magical in its effect, and a briefing which held many seeds of suspicion went supremely well. The Americans knew that the Europeans needed to feel they were being consulted, needed actually to be consulted, and needed to be reassured that the American President appreciated he was dealing, to a high degree, with Europe's own future. And it happened.

There will always be difficulties in the transatlantic relationship. I've previously discussed the American sense that Europe is a great deal richer than it used to be and still exerts itself inadequately for its own defence, relies too much on American effort and the American taxpayer; and this sense can always periodically lead to an American urge to pull back forces and jerk Europeans into doing more by that compulsion. I was always rather doubtful whether that would, in fact, be the outcome, but the shadow was always there, and European words and actions could only too easily deepen it. Nor was American suspicion without substance. I could understand their irritation at, for instance, the low levels of military stocks some European nations maintained – making nonsense of conscientious American adherence to far higher – and NATO-stipulated – levels, consistent with that increased concentration on conventional arms and conventional battle-readiness which the Alliance had agreed. We managed to get endorsement of a plan to correct this, but it was a symptom – a symptom of American suspicion that Europeans were inadequately serious about their own security.

Then again, Europeans tended to be quietly critical of aspects of the American system of government, or the American Presidency. They would say that the rivalries between the State Department, the Pentagon and the National Security Agency in the White House led to difficulties and confusions for America's allies; and sometimes there was something in it. They would say that an American President was weak, and ask how the free world could be expected to function if led by someone who didn't know where he was going. Alternatively they would say that an American President was dangerously strong, pushing his allies around.

It's not easy for America. In my experience the United States has, however, handled its end of the relationship – and regarded the relationship itself – with exemplary tact, steering an intelligent and careful course between overdominance on the one hand and inadequate leadership on the other. It has been well served in its representation in NATO – I think of Ambassador David Abshire, a man who really knew his way around the American machine of Government and the Congress, a man who was trusted, helpful and eminently sound; and there have been plenty of others. It is also a matter of proper gratitude by the rest of us that the United States has produced for Europe a series of magnificent Supreme Commanders, of whom Bernie Rogers, in my own time, was invariably inspiring, forthright and wise.

I have said that the sense that the Allies are seeking ways to reduce both tension and armaments is a necessary ingredient in producing NATO's acceptability to the electorates of the member nations. This applies, of course, not only to nuclear weapons. Enormous armies, navies and air forces also confront each other and the knowledge that they do so is an additional source of unease as well as expenditure. To seek to reduce them on a mutually agreed and balanced basis, consistent with the security of both NATO and the Warsaw Pact, is another desirable element of *détente*.

It is also particularly difficult to achieve. Nuclear arms reduction is hard enough, with the necessity for laborious and sophisticated searches for an agreed basis of comparison, some concord on what equivalence means. In the nuclear field bombers, ballistic missiles, Cruise missiles, warheads, delivery systems, ranges, orders of lethality – all this is hard but possible to reduce to some sort of data base; although even that is but the start of the argument, which has to be about what constitutes a fair and stable balance thereafter. For conventional weapons and forces, however, the difficulty is much greater. The weapon systems themselves are extraordinarily difficult to compare. Men can be counted – but in some countries vital jobs are done by civilians, or contracted to non-military firms, which elsewhere are performed by people in uniform. Then there is geography. So far the Mutual and Balanced Force Reduction talks in Vienna have been concerned only with Central Europe – with the Central Region of Allied Command Europe; and after fourteen years of discussion the two sides have not yet (at the time of writing) agreed the basic data! And it is proposed – not illogically – that this is anyway too narrow a scope of consideration, that Soviet forces (for instance) may be moved, rapidly, from one part of the Soviet Empire to the Central Front without difficulty. Where does one start counting? And what (from the Soviet point of view) about a large Turkish Army, nowhere near the Central Region, but in being? And – again from the Soviet point of view – therefore requiring 'covering' by Warsaw Pact forces in appropriate strength. Then there is quality – some NATO nations' forces are, if only for economic reasons, very much better equipped than others. Should they receive a 'quality bonus' on that count – and how is it to be investigated, assessed and agreed with a Soviet side who are, anyway, generally paranoid about information security? To what extent should French forces be counted – not assigned under present conventions to Allied Command Europe? And to what extent is it reasonable to count a large Spanish Army – not in any way integrated into the NATO Command Structure, but at the disposal of a NATO nation?* Then, in dealing with the considerable disparities, how does one propose to set about bringing into balance 50,000 Warsaw Pact tanks with 20,000 NATO tanks? Does one dig in on a refusal to reduce by one tank until the opposition has reduced to 20,000 – in which case they never will? And what factors should one inject for communications – the advantage given to the Soviet Union by a land-line of communication, making reinforcement by road and rail a comparatively rapid matter compared with the physical problems of NATO, and its diversity?

France has pretty consistently taken the view that the problem is so complex that it is insoluble, and that to attempt agreement over MBFR – or any variant of it – is merely to

* Spain confirmed at a referendum her membership of the Alliance during my time – no small achievement of the Spanish Government.

arouse expectations, expend energy and produce disappointment. There is much to be said for their scepticism. The French political consensus on defence perhaps makes it easier for them to take so robust and commonsensical an attitude, although the French have now (1988) decided to participate in a new set of negotiations on conventional forces in Europe. For the rest of us, I suspect, the fragility of public support for a sufficient defence effort by every country makes it expedient to go on trying. It is part of the laborious effort to keep the world at peace. Nor should one be purely cynical. Few men, however pugnacious their temperament or resolute their commitment to defence, would not rejoice in a world less teeming with arms and all the apparatus of war.

This entire question of arms control dominated the latter part of my time at NATO. Highly technical, it cannot usefully be discussed in any detail in a book which is likely to be published after further significant changes have occurred. At every stage in an extended negotiation of the type on which the United States and Soviet Union have embarked there has to be caution, and at every stage a judgement has to be made on whether the political desirability of the next step is realistically consistent with the continuing requirements of deterrence. Deterrence implies stability; it necessitates strength and balance at every level. It also demands that the perceptions of the parties – potential adversaries and allies alike – are clear about that balance, so that there could be neither temptation towards some sort of a gamble on the one hand nor discouragement into a kind of surrender on the other. Yet NATO's achievements stand, and my reflection on my time there is outstandingly one of gratitude – gratitude that the nations of the West have at last come together to combine their strength and to discuss their difficulties in a continuing way unprecedented in history; and I include in this grateful reflection the achievement of the European Community. The work of neither organization is complete, but the longer our memories, the more remarkable each appears. I can never forget 1945.

*

I am sometimes asked whether my political – and international – life has made me a pessimist or an optimist, and I shall end this book by trying to answer the question.

On the debit or pessimistic side there are, obviously, disagreeable aspects to the present era. I grew up when it was, on the whole, safe to walk the streets of big cities – anywhere, and particularly in England. The idea that public transport in London, anyway after a certain hour, might carry risk to the traveller would have been thought so incredible, so monstrous, that the contrast with our own day is glaring and uncomfortable. The incidence of violence was very much less in my youth, and although that peaceable period was probably short-lived – the eighteenth and early nineteenth centuries were acknowledged as rough and brutal – the decline of personal security is marked and odious.

A certain national decline must be admitted and it has been matched by a very evident deterioration of manners. One of my generation has spent most of adult life in a period of retreat for our country, of diminution, shrinkage, apology and dwindling confidence in ourselves, our history and our destiny; of disappointing economic performance with consequent lowering of standards. And this has been accompanied by – at worst – a sort of snarling and bitter self-mockery and introspection on the one hand and a greatly increased level of oafish insensitivity on the other. I don't think it is entirely because I am approaching seventy that I find too much British behaviour and too many British attitudes loutish, compared with those I remember from other times, and that this has lowered our standing is sadly beyond dispute. I sometimes have the impression that British manners have become the worst in the world, and it is a very disagreeable impression. National reputation used to rest on strength, diplomacy and commercial success. It still does, although the commercial success has been variable, to put it mildly. But national reputation is also made or wrecked by the decent manners and personal integrity of our people, especially when abroad, and on that count we have a deservedly poor name compared to that which once was ours. Patriotism, of course – and I believe the British are still patriotic, love their country – has always had several voices and one of them can easily become noisy and vindictive.

But on the optimistic side there is much, and although it is chiefly material it is still greatly to be welcomed. I recall Harold Macmillan's remark that it is the business of politicians to try to create conditions in which prosperity can flourish and that if it is accompanied by unattractive moral attitudes or by a diminution of true contentment that is sad, but essentially a matter for individuals. I agree with that, and it is easy to exaggerate the unattractive moral attitudes, to notice here and there the diminished contentment, and to take for granted the real benefits. They are indeed real. The material condition of our people has been totally transformed within my lifetime despite many economic failures and our slippage in the prosperity league tables of the developed world. The great majority of the British can take necessities, even entertainments, for granted in a way which would have astonished earlier generations. Of course there is still bad housing – and shortage of housing. Of course there are still patches of poverty. Of course there is disfiguring – here and there increasing – ugliness. But words themselves have in many cases different significance. Even unemployment – and I accept that the lack of dignity and satisfaction endemic in not working when one wishes to do so may well transcend material hardship – is a different phenomenon to that I remember and that suffered by many of the soldiers I first knew and admired. In those days to be out of work was to be hungry. That is mercifully rare today and the change is a mighty change for the better, just as the violence and insecurity which makes life miserable for some, particularly for some living in our cities, is a mighty change for the worse.

But there is one source of optimism in which I believe strongly and which colours my mind greatly and moves it to the credit side of the balance. I do not believe that we shall again suffer a major war, with all its destruction, cruelty and misery. Local wars are likely to continue, and it must remain the object of statesmen to eliminate their causes, to prevent their outbreak, and when they occur to contain them in scope, scale and duration as much and as urgently as possible. But I do not believe that these will again reach the sort of awful proportions which devastated a large part of the world forty-five years ago: and I do not believe that they will happen in Europe. My belief, my optimism is, however, conditional. It depends upon no sudden upsurge of irrationality or insanity; and it demands a certain physical balance between East and West, between opposing systems, between possible contestants – a balance which can continue to make clear that there are no profits, that there are instead terrifying and unacceptable dangers, attendant on the use of force. Only strength can deny to another temptation. We have tried to create it. We must retain it and cherish it. Provided we do so we will, without question, have peace. Nobody thinking thus can be grossly pessimistic.

In these pages I have reflected a little on things past, on the tribulations, triumphs and altercations of yesterday; and when one does so, as Swift observed, these things often arouse our wonder at the excitement, the enthusiasm or the alarm they once generated. Time has passed now. We know how the story ended. The consoling perspective of history removes all suspense and often injects no little absurdity into events long since enacted, whether the outcome of a passionate political battle or Uncle Charlie wielding his horsewhip on the steps of the Conservative Club. We can smile at the immoderate reactions of our predecessors, or of ourselves when young. Today, on the other hand, seems singular in its importance, its dramas momentous in a way previous generations could hardly have conceived; and at our contemporary concern 'we wonder not at all'.

Yet the trials of each age tend to be repeated in one form or another. I have seen enough to feel that I've seen some things many times. Few circumstances, particularly in politics, and fewer still in international affairs, are original or without precedent. Patterns recur. The past often teaches. Horses can run true to form. And the fearful preoccupations of our own day will here and there seem as disproportionate in the eyes of our successors as our efforts to deal with them will sometimes appear sadly ill-judged. We cannot see the future. To reflect on things past, on the scepticism they teach about human wisdom, may be as sound a support as any in meeting that future with a measure of equanimity.

INDEX